D1252893

Bd. Heckman 10/5/73

FATHER DIVINE

15-7

FATHER DIVINE

BY SARA HARRIS

with the assistance of
Harriet Crittendon

Newly revised and expanded,
and with an Introduction by
John Henrik Clarke

COLLIER BOOKS
NEW YORK, NEW YORK

Copyright, 1953, by Sara Drucker Harris and Harriet Crittenden
Copyright © 1971 by Sara Harris
Copyright © 1971 by The Macmillan Company

All rights reserved. No part of this book may be reproduced or
transmitted in any form or by any means, electronic or
mechanical, including photocopying, recording or by any
information storage and retrieval system, without permission
in writing from the Publisher.

The Macmillan Company
866 Third Avenue, New York, N.Y. 10022
Collier-Macmillan Canada Ltd., Toronto, Ontario

Father Divine: Holy Husband was originally published by
Doubleday & Company, Inc. and is reprinted in an updated
edition by arrangement.

Library of Congress Catalog Card Number: 78-146617
First Collier Books Edition 1971

Printed in the United States of America

BX
7350
.H37
1971

TO ARNOLD

ALMA COLLEGE
MONTEITH LIBRARY
ALMA, MICHIGAN

ALMA COLLEGE
MONTEITH LIBRARY
ALMA, MICHIGAN

CONTENTS

Preface by John Henrik Clarke   ix
Introduction   xvii
1   John Doe, Alias God   1
2   House of Joy   17
3   David and Goliath   31
4   "Let God Pay His Own Bills"   45
5   Depression Flood Tide   59
6   "God! He's Just a Natural Man!"   73
7   Root of All Evil   85
8   Sex and Segregation   97
9   "Let the Dead Bury the Dead!"   119
10   "Just to Hear You Tap Your Beautiful Feet"   133
11   Do Not Love Anyone . . .   149
12   "Happy as the Rambling Piano Keys on Easter Morning"   171
13   "Every Tongue Confess!"   193
14   Miss Holy Gets "Book-L'arned"   211
15   One Little Nay?   227
16   God in Bedlam!   247
17   God Takes a Bride   265
18   The Prodigal Son!   287
19   "There Is Only One Fact——"   303
20   "—Rosebuds of My Heart"   319
21   "Intellect Stands as a Bar!"   331
22   "Father Can't Never Die!"   341
Afterword   353
Index   369

PREFACE

This is a serious book about a serious subject. Father Divine was not a character in a comic opera. Quite the contrary. He was a player in a human drama that affected the lives of millions of people, black and white. He was the product of his times, and there is no way to understand him without some understanding of the interplay of the forces of human deprivation and social dislocation that produced the atmosphere in which he thrived. He gave hope to the hopeless, and he fed the hungry and restored their sense of worth and belonging.

No matter what he was to the rest of the world, to the people who found new life and lived again, stimulated by his presence and credos, he was real; he was father; he was God.

Father Divine and his movement did not emerge overnight. A special atmosphere, time, and situation were created to accompany his emergence. He was the beneficiary of this atmosphere, time, and situation that he did not create. This man's success with a large number of black and white people has deep historical roots. These roots are deep in Europe and even deeper in Africa. The white man's approach to religion has failed among a large number of white people. The western black man's approach to religion, which is a colorful stepchild of the white man's approach, has failed among a large number of black people because of poor communication and the inability of this religion to touch the blacks' innermost psychic being.

Christianity, an Eastern religion, was refashioned by Europeans for their own purposes. This religion was the handmaiden that furnished the rationale for their rise to world power in the fifteenth and sixteenth centuries. In many ways, the white man's relationship to Christianity is a contradiction. His very method of taking over the world belies the basic principles of Christianity. The black man's relationship to the white man's concept of this religion, in the light of the white man's use of it to justify European expansion into Africa, Asia, and the broader world, is a much bigger contradiction. The black man's contradiction has the more glaring and tragic overtones mainly because he is a victim of the white man's violation of such basic Christian tenets as the advocacy of brotherhood and brotherly love, and the prohibition of the killing of one's neighbors. In the light of these contradictions, it is not difficult to understand why a large number of people, black and white, seek new religions and new gods outside of the realm of what is considered to be orthodox.

Father Divine's movement had its greatest development in Harlem, the world's most famous ethnic ghetto. To understand this movement, it is necessary to understand Harlem and why other men and movements have flourished there.

When Father Divine arrived and began to set up his heavens, or kingdoms, around 1933, one era was ending and another was beginning. The period of the Harlem Renaissance was over, and it was followed by a national depression. Father Divine moved into a vacuum left by the decline of the Garvey movement and the passing of the first of the colorful cult-leaders in Harlem, George Wilson Becton. Both of these leaders gave large numbers of black people a sense of themselves, their identity, and their value as human beings for the first time. Marcus Garvey gave them a sense of nationhood, made them cooperative owners of a shipping line, and brought about cooperative ownership within their own communities. The decline of his movement left a multitude of people stunned and suspicious of other leaders and their promises.

In his book, *Harlem, Negro Metropolis*, the Jamaican poet and novelist Claude McKay gives the following picture of Harlem on the eve of the emergence of Father Divine:

The church leaders of the community had gone a long way toward letting the people take extreme license in spiritual matters. No matter what their personal feelings, they knew that they had to cater to the emotional needs of their congregations. In spite of this catering, the regular churches were not adequate outlets for the burning religious energy of the black masses. The presence of a great depression, when economic questions had to be answered as well as religious ones, made this situation more acute. Cults were multiplying in Harlem. Some of the "New Messengers" had only a small following, a banjo and a tambourine. The sidewalks of Harlem were their churches.

One of the most colorful of the new message-bringers was a tall and stately figure who was referred to as the Barefoot Prophet. In winter and summer, he walked the streets of Harlem barefooted. He was a striking figure, with a large head of bushy white hair. He met his forever-changing congregation on the streets and in the poolrooms and saloons of Harlem. He inquired about his people's relationship to God, and the status of their souls. Then he accepted contributions for his own well-being.

During the early 1930's a diversity of cults were competing for space and followers on the streets of Harlem. There were such sects as the Crossbearers, who were mostly women; the Ordeal-by-Fire Disciples, who licked flames with their tongues; Daddy Grace and the radio artist Mother Horne; the Moorish Science Templars, forerunners of the Black Muslims; and the Black Jews. Most of the attention during this period was going to the World's Gospel Feast, which was promoted by George Wilson Becton, and to the Peace Mission of Father Divine. Among the cult leaders, Becton was the star, and Father Divine was, figuratively, waiting in the wings.

Claude McKay has this to say about him in *Harlem, Negro Metropolis*:

George Wilson Becton was the first of the great cult leaders to excite the imagination and stir the enthusiasm of the entire Harlem community. He was the supreme Godsman. He started his career in Harlem just when the high tide of its carnival was receding. That was in the beginning of the nineteen thirties.

Harlem was the wild playground of New York. A territory abandoned to big lawbreakers, it was the "widest open" spot when Prohibition was in force and was the headquarters of the great gangsters trafficking in bootleg booze and narcotics. At night, its speakeasies drew together around the same bar the sophisticates and aristocrats of New York, the hoodlums and criminals. Like gypsies summoned for the divertissement of distinguished guests, Negro performers provided rare entertainment. The spirit of the times was reflected in the state of hectic ferment among Negroes.

Becton invaded the notorious realm of freebooters with his twelve young disciples and a splendid orchestra. Becton was tall, handsome and college-educated. Harlem cultists before his time were all illiterates. But Becton spoke the language of the educated Negroes, although he knew how to reach the hearts of the common people. He styled his mission "The World's Gospel Feast." His meetings were not the loose corybantic revels of Father Divine's "kingdoms." They were patterns of order and grace. The congregation waited in a hushed silence which was broken by soft strains of music. Pages in fine robes led the singing. The orchestra plunged the congregation into joyful swaying, as they sang gospel hymns to the titillating music of the dance hall. And Becton's commanding presence dominated the scene. Women, responsive to his agile movements and his well-modulated, persuasive voice, swayed like reeds.

Becton's consecrated dime ceremony diverted tens of thousands of dimes from the numbers racketeers to the church collections. Though the assumption is hard to prove, this ceremony may have been the cause of his untimely death when his fame was at its peak. One night in Philadelphia, May 21, 1933 to be precise, he was kidnapped by two white men and literally taken for a ride in his own car. When the car was found, Becton's body was punctured with bullets. He never became coherent enough to give any description of his abductors, or why they wanted him dead. Four days later he died in extreme agony.

The death of George Wilson Becton left the field of Harlem wide open for Father Divine to conquer. He now became the main attraction among Harlem cult-leaders. The glorious domain of his Kingdoms of Peace was expanding. This was the beginning of his triumphant years in Harlem. For him, it was truly wonderful.

In the fall of 1933, the people of New York City were in the throes of a three-way election battle to decide who would be Mayor. One of the contesting candidates saw fit to seek overtly the support of Father Divine and his followers. On November 4 of that year, Father Divine was holding a vespers banquet in the Rockland Palace. To the surprise of all, in walked the candidate, Fiorello La Guardia. "I came here tonight to ask Father Divine's advice and counsel," he said. "Peace be with you all." This incredible event, the arrival of a white candidate in the role of petitioner at a Divine gathering, was an early launching point of Father Divine's influence. Thereafter, candidates of every caliber sought his endorsement. Though he was never overtly political, he did encourage his followers to register and vote for their own benefit and for that of their community. The political structure recognized the potential strength of this voting bloc to such an extent that it even waived the stipulation that people use their given names as they registered to vote, and allowed Father Divine's followers to use such names as "Mother's Delight," "Brother of Good Faith," and "Sister Who Stood by the Way."

Father Divine based his entire spiritual concept on the soaring belief that race should not be a factor in human relations. He refused to accept the concept of race as being valid, and permitted no form of it to exist in his kingdoms. To this day, very few people are aware that Father Divine not only believed in but indeed created, among his followers, a society based on the fundamental principle of the brotherhood of man. He gave stimulation and status to people who had nothing by involving them where their status and humanity mattered—in the human family. His people had few previous allegiances. Father Divine was, for them, the bringer of light to the universe, and all praises were due to him. His followers developed skills, worked in the movement, and were sought after as domestics and workers because of their high principles of honesty and cleanliness.

By 1935, the mystery surrounding Father Divine had deepened, and his followers had multiplied. In an article by Claude McKay ("There Goes God! The Story of Father Divine and His Angels," published in *The Nation*, February 6, 1935), we get the following picture of Father Divine during the formative years of his power:

In his sumptuous living quarters, African in the gay conglomeration of colors, Father Divine in a large easy chair appeared like a slumping puppet abandoned after a marionette show. He seemed to have shrunk even smaller than his five feet four, which is not unimpressive when he is acting. He pointed to a seat near him, and said he thought he had said enough at his meetings to give me an idea of his work and mission. I told him that I was interested mainly in his ideas about social problems and inter-racial relations and would like a special pronouncement from him as a Negro leader and pacifist. Father Divine replied: "I have no color conception of myself. If I were representing race or creed or color or nation, I would be limited in my conception of the universal. I would not be as I am, omnipotent."

I said that I accepted his saying that he was above race and color, but because he happened to have been born brown and was classified in the colored group, the world was more interested in him as a Negro. And I asked him what was his plan for the realization of peace and understanding between the masses and the classes. Father Divine said: "I am representative of the universal through the cooperation of mind and spirit in which is reality. I cannot deviate from that fundamental. The masses and the classes must transcend the average law and accept me. And governments in time will come to recognize my law."

I drew his attention to an editorial in the *Daily Worker* referring to the demonstration against war and fascism, in which the Communists had paraded in company with Father Divine at the head of thousands of his people in carrying banners bearing the Divine slogans. The editorial was an explanation to critical readers of the necessity of cooperating with Father Divine and his follows, "carrying such strange and foolish placards." Father Divine said that he was always willing to cooperate in his own way with the Communists or any group that was fighting for international peace and emancipation of people throughout the world and against any form of segregation and racial discrimination. But what the Communists were trying to do he was actually doing, by bringing people of different races and nations to live together and work in peace under his will. He had come to free every nation, every language, every tongue, and every people. He did not need the

Communists or any other organization, but they needed him.
For he had all wisdom and understanding and health and
wealth. And he alone could give emancipation and liberty, for
he was the victory. I thanked Father Divine for the interview,
and he dismissed me with the gift of a pamphlet.

To most Divinites, 1936 was a year of great joy in
righteous government. Trouble came to the kingdoms the
following year. It came thick and fast over two issues that
were not supposed to be in dispute in the kingdoms—
money and sex. About noon on April 20, 1937, two white
men entered Headquarters Kingdom at 20 West 115th
Street while Father Divine was giving one of his messages
of inspiration to the angels. One of the white men was a
process server. This intruder was badly beaten and driven
from the kingdom. Later that day, a police search failed
to find Father Divine in New York. An order was issued
for his arrest, charging felonious assault. Three of his
angels were held on the same charge. Three days later
Father Divine was discovered in one of his kingdoms in
Connecticut and brought back to New York. In Los Angeles, the same week, John West Hunt, a wealthy white
disciple whose cult name was the Prodigal Son, also called
St. John the Revelation, was arrested under the Mann Act
for the seduction of a young follower named Miss Delight
Jewett. The most serious and least expected trouble came
when Faithful Mary, the star angel of the movement, de-
fected. Nineteen thirty-seven was indeed a year of tribula-
tion for Father Divine and his followers.
Incredibly, 1938 found the movement recovering and
Father Divine once more in triumph. The wayward angel,
Faithful Mary, returned to the good graces of the kingdom. Father Divine and his followers acquired the Krum
Elbow estate and became the neighbors of President
Roosevelt at Hyde Park. This event was accorded national
attention. In the years between 1938 and 1946, when the
Divine movement began to show signs of decline, Father
Divine gave thousands of people who were lost from their
moorings a sense of security that they had never before
envisioned. A study of this movement is essential to understanding the interplay of the forces of human deprivation and social dislocation in black America after the de-

Nation of Islam (Black Muslims) and the civil-rights
cline of the Garvey movement and before the rise of the
movement. This is why the present reprint of the book
Father Divine is important. I repeat, this is a serious book
about a serious subject.

—John Henrik Clarke
July, 1970

INTRODUCTION

This book was conceived in 1950 many years before the black revolution had acutely become America's concern. As a student of American sociology I'd heard and read somewhat of Father Divine as the black Messiah who, like Marcus Garvey before him, was a utopian seeker of magnificent proportion. I didn't know much about him at the time—only that while his followers included white and sometimes even wealthy people, the bulk of them were blacks out of the hard, remorseless, poverty-stricken world of depression Harlem. I knew that Father Divine had loomed into eminence in 1933, the year so many Harlemites existed on charity that this slogan of humor rooted in bitterness, was evolved there: "Jesus'll lead us and the relief'll feed us."

I also knew that Father Divine, the antithesis of Garvey in so many pregnant and pithy ways, had nevertheless succeeded as well as, if not better than, Garvey in decoying vast numbers of Harlem's black masses into the belief that they had reason for hope and optimism despite their marks of oppression.

In a very real sense, of course, it was Garvey who, though unconsciously, helped set the stage for Divine's emergence as the reincarnated God when Garvey climaxed his brave dream of an all-black nation with the even bolder illusion of an all-black religion: the Blessed Virgin Mary as the Black Madonna, Jesus Christ as the Black Man of Sorrows and God as the Black Lord God. Was it any wonder then, that, when he went on trial for having used the mails to defraud black people by selling shares for the Black Star Line (his black merchant marine), Henry Lincoln Johnson, the black attorney who represented a codefendant, could claim compellingly:

"If every Negro could have put every dime, every penny into the sea, and if he might get in exchange the knowledge that he was somebody, that he meant something to the world, he would gladly do it. The Black Star Line was a loss in money but it was a gain in soul."

I often wondered to myself, therefore, before I ever met Father Divine and had the opportunity to raise these questions which had intruded my mind and imagination, how much of a "gain in soul"—as Henry Lincoln Johnson seemed to have meant those words—Father Divine's heavens offered to black, lower-class people during the 1930's to 1940's. What were they after anyhow, those vast numbers of blacks who followed Divine? Was it the expression and release of emotions too overwhelming to be contained or controlled in other fashion? Perhaps they sought an answer to the acute and compelling problems of daily living no temporary release of pent-up emotion could alleviate.

I knew, even before my first meeting with Divine, that he offered the angels both emotional release and the practical solutions to their living problems. Not just in feeding the hungry and housing the destitute, but also, more significantly, in alleviating to a great degree what psychiatrists Abram Kardiner and Lionel Oversey called "the Negro's most vulnerable psychological handicap, his depressed self-esteem."

If Garvey could have inspired black race pride merely by saying that everything black was superior and not inferior, how much more effective, then, was Father Divine's creation of a heaven presided over by a black God? There was no need for preaching black superiority since God, Himself, signified its prime "sample and example." And though whites did exist in utopia, they were the ones to be tolerated by the black angels instead of vice versa. Obviously, they had profited so much as individuals from their affiliation with Divine that both men and women had been willing not only to turn in all their earnings to heaven but also to renounce sex, marriage, and parenthood at Father's command. I asked myself why this should have been the case. Did the women, for example, embrace the prohibition out of love for Divine or, rather, from resentment against black men as ineffectual providers? Could the proscription have served as a catharsis for a pressure point of sexual maladjustment in lower-class black women's personalities, or had it actually, as I supposed they believed, been undertaken for God's sake?

How and why did the black men submerge their sexual instincts when they came to live in heaven? And what were the motivations of the white and wealthy followers, not only for celibacy, but also for their acceptance of the poor, black angels?

What about Father Divine's own marriage to the voluptuous, young blonde known as Sweet Angel in Heaven? Was she really "a spotless virgin bride" as Father maintained? And why, when all was said and done, had he chosen to marry a *white* woman?

But my speculations about these matters did not obsess me. The one fact that constantly intruded my imagination, creating effects and raising questions I felt compelled to answer was this: how and why had Father Divine demanded and succeeded in causing black people to submerge their natural resentment and hostility toward white America so blacks could mouth and mean his incantations of "no rage" and "no hate" and "no war." How divorced were the angels from the real world, where black was black and white was white and the gap was so overwhelming, as we all—even in those years—knew it to have been, when the angels maintained that there was no such thing as race or color? And where did Father Divine actually fit among the black leaders of his period? Should he, in fact, be regarded as a black leader at all, or was he, rather, jeopardizing the whole cause of integration to which all the black leaders of that period were committed?

Having decided I'd like to explore all these questions, and especially the one of Father's stand in regard to the social action and protest of his time, I wrote to request a meeting and said I hoped it would result in my writing a book. The following are a few relevant points out of the nineteen-page letter Father wrote in answer:

Now, in reference to that which you deem to name my activities on the "Negro protest front," I wish to say it is true, equality is a thing requested, yes, demanded by Me and must be fulfilled; nevertheless it may not be immediately legalized but whether it is legalized or illegal, I have the answer to the problem for, as all of my followers say:

"Father's love is stirring up the nations. It is bringing all mankind into the unity of the spirit of mind, of aim, and of purpose: therefore, when GOD gets inside of a person, GOD will change the condition of the mind of the children of men with whom that person is concerned."

We have two races on the earth now. We have the Angelic race and we have the human race. These are the only two races we know anything about—the Angelic race and the human race. We shall bring the human race into the Angelic race until all will be Evangelized and Angelic as well as I and my followers are. That is what it is all about.

You know those poor creatures in the South: I mean those who think they are in authority, the poor creatures bound down with prejudice and hate and debauchery of every kind—when GOD shall have reached out HIS long Arms . . . I am reaching them now; I shall cause the nations of the earth to love one another even as they love themselves, and when this is accomplished, there shall be no more division, there shall be no more strife: by interpretation, there shall be no more sickness, there shall be no more sorrow; there shall be no more pain and there shall be no more death; for the TABERNACLE of GOD is with men, and HE shall dwell with them. GOD Himself shall be with them, and shall be their GOD and they shall be His people. That is what it is all about.

As to my writing a book, Father wrote that he:

does not need mortal books written about ME since the Bible has already told all of that, already written all that needs to be said about ME. But I will be glad to see you for a few minutes if you wish to come to my headquarters of the world in Philadelphia. Now, I generally grant five-second interviews to people but if you see fit to come, why it may then well be that I will extend my time with you to more than five seconds.

Father ended his letter:

The above I wrote so that you and all may see and know the foundations upon which we are standing on this subject you deem to call "Negro social protest," a term we do not recognize as we do not recognize any color or race so that you and all people who are concerned might be even as I am, for this leaves Me Well, Healthy, Joyful, Peaceful, Lively, Loving, Successful, Prosperous, and Happy in Spirit, Body and Mind and in every organ, muscle, sinew, joint, limb, vein and bone and even in every ATOM and Fibre of MY BODILY FORM.

> Respectfully and Sincere, I AM
> Rev. M. J. DIVINE
> (Better known as Father Divine)

I arrived at the beloved Mecca in Philadelphia, Father's "headquarters of the world," an old-fashioned brick building somewhat on the shabby side, just as Father and Mother Divine drew up in their chauffeur-driven Cadillac. A crowd of a couple of hundred whites and blacks were massed on the curb to see them. They screamed and jumped like children when short, bald, squat Father, and Mother, dressed all in blue as an accentuation for her blond prettiness, emerged from the car.

After Father and Mother had entered the headquarters and the nerve-shaking tautness had abated somewhat, I showed my letter from Father to the thin, young, red-haired white woman, Dorothy Darling, who was then Father's personal secretary and has remained until today as Mother's secretary and right hand. She seemed impressed primarily with the fact Father had said he might see me for more than five seconds and offered to set up an appointment for me. A woman chauffeur drove me to the Divine Lorraine, a first-class, though not luxurious, hotel owned by the movement. I was shown to an impressive suite which had a huge living room, bedroom, and bath, and for which I paid the same price as out-of-town followers would have been charged—fifty cents a night.

After I'd rested somewhat and freshened up, the woman drove me back to headquarters and escorted me to the dining room for the banquet at which, she said, Father and Mother were expected to appear. It was a huge room, set up to accommodate hundreds of diners. Though the main table that I assumed to be reserved for Father and his entourage was empty, the others, arranged horseshoe style, were full. Standing behind the diners were great crowds clapping, singing, and offering personal testimonials to Father Divine. It was all very joyous and impressive, and I was almost sorry when, a little after ten o'clock, a bell rang and a deep voice announced, "Peace, everyone, Father and Mother are coming down to the banquet hall now." Again, as had been the case on my arrival at heaven, the air was filled with shouts and screams of delight and nervous anticipation.

Well, when Father (wearing a blue suit, white shirt, and red tie) followed by Mother (in a pink dress) and the twenty-six young secretaries, both blacks and whites, walked to their places at the head table, all sound ceased, and you really could have heard a pin drop. Father, Mother and the secretaries took their seats; Father sitting first, then Mother, and finally the secretaries in what seemed to have been rehearsed unison.

Then bedlam burst. Men and women danced and screamed and threw themselves on the floor to express their overwhelming love for Father. Every person expressed himself in his individual way, as the spirit moved him. Nobody seemed especially conscious of what anyone else was doing, and Father himself seemed less aware than anyone of the various forms the followers' adoration took. In the midst of the testifying and singing, he looked in my direction and raised his hand summoning me to take a place at the head table three chairs away from his own.

An old lady to whom I'd been talking for some time looked at me with new eyes of attention, grabbed hold of my arm so tight she left a mark, and whispered, "Oh, how Father condescends to you!" Moved by her fervor and passion I found myself thinking he was "condescending" to me and wondering how I'd manage to make suitable conversation.

Actually, though, there was not much time for talk, because the food was brought in by a team of black, and white, waitresses in crisply starched uniforms practically before I'd been seated. What a fantastic feast it was: fricasseed chicken, roast duck, boiled beef, spareribs, fried sausage, lamb stew, liver-and-bacon, stewed tomatoes, spinach, brussels sprouts, string beans, asparagus tips, fruit salad, ice cream, and chocolate cake.

Next to me, a young black girl named Miss Love Dove, a high-ranking secretary, told me that people paid what they wished for the sumptuous feast, and those who couldn't afford to pay ate free. She also said, though not in so many words, that any person so blundering and unhandy as to cause a platter to touch the table would be looked upon by the angels sitting in the farther seats as having broken the "chain of blessings begun when Father touched a dish, and maintained only so long as it passed from hand to hand in constant flowing motion." Apprehensive that I would be the one to break the chain, I passed up the delicious-looking foods on the large, heavy platters and concentrated on such concoctions as salt-free turnips, which came on small, easy-to-wield plates. Needless to say, I didn't relax until the dinner was done at five minutes to one, which was about two hours and fifty minutes after we had first sat down at the table.

Father Divine expounded for an hour and twenty minutes delivering a sermon, Miss Dove informed me, he had preached for the first time in 1936.

Peace everyone. Good health, good will, and a good appetite with a heart full of merriness and bodies filled with enthusiasm, by the realization of this victory I have so freely given. Upon this foundation you have been established this evening.

When I say righteousness, truth and justice shall be legalized universally, just as it is under my personal jurisdiction. It is a privilege to realize that that which you surmise, and that which you visualize, can be materialized. You have visualized negation, lacks, wants and limitations. You have visualized segregation and every other detestable expression. You have experienced that or those things in your daily experience by bringing those conditions into materialization by vivid visualization.

By vividly visualizing, you actually materialize that which you visualize, and cause yourselves to be the outward expression of the personified negation that you were visualizing. I come as I came, emphasizing, stressing and demonstrating that which is essential for your visualization. Since you have visualized the negative through the ages—visualized yourselves as individuals in poverty, lacks, wants and limitations, visualized yourselves as the preys to the prejudiced minds of our present civilization—you have imposed them upon yourselves. You reincarnated them and became the personification of that which you were visualizing. Therefore, you have actually personified misery. But I came to reverse that unjust decision. And this is accomplished by the Appellate Division of the Supreme Court of Heaven. Now isn't that wonderful?

Two tape-recorders were on and Father's twenty-six secretaries were recording his message in shorthand.

There are courts in the heavenly state of expression and remember there is a supreme one, as well as there is a Supreme Court in and on the earth plane. For this cause, I am stressing, this evening, the significance of the positive visualization. I have brought into actuality in this great city something you all have been seeking through and from the early existence. Oh, it is a privilege to realize. God's words, yes, his words through prophecy, cannot fail.

Speaking of God, you all believe in God, but you do not believe in the mere mysteriousness of a mystical God in the imaginary Heaven. You only believe in the tangible-ated God. A God that is a present help in the time of need. A God that has lifted you out of depressions. A God that has lifted you out of ignorance. A God that has lifted you out of superstition. A God that has established your going in the land of the living. That's what you are talking about. You are not thinking about a God in the mystical Heaven. All that they have surmised and all that they have striven to get you to visualize. I have brought it down from the sky. We are not studying about a God in the sky. We are talking about a God here and now. A God that has been personified and materialized. That's what I am talking about.

. . . Not the kind of a God that *they* are talking about in the sky . . . According to their version, they have kept you in bondage through believing in that God. To keep you submissive, meek and obedient to their slavebound and slaveric minds and desires to keep you in bondage. . . .

After Father finished speaking, Mother rose to smile at Father, the angels, and me, and sang this song in her high, pretty voice:

> *Goodness and love and justice and truth,*
> *Shall have access in the land.*
> *These together with mercy,*
> *Shall govern every man.*
> *Now we have a righteous government.*
> *Now we have a righteous government.*
> *Now we have a righteous government.*

After Mother was done singing, the angels joined her in other songs, singing their hearts out and clapping and stamping in accompaniment. Their spirit was even warmer and more contagious than it had been earlier, and I was infinitely moved. Suddenly Father, who hadn't been attending to me from the time he'd first summoned me to sit at his table, said, without really looking in my direction, "We have a visitor today and if she would, by chance, wish to say a few words why, she should feel welcome to do so."

And, perhaps because I'd been so penetrated by the mood of the banquet and heard in my mind the words of the old lady who'd told me "Oh, how Father condescends to you," with such ardor, I panicked. I stayed seated, the tape-recorders continued, the twenty-six secretaries had their pencils poised to record my speech, and I was at a loss for words and couldn't even summon the equanimity to rise and acknowledge Father's invitation. After what must have been two or three minutes that seemed hours to me, Father said ungrudgingly, even graciously, "If I came to heaven when earth had been my abode and someone asked me to speak a few words, why, it might be I would not function in that expression either. By the common phrase quite often used, and I believe I may be justified in using it to convey the thought to you, Mrs. Harris, you are welcome to our home, even if you do not see fit to express yourself to us at this particular time." He nodded his head at me and left the table followed by Mother Divine and the secretaries.

The angels were in no way so ungrudging to me as Father, himself, had been. Where I'd formerly been treated with warmth and friendliness, the atmosphere now was sullen and glum. I asked Dorothy Darling at what hour that night she'd scheduled my interview with Father and she replied, "What interview? Father doesn't schedule interviews since there are so many people in the world clamoring to see him. He takes them in turn as their time comes and so, if you wish, I will put your name on the list for five seconds with Father."

I asked whether she could predict at what time I might count on being called in for my five seconds since it was already so late and she said, "Perhaps some time during the night tonight or tomorrow or next week sometime. People have come to heaven and waited a month or more for their seconds with Father."

I committed the error of saying, "But I've come all the way from New York to see Father Divine."

Dorothy Darling literally looked down her nose at me and said in a sharp, tart tone, "People come all the way from Australia to see Father Divine and they do not expect special consideration because of it." She hesitated a long moment, then asked, "Well, shall I put your name on the list after all or do you think you'd better be heading back to New York now?"

Of course, I asked her to list my name, and I sat down on a wooden bench where several black and several white women angels were also waiting their turn to enter Father's office. And many others, easily a hundred, stood waiting in groups or walked around the stuffy hall, stopping to chat with their friends now and then. As had been the case at the banquet, there seemed to be an iron-clad separation between the sexes. No man sat on the women's bench I was sitting on, and there were no women on any of the men's benches. As for those who walked around, men and women who happened to catch each others' eye nodded and said, "Peace," but there was a concerted effort to keep from seeing one another.

I waited on the bench for four hours while angels whose names were Miss Beautiful Peace, Miss Little Child Again, Miss Buncha Love, Mr. Humility, and Miss Universal Vocabulary were called for their five-second interviews with Father and then emerged radiant. Sometime after five in the morning an elderly white angel, Miss Moonbeam, suggested I return to my hotel room, saying she'd phone me there if and when my name was called. Since a person wouldn't be permitted access to Father until almost an hour after he'd been called, there would be ample time, provided I lay down without undressing, to return for my audience.

She didn't call me, or perhaps she did and I was so deeply asleep that I didn't hear the phone ring. But the fact is that when I returned to headquarters the next morning at nine, Dorothy Darling told me that my name had been called at seven and when I hadn't responded, my place had been taken by the next person on the list.

"Do you want to be listed as of now?" she asked. "I must tell you there are many people ahead of you so far."

I thanked her and declined her offer for then, saying I'd return to heaven in a week or thereabouts after I'd talked again with Crown Publishers, who were considering my outline for the book.

Back in New York, the Crown editors told me that they'd decided, after consideration, to turn the book down because I seemed to them to be insufficiently objective and too favorably disposed toward Father Divine. Doubleday then accepted my outline. And Crown, soon after its decision, was "punished" in a way that I knew Father, when I told him the strange facts, would be certain to characterize as "retribution against God's enemies." For, as it happened, Crown's editor-in-chief died of a sudden heart-attack, and Crown was sued for a vast sum of money for having published some allegedly libelous statements.

On my return to Philadelphia with my news of Crown's adversity, I was met by a prime leader of the movement, a handsome, socially prominent white architect in his middle forties, who had left his family and former life in order to become an angel. His heavenly name was John Germaine. At our meeting during my first visit to heaven, he'd pointed to his neck and told me about a nonexistent scar: "I got this scar over two thousand years ago when I first came to earth with Father Divine, who happened then to have been traveling in the Sonship rather than the Fatherhood degree. As you can imagine, it's a badge I bear with pride and joy."

When I told John Germaine what had happened to Crown simultaneously with their having turned the book down, he said, "Well, naturally, all those catastrophes had to happen to those publishers, who, in rejecting your book were also repudiating Father. They thought negatively of God. And so what could they expect after that—that Father would permit them to go on living as though they'd never committed such a crime? It couldn't happen."

Whatever question had been left in my mind about

whether or not Father Divine was an opportunistic defrauder, or so deranged himself as to believe passionately in all the tenets he laid down for his angels, it was answered once and for all when John Germaine told my story to Father. He reacted with such artlessness and gullibility as I wouldn't have believed if I hadn't myself experienced it. He spoke to me, and to hundreds of angels gathered at the second banquet I attended, in the same mood and with practically the same words I would hear him use time and again, whenever his colossal ego was offended, as it was now:

If one man sinneth against another, the judge shall judge him. But if a man sinneth against the Lord, who shall intercede for him? In the case of the publisher, who would not accept your book which would undertake to state more or less of the truth about my works here on earth, it was retribution that an editor on their staff should suffer a heart attack and pass on though he had not, to your knowledge, been a sickly man. Those publishers classed me with themselves as no more than any other man and so I had no choice but to show them what would happen to mortals who would compare me to other men and find me lacking by comparison. Who would dare to say that God's works do not merit having a book written about me while men's works do not merit such a thing? What says the word in the Ten Commandments? "Thou shalt not bow down thyself to them, nor serve them. For I the Lord thy God am a jealous God, visiting the iniquity of the fathers upon the children unto the third and fourth generation of them that hate me."

And, as you say, there has been a suit for over a million dollars leveled against them. Things don't just happen, but they happen just. Anybody can see that those critics among the publishers were cursed and that their cursings against God were returned to them even as they never left them. What they intended for me when they forbade you to write a book about my miracles and good works on earth came to them heaped up, pressed down and running over. Such is the love of the spirit of life. And if prejudice rules in their hearts and they divide themselves from me, as they have done by forbidding this book, prejudice afflicted them. And the law of retribution brought justice and judgment against them accordingly. For retribution is sure and retribution is assured, for truly has the word declared: "God is no respector of persons."

Thus, retribution rolls on, striking here and there at those who think they can criticize and slander me. But none can reach me to destroy the fundamental principle of my life and of my teaching. They are destroyed who run against the un-natural law of life. Hence it does not pay to defy my name, as the story of those publishers clearly shows.

Next Father Divine told—commanded—the angels to answer all my questions and talk to me freely about their lives before and after they'd entered heaven. He even lifted the ban governing separation of the sexes. He in-formed the male angels that not only would they not be sinning by talking to me, as would be the case with other women, but also that they would be more pleasing to God if they contributed to my knowledge and understanding. Often, therefore, I heard men who might have been con-versing with me for hours without any seeming restraint explain to their colleagues after we were done talking, "It was surely hard to speak to that lady and answer all of her questions. But what *wouldn't* one do for Father's sake?"

The women angels were a different story from the men. They were avid for conversation. I found them not only persevering in recalling every detail of their former lives, but also astonishingly analytic in bringing out their rea-sons for having become angels.

Of course, I spent a lot of time with Father's secre-taries, evenly divided between black and white, and some of them very young—in their teens and early twenties. They were Father's "inner cabinet," and they loved him so much they desired nothing more than to become anony-mous—shadows of Father Divine. Known in the move-ment as "Father's Sweets," the secretaries, though edu-cated and intelligent, were more valued for their "spotless virginity" than any other reason. I learned, only after I had been among them for a time, that one could aspire to become a "Sweet" even if she had not been a physical virgin in the world outside. For Father, being God, could, if he would, restore a person's lost virginity. He once let it be known through an intermediary, a favorite secretary, that my own virginity could be retrieved if I would make some rather simple moves—like learning shorthand so I could become one of heaven's recording secretaries and leaving my husband to whom I'd only been married a short time.

I spent a lot of time with Sweet Angel, Father's bride, who had been a Sweet and a secretary, before her marriage. She told me, and I am still sure today that she believed every word she said, that she was, in reality, a reincarnation of the first Mother Divine when Father had married her. She was as much a spotless virgin now, seven years after her marriage, as she'd been on the day the wedding had taken place.

And last but not least, I had almost, if not quite, the same access to Father Divine as the Sweets and Mother in the Second Body did. We talked of many matters, and though I was inhibited at the beginning by the knowledge that our intimate conversations were being taped by two recorders and taken down in their entirety by the secretaries, I gradually overcame my uneasiness and questioned Father as freely as though he and I were alone together. All the chapters of the book except the first, "John Doe, Alias God," were written from notes I took over the year and a half I lived and visited in the various heavens. When the time came for me to leave Philadelphia and Father, I told him, in all honesty:

"I must tell you now that I have never in my life met such happy and fulfilled people as your followers. A part of me is envious for their contentment and peace of mind. Nobody who knows them could fail to be impressed with you and all you've done for them. I must, however, write my book from where I stand—in the mortal version."

I believed that Father realized that my language meant:

As hospitable and, on the whole, communicative as you and the angels have been, I must still describe you and your movement with objectivity and attention to its negatives as well as positives as I observed them. I am regretful that I cannot concentrate on the positives alone, as you doubtless trusted I would do under the circumstances of the image I presented—sometimes with deliberation, of course, but more often, spontaneously, since I really was tremendously moved by the atmosphere surrounding you.

On the positive side, I am first of all going to report, in their words rather than mine, the enormous individual help the black angels in particular received from their alliance with you and your movement. So many of them struck me as having been completely incapacitated for existing in the reality world and might well have been in mental hospitals or jails if you had not come into their lives. Your movement, unlike the religions most of them left behind when they came to affiliate with you, does not impose penance or atonement. And there is no breast-beating, of which they must surely have had enough in their lives. And how wonderful for your black angels, especially the women, that you are, as you yourself would say, so "superlative a sample and example" of a father figure. I am convinced that no one else could or would so completely gratify—satiate rather—the thwarted longings of the majority of your black women angels for a concerned and caring father. Disposed by their early and later lives to anxiety and timidity with people, they are enabled, now that they've become angels, to be brave and fearless in their relationships in and out of heaven. They've come to value themselves in a way they never could have before because they know that you hold them so dear. I am touched and impressed whenever I stop to contemplate how very much the black angels, especially the women, have gained from you on the levels of identity and selfness.

However, Father Divine, as one leading a movement toward black awareness and social protest, I perceive you. . . .

This book, as I said, was written eighteen years ago when the common goal of the entire black leadership was the complete and equal integration of black people into white American society. And Father Divine, judged even by those aspirations, was obviously not only of no consequence in the white power-structure; but also he was in direct, if unconscious, resistance to every objective for which the black leadership fought.

As I suspected would be the case when I first tried to clarify myself to him, Father ignored the negative connotations of what I tried to tell him and said, in vehement answer to my talk:

Though you may not be aware of the moment and may not even begin to know it yet within your conscious mentality, God has acted upon his own impulse and more or less revealed himself to you, though you may not know it. Yea, you have human information and human intelligence but in order to

know God as he is—you should and must and *positively will*
relax your human mentality wholeheartedly and completely
for the Christ. Then, though your human mind does not know
it as yet, why, you will be unable to write your book from the
mortal version in the which is where you say you stand. But
rather you will be led to write from the version where you *do*
stand in actuality in the heavenly—not earthly—reality of the
angelic life.

He contemplated me a long moment and benignly continued:

It is the same with you as it was in the beginning of creation—
even the scientists and astronomers cannot tell how the earth
was spoken into existence although, as you may remember from
your Biblical training, it was without form. In the creation,
God said, "Let land appear." He spoke the earth into existence.
And he is speaking your book into existence as he did in
ancient times. God said, "Let this book be written from the
Angelic life—let that be the version." Your time has not come
as yet but that does not mean to say it will not arrive at all.
And, as a consequence, when it does arrive, then it will come
as a transmitted message to the children of this earth through
you. And all you have to do is dial in on Him, the Fundamental, for *I am a live wire and you will not write your book
from the mortal version as long as I will not to have it so.*

Father was both pained and incensed, therefore, when
the book appeared, and he responded, some six weeks
after its release, with a blast at me, my publisher, the
reviewers, and the readers. The followers named it "the
most glorious and gorgeous curse Father ever delivered
himself of." It consisted of six closely-printed pages in
the *New Day*, the movement's weekly newspaper, and
included pertinent references to the Bible. It stated in
part:

DIVINE PROPHECY, PREDICTION, DECLARATION AND
ULTIMATUM!
Re: The Book, "Father Divine, Holy Husband" . . . Attention:
The Writers, Publishers, Republishers and All Concerned,
All Publications, Readers, Sympathizers, Harmonizers, Be-
lievers, Critics, Followers, Preachers and Priests, as well as
Nations and others that Coincide with those Lies Published
in that book:

I THIS DAY, IN THE NAME OF ALMIGHTY GOD, I CURSE YOU BEYOND YOUR REASON TO GET CONSIDERATION WITH MERCY OR COMPASSION FROM ANYBODY. THIS IS JUDGMENT DAY . . . I have cursed them down to the bottomless pit of earth . . . Thousands and thousands will be burned beyond recognition while they are Living on the Topside of This Earth For I Curse them.

. . . I am cursing them from the Rivers to the End!—From Shore to Shore and From Land to Land. . . .

You Can See Them Dying On Every Hand! Accidents, Diseases and All Sorts of Catastrophies . . . Many of them Will Have Accidents and Be Broken Up! Many of them are Cursed With Infantile Paralysis! I am Cursing them Now! Many are Cursed With Paralytic Strokes and Other Ways Whereby They Will Be Cursed. Yea, I Am Cursing Them! Misery Shall Follow This Generation As Never Before.

I Am Cursing Their Children and I Am Cursing Their Children's Children In the Fulfillment of the Prophecies. . . .

I Set Before You a Blessing and I Set Before You a Cursing. And Those Who Will Accept of Me and My Plan and Purpose. If You Are Dead You Will Be Made Alive! But You Had Better Not Read That Book Or Any of Those Prejudiced Newspapers That Are Carrying Reports of It. I Curse You! If You Read It! I Curse You If You Read It! Now That You Know I Am God! I Hold The Wealth Of The World In My Hands! I Hold Your Energy! I Hold Your Breath!—Every Beating Pulse! And I Curse You Until The World Shall End.

I naturally avoided Father and the angels after the curse was proclaimed and knew no more about them than I read in the newspapers—less and less as time passed. Then in September of 1965, I had calls from newspapers and Philadelphia's TV station WCTU informing me that Father Divine had died and soliciting my recollections of him. They all said that their interviews with Mother and the angels revealed them to be as bitter and hostile toward me then as they must have been on the night Father damned me.

When the time came to update the book, therefore, I knew that I would be no more welcome in Divine's heaven than the proverbial rich man in the Biblical one. I had to find a stand-in, a person to investigate all that had occurred in heaven since I'd left in 1951. I am very fortunate that my husband, Arnold, and a friend, Paul A.

Fine, formerly a professor of Sociology and Psychology at Rutgers University, agreed to go to heaven on two separate occasions and talk at length with Mother and the angels. The last chapter is their version of the contemporary movement. I am, of course, deeply thankful to them.

—Sara Harris

FATHER DIVINE

JOHN DOE, ALIAS GOD

Father Divine claims that twenty million people call him God. He says:

"I am their life's substance! I am their energy and ambition. They recognize my deity as that which was in the imaginary heaven, and if they can only get a word with me, they feel like they are in heaven!"

Father Divine is not exaggerating what he is to his followers, both Negro and white, ranging from the illiterate to those with college degrees. The general impression that all of the followers of Father Divine are Negro women, most of them unable to read or write, is in error. In all the heavens, especially in the beloved Mecca in Philadelphia where Father Divine has his headquarters, there are white followers who are doctors, engineers, teachers, nurses. Many colored followers hold office jobs, some are registered nurses, others are teachers.

When Father walks across the hall from one of his offices to the other, followers run after him. Some jump up as high as they can, like children, others try to suppress the tension in their faces, but they have to join in the screams bursting from the throats of those crowding around Father. No one would dream, though, of touching even the sleeve of his jacket.

"Just to look at him is enough of a blessing. That is enough—more than enough—just to look and look at him." One of Father's secretaries stands aloof from the crowd and clasps her thin, white hands as if in prayer:

"Bless his holy heart!" she murmurs.

When Father drives up to any one of the heavens in his car, young women shriek and push through the crowd massed on the curb to see him, and fling themselves at the slowing Cadillac, running alongside, grabbing at the door handle, to peer in at the adored face.

At huge banquet tables, set to accommodate hundreds of diners, crowds fill every inch of space. Most of the followers like best to stand behind the diners, singing their hearts out, stamping and clapping until the very walls vibrate.

"I haven't eaten at any of the tables where Father serves," says Miss Universal Vocabulary. "I ain't learned yet to eat and love at the same time."

A pallid, grandmotherly old lady begins a song in a palsied voice:

> *Just to look at you,*
> *I wish I was in heaven ten thousand years*
> *Just to look at you.*

She throws up her purple-veined hands and begins to spin like a top, her bifocal, rimless eyeglasses striking against jutting shoulders, but nobody pays her any mind at all.

"Just to see you smile your beautiful smile——" Every voice joins in. Hands clap, feet stamp until the floor shakes.

> *Just to see you smile that beautiful smile,*
> *I wish I was in heaven ten thousand years,*
> *Just to see you smile that beautiful smile.*
> *Just to see you tap your feet, your beautiful feet,*
> *I wish I was in heaven ten thousand years,*
> *Just to see you tap your beautiful feet.*

Over and over they sing the refrain, adoring Father's beautiful hands when they clap, Father's beautiful head when it nods.

Father Divine is barely five feet tall. He is squat. He is African of feature, completely bald, and has the short-legged gait of a conquering hero. One who looks less like a divine being would be hard to imagine.

Father Divine has turned his liabilities into assets. He asks rhetorically:

"Why is it that God comes in the most insignificant, the most illiterate, the most underprivileged, the most downtrodden among the children of men? He comes among them that He might lift them and bring down the loftiness of the mighty, the self-exalted. Do you see the mystery?"

"So true, Lord, so true!" they shout in response.

The golden blond, twenty-seven-year-old Mother Divine, Father's second wife, who always sits at his right at the banquet table, smiles adoringly at him and joins in the chorus:

"So true, Father dear!"

With the impact of earth tremors on a seismograph, so does Father Divine affect his followers. A woman in a white blouse outlining unbrassièred, pendulous breasts, gives a deafening shout. She stiffens her spine, spreads her bare, dark arms as if crucified. Then she throws her torso backward and stands rigid, her outthrust stomach hitting the woman in front of her.

She lets her arms fall and stands upright again. Her voice is strident:

"I used to spit blood. I spit blood from the t.b. Nobody want to have me around. My so-called husban' don' want nothin' to do with me. 'Go on away.' He turned me outen the house. But you put your spirit in me, God. You healed me. You got no man in you, God! I know you, God!"

A trembling woman in a skintight, black satin dress keeps whispering, "I love you, Father. I love you, my sweetheart, I love you. I love you." Her whispering voice is the softly abandoned voice of a bride. Her body jerks in spasms.

A middle-aged woman in a red coat starts to snake her way up and down the aisle of standees. She is half dancing, half stumbling. She cries, "God, God, God!" Her voice is shrill. "God!" She moves blindly, in a trance. Then she grabs hold of a young woman sitting at the table. She nuzzles her face in the seated woman's neck and stays that way. Nobody pays any particular attention. Father, being accustomed to the peculiar form his followers' adulation often takes, pays less attention than anyone.

"They love, love, love me so much," he says.

Because Father's followers love him as much as he says

they do, they have banded together to prove their love in material form. They have placed all their money and all their services at his disposal. Today, Father Divine runs one of the biggest co-operatives in the country, and its real estate holdings in New York, Philadelphia, and Newark alone are worth over six million dollars. He is virtual owner of hotels and mansions in the finest white neighborhoods.

Father Divine has never paid one cent of income tax, though. Indeed, he has never even filed a return. He insists he owns nothing "not even my clothes." Many of his critics have prophesied that, sooner or later, the government will be able to find evidence that will force him to pay an income tax. Thus far, T-men have not been able to crack down on him. Not for lack of trying, but because Father is telling the literal truth when he insists that there are no properties, businesses, or bank accounts in the name of God, Father Divine.

He rides around in a Cadillac driven by his private chauffeur and wears custom-made suits and the finest of haberdashery, yet he does not need a penny to buy them with. The followers press upon Father anything he needs or wants, as their love offerings to God.

How did Father Divine attain his glory? How did this man born in the squalor of a shanty in the deep South end up as God?

"Except a man be born again," Jesus told Nicodemus, "he cannot see the Kingdom of God."

Father has commanded that a thick veil of mystery should hide his past life. When he tells the mortal world of the day that he was born out of his fleshly body, he says:

"I was combusted one day in 1900 on the corner of Seventh Avenue and 134th Street in Harlem."

To the followers, Father is ageless. Mother Divine says, "He does not live in time or seasons——"

Some say he married the first Mother Divine, the predecessor of his present wife, in 1882, which would make him at least ninety. He looks only middle-aged, however, and his actual age is probably in the late seventies.

Today, he says, "I might as well be forty-one as anything else," cheerfully ignoring the fact that he has given his birth date several times to officials as being 1880.

In 1949, a national radio program, conducted by Bruce Chapman, the Answer Man, answered a questioner who wanted to know when and where Father Divine was born. Was he married, and, if so, did he have any children?

The Answer Man quoted from Father's own letter which gave, Father wrote, "the true and open facts."

"Where was I born? I came to America that I might be called an American, but see St. John——" Father went on to quote from the Bible. "Before Abraham was, I am." He frequently answers that way when people ask how old he is.

The Answer Man's listeners must have been even more surprised to hear the rest of Father's answer:

"Am I married? Yes, but not for self-indulgence or sex indulgence, neither for physical propagation, therefore I do not have any natural children through physical propagation."

Though Father's version of his life is memorable, the available information about his rise from utter obscurity to his lofty pinnacle is even more impressive.

The best evidence to be found indicates that he was born around 1880 on a rice plantation on Hutchinson Island in the Savannah River. His name was George Baker, and his parents were sharecroppers. He had sisters and brothers. Nobody knows how many.

A man named Joe Jones who lived in South Carolina until recently claimed to be his brother. He never proved the relationship.

An old Kentucky lady named Maybelle Reid claims to have played with Father Divine. She tells, "He couldn' never be ascared of nothin' nohow. He was a real warm boy for the girls."

One biographer, John Hoshor, says that George Baker was married at seventeen and that he had four children whom he deserted. This has never been proven either. The first really authoritative details known about Father Divine start with 1899.

Bishop Saint John The Vine Hickerson, the only person

alive today who knew Father Divine before he became God, tells about those early years:

"Sure, he was just plain little George Baker in 1899. He lived in Baltimore, Maryland. You know what he did? Gardening. Working around the white neighborhoods for fifty cents a day. He used to live for Sundays because he used to teach Sunday school and be an assistant preacher in the church of Reverend Mr. Henderson. It was 'Baptist Church Colored.'"

During the days when Father Divine was George Baker, his sermons were pedestrian ones. They never indicated that he thought he was God, Bishop Hickerson says.

It was at Reverend Henderson's church that Father Divine first met the man who, more than anyone else, was responsible for his present ideology. His name was Samuel Morris. He was a mulatto, so fair-skinned that he might easily have been mistaken for white. He was tall and very attractive.

Samuel Morris lived in Allegheny, Pennsylvania. On Sundays, he served as a lay preacher there. On weekdays he worked as a steel-mill laborer. He hated his weekday job and longed to get away from it. He could not though. How would he support himself if he left his job? How would he eat? How would he sleep? These mundane problems seemed unsolvable to him. Until one night, in the middle of reading his Bible, he came on a verse in the third chapter of First Corinthians that staggered him and made him know that a man of his stature could afford to ignore worldly practicalities like eating and sleeping.

"Know ye not that ye are the Temple of God, and that the spirit of God dwelleth in you?" the Bible asked.

Didn't the Bible speak plain as day that if the spirit of God dwelt in him, and if the Spirit and the Word were one, then God Himself dwelt in him? And if God dwelt in him, then his body was God's body—and he, Morris, was God.

Morris was convinced his truth was the greatest ever revealed. And when, one night, he dreamed he heard a heavenly summons: "Go to Baltimore and save souls there," he could no more have ignored the dream than he could have stopped living.

Having arrived in Baltimore, he contacted Reverend Henderson whom he knew slightly. When Reverend Henderson invited him to preach a guest sermon in his church, he accepted with alacrity.

"The night Samuel Morris came to Henderson's church was sure enough Divine's lucky night," according to Saint John The Vine Hickerson.

It was a rainy night, but the church was filled to its capacity. Reverend Henderson had done a good job of advertising the guest preacher.

Samuel Morris started to preach in the ordinary way. He had a deep, resonant voice and wonderful fluidity of body. The congregation was delighted. Suddenly, though, in the midst of a profound sentence, he stopped and stood stock still in the pulpit.

"I am the Father Eternal!" he shouted, thudding his fists against his chest and reaching toward the rafters. "I am the Father Eternal!"

Several muscular men rushed him, picked him up, and deposited him bodily on the sidewalk, with the enthusiastic approval of the other members of the congregation —except one. That one helped Morris to his feet and took him home to his boardinghouse, run by a lady evangelist named Mrs. Snowden. Morris' Good Samaritan was George Baker. To George Baker and Mrs. Snowden, Morris revealed the great truth that had been revealed to him in Allegheny.

After George Baker brought Morris there, a room in Mrs. Snowden's Baltimore boardinghouse was turned into a modest mission that attracted a few people. Though the small congregation had their doubts about Morris' being God, his electrifying shout "I am the Father Eternal" brought them to their feet, thrilled out of their everyday doldrums at being under the same roof with one who could proclaim himself God and not be struck dead on the spot.

George Baker addressed Morris' meetings. A few weeks after Morris' coming he became recognized as his legitimate assistant.

Around 1907, Samuel Morris announced that he had been born again. He took a divine name as befitted his divine status—Father Jehovia—"Jehovah with one letter added and another letter removed." He instructed his disciple, George Baker, that the time had come for him also to achieve heavenly recognition even if on a smaller scale. George Baker was reborn as the "Messenger." Father Jehovia announced himself "God in the Fathership Degree" and he conferred on the Messenger the title "God in the Sonship Degree."

While they preached every night, both men earned their livings during the day. The Messenger still hedge clipping and mowing lawns, and Father Jehovia driving a wagon gathering junk.

In 1908, St. John The Vine Hickerson joined them. He must have been an impressive figure, for even today he is still imposing. Tall, ascetic, he looks like the old masters' paintings of Jesus, except for his tan complexion and advanced age.

As a young man, he had fought the devil in Pentecostal Holiness and assisted Elder Robertson's Live Ever, Die Never Church in Boston. He was a born preacher with an electrifying style when the spirit was in him.

He would begin preaching in a low quiet tone, all the while ambling about the lectern slowly. As his voice grew louder and his words faster, he would break into a lope, and suddenly he would leap straight up into the air and land shouting.

For four years, the three men, Father Jehovia, the Messenger, and St. John The Vine Hickerson, worked together under Jehovia's leadership. Although their congregations remained small, they became known throughout the city as the most colorful religious team ever to have hit Baltimore.

Around 1912, the trio split up because Hickerson became dissatisfied with Jehovia as his superior and expressed his feelings. He was willing to let Father Jehovia keep his Fathership Degree, but, he asked, what about the biblical admonition, "The Spirit of God dwelleth in you"? That, he told Jehovia, meant that anybody who read the admonition was the "you" and could be God too.

Father Jehovia objected to the challenge of his divinity. The Messenger was satisfied with his title of God in the Sonship Degree. Why couldn't Henderson be?

Hickerson could not be satisfied, though, and he left Father Jehovia to come to New York. He wanted to found his own church there.

Shortly after St. John The Vine Hickerson left Baltimore, the Messenger decided that if Saint John could be God, so could he be. He left Baltimore too and began to travel South.

All along the way, he did odd jobs to support himself and preached on street corners or in Negro churches. As he traveled, he recruited disciples to travel with him. These came slowly. In two years, he had no more than a handful.

In 1914, the Messenger and his small coterie arrived in Valdosta, Georgia. Here, for some unaccountable reason, he became a huge success. The entire Negro community, especially the women, responded to him.

"I be God," he shouted to crowds of tired domestic workers, "you be God. Drop your yoke of bondage."

"Amen," they shouted back.

The Messenger stayed in Valdosta for many weeks. Night by night, his street-corner congregations grew larger. On Sundays, they were overflowing. People, especially women, came from the legitimate Negro churches; they came in such numbers that the town's ministers grew resentful. They tried to woo their congregations back. The people, especially the women, would not be wooed. They tried to intimidate them into coming back. They would not be threatened. Finally, in desperation and as a last resort, they had the Messenger arrested as a public menace. They charged him specifically with claiming to be God and stated that he was obviously a lunatic. Their accusation was strengthened by the fact that when the police officer who arrested him asked his real name, he denied he had any name but the Messenger. When the same officer asked one of the disciples who traveled with him whether the Messenger had another name, the disciple answered, "He got another name all right. It's God. That's what's his real name. God. 'Cause that's him, God. He ain't nobody but God."

The writ that brought the prisoner to trial identified him as John Doe, alias God.

The two chief witnesses against John Doe, alias God,

were ministers. One was a doctor named Stafford who was pastor of the Holy Roller Church. The other was the Methodist pastor, Dr. White. Dr. Stafford testified that thirty or forty people in Valdosta had been encouraged and did believe that the Messenger was God. Therefore, concluded Dr. Stafford, the Messenger, in his opinion, was crazy. Dr. White reiterated Dr. Stafford's testimony.

That the Messenger's attorney, J. P. Copeland, believed jealousy of rival ministers to be the cause of his client's arrest was apparent in the way he questioned the main accusers. He asked Dr. Stafford, the Holy Roller minister, if he thought a person of sound mind could believe the Methodist interpretation of certain parts of the Bible. Dr. Stafford said he certainly could not. Then he asked Pastor White to tell what he thought of Holy Rollers' sanity. Pastor White said he thought all Holy Rollers were crazy.

Mr. Copeland addressed the jury. "Gentlemen, the two principal witnesses against the defendant have testified that they consider each other to be of unsound mind because of the same religious prejudice which is the basis of this complaint." The jurors smiled.

They were not amused, however, by other witnesses whom the two main accusers had gathered. John Burns, colored handyman around town, called the defendant "one of them crazy preachers what send the wiminfolks crazy." He called him a preacher who "made trouble by playin' on wimin's feelin's." He quoted one of the Messenger's oft-repeated statements: "My followers are not entangled with a yoke of bondage."

The jury was certainly not amused by the picture painted for them by several other witnesses, men whose wives, formerly hard-working and satisfied with their lives, were depicted as having suddenly begun to talk bitterly of their "yoke of bondage." They had worked in the fields when they were children. They had been uncomplaining. As soon as they'd grown, they'd begun to clean and cook for local families. They had remained uncomplaining. Then the visiting preacher had come. These satisfied workers had begun to call him God and say that he would "change their troubles into happiness."

There was the fat, brown-skinned woman who had been such an efficient cook. Her husband told the court that after the Messenger's advent, she lost interest in her work. She often cried out, "Hallelujah, God has revealed himself!" She took to running through the streets, yelling that God was walking in Valdosta. Her value as a cook had naturally decreased. Wives of other witnesses had been infected in exactly the same way.

There were the domestic workers who had suddenly instructed their husbands that they didn't care to work in other people's homes any more, and the fieldworkers who complained that salaries were too low to pay for their services.

M. General Washington stated, "All my wife does now is stand around droolin' at that man. She won't work no more. The meetin's keep her up so late, she can't be gettin' up in the mornin'."

These emotionally rendered testimonies proved to the jury that the defendant was a community menace. Their verdict was "guilty."

They said that the Messenger was of unsound mind. Not crazy enough to be sent to the State Sanitarium but crazy enough to be ordered to leave the state of Georgia at once. The Court accepted the recommendation.

Crazy or not, before he left Valdosta to come North the Messenger garnered several new disciples. There was a disciple named Michael and one named Gabriel. There was also a very pleasant-looking stout lady named Peninah. From the day she entered his group, it was apparent to the other followers that Peninah or Sister Penny, as the other disciples called her, was a favorite of the Messenger. He spent a great deal of time with her and permitted her to accompany him wherever he had to go. Most of the disciples, before the group left Valdosta, began to accept Sister Penny as the Messenger's second in command.

The Messenger and his disciples made their way North from Valdosta in easy stages, making stopovers in towns en route so that the disciples could find jobs as domestics and earn money for living expenses and fare to the next town. While the followers worked, the Messenger preached. In some towns, he garnered new disciples to take North with him.

In 1915, he arrived in New York City with his entourage of about a dozen devoted followers. One of the first things he did was to seek out his former friend, St. John The Vine Hickerson. Hickerson was conducting a flourishing church called the Church of the Living God, on Forty-first Street. His dynamic preaching of the indwelling God had brought auxiliary Gods flocking around . . . Joe World, Steamboat Bill, Father Paul, Father Joshua, Elijah of the Fiery Chariot, Father Obey were just a few of them. The Temples of God, as the men followers called themselves, wore crowns festooned with gold and silver, and they shouted:

"God in you, God in me, Everybody be God. God lives in this Temple and I'm so glad, so glad. Can't never die!"

The Messenger often attended The Vine's church and sometimes St. John Hickerson came to the apartment on West Fortieth Street which he and his followers rented.

"He used to invite me to that apartment on Fortieth Street," Hickerson tells tartly today, "and give me good to eat and all like that, but you don't catch him lettin' any of them folks of his come to my church. Then, while I'm eating, he says, 'How do you do this? How do you do that?'"

Cannily, the Messenger kept his disciples away from the Church of the Living God, even while he, himself, kept contact with Hickerson in order to question him about the practical management of his cult.

"He learned and didn't give nothin' in return," Bishop St. John says. "Divine started out to be a son to me. Me, the father. Him, the son. Me, telling him about things. Him, learning. That's how it goes. Intelligence is the father. Obedience is the son. Me, the father. Divine, the son. Then, he started in peckin' at me behind my back. I didn't care, though. I still consider him a son, account of all he had to learn from me, but a crooked son."

Actually, the Messenger learned more from Bishop St. John The Vine than St. John, himself, knows. He learned from watching St. John The Vine that the doctrine of the indwelling God, which he had started to preach down

South, could not possibly work in favor of its leader. He learned that it could not possibly make for the kind of disciplined church he envisioned.

In St. John's church, there was no control. The members did as they pleased and never heeded their spiritual leader. Gradually, the Church of the Living God began to fall apart. Since each member of Hickerson's Temple of God considered himself as important as his Bishop and more important than anyone else in the community, the Temples of God and ordinary citizens who lived in their vicinity often had the most violent disagreements.

"God be in me, he not be in you," the holy ones would taunt their neighbors.

The West Forty-seventh police precinct reports recorded many instances of violence between Temples of God and unaffiliated neighbors. There were fist fights and even stabbings. And, when St. John The Vine Hickerson attempted to control his congregation's violence, he was no more adhered to than was anyone else.

The complete disintegration of the Church of the Living God proved to the Messenger that, no matter what, no auxiliary Gods must ever be permitted to function in his heaven. He left the West Fortieth Street neighborhood and moved his disciples into a four-room flat on Myrtle Avenue in a Negro section of Brooklyn. He severed contact with his friend Hickerson and proceeded to use what he had learned from him. Not only did he make it clear to his followers that he was their only God, he also went so far as to demand that they give up every loyalty except the one to himself.

All ordinary mortal feelings must, he dictated, be cast out. Followers must discipline themselves to reject any attachment which they might feel for members of their families or for friends who had been part of their former lives. He demanded that parents give up any thought of their children and that children give up any thought of their parents. He commanded husbands never to think about their wives and wives never to think about their husbands. And he proclaimed any sex expression, even between husbands and wives, a glaring black sin. Strangely, from then until today, all followers except for very occasional backsliders obey these rules to their letters.

Illogically, at the same time that he officially outlawed sex among his followers, the Messenger took a wife himself. She was Sister Penny of Valdosta days.

Sister Penny's position, after her marriage, did not change very much. She remained what she had started to be in Valdosta, the Messenger's first lieutenant, in full charge of the physical details of running his establishment. Maids and cooks took their orders from her.

The Messenger assured his followers that he and Sister Penny were no more subject to "carnality and bodily lust" than he wished his angels to be. That is why they occupied separate rooms, Sister Penny sleeping in the women's dormitory and the Messenger himself sharing sleeping quarters with his male disciples. The followers never doubted that Father and his wife were as chaste as they claimed to be. And Sister Penny's appearance did much to aid Father's claim. Looking more like the Messenger's mother than his wife, she was not the kind of woman a mortal man could have desired lustfully. It was only because the Messenger was God, the followers felt, that he was enabled to see beneath the homely body to the beautiful spirit lodged inside it.

Sister Penny helped the Messenger considerably during those early days of the movement but never obtrusively. She adored him and was never demanding of him. She was always available for any routine task he might assign her and she always did it well and with no fanfare. Although she was uneducated as the Messenger himself, she, like he, had a natural shrewdness and ability. And she was a marvelous housekeeper.

It was in Brooklyn that the Messenger first made himself available to the non-affiliated. He opened his flat to outsiders for meetings and meals. Peninah's dinners, banquets really, became the talk of Fulton Street. They were lavish, they were good, and they were free. Many people, aside from his disciples, began to think and to talk about the Messenger. And to come to the free banquets.

After a good meal the Messenger would address the

gathered group, followers and visitors alike, made up almost entirely in those days, of colored domestics. He talked about racial equality, stating that he had come from another world to achieve it.

It was a new kind of chauvinism the Messenger preached to his early New York followers and friends. He went a step beyond what even Marcus Garvey, the most aggressive Negro chauvinist of recent years, had ever dared to say. Where Garvey had said that black was basically superior and white was basically inferior, the Messenger exemplified that statement. He said, I am a Negro and God dwells in me. You are a Negro and you are like unto me. Therefore, you are superior to white.

Some of those who came to listen to him expostulate his doctrine of racial equality and to eat his good free meals stayed to affiliate with him. Before his first year in the Brooklyn flat had ended, the original twelve disciples had increased to twenty. Now, the four-room flat was no longer an adequate headquarters. The Messenger began to feel cramped. He decided to seek new quarters.

In his search for an apartment, the Messenger grew discouraged. There were few desirable apartments for rent in the Negro area. Those which were available were priced too high. Outside the Negro neighborhood, no landlord would rent to him. He conferred with Peninah and made an important decision. He would buy a house out of New York City but within commuting distance. In the long run, it would be cheaper than renting an apartment and it would make for pleasanter living.

After a long hunt the Messenger found a house. It was a two-story frame house of twelve rooms on a sixty-foot lot. It was located at 72 Macon Street, in the very center of an unpretentious middle-class white area in Sayville, Long Island. The Messenger paid $750 in cash and the remainder of the purchase price of $2500 in mortgages. On the deed appeared the name Major J. Devine—The Messenger's newest acquisition—and also the name of his wife Peninah.

[2]

HOUSE OF JOY

Macon Street houseowners did not approve their new neighbor. They thought that he would cause the town to be overrun by Negroes. They presumed that, because of Devine and his colored followers, Sayville, which catered to summer visitors, would soon be dead as a resort and that they, themselves, would be forced to sell their homes at low prices and to flee the town.

Those few people who were not disturbed about the color of Major Devine's skin were troubled about other things. They thought he and his followers were peculiar. They thought they might be dirty or unhealthy and that they might infect the whole community. They thought they might proselyte some Sayvilleites to their fantastic beliefs. Above all, they were sure that 72 Macon Street would be a noisy house.

Major Devine did none of the things his neighbors had feared he might. He did his best to operate as a good neighbor. He was always polite to anyone who passed his door. When he met people, he greeted them enthusiastically. He made it known that he would be a hospitable host if any of the neighbors would care to make his acquaintance. Above all, he did all of his shopping, and ample shopping it was, in the Sayville shops, even though he might have saved money by buying outside of town. He seemed, after the neighbors grew to know him slightly, to be an exceptionally gentle man. He worked around his grounds a great deal, clipping hedges or raking leaves.

Devine operated an employment agency in Sayville just as he had in New York. He used to insert weekly ads in the *Suffolk County News*, offering "reliable colored help" for all kinds of domestic work. When prospective employers replied to his ad, he would go to see them. Appearing on their doorsteps, hat in hand, he would laud his clients in the most flowery terms.

"She has a wonderful character," he would say, "and a kind heart that is kinder than other people's hearts with uprightness in and out of season."

The disciples, like their leader, seemed decent and orderly, no different from the other people in the neighborhood. Most of them left the house in the morning, as other working people did, and returned to it again in the evening. They were happy people who sang sometimes, but never loud enough to annoy their neighbors and never after 9 P.M. Most important, between 1919 and 1927, the original twenty disciples, instead of overrunning the community as it had expected they would, had slowly increased by twos and threes to a membership of only forty.

It was not until the very late 1920's, a good ten years after Major Devine first moved to Sayville, that he did give his neighbors cause to regret his presence. For, at that time, he undertook a program to increase his following. He began to publicize himself in New York and in Brooklyn and the Bronx. He set aside Sunday as a proselyting day, when outsiders—the more, the better—were invited to avail themselves, free, of the most generous hospitality they'd ever heard of. They came, to the chagrin of the neighbors, in droves.

"Every Sunday was like Christmas," long-time follower Sweet Notion recalls today.

The tables were set with the finest of platters of chicken, ham, beef stew, corn, mashed potatoes, rice, hominy, beans, tomatoes, cole slaw, spinach, mountainous bowls of ice cream, cakes as big as automobile tires but higher, piles of cheese, tea, coffee, postum, milk, and chocolate milk.

After dinner, Major Devine spoke to convert the strangers.

"Peace, everyone, righteousness, justice, and truth. When you started out to find a Better Home, here is the Place that you have found it where the trials of the world cannot come. You will be so happy here where there are no sorrow, pain, nor death in the presence of the Lord all the time. Aren't you glad?"

The guests, all profoundly impressed by the beneficence, returned to their homes to start the flow of word-of-mouth endorsement of Major Devine. Some of them, learning that he could get them jobs, remained in Sayville.

In 1928, about a year after Major Devine began his conscious recruitment campaign, his less than forty disciples had increased to better than ninety skilled and unskilled laborers, who contributed their entire earnings, an average of fifteen dollars per week apiece, to the upkeep of God's dwelling.

By 1930, he began to make progress among the servants of wealthy families, who earned as much as a hundred dollars a month. In the same year, he converted his first white followers—a whole busload of them. They came from West New York, New Jersey. They had been Holiness people.

The year 1930 also heralded the spectacular conversions of a few wealthy, well-educated white women, and of a white man with a college degree from Boston University, named J. Maynard Matthews, who gave up his automobile agency to become Brother John Lamb, Father's executive secretary.

That year of his first real triumph, 1930, was the year when Major J. Devine was reborn a third and last time. That was the year when George Baker, alias the Messenger, alias Major Devine, formally took the name which, he felt, best exemplified his personality—Father Divine.

As Father Divine, he grew more and more important in Sayville. His fame spread in white communities, in more secure colored communities, and most especially in the communities composed of lower-class Negroes who came to Father Divine and stayed with him and accepted him as God because they needed him to be God.

Today, those who, having come during Sayville times, are still happy with Divine tell how it was and why it was that they were irresistibly drawn to him. It was more than the free banquets that lured them. They say they came to Father because they were poor, they were Negroes and thought they were inferior, and because they knew that through all their whole lives long they would have no hope of being anything but inferior. They say that they knew they could not live in the same houses as white people lived and did not expect to live in those houses. They knew they could not attend the same schools as white people attended and did not expect to be allowed to attend those schools. They knew they could not hold the same jobs as white people held and did not expect to hold those jobs. Therein, they tell today, lay the tragedy of their frustrations—not in what they did not have but rather in what they could not expect. It was not the reality of their lives that was so unbearable. It was the hopelessness behind the reality.

For young as well as old lower-class Negroes in the 1930's, Divine became a symbol of righteousness and justice. It is to his credit that, for most of them who came, like Lillian Wilson did, in the 1930's, he has remained until today the same symbol.

"I gave my heart to Father twenty-two years ago, reckoning by your mortal version," Lillian Wilson feelingly tells today, "and I could never take it back. Oh, the wonderful life he's given me in return!"

Lillian Wilson was born in the drab section of Brooklyn's Harlem on Fulton Street. Her father had walked out on his six children, and her mother had had to do domestic work by the day in order to feed her family. Since there was no supervision, the children often played hookey from school. Lil never did, though. Her teachers said she was one of the brightest in the class.

Lil's mother was proud of her daughter's being smart enough to want to take up typing so that she could get an office job. She was even prouder of having raised a God-fearing girl. Lil went to the store-front church with her mother. They were the only ones in the family who were churchgoing, and they prayed for salvation for the others.

In high school Lil worked hard at her typing because her mother and the preacher told her typist jobs paid well. Lil graduated from high school, but when she applied at an employment agency, they told her there were very few jobs that didn't specify "white," and times were so hard that even white typists were out of work. After she'd been to every agency she heard about, the situation looked hopeless and Lil felt forced to take a job as a live-in maid. Her pay was small.

Lil's mother advised her to quit her job and get married. She retorted bitterly that if that advice was as good as her mother's former advice about typing, she was not taking it. She pointed to her sisters, all married to men whom they had to support. They all had a houseful of children too. There were just no sort of men around but the shiftless ones, as far as Lil could see. Her mother said she was crazy. Lil said her mother was crazier than she would ever be.

It was actually to spite her mother that the girl took the free bus trip out to Sayville one Sunday. Her mother had been telling her, the night before, that the preacher was saying that Father Divine was the Antichrist. Just to start an argument, Lil had defended Father Divine.

The people in the bus going out to Sayville were not much different from the congregation Lil had worshiped with all her life. They sang and clapped and praised God. Their God, though, was Father Divine, and Lil was shocked. An old lady who sat next to her in the bus told her about the time when Father Divine had lived in Brooklyn.

"I used to get heart attacks. Father opened the heart and laid it open," she said, "and then he closed it again. I never had heart attacks after that." Tears rolled down her face as she related how wonderful it had been.

At the Sayville house, the spirit of warmth and kindness made Lil's wait for a seat at the dinner table a pleasant one. As she watched Father pour coffee from a silver pot, she heard a woman, close to her in the standing crowd, explain that she had seen, with her own eyes, Father pour more than two hundred cups of coffee from that very pot that "you'd think wouldn't hold no more than twelve cupfuls."

Some people finished their meal and Father rose to speak. Lil thought that he was going to ask for donations, but he said, instead, "Peace, everyone."

"Peace, Father," came the answering shout.

Father's eyes seemed to be upon Lil, in concern over her long wait for her meal. At last he said graciously that those who were standing were welcome to fill the emptied seats.

As Lil sat down, Father continued speaking.

He talked for a long time, and though Lil could not understand many of the complicated words he used, she did not mind. She was too busy thinking about one thing he said . . . the words he used when his voice rose in flaming indignation.

"Out of all the higher education, it does not profit until you get away from racism. Until we get away from a race or color, our representatives need a higher degree! I desire to give our representatives in government a new birth of freedom, under God, so that they might represent one nation, indivisible with liberty and justice for all! That is my work and my mission."

Lil's curiosity overcame her shyness. After the banquet, she pushed through the crowd around Father and said she wanted to pay for her good meal. He looked straight at her, and she saw that his eyes, set far apart, had a magnetic quality.

"Sister, everythin' is free to anyone who wants it." He had a ready laugh that put her at ease. "I see you are puzzled, sister. The Spirit of the Consciousness of the presence of God is the source of all supply and will satisfy every good desire."

Lil wanted to ask him whether his words at the banquet table meant that he promised to change things so that she could get an office job even though she was colored, but others crowded her away from the coveted spot.

The following Sunday she returned to Sayville. It was nicer there, surrounded by trees and flowers, than it was in the hot city. She liked the inside of the house too. She was deeply impressed by the picture over the mantel of Booker T. Washington having lunch on the White House lawn with former President Theodore Roosevelt with the word "Equality" printed underneath. She liked the sign on the stairs: "Peace—cigars cigarettes and intoxicating liquors not allowed." She knew that meant there would not be any drunken men in Sayville of the kind she had seen all her life.

On her second Sunday at Sayville, Father spoke against the lusts of men:

"Human indulgence through the sex affections—those desires will leave the people and they will not have a desire such as they have had. For the atmosphere in which they are breathing will be contagionized with the spirit of temperance, with the spirit of morality, with the spirit of modesty, the spirit of righteousness, the spirit of truth, the spirit of justice, and even the spirit of virtue such as was brought to fruition in the body of Mary. Do you see the mystery?"

"Yes, sweet Savior!"

The followers broke into song.

> *Father Divine is my Father,*
> *Father Divine is walking in the land.*
> *Father Divine he is my Father*
> *Got the world in a jug*
> *And the stopper in his hand.*

Lil found herself singing the reassuring song as she worked on her job. After her sixth Sunday in Sayville, she never went back to the store-front church. She felt that she belonged with Father. When people she knew, those who had never seen Father, called her queer, Lil told them that the followers were not so different from the people in other churches.

The woman who leaped to her feet to testify at the banquet table one Sunday night might have been one of Lil's mother's friends, the one who was always shouting at the store-front meetings about having been healed of a tumor.

"Thank you, Father," shouted the follower. "Father, you gave me your own blood transfusion. I bled till there was no more blood. My intestines were rotten . . . I was nothin' but the skin and the bones. Father—you raised me from the dead. God . . . you gave me that blood transfusion!"

Her emotions could be expressed only by a song.

"Father is the doctor," she sang, and the other followers clapped and stamped the rhythm.

> *Father is the doctor,*
> *Father is the doctor*
> *Father is the doctor*
> *Bless his holy name.*

That was the evening when Lil found herself sitting between two white women. One lady told Lil that she was through with the Holiness people and was going to become a Divine follower. The other white lady was from Long Island City. She had been a Christian Scientist, but she had recently lost a child. She told Lil that Father's healing was like Christian Science, only much better. If she had come to Father before, she was sure that her child would never have died. Her name was Sister Everjoy.

The strain that Lil always had felt when she'd talked to white people slipped away. Light- and dark-complected people, as Father insisted they be called, were alike in the "House of Joy," Father's dwelling. They ate together, worshiped a dark-complected God together, and slept together. She had her answer to the question she hadn't had the chance to ask Father on her first visit. He hadn't only preached about race equality. He was bringing it about.

Lil made up her mind to ask Father for some advice. She told him that she wondered if she was crazy to want to try to get an office job. Father told her that he had worked long and hard so that his followers might be sought after by employers, as being trustworthy and reliable employees.

"The more profound your devotion to me," Father smiled, "the greater will be your expression and reproduction of my mind and spirit."

When Lil applied for a job, in answer to an ad for a typist, she did not anticipate defeat before she started. She felt almost confident, believing in Father's words—that employers welcomed followers. After her interview, she rushed breathlessly to Father with the news that she had been given the job.

He did not need to tell her that he had blessed her with

an abundance of all good blessings. She had known it all along.

Lil's mother was delighted about the job, but she flew into a rage when Lil told her that Father Divine had revealed himself to her as God.

"Why, he's nothin' but a racketeer!" her mother stormed. "People are sayin' he's got a counterfeit plant out there that changes five-dollar bills to five hundreds. You must be crazy!"

Lil could afford to pity her ignorant mother. Didn't she know how many lies jealous people told about Father? Banks in Sayville tested the bills that Father spent, and nobody could say that Father's money wasn't as genuine as he was himself.

"I was crazy before I found Father," Lil said quietly. "Father was the only one who helped me. All you ever did was talk. I never want to see you again." Lil's mother tried to see her even after their quarrel. At first, Lil thought she might try to convince her of Father's divinity, but soon she realized that it was no use to try to explain her new religion to a woman with such set ideas. Her mother called Father bad names, accusing him of farming people out like slaves, taking all their wages, in exchange for just their board and room. Lil was so shocked and angry that she told her mother, and meant it as she hadn't the first time, that she never wished to see or communicate with her ever again. She told her mother that it was a privilege to be blessed to help contribute her money toward Father's work and mission on earth. She had everything she wanted right there in heaven so she did not need any money; and, more important than material things—she had Father Divine.

By the spring of 1931, Sayville had become a lodestar to thousands of Negroes like Lillian Wilson. They converged on the town every Sunday. They came in anything on wheels that they could borrow or beg . . . private cars, sightseeing buses, moving vans, ice trucks, motorcycles. They came from the Bronx and from Brooklyn and from Richmond. The great bulk of them came from Harlem.

In Harlem, bus-owners ballyhooed every Sunday, "Drivin'

right out to Father Divine's heaven in Sayville. $2.40 a round trip with all the fixin's for nothin'."

Father stopped them, though. He himself bought buses for the transportation of people with no other way of getting to see him.

Week by week, the crowds increased. Such traffic jams were created that Sayville's traffic officers, whose lives till then had been leisurely, had to work overtime.

Although no alcohol was allowed on the Sayville premises, followers grew drunk on the strong brew of the abundance of physical and spiritual blessings of the Great Provider. They reeled and danced in the big yard of the House of Joy, and some streamed exuberantly out into Macon Street. Inside the house, the singing, clapping, and stamping went on until all hours, and the heavenly din drowned out any banging at the door or telephone calls from the outside world where Father's neighbors resided.

Most of the homeowners in the vicinity wished that they lived anywhere but on Father's block. The plight of Father's neighbors became the talk of the whole town, fanning the fears of those who had predicted from the beginning that Sayville would have cause to regret Father Divine's becoming a resident. The people who owned properties in the summer colony, near the waterfront, also grew concerned. They concluded, as Father's neighbors had, that Father Divine gave the town a reputation as a cheap, noisy Harlem colony, frequented by a sprinkling of insane white people, and that, if he were permitted to remain, their real estate investments would be doomed.

A committee of leading citizens was organized with the purpose of ridding Sayville of Father Divine. It was headed by Mr. Rogers, president of the National Bank in Sayville. Its most vociferous members, naturally, were Father's closest neighbors, Fred Gutley, who lived at 71 Macon Street with his father and mother, and August Schwaner, who lived at 75. The large hotel owners were also affiliated.

One of the first activities of the committee was the planning and carrying out of a mass meeting which was held on September 27, 1931, at the Sayville high school. Thomas Guthrie presided.

"The reason we are here," Guthrie stated, "is to do something to get rid of the noise on Macon Street and the inconvenience and the racket. It calls for community spirit."

He outlined the problems of Father's neighbors. Then he discussed the problem of the community's businessmen who "are having a hard enough time in the community to make a living out here in the winter without having a nuisance of this sort in town which is chasing the people away." And he talked about real estate values.

After much heated accusation, the committee got down to practical business. They appointed a subcommittee to call upon Father.

The subcommittee called. It identified itself as speaking for "Sayville at large" and requested Father Divine to leave town.

Father refused. He was polite to the committee but sure of himself. He said that he had bought the house at 72 Macon Street in good faith. He spent thousands in local stores, paying cash. He was law-abiding and so were his followers. He believed in the Bill of Rights and the Constitution of the United States. Therefore he believed that American citizens had the right to worship when and how they liked.

"Then you will not move?" the spokesman asked.

"I desire peace," Father said, "but I cannot do what you request. In fact, I am negotiating for the purchase of three more houses in this block."

His manner as well as his words convinced the committee that it would be useless to argue. They left, surprised at his self-confidence and certain that he must have mysterious, influential backing to enable him to act so independently.

They speculated and almost began to believe wild rumors about Father that had been around town for months. "Capitalists" were financing the movement, some Sayvilleites insisted. Others said that Father's funds came from "Moscow gold." A wealthy white woman was supplying Father with thousands of dollars, according to many, and so was John D. Rockefeller. The unnamed woman and Rockefeller were backing Father because they wanted him to divert the masses from revolution.

On a Sayville street corner, an argument developed between a native and one of the brothers.

"I hear tell Rockefeller put Father Divine up to telling you black folks not to sleep with your wives because he don't want no more black folks born."

"Peace," the brother answered with superb self-control. "You been hearin' a bunch of lies. Sure Rockefeller hisself been to see Father, but it was to get healed. The doctors couldn't do nothin' for him, but Father he cured him. Rockefeller and other millionaires they want to pay Father so they can keep him to theirselves . . . to keep 'em from dyin' . . . but Father wants to heal everybody, not just rich folks."

When the members of the committee were certain, as they were after their first interview with Father, that they could not make a dent in his stubbornness through personal contact, they determined, wishfully, that he must be breaking the law in one way or another and worked to secure evidence of his wrongdoing. They started an organized program.

First, letters began to arrive at 72 Macon Street, addressed to Father Divine from senders unknown to him. Enclosed in these were cash, money orders, and checks. It was a farfetched attempt, but they hoped he would take the strange money and thus lay himself open to suspicion of using the mails to defraud. Father returned all these letters and monetary offers. "God will provide," he wrote in answer to them.

Then Sayville police began to crack down on Divine disciples' cars, tagging them with parking tickets. Father countered by turning the grounds of his property into free parking spaces.

The citizens' committee communicated with the Suffolk County District Attorney in Riverhead. They voiced their fear that the economic life of Sayville was threatened. Something must be done, they said.

It seemed a good idea to plant a detective, posing as a follower, in heaven to find evidence on which to base a criminal case against Father. The District Attorney hired a female operator from New York City. Her name was Rose Burrows.

Miss Burrows had a voluptuous oriental type of beauty, partly Spanish, partly Egyptian. From experience, she was confident that she could lure any man.

Her assignment was to find out from where Father's funds emanated. (He had often been seen, people said, carrying a satchel full of thousand-dollar bills.) The District Attorney also hoped to obtain evidence of immorality among men and women angels.

Rose Burrows posed as a destitute mulatto girl, out of work, abandoned by a worthless husband. She went to a Sayville banquet where her story was believed and she was warmly welcomed, as was anyone who seemed to need help. Her shabby clothes, bought secondhand, lulled any suspicions there might have been about her.

When she arrived in the Sayville heaven, Rose was fed lavishly and conducted by Sister Penny to a clean dormitory room, furnished with several double beds. She was outfitted with clean clothes, altered to fit her by a handy sister.

Rose became a willing member of the working staff around the house, performing cheerfully more tasks than were assigned to her.

She talked a great deal with the white sister with whom she roomed.

"Isn't Father Divine wonderful?"

"Child, he surely is."

She attempted to probe into the reason why none of the sisters seemed "to hanker after" any man. Long-time followers told her that ever since Father Divine had shown them the light, they found that no such thing appealed.

"Don't even Father and Mother Divine sleep together?"

"Oh no, honey, that would be a big sin."

Rose tested the truth of the sisters' words upon the male angels. She altered a couple of her dresses to reveal her luscious curves. Whenever she strolled past a brother, she swung her hips. To her astonishment, no one gave her a second look. Then one day came the real test . . . Rose's chance to be alone with Father.

She was cleaning his study when he came in.

"Peace, Father," she said.

"Peace," he answered.

He busied himself at his desk, and if he noticed that the pretty new worker stooped over more often than her work required, her plunging neckline spilling over, her skirt tightening against her shapely thighs, he gave no sign.

Three weeks after Rose Burrows started to investigate Father Divine, she reported to the District Attorney that she had not been able to discover a shred of evidence of immorality or fraud. On the contrary, she had seen many down-and-outers welcomed and given shelter, clothes, and plenty of food. When she had asked Father, "How can you afford to feed so many people all the time?" he had answered, "God provides through my personal body."

When the Sayville people who wanted to oust Father Divine learned of Rose's failure, they were discouraged. However, they still meant business and they decided to use the weapon that they found available . . . Father's neighbors' complaints about the noise emanating from 72 Macon Street that went on "until all hours." They decided to have Father arrested as a public nuisance.

3

DAVID AND GOLIATH

At midnight, on Sunday, November 15, 1931, Officer Tucker of the Sayville police force knocked at the door of 72 Macon Street. There was a great crowd gathered there that night and there was loud singing. The officer had to knock many times before he was heard and had the door opened to him. A man whom Tucker knew to be Saint John, a close assistant of Father's, answered the door.

"I want to see Father Divine," Tucker said.

"You can't see him now," Saint John answered. "He has got a spirit."

Tucker said, "You're all making too much noise in there. The neighbors are complaining."

"I can't do anything about that," Saint John answered.

Officer Tucker left 72 Macon Street. When he returned, about two hours past midnight, he was accompanied by Suffolk County District Attorney Mr. Arata and by bank president Rogers. Also with him were six troopers from the Bay Shore barracks, and six deputy sheriffs. They forced their way in and arrested Father Divine and eighty members of his congregation, fifteen of them white, for "disturbing the peace." They took them in three buses to the court of Justice Charles Duryea.

On the whole, the arrest was a peaceful one. Father Divine accompanied the officers quietly to the waiting bus. He did not seem perturbed or indignant. Neither did most of the followers. The only disturbance was caused by four women whom the police officers were never asked to identify. These resisted arrest and had to be hand-cuffed. One woman became hysterical in the police station. She fell on the floor and kept rolling there over and over again. Father would not permit police officers to touch her.

"Leave her alone," he warned in the impersonal manner of a doctor who knew his patient better than anyone else did, "and she'll come to herself."

The woman did.

Fifty-five pleaded guilty of disturbing the peace. These were fined five dollars each and dismissed. Twenty-five pleaded not guilty. These were ordered to report for trial.

Father himself pleaded not guilty. He stated that he resented the indignity of the charge. It was unfair. He was being discriminated against because of the color of his skin. Polysyllabically, in words that Justice Duryea could not understand, he referred to the Constitution of the United States and the Declaration of Independence, which were being "spotted black as my patent-leather shoes" by this arrest. He would rather be thrown into jail to "rot there" than to admit to such an unfair charge as disorderly conduct.

The Negro press reported Father's arrest and his reaction to it. The white press picked it up. Practically overnight, the case of Sayville vs. Father Divine acquired national significance. Neither Sayville nor Father Divine had ever rated nationwide limelight before. Sayville cringed from it. Father Divine basked in it. He enjoyed the picture which he had created of himself as a martyr to racial discrimination. Liberal people and groups throughout the country, white as well as colored, accepted his picture of himself. They wrote to endorse his stand. Many offered to help him fight "Sayville's vested interests." Father answered all of his letters personally. Some days, he and his secretaries started corresponding early in the morning and did not finish until long after midnight.

James C. Thomas, brilliant Negro lawyer, who had served a term as U.S. Assistant District Attorney, telegraphed to offer his services at Father's coming trial, free if need be, to "combat the infringement of property rights and privileges so sacred and won at so great a cost."

Father graciously accepted Attorney Thomas' offer.

In Sayville, outsiders' interest only fanned Father's

neighbors' hostility toward him. It was all very well, they
said, for outsiders to "butt into the town's problems," to
write letters to the papers talking about civil rights and
democracy and every man has a right to live where he
wishes. But would they be so free with their talk and
letters if they were directly concerned?

Formally, the Sayville Committee stated that there was
only one reason why they wished to oust Father Divine—
he was a nuisance to his neighbors. They avowed that the
color of his skin had nothing to do with their dislike of
him. Informally, though, they played upon strong feelings
against Negroes.

Two contradictory facts were true in the case of the town
of Sayville vs. Father Divine. On the one hand, Father
Divine, pure and aside from the color of his skin, was
undesirable in the eyes of his neighbors. The stable, middle-class Macon Street block, with its set pattern of rising
at seven in the morning and going to bed at ten in the
evening, with its rigid concepts of black and white and no
gray in between, with its lack of worldliness and imagination, would have understood a white Messiah as little as
they understood this black one in their midst. And they
would have condemned him as completely. On the other
hand, the color of Father Divine's skin did matter in
Sayville—and matter terribly.

When, on May 24, 1932, Father Divine went on trial
before Supreme Court Justice Lewis J. Smith in Mineola
as a public nuisance, the two aspects—the honest motivation of the attack against him as a public nuisance and
the overwhelming prejudice against him as a Negro—were
each apparent, particularly where Judge Smith himself
was concerned.

The courtroom was crowded. On one side were aroused
Sayvilleites gathered to see "justice done." On the other
side were Divine adherents, those who were connected
with the movement, tense about what was going to happen to their Lord, and those outsiders who were reacting
to Father Divine as a symbol, no more no less, of racial
discrimination.

Judge Smith, immediately the trial began, betrayed his
antagonism toward Father. Although this was contrary to

usual procedure, he had Divine locked up in jail for the period of the trial by ordering his bail canceled.

District Attorney Alex G. Blue and Assistant District Attorney L. Baron Hill of Suffolk alternated in conducting the case for the people. Attorney Thomas represented Father Divine.

The Bill of Particulars against Father as charged by District Attorney Blue stated:

Defendant claimed to be the Messiah returned to earth; conducted so-called religious services, at which services colored and white people did congregate and mingle together in large numbers; and did then and there exhort people in loud tones of voice and did then and there encourage, aid, and assist those present in shouting and singing in loud tones, annoying neighbors in the vicinity of the defendant's place.

And did then and there permit and encourage large numbers of people on foot and in autos to gather around his place in the highways, thereby preventing and obstructing the streets and highways in and about his place; and did encourage said singing, shouting, exhorting, and stamping to continue past midnight, keeping them awake at all hours of the night and morning.

District Attorneys Blue and Hill produced twelve witnesses, all close neighbors of Father Divine, who claimed with varying displays of emotional involvement that there was loud shouting and singing at 72 Macon Street and that they had often heard followers give praise to Father Divine as people normally give praise in a church. They asserted that Father's followers, even without the singing and shouting, were disturbing neighbors.

Miss Claire Swettman was a prosecution witness. She said she lived on Macon Street, directly across from the defendant, and has been living there for better than one year.

"I used to hear shrieks and horrible moans," she said. "People were always screaming 'Oh, Father!' The place is very run down. Divine has a lot of women and children there. Sickly people. One man is always holding his nose; another man is always slobbering. There was one man who seemed almost in the last stages of t.b. tottering along. This man coughed and spit all over the street and it almost turns your stomach to watch."

Annie Halleck, who lived at 60 Macon Street, was another witness. She claimed to have been "driven almost crazy" by Father's followers. "All you hear is 'wonderful, Father, peace.' That is all you hear all day long."

A third witness, named Mrs. Connely, described the activities at the Sayville heaven as "first cousin to a summer Sunday at Coney Island." She testified that the followers' loud religious services were interfering with her enjoyment of her home. She testified to the followers' belief that Father Divine was God since "I have often heard them screaming it."

The next witness was the daughter of Mrs. Connely, who lived with her mother. She said that one night, when the noise was at its loudest, she telephoned and got someone on the line at Father Divine's.

"Do you know who you're talking to?" the unidentified voice told her. "This is God himself."

Fred Gutley took the stand. He said that he and his parents had owned their house at 71 Macon Street for twenty years. Although it had been used as a summer home for many years, in 1930 he had had it converted for all-year-round use. Recently, however, he had given up his house.

"A nuisance of this sort in town chases people away. I sold out, and we [his parents and himself] moved to New York against our will. We wanted to make it an all-year-round residence."

Peter Gutley, Fred's father, was also a prosecution witness. One night, he said, after he and his family had been driven "almost crazy" by the noise in Father's house, he went over there and asked to see Divine.

"Give us people a chance to get some sleep or peace," he said he politely asked Divine. "Divine starts to laugh at me. He says, 'I'll see about it.' I say, 'You better do something about it.' He said, 'Go see what you can do.'"

Father's followers, who took the stand on his behalf, completely disclaimed the prosecution's accusations.

Follower Joseph Mahood, a Flushing undertaker, maintained, with imperturbable adamance that the District Attorney could never shake, that noise at 72 Macon Street was practically unheard of.

"Several times," he said, "I can't get in the dining room. I would be at the window. I have been to the fence. I have been out in the garden walking around looking at the vegetables and so on. I would have to get up to the building and put my ear to the screen to hear what was going on. Twenty-five others were also trying to hear."

Mr. Mahood's voice, as it addressed the Court, was contemptuous of the "liars" who claimed they heard noise emanating from Father's headquarters. How could they, who were houses away, hear noises that he and twenty-five other objective witnesses could not hear even by putting their ears to an open screen?

Judge Smith addressed the undertaker. "Your hearing, is it good?"

"I think so," Mr. Mahood replied. "No doctor ever said it wasn't."

Judge Smith did not like Mr. Mahood. This was apparent in the tone he questioned him with and in the disapproving way he looked at him. Judge Smith did not, as a matter of fact, like any of Father's followers who appeared in his behalf. He, himself, participated actively in questioning witnesses for the defense. The way he questioned Mrs. Lillian Cox of East Orange, New Jersey:

"Peace. Peace, Father," she began in a hoarse whisper.

The Court said sternly, "No. No peace. Just answer the questions."

The lady testified that Father had cured her of a petrified limb.

"What is that, petrified?" the Court interjected. "Do you mean 'turned to stone'?"

"Yes, that was what mine was."

"Your leg had turned to stone?"

"Yes." The witness swore that she had had to use crutches for three years and that her doctor had been unable to help her.

"Did you ever shout in the meetings?" she was asked.

"No," she answered hoarsely. "I've had laryngitis for years. Can't you tell?"

Asked why she had not been healed of her laryngitis by Father Divine, she retorted that she had never brought her laryngitis to him.

The only person in the court who did not smile at her answer was Judge Smith. He went on questioning Mrs. Cox.

When it came time for Father Divine's white witnesses to appear, Judge Smith took charge of their cross-examinations.

John Lamb was questioned by Judge Smith.

"You don't belong to his [Father Divine's] race, do you?"

"Well, not as you might put it," John Lamb answered. "I only recognize one race."

"I don't care what you recognize," the judge snapped. "I say you don't belong to the same race as he is. You are not a Negro."

John Lamb smoothed his thin blond hair back from his forehead. "No," he answered.

"All right," Judge Smith replied. He asked John Lamb whether he considered Father Divine to be God.

"I consider Father Divine the perfect expression of God," Mr. Lamb replied.

Judge Smith then asked, in the manner of a magician pulling a new trick out of his hat, where Father Divine's money came from. Without stopping to think, Mr. Lamb replied that he believed Father's money was supplied by the Universal Mind Substance.

"What do you mean by that?" the Court demanded.

"Another way of expressing it would be God," the witness answered.

"You believe God sends money directly to him?"

"Yes."

"Just how is that physical act done?"

"That I have never inquired into," was the bland reply.

Judge Smith ordered John Lamb off the stand.

If John Lamb irritated Judge Smith—and he did—the white women witnesses for Divine who followed Lamb were even more provoking to him.

Agnes Hunt was called to the stand. Like Lamb, she refused, until she was openly forced, to recognize color. Asked whether the inmates of heaven were of both sexes, she said that they were.

"White and colored?" the Court asked.

"I don't recognize color."

"I beg pardon?"

"I only recognize one color," replied the witness.

The Court snapped, "I didn't ask you what color you recognized. I asked you, white and colored?"

"As you express it, yes," Miss Hunt replied.

It remained for a twenty-six-year-old white secretary of Father's, a girl named Helen Faust, who had joined the movement in 1929, to climax the white followers' belief in Father Divine as the Deity.

Miss Faust had attended Boston University. She had studied for a year in business school. Her mother and sister both were followers.

"Do you believe Father Divine is God?" asked the Court.

"Yes, sir, I do."

Judge Smith challenged:

"Do you mean to testify in the court that you believe the defendant is God?"

"Yes, your honor, that's what I mean."

"What salary do you receive?"

"I don't receive any salary, your honor. I live and board in heaven and get the clothes I need. I'm working for the cause."

"What cause?"

"Peace and the brotherhood of man."

Judge Smith instructed that Helen Faust come to his chambers after the testimony. He wished her to make a statement to his private stenographer.

"Are you twenty-six years old?" he asked Miss Faust.

She replied, "Yes, your honor."

"Are you sure?"

"Yes, your honor."

"You don't look twenty-six years old to me. You look younger than twenty-six years old. You look under twenty-one, as a matter of fact, under age."

Miss Faust insisted that her age was twenty-six.

The judge insisted that he did not believe her. He turned to his stenographer. "Record this," he said. "If we find this girl is under age, the D. A. will know what his duty is in respect to her."

Judge Smith's prejudice against Father Divine, clearly shown as it was in his questioning of defense witnesses, was even more clear in the manner that he permitted the District Attorney to ask immaterial questions that were prejudicial to the defendant. The most glaring of these related to District Attorney Blue's attempts to prove to the jury that Father Divine conducted himself in such a manner as to cause people under his jurisdiction to become insane. He had no proof of this fact but his questions to three witnesses were voiced in such a way as to imply the truth of it. And in every case Judge Smith overruled the objection of Defense Attorney Thomas. As he did when Attorney Thomas objected to the way the District Attorney was questioning his witness, Arthur Madison.

Arthur Madison was an able Harlem attorney who worked for Divine. While not a follower in the strict sense, he tremendously admired Father. He maintained that Divine was the most profound man he'd ever known.

"Now," District Attorney Blue asked Mr. Madison, "do you know whether or not any person was ever committed to the Central Islip from this defendant's place?"

Attorney Thomas objected to that question. It had no place in the testimony, he said, and District Attorney Blue was not basing it on evidence. The Court overruled the objection.

"No, I do not," Mr. Madison answered.

"Do you know what Central Islip means?" the D. A. asked.

Mr. Madison answered, "Yes. It means an institution for the mentally defective."

"Do you know whether or not any person was ever committed to that institution from the defendant's place?"

"No, I do not."

"Have you heard that any person was so committed?"

"Not from his place. Not that I can recall."

"Do you know whether or not any person was committed to *any* institution for mental defectives from the defendant's place?"

"No, I do not."

"Have you heard it said that some person was so committed?"

"I have never heard of anyone."

For the duration of the trial, the jury's minds were never free of the suspicion Mr. Blue raised. Judge Smith refused to have it combatted.

The judge's prejudice throughout the conduct of the Divine trial was a mere prelude to the prejudice he displayed at its conclusion when he charged the jury before they left the courtroom to consider their verdict.

He said that he believed Father Divine to be a bad influence whose teachings disrupted homes and even affected the minds of his followers. He mentioned uncorroborated testimony to the effect that two individuals had been taken from the Divine home who were said to have escaped from a nearby insane asylum.

He said that Father Divine had told a probation officer and a psychiatrist who had been directed to examine him that he was fifty-two years old, born in Providence, Rhode Island, as Major Morgan J. Devine; had no education, was Protestant, had never before been convicted of a crime, did not know who his parents were or whether they were living, and knew nothing of worldly things since he moved only in the world of the spirit and his money came from God.

Judge Smith excoriated Father. "I find the defendant is not an ordained minister. I am informed his name is George Baker and not Devine. That he was not born in Providence but in Georgia. I am informed that, as to his income, he obtains work for people and uses their wages, and that to others who come under his spell, that they are induced to transfer property to him. I am advised that this defendant is not a moral man but is very immoral. I am advised that Mother Divine is not his legal wife. While some may believe this man to be God, there are many who do not believe him to be God and those who do not believe him to be God are entitled to have their rights protected . . . one cannot use religion as a cloak for the commission of crime."

The jury found Father Divine guilty as charged, but recommended leniency. Judge Smith ignored the jury's plea for leniency. A few days after they issued their verdict, he sentenced Father Divine to the maximum penalty —one year in jail and five hundred dollars' fine for being a public nuisance.

In the courtroom, an angel started keening. The torn sleeves of her black dress showed much of her heavy woolen underwear. One of her eyes was closed as if there were something wrong with it. Her expression went from despair to exultation as she moved her gray head from side to side, her good eye staring from Judge Smith to Father and back again.

"That jedge, he don' know who he monkeyin' with," she mumbled.

Indeed Judge Smith did not know "who he was monkeying with."

On the Wednesday following the Saturday he had sentenced Father, Judge Smith dropped dead. He was only fifty years old and in apparent good health.

Throughout his incarceration, Father had maintained a silent dignity. Now he spoke from his cell: "I hated to do it."

Followers' reactions to Judge Smith's death ranged from jubilation to dazed wonder. Those who had known Father to be God realized that he could strike dead those who opposed him, but to have seen Father's awful powers of retribution in action for the first time was cataclysmic.

A white angel, a Civil Service stenographer, explained it to a curiosity-seeker in Sayville.

"Father has the power to heal the sick and the reverse is true too. He can make the well sick but he hates to do that. Father said he hated to make Judge Smith die because Father seeks no adversities."

But, the angel went on, the jurist, by his prejudicial handling of Father's case, had brought doom on his own head.

Judge Smith's "doom" was the first demonstration of Father Divine's powers of retribution. The coincidental death of the jurist was fated to be the foundation for one of the most important tenets of the movement, a tenet which would enable Father Divine to attract new converts and, just as powerfully, it would enable him to keep established followers in line.

Judge Smith's death gave birth to intriguing legends about Father. The most colorful of these was one follower's version of Father's stay in jail. The followers said that Father refused the ordinary prison fare, preferring to "materialize" his own breakfast of platters of bacon and eggs and fried chicken. Father's jailer, the story went on, fell on his knees and asked Father please to leave his jail.

After a thirty-three-day incarceration, Father did leave the jail. On June 24, 1932, his release on bail was effected. And, afterward, the Appellate Division, holding that Father had been tried prejudicially, reversed Judge Smith's decision.

Father's imprisonment and Judge Smith's death had a most peculiar effect on the Divine Peace Mission movement. Where, before the Sayville incident, he had been proud to count his followers by hundreds, now, all of a sudden, so many new people had flocked to his banner that he could count them by thousands.

"I didn' believe Father Divine was God before," comments follower Lovely Heart, who was recruited in the period following Judge Smith's death and is still with him today. "It took a miracle to show me, me and all them other unbelievers, but Father shown us who he was even though he had to kill off a mean-hearted judge just in order to make us know."

June 25, 1932, may well be reckoned as the most important date in the fabulous Divine career.

If Father had known his Shakespeare as well as he knew his Bible, he might have pondered:

"There is a tide in the affairs of men which, taken at the flood, leads on to fortune——"

His exemplification of immortal retributive powers coming, as it did, during the third year of the black depression, which wreaked havoc throughout the country and reserved some of its cruelest blows for Harlem, was the tide which initiated his "fortune."

Only a few hours after Father's release from prison, established followers as well as thousands of new recruits swarmed into New York's Rockland Palace at 155th Street and Eighth Avenue for a "Monster Glory to Our Lord" celebration. Seven thousand men and women filled every seat and, in defiance of Fire Department regulations, overflowed the standing room. Hundreds had to wait outside.

Father boiled over into impassioned words.

"You may not have seen my flesh for a few weeks but I was with you just the same. I am just as operative in the mind as in the body. There were many who thought I had gone some place but I'm glad to say I did not go anywhere. I held the key to that jail all the time I was in it and was with you every time you met. They can prosecute me or persecute me or even send me to the electric chair but they can never keep me from you or stop me from doing good."

"Hallelujah!" the crowd cried. "God Almighty! Hallelujah!"

Father responded to the wild applause. He leaped and cavorted in revivalist style.

A young woman jumped up from her seat.

"He's God Almighty!" she screamed. "I know it. From my heart down I was a lump of ice. No doctor could get this disease off me. And then I heard Father say, 'Take up your bed and walk.' I don't know why he bothered with me. But he raised me up again. My, my, my."

"Hallelujah!" the assembly shouted.

The young woman had not yet finished her testimony.

"One of my neighbors, she told me, 'Father Divine is nothing but a M-A-N'!" (The follower spelled out the word.) "That neighbor she got the same disease I did—but she died. She died because she called God Almighty a M-A-N."

She raised her arms and shouted, "Godalmighty!"

It seemed as though the testimonies to Father would never stop. No sooner did one person take his seat than another leaped up to tell of Father's retributive and healing powers. An acquaintance of a follower had mocked at Father, and as a result he had broken his leg. A friend of another follower, a hopeless cripple for many years, had been inspired to call for Father's help. On the day before the Palace meeting, she'd been enabled to throw away her crutches.

Suddenly the tone of the testimonies changed. An old man pushed his way down the aisle.

"I could tell about them who died," he shouted. "They

hurt Father and they was done in just like that judge was done. But I ain't gonna tell that. I'm only gonna tell about we're cold and hungry. We need you to take us outa the cold, Father!"

The crowd went wild. "It's true," they screamed. "God Almighty!"

"Need you, Father!" The old man made a chant out of his lament. "Need you. Need you. Need you, Father."

The old man had unleashed a mighty torrent. Men and women who had tried to lose themselves in talk of "miracles" stopped trying and talked about their real troubles. Their yokes of bondage had always been heavy, but never as heavy as they had been during these last depression years. Now they were colder and hungrier and sicker-to-dying than they had ever been in their lives.

"Need you, Father!" The old man's refrain was echoed many thousands of times over inside their hearts. "Need you, Father!"

In all of his meteoric career, Father Divine had never received an ovation like this.

At the Rockland Palace meeting he came to a conclusion . . . a conclusion that was to become one of the most important decisions of his career.

For the present, he would not attempt to build heavens in hostile white communities like Sayville. For the present, he would live and work in depression Harlem.

4

"LET GOD PAY
HIS OWN BILLS"

Father Divine opened his first Harlem heaven in 1933. That was the year when so many of Harlem's residents existed on charity that a slogan—out of humor rooted in bitterness—was evolved there:

> *"Jesus'll lead us,
> The relief'll feed us."*

It was the year when men and women, disgusted with four years of ineffectual striving to care for their families by honest work, turned to crime, petty mostly.

"I needa get some bread for them four kids I got," Robert Jackson, twenty-one years old, an active church member with an excellent previous record, told a policeman who caught him in an attempt to hold up a white man.

Nineteen thirty-three was the year after the year of the huge Negro migrations from the South. They came to Harlem from the rice swamps and the cotton plantations and the sugar farms, men without money or trades and their women and children. They lived in dreary, unheated tenements that most white people never suspected existed. Roaches and rats were considered ordinary occupants of Harlem apartments. Negro newspapers of the period record many cases of children who were bitten by rats. There was a little girl who, because of a rat bite, lost the third finger of her right hand, and a five-year-old boy whose foot was badly bitten. A private bath in a Harlem apartment was a luxury practically unheard of. There were washtubs in the dank kitchens which served as bathtubs (those family members who wanted privacy hung sheets around the washtubs on bath nights). A single toilet, wooden-slatted and with no window, serviced three or four apartments.

"Never had no toilet for just our family," comments Divine follower Happy Heart. "I usedta live on 137th Street off'n Lenox Avenue, on the fifth floor. There was four other families livin' on that floor, too, and all five of us, twenty-six people sharing the same toilet. Most times you want to get in—somebody else got there first and you got to wait. Some hours, like early in the morning, you want to go out looking for a job, there is a line out in front of the toilet. Only the pushers knows how to push other folks around can get in there in the mornings. Me, I never used to get in. Used to be a public toilet on 125th Street, you got to walk down steps like to a subway, I used that all the time. It wasn't never so crowded as the one in our hall. And the plumbing was O.K. most of the time which is more than I could say for the plumbing in our toilet."

That was the way it was in most of the Harlem apartment toilets. The plumbing was more often out of commission than not. When tenants complained to their landlords, their complaints were seldom taken seriously. For landlords knew there were ten Negro tenants to take the place of the one disapproving one who might leave.

Restrictive covenants and neighborhood prejudice, barring Negroes from almost every section of the city except Harlem, resulted in the most flagrant violations by landlords of city building and sanitary codes. It resulted in phenomenal rentals which single families could never meet. They had to band together, three and four miserable, ill-assorted families, to pay the tremendous rentals asked for an apartment that could hardly have accommodated one of them. While white families paid 20 to 25 per cent of their incomes for renting desirable apartments, Negroes had to pay 40 and 50 per cent for miserable railroad flats laid out room to room in such a way that privacy was an impossibility. Little children learned far too early and graphically everything there was to know about sexual behavior, in all its phases.

In 1933, 50 per cent of Harlem's Negro families, with employment opportunities as closed to them as housing, were forced to apply for unemployment relief.

Prostitution was rampant in Harlem. Many of the prostitutes were young, girls in their early and middle teens who knew one thing: that this, the selling of their bodies, obviously valueless anyhow, was one way of eating and sleeping and of helping their families. They used to accost men, by day as well as by night. Sometimes young children would solicit for their older sisters or their mothers, openly, without shame, lauding the charms of the women in their families, competing among themselves for the few likely male prospects.

According to the record, Harlem, during the depression years, faced by far the most acute problem of juvenile delinquency of any section of New York. During the period from 1930 to 1935 alone, six thousand Negro youngsters under sixteen years of age were declared to be delinquent, and three thousand more were declared to be neglected. Boys and girls congregated on the street corners, taking their values from one another and from the successful older gang members whom they would see occasionally, the only prosperous-looking men in all of Harlem. They stood on the street corners and admired the successful men and compared them to their tragic, broken-down fathers, and found the fathers sadly lacking. They emulated the gangsters—stealing when they could, drinking cheap liquor in low dives, smoking big black cigars, smoking marijuana when they could get that. At twelve and thirteen and fourteen, they were muggers and thieves and pimps and prostitutes—and proud to be those things.

It was the "good" Harlem girls and boys who were ashamed of their goodness. They were failures in the eyes of the others, "scaredy-cats" like their "old men."

The children's homes couldn't combat the outside influences. Most of the fathers didn't try. The idea of their ineffectuality was too strong within them. Most of the mothers couldn't try. Almost every Negro mother had to seek work outside the home to increase, in some cases to supply, the family income. They served, most of them, as by-the-day domestics. Domestics worked long hours. Mothers left their homes before breakfast, such as it was, and did not return until long after time for dinner. They did not even know the strange values of their strange sons and daughters.

They did not want to know them. The children's schools
didn't combat the outside influences. How could they, when
overcrowding caused them to operate three-shift systems in
Harlem?

In 1933, almost all of Harlem was tired and hungry—
and sick. The tuberculosis death rate was fantastic—four
times higher than that for the city as a whole. The number of recorded cases of syphilis was seven times higher
for Negroes than it was for whites. Twice as many Negro
mothers as white died in childbirth. In all of Harlem, with
its more than 350,000 Negroes, there was one hospital.
And most of Harlem's residents were limited to that one,
because many other hospitals had policies of racial segregation.

Desperately, Negroes sought for ways out of their
dilemmas. There were more drunks in Harlem than in
other parts of the city. There were more dope addicts.
There were more family deserters. How could there not
have been? And there were more "fake" healers who, for
hard come by nickels and dimes and quarters, promised
Harlemites all success and futures that, unlike their
presents, would be full of good fortune.

Every Harlem side street had its quota of charlatan
preachers and "spiritual contactin' folks" who rode riot-
ously on the shoulders of Negroes fresh up from the
South. These established themselves in madly decorated
back rooms where the shades were always kept drawn,
and sold people magic answers to the acute problems
there was no answer for. For small fees, they sold charms
guaranteed to bring good luck. For slightly larger fees,
they sold numbers "absotively posilutely" guaranteed to
win on the next day's policy wheel. They gave advice to
deserted wives and sold "love potion" miracles to elderly
men who had begun to doubt their virility. They held
meetings where people could shout and sing and throw
themselves on the floor in orgies of wonderful relief for
pent-up tensions. They claimed personal contact with "the
spirit world," and they promised to put their clients into
contact with that world for a mere twenty-five cents a
head. They sold pills to "attract the goodest spirits and
cast out the worst." And Harlemites did without food and

made their children do without in order to buy those pills.

During the thirties, the profits of these panacea-men were estimated to be in the neighborhood of a million dollars a year. The more successful among them were able to interest groups who functioned around them on a permanent level and did not have to depend on the transients. These became wealthy.

One of the most successful "spiritualists" during the thirties was Madame Fu-Fu-Tan. Madame Fu-Fu-Tan was part-Negro, part-Chinese. She looked exotic and emphasized her exoticism by wearing filmy, varicolored veils. She used to trail delicately into a dimly lit receiving room and allow her audience to catch a small glimpse of her. Then, like an ascetic strip-tease artist, she would retire behind a black velvet curtain. From behind the curtain, she would speak in sepulchral tones, summoning spirits, conversing with them in a language nobody understood, and transmitting their messages in good, ordinary English with an occasional bit of Harlemese thrown in for good measure. A low tom-tom would beat out a rhythm in accompaniment to her every word.

Madame Fu-Fu-Tan's prime competition was a tall, handsome spiritualist named Sufi Abdul Hamid. In 1933, she ended the competition by marrying him. They combined forces and bought a house at 103 Morningside Drive, which they named the Buddhist Universal Holy Temple of Tranquility.

Sufi Abdul Hamid was known to some people as His Holiness Bishop Amiru Al Munimun. But his real name was Eugene Brown, and white Harlem business people feared him as a man with a fighting desire to rid Harlem of every white face. They called him the Black Hitler. "His Holiness" Sufi presided over his Temple of Tranquility in gold-brocaded robes and attracted a huge number of followers. For it was thought that he, more than any of the other spiritual leaders, knew the secret of the numbers racket. Hungry Harlemites were certain that the "good spirits" transmitted "tips" to Sufi Hamid which they would give to nobody else.

Of all the flourishing Harlem cult leaders of 1933, the

most successful was a man called Daddy Grace. Daddy was, and still is today, an imposing man whose prime characteristic is unashamed, prideful male virility. He was broad, and six feet, two inches tall. Strangely, he wore a pince-nez.

"Daddy," as he was known to all the women of his flock, who comprised his adoring majority, boasted that he could make the blind see, the lame walk, and cast out evil from the soul.

It was not only the cult leaders who flourished in Harlem in the thirties. Desperate people who needed outlets began to seek solace more frantically than they ever had before through the medium of the legitimate churches. Honest, dedicated ministers had to work long hours. Some hardly took time out to eat or to sleep. They fed church members and housed them sometimes and served as social case workers in suggesting ways to help them solve their personal problems. But these ministers could not do enough. Whatever services they gave, and they did give inestimable services, they could not ever give enough.

In the midst of all the honest hopelessness and the overwhelming chicanery, Father Divine came to Harlem. In 1933, he rented a building at 20 West 115th Street and dedicated it to the service of Harlem's needy. It was there that he first began to serve the tremendous banquets which would, in later years, become his trademark. Hungry Harlemites, who hadn't had good, hot food for more time than they wanted to remember, came and ate: fricasseed chicken, roast duck, spareribs, fried sausage, lamb stew, liver-with-bacon, rice, hominy, boiled and fried potatoes, stewed tomatoes, spinach, brussels sprouts, string beans, boiled beef, asparagus tips, fruit salad, ice cream, and chocolate cake. Those who could afford to paid fifteen cents for these amazing meals. Those who could not ate free.

Father welcomed all who came. He was a kindly host in those days, with a warm, genial smile and a real urge to please. He sat at the head of the table and blessed the food before his guests received it.

"Do not fast!" he counseled warmly. "Eat your fill!"

Thousands of people came and ate. They trooped into

20 West 115th Street, hundreds of them at a time, and none was ever turned away. From early morning till late at night, banquets were served, and Father's staff never stopped working until the last person was accommodated. Some who came, the less desperate among them and the more sophisticated, ate and scoffed. The vast majority did not scoff, though. Most who came to eat stayed to marvel.

Talking today about his Harlem period, Father pridefully says, "Yes, we had 2500 to 3000 fed daily in our places in 1935 and '34 and 1933—around that time—and about 2500 to 3000 daily in New York City absolutely gratis, as those of the people that did not have employment—and also thousands, untold thousands, fed at ten and fifteen cents a meal."

According to qualified observers, Father is exaggerating somewhat the number of people whom he serviced . . . but he is not exaggerating very much.

Mrs. Elaine Goldberg, a social worker in Harlem in the thirties, says, "Father Divine rendered an inestimable service to Harlem's unemployed from 1933 to 1937, and he did it with a genuine goodness that I, as a social worker, could hardly help but admire."

Where did Father Divine get the money which he spent so lavishly? That was a mystery to people outside the movement. Actually, there was no mystery at all. Today, the Divine financial setup is a simple though brilliantly constructed one. Then, it was even more simple. It was merely an extension of the Divine manner of collecting money from true followers which had begun in Brooklyn and in Sayville.

In Father's early Harlem days, all his true followers voluntarily put all their money and all their labor into extending the movement. Father ordered followers to form groups large and small to set up businesses of all kinds, as "Divine Peace Mission Movement Co-operatives." They were to function under a set of rigid regulations imposed by Father. The most important of these was that, while followers gave all their money and all their services to establishment of communalism, they were to take out no profits from their investments but only money enough to supply them with the barest necessities.

"When you turn your bodies and minds over to God for his use which is your *reasonable service*," Father told his early Harlem followers, "God then presents you with the key to his infinite storehouse and you have access to limitless blessings."

Followers did as Father directed. In old Harlem lofts, stores, and abandoned factories, businesses began to spring up. There were dress-making establishments and men's tailors and barber shops and restaurants and boardinghouses and new movement extensions which began to be known as heavens. Father's critics called his communalism "chain-store religion." Father himself named it "God, Incorporated."

The way that the largest Harlem extension, the "Faithful Mary Extension Heaven," was maintained was typical of the way all other Harlem heavens and Peace Mission co-operative businesses functioned.

The Faithful Mary Extension Heaven consisted of a row of seven four-story brownstone houses on 126th Street between Sixth and Lenox Avenues. The main building, a Turkish bathhouse, spacious but somewhat dank and decayed, devoted most of its space to the large banquet hall, meeting rooms, and, on the top floor, offices and an apartment for Father's use. One floor was given over to sleeping quarters. Since the roomers were important angels who paid no rent, the building made no profit. However, it was self-sustaining.

The other six buildings in the row were utilized, to the last inch of space, as rooming houses. Fifty followers lived in each house, and the houses were always filled to capacity, the main reason being the cheap rent—about a dollar a week for sleeping in double beds, lined up in dormitories.

The roomers were satisfied with their living conditions. They ignored the remarks of outsiders that they were being overcrowded just as badly as they had been in their former tenements and for the same reason—big profits for a landlord. Where else but in Father Divine's heaven, they asked, could they enjoy such clean, cheap accommodations—such big meals for only ten to fifteen cents apiece? How could Father be making any profit out of them?

As a matter of fact, the Faithful Mary Extension Heaven, and other heavens throughout Harlem, brought in a tidier profit than the roomers suspected. A minimum of $200 a month rent from each of the six houses, making a total of at least $1200 a month, was collected. From this, a rental of $450 a month for all six houses had to be deducted. A gross profit of at least $750 a month remained. Little had to be spent on maintenance, for all the work was done by followers in exchange for their board. All food was purchased from Peace co-operatives at "evangelical prices."

Between 1933 and 1937, Father Divine became Harlem's outstanding lodging-house keeper. Dedicated followers leased, for his use, three apartment houses, nine private houses containing fifteen to twenty flats arranged in best profit-making tradition, dormitory style, and three meeting halls with dormitories on upper floors. He also ran twenty-five restaurants serving ordinary meals of one piece of meat, potatoes, bread, butter, and coffee for fifteen cents; two groceries; ten barber shops; ten cleaning stores; and twenty or thirty huckster wagons, which made the rounds of Harlem with vegetables, fruit, and fish to be sold at evangelical prices. There were signs on all of the huckster wagons: "Peace, Father, Clams and Oysters," and "Peace, Father, Fresh Vegetables." There was also a Divine coal business which owned three trucks and operated them between Harlem and the coal fields of Pennsylvania. They would buy coal at the then-wholesale rate of $4.00 a ton and sell it to followers or outsiders at $7.50 a ton. The general market in those years sold coal for $8.50 a ton.

Besides his Harlem extensions and businesses, Father Divine in the thirties acquired properties in Newark, Jersey City, Bridgeport, and Baltimore.

In Newark, a former bathhouse at 122 Howard Street was purchased by the followers for $15,000 in cash. It was remodeled to contain a church auditorium, an apartment for the use of Father Divine, a restaurant, and a large dormitory for transients.

In Bridgeport, Father's followers combined their incomes to purchase a $30,000 building. They placed a tremendous sign on the front which read: "Fear not little flock, Father has given us this building."

As Father's obvious wealth increased, his flock also grew by leaps and bounds. By 1935, he figured he had two million followers. The actual count is nearer to half a million. His weekly income from his business establishments—impossible to check because then, as now, he kept no records—was reputed to be $20,000.

Father seldom spoke about his wealth, but he often spoke about his followers and the irresistible magnetism he could not help but exercise on all who had contact with him.

"The way it is about our church meeting," he proclaimed publicly, "they crowd in and block the stairways and doorways and halls and lobbies and the like and we have to be very careful so we do not break the laws of the fire ordinance."

Father's recognition of his magnetism was based on fact. It was true that, whenever a Divine meeting was held, many thousands filled the huge hall and many more thousands had to be turned away.

More and more people came to affiliate with Father. They came from the legitimate churches and they came from the store-front churches.

The legitimate ministers were indignant about the way Father was taking their congregations away from them. The cult leaders were also indignant. For the first and only time in Harlem's history, ministers and cult leaders had a point in common. Their hatred for Father Divine was even greater than their dislike for one another. Sufi Abdul Hamid and Daddy Grace fought Father Divine. Bishop H. C. Lawson, still today one of the most highly respected of the orthodox clergy, who had, by the time Father arrived there, been preaching in Harlem more than a score of years, also fought Divine.

Poor Sufi Hamid's fight with Father was not a long-standing one. "Snoofy," as Father's old-time followers still contemptuously refer to Sufi Hamid, died before he could conclude it.

"I'm a bona fide member of the gospel," Snoofy used to scream out, "and there'll be no tangles with the law." His followers always laughed when he said that, because they knew Sufi Hamid was referring to the tangles Father Divine had had.

Snoofy said, "No tax evasions here!" And everybody understood he had reference to the attempts of the Internal Revenue Bureau to prove that Father Divine was evading payment.

One of Sufi Hamid's favorite expressions used to be, "I'll take that fake Divine and I'll drive him out of New York City."

Once, in order to compete with Father, Snoofy purchased an airplane and announced he would reach higher mysteries than Father had ever thought of reaching. Father's followers knew that that was his undoing. On July 31, 1938, while he was learning to fly, his plane crashed and he was killed.

Father lost no time in interpreting Sufi's death to the world. He said:

"Sufi Hamid opposed me and was supposed to drive me out of New York City. But the first time he went up in his airplane, he fell and was killed instantly. He called himself a great leader. But as he thought himself great and admitted to a desire to destroy me personally, he destroyed himself. They that would rise up in opposition against me from time to time and everyone who will rise, they will be cut down in the same way. When Sufi Hamid, he rose up against me, he went down so quickly, body and all his power was killed immediately with him."

Daddy Grace continued to fight against Father Divine where Sufi Hamid left off. He was a formidable rival. By 1935, he had established his "Houses of Prayer" all along the East Coast. And, in the South, he was much more popular than Father Divine would ever be able to become. It was said that in Savannah, Georgia, during one two-week session, he had baptized two thousand candidates at a dollar a head.

Daddy was responsible for one of the most humiliating moments Father Divine has ever known. He put Father out of his own heaven. It all happened because Father's main headquarters at 20 West 115th Street had been rented instead of bought and because Daddy Grace was aware of this fact. He went to the owner of the building and offered to buy it from him, and to buy it with cash if the sale could be concluded immediately. The owner sold on Daddy's terms. Since Father had been kept in the dark about the change of ownership, he was greatly surprised when, one morning, the new landlord announced his status and insisted the premises be vacated immediately. Father found himself reduced to importuning Daddy Grace for a delay, to permit him to find other quarters. Daddy Grace refused any delay.

On moving day, the angels lugged beds and other furnishings out of heaven while Father supervised. Daddy stood and watched. Being publicity-wise, he brought newspaper reporters from the Harlem weekly, the New York *Age*, along. Strutting up and down the sidewalk in front of heaven, he loudly proclaimed:

"Look at me, the man who, though not God, ousted God from his erstwhile kingdom."

After Father left 115th Street, Daddy started to operate there in an attempt to take over the followers. He redecorated the former heaven. He draped himself in garishly colorful costumes which accented his obvious virility, and held revival services every night. The revival services always held the same theme—a new day would come and Father Divine, this false God on earth, would no longer be worshiped.

Daddy's attendance stayed low. All the faithful had moved with Father Divine to a new headquarters at 123rd Street and Lenox Avenue.

There are some old-time Harlemites today who are inclined to believe that Daddy Grace might have had a chance against Father. In the very middle of his feud with Father, however, various personal troubles, including the fact that the government was "persecuting" him about a small problem of income tax evasion, caused him to throw in the sponge and flee to Cuba.

Legitimate ministers took up the cudgels against Father where the cult leaders dropped them. Bishop Lawson began a militant crusade.

He attacked Father not only from his Refuge of the Christ Church pulpit but on the air and in the Negro press. He called him a "faker" and a "racketeer." He wrote letters to the New York *Age*, in which he asked what the source of Father's money was and implied that he had a few rich "students" who were giving him everything they owned. He said that Father pretended to heal people when he knew nothing about healing. He said that he knew for a fact that Father Divine was having illicit relationships with his women followers. He named a woman, Jessie Birdsall, who claimed to have "cohabited with God. Divine said it was to make her good. She was God's girl friend on the side." He said that Divine was illiterate and unintelligent.

"Many false Christs shall arise," he still says today, in reference to Divine, "and they must be exposed."

It is significant to note that while Bishop Lawson alone carried the brunt of his battle, Father did not have to carry his. The followers did it for him. Father wrote one letter in answer to the Bishop's accusation. It oozed humble meekness. Then, followers took over for him. They wrote scathing letters to Bishop Lawson and had them publicly circulated.

Priscilla Paul was Father's most vociferous defender. An insider, a woman with the movement since early Sayville days, she had always functioned close to Father. She wrote the Bishop so many letters that he hardly had time to read them. All of them contained the same sentiments and compared Father Divine and what he was doing for his people to Bishop Lawson and other ministers like him.

One letter started with the statement that Miss Paul "would rather consider" the Bishop's Refuge Church of Christ "your Refuse Church of Christ." She wrote the Bishop that "thoughts are like chickens, you may send them into your neighbor's backyard, but at sundown they will come home to roost. Thoughts are things, you think thoughts and they rebound as things. Now the Bible says, 'It is better that you shall have a millstone around your neck and be cast into the depths of the sea than that you should offend one of my little ones.' Now I will ask the readers of this paper, not by Father Divine's words but by his works, don't you think he is one of the little ones?

Father Divine is not preaching the life as Bishop Lawson is, he is living the life before the world . . . If Father Divine was a natural and carnal-minded man like Bishop Lawson, he would not be the shepherd of the sheep . . . It is a known fact Father Divine has not taken up any collection. He says ministers say they are working for God, then why charge it to man? Let God pay his own bills. He is able . . .

"Now in re Father Divine's money and where he gets it. I don't see why Bishop Lawson should worry about that. One thing he can feel good over. Father never got any money from him. He said Father Divine got his money from some wealthy, deluded students (?). Now I wish to say that is an unnecessary, uncalled-for lie, but if it were true, which one would be justified in his works—Father Divine taking it from the ones able to give and using it for good works or Bishop Lawson preaching death as the gospel of Christ, heaven above the sky, hell below the ground, *nothing that man can reach in this life,* yet charging for that and robbing the widow and the orphan . . .

"In re: to Father Divine's being a sham. For of a truth I can say he gives me real clothes to wear. They fade not away. I don't see anything like a sham about that. He gives us the best food to eat and an abundance of it. He gives us real beds to sleep in, real light to see by, plenty of large, comfortable bathrooms, plenty of soap that we might keep clean for cleanliness is next to godliness, all without money and without price or collection. He gives us light where other leaders have given us and are still keeping some in darkness. He gives us understanding that no one is able to give but himself. He gives us the gospel. He does not speculate on the word as Bishop Lawson does. Father Divine is not teaching far-off heaven or hell but is teaching that God is not far-off but is at hand. So if God is at hand, heaven is at hand for God is in heaven . . ."

5

DEPRESSION FLOOD TIDE

Priscilla Paul's letter to Bishop Lawson was meaningfully echoed by all of Father's Harlem followers. It is still echoed today when a stranger mentions Bishop Lawson to any one of them who was with Father during the days of the feud.

"It's like Priscilla Paul said," Miss Jonathan Matthew tells, "Father give us understanding when we came to him in them depressing days. He give us heaven and a God at hand when nothin' else was there to hold on. Like when he come to me—I reached the end of my bein' able to take my troubles. I wasn' able to step over things. I got no food to eat."

Father Divine revealed himself to Jonathan Matthew in 1933. She is in her fifties now and has spent thirty-five of her years cooking and scrubbing for white people.

She cannot contain her glee at being what she is now instead of what she used to be before she knew Father Divine was God. He has blessed her with an abundance of good things, even a vacation. She spends her days off visiting the Philadelphia headquarters where she can see and praise Father.

Every bit of her chunky body bounces as she testifies at the banquet table or at meeting:

"God, it is just so sweet!" She couldn't help crying it out if a gun were pointed at her to stop. Everyone must know. "I used to go on my knees. Now I ain't gettin' on my knees for nobody! God, it is just so sweet! Now I don't get on my knees for anything!"

Nellie Barnes, as she used to be called before Father came into her life, was one of a group of women of all ages, yet alike in their frightened misery, who used to stand on a Bronx corner no matter what the weather, to try to get a day's work in the thirties. Nellie, young and strong enough to give a good day's work, never thought she'd ever have to stand in what was called the "slave market," like a beggar, holding up a penciled sign, showing how cheap she would work. Nellie was luckier than most of the others who stood with her. She managed to get work almost every day, even though it did pay only twenty-five cents an hour, no carfare, and a sparse lunch. When she had the good luck to work for an employer who gave a good hot lunch, Nellie would do just about any special jobs assigned her—even men's work. She often had to clean windows three and four stories up because she needed that hot lunch so badly. After all, her $1.50 a day earnings did not leave much with which to buy food at home.

Nellie had been born and reared in Harlem—in the same flat, in fact, where she and her husband still lived. She'd had her baby in that flat and he had died there before he was six months old. He'd needed a doctor, and Nellie, superstitiously frightened of hospitals and doctors, as was almost everybody she knew, finally realized there was nothing else she could do but take him to Harlem Hospital.

The waiting room was so jammed with sick children and parents that she had to stand for hours, holding her baby. But harder to bear was the fear that the doctors and nurses at the hospital had no time to bother about her child. When the baby died, her bitterness confirmed her fears of hospitals.

When Nellie married, her husband had had a job in a steam laundry and they had talked hopefully of getting a flat for themselves, instead of living with Nellie's parents, too infirm to work any longer. But when Nellie's husband was one of the first to be laid off at the laundry, they stayed in the old flat.

The whole family had to sleep in the single room, with a blanket hung as a partition. The toilet was in the hall, used by five families on the floor. And the plumbing usually leaked through to the flat below, while in winter it often froze for weeks at a time. Nellie and the other tenants knew the building was a firetrap. Though the rent was forty-five dollars a month, the landlord never fixed anything. But Nellie's husband was handy, and he could fix some of the worst things. Nellie used to consider herself lucky on that score too.

Then, one day, after nine years of marriage, Nellie's husband died. It was after the death of her husband that she began to really know what troubles were. It wasn't only the way she missed him, but also, shamefully, the way she missed the small pay he'd sometimes brought home. Now, the support of her old parents and herself was Nellie's problem alone.

Nellie was not one to talk about her troubles though. She always said, "You got to step over that."

Nellie was a churchgoing woman who tried to do right, as the minister instructed her. One day, though, she was so hungry that, while working on a job, she tried to hide a bottle of milk and some leftover chicken under her jacket to "tote" home. Her employer saw her. She grabbed the food and looked at Nellie as if she wouldn't wipe her feet on her.

"Niggers are all thieves!" she cried.

Then Nellie heard of that place called Father Divine's where anybody could come and eat plenty of good things for nothing.

She took her parents to 115th Street, and they joined the crowd in the dining room waiting for places. Nellie thought Father Divine must be a good minister, as she watched the food being passed in a chain. When she saw her parents eating as much fried chicken as they wanted to, her eyes, black-circled before her time, filled with tears. She remembered how often she had shuddered at the thought of their ever having to shuffle into alleys, like some old people that she'd seen, digging into garbage cans to keep from starving.

Instead of going to the Baptist Church on following Sundays, Nellie and her parents kept coming back to Divine's. They heard Father say:

"Why believe in something that they claim to save you after passing from this existence to keep you living in poverty, debauchery, lacks, wants, and limitations while on this earth you are tabernacling. I will not only lift you as my true believers but I shall lift all humanity from all superstition and cause them to forget all about that imaginary God I am now eradicating and dispelling from the consciousness of the people. Aren't you glad?"

Nellie did not join in the answering shout: "So glad, Father dear." It hurt her inside to hear that maybe the God she had worshiped all her life was just imaginary . . . but she began to wonder. Could Father Divine lift his true believers out of all their misery and trouble after all?

She talked to the neighbors.

"If he can do what he says, he ain't nobody but God."

Most of them laughed at her. "No God could look just like us, could he?"

"No matter what he looks like he's good," she cried.

Still Father Divine did not reveal himself as God to her until the "miracle." It came when she couldn't "step over" her troubles any longer. She was washing windows on a third floor, when she lost her balance and fell. Her fall was broken by a clothesline but, even so, her foot was "almost broke off." Today she tells how the doctor in Roosevelt Hospital, where she was taken, told her he would have to "cut it off."

She lay in bed under opiates. There was a dim blue light at the end of the big ward. In all of the twenty-two years since Father first came to her, Nellie has never tired of telling of the "wonderful miracle," in her deep rumble of a voice.

"I saw this beautiful, brown-skinned man as he came in the door. He had somethin' made of gold reachin' from his head to his heart. He had on a brown and white suit, a blue tie, and tan shoes."

She recognized him. It was Father Divine.

"He walked to my bed," she says, "and put out two hands and said, 'You are better. You are so much better.'"

The sweetness of Father's healing love brought the breath back into Nellie's body. Next morning she dared not believe what she had seen. But she maintains that two ladies in the beds beside hers said that they had something to tell her.

"You know the pretty little brown-skinned man was here," they told her. "He was dressed in gold. He stayed by you until six in the morning."

Then Nellie knew. Father Divine was God. "So sweet, God. So sweet, Father," she cried.

She would not let the doctors cut off her foot. They had to put it into a cast, and, of course, Father Divine made it whole again so that she did not even limp.

After "the miracle," her body and soul belonged to Father Divine. And her old worries became ridiculous.

She no longer had to struggle to pay forty-five dollars a month rent. She had only to pay $1.25 a week for a clean, comfortable bed in Father's heaven. When she came home from work, there was no housework for her to do, and she could rest and then eat a hot dinner for fifteen cents. Her infirm parents lived on different floors in the same extension in which she lived. Nellie paid their small rent and smiled blissfully when she said Peace to them, for they were off her hands and under the loving wing of Father Divine.

Best of all, though, was Nellie's knowledge that "nobody could wipe their feet on me again." She could say that she wouldn't wash windows or "get down to scrub until my knees gave way under me." If the lady of the house did not approve, Nellie could leave and find a better job. Meanwhile, her savings could carry her at Father Divine's.

No wonder she cries out her praise: "I used to go down on my keees. Now I don't go on my knees for anything!"

Today she is irrepressible in her pride in the life she has been blessed by Father to live. For many years she has worked for "doctors' and lawyers' families" and never earns less than a dollar an hour. And she saves because Father teaches his children not to spend their money on sinful things like movies, cosmetics, smoking, or drinking.

"I never knew what a vacation was," she says, "but last May I took a month off and went to Niagara Falls."

Her exuberant laugh reveals what a fine time she had.

Small wonder that Nellie pities stupid people who are living as she used to live, clinging to the old churches that give them so little contrasted to what Father Divine gives so fully. Wholeheartedly, she agrees with Mr. Henry Lee who recently took an ad in the *New Day*, the newspaper of the Peace Mission movement, to proclaim his faith:

"Bless your Holy Heart, Father dear. Your children are happy knowing You are God at hand and not a sky-God afar off."

Who but the blindly stupid would want a sky-God when they can have a God in the flesh? Not Henry Lee certainly!

During the depression, Henry Lee came to Harlem from the South. Henry was no different from the thousands of other Negroes who came because they had been dispossessed from farms they had worked as share-croppers, and who found themselves with no other work available to them. When he arrived in Harlem, he could neither read nor write.

His older brother, Jim, had preceded him to New York. Jim had become a success with a "big job." The nature of Jim's "big job" was a mystery to Henry who knew nothing about city life or city racketeers. Jim worked for a racketeer selling policy numbers.

Through his brother's influence, Henry soon found a job, dishwashing and scrubbing in a lunchroom. The pay seemed large to him, until he tried to make ends meet. Then, he had troubles. But they didn't matter too much. Badly off as he was, there were so many people in worse circumstances. And Harlem, with all its color, intrigued him. And his brother Jim was interesting company. Living was fun for Henry until Jim packed up one day after an outbreak of stabbings over the numbers racket and left New York. Henry missed him more than he'd ever known he could. He felt an aching need for Jim or for a real friend of his own. The people he met at work never stayed there too long. They came and went out of his life with bewildering rapidity. He began to think about the good companionship he'd had in the South. There were all the friends he'd made in church for example.

Nostalgic memories of Southern church congregations that acted like one big, happy family urged him to seek companionship in one Harlem church after another. He went to the store-front churches first, because he was tempted by their lurid posters guaranteeing to save his soul from the devil. He listened to the acrobatic preaching and bought the good-luck charms.

But he met no one in those churches who took an interest in him, and his loneliness continued unabated.

Until one day, at a new church he'd never tried before, he met a young woman named Myrna.

"You ain't a drinkin', gamblin' man," she said the first night he met her. "I can smell the drinkin', gamblin' ones a mile away." It turned out that Myrna was married, but that her husband did drink and gamble and that she'd been hoping to get "shed of 'im." She liked Henry almost from the first meeting, and he fell head over heels in love with her.

After Henry met Myrna, his worries changed. Now he could have companionship and even love, which he had never dared dream about, but he had no money to spend on Myrna. Frantically but unavailingly he hunted a better job. He grew tense and worried with the strain of it. Then, unaccountably, four months after he met her, Myrna told Henry that they could "go housekeeping" together.

"I ain't got enough money," Henry admitted unhappily.

Myrna told him that it was all right, that she had a steady day job with a lady on Park Avenue and that her wages coupled with his would carry them until he could find something to support them both. She had thrown that "no-count rag" of a husband out, and Henry could move into her room.

For almost a year, Henry and Myrna lived together. Every day, Henry learned to love Myrna more. He felt she was everything a woman should be. Someday he would give her all the things that kind of girl deserved. He made this promise as regularly to himself as he did to Myrna.

One day, though, with no warning, Myrna picked up and left Henry. Whether she got tired of his abject devotion, or whether it was because he never was able to better his low wages, he never found out.

Trying to forget Myrna, he began to drink corn whiskey and get himself a different girl every Saturday night.

He quit worrying about his dishwashing job. He was often late for it and sometimes absent. Since there were scores of men available to take his place, one Saturday afternoon he went to receive his paycheck and found a dismissal notice in his envelope.

Henry remembers well that bleak winter he lost his job. He remembers the bitter months when, in a panic, he made the rounds everywhere, anywhere, trying to find something to do. He often had to beg on the streets for a meal. Clearly he remembers the bread lines.

"Cops rushed us in and out," he tells, "after we stood for hours in the cold without no coats, waiting to get in. They gave us stale coffee an' oatmeal without no sugar or milk at all."

He had virtually abandoned all hope, except the one of warmer spring weather, when hope was reborn within him . . . a hope that came with a Father Divine parade, that streamed up Lenox Avenue a few days before Easter.

Henry was among the loungers on the street, when the first blare of trumpets, swinging out the "Dark Town Strutters' Ball," heralded the marchers. Then they came, the hundreds and hundreds of paraders, and, for the first time, Henry heard the shouts of, "Peace, Father. It's wonderful! Thank you, Father!"

Everyone was screaming and calling out to a man who was riding at the head of the oncoming parade, in a shiny limousine driven by a chauffeur. Henry asked the fellow next to him who the little man was.

"You mean you never saw Father Divine before?" the answer came. "He feeds the unemployed for nothing. I go over there all the time. He's a good preacher—but he ain't God, though."

Henry made out the words the marchers, following the limousine, were chanting:

"He's God, he's God. Father Divine is God."

What the marchers were chanting made no sense to Henry—but he was struck by their well-fed, happy air. He had never seen people as happy as that in his life. Although there were between five and six thousand marchers that Easter of 1933, to Henry there seemed to be almost a million of them. Long after Father Divine's limousine was out of sight, they still came, marching out of step, but chanting in unison, "Father Divine is God, the true and living God."

They held signs aloft. "Father Divine raised me from the dead," and "Father cured me of sniffing snuff." The dozen or more cars with California, Colorado, Virginia, and Pennsylvania plates that brought up the rear of the parade convinced Henry that Father Divine must be rich enough to feed the unemployed free, as the man next to him had said. So he trailed the parade until it wound up at what the marchers were calling heaven.

Henry was one of the down-and-outers who flocked to the free banquet that evening. He found himself wishing that someone had told him before about Father Divine. If he'd known, he would never have wasted his time in other churches, for he still remembers the glow of hope that relieved his misery when he saw Father Divine feeding the unemployed free the way he did.

"He gave us a good meal. I knew it was somethin' that never happened before in the world. In the world I knew, churches had never given such to the downtrodden. That opened my eyes."

Henry came back every day to fill his long-starved stomach, but he would suspend even a succulent piece of pork halfway to his mouth to listen more closely when people would tell their stories of how they had been saved from vice and crime.

One flashily dressed woman knelt in the aisle, her arms outstretched to Father serving the food from the head of the table.

"I came here thinking evil. And when I entered your presence I tried to fix you—you fixed me instead. You saw straight through me, Father, the lust that was in me, and you drove it out of me into the Gadarene swine."

A man stormed from the clump of people in the rear, pushing and knocking them aside so that he could get close to Father. "I used to take a Jew-man's furniture and then change my address and sell it. I don't do that no more. I mean to pay back all I stole. I concentrated on your spirit, Father, and you guided me."

Night after night, as Henry listened to followers' confessions, he felt guilt stirring in his own mind. Look how sinful he had been with Myrna. She'd been married and he had lived with her anyway. That was why he couldn't get any honest work.

He wanted to confess as the others did, but to do that was as difficult for him as it had been to beg on the streets for the first time. One night, though, he overcame the difficulty. He pulled himself to his feet at the banquet table—confessing—knowing it was the only way to get the curse of bad luck off him. Perspiration broke out all over him. His voice shook.

"I found one woman that was different. I wanted her, Father. She was married. I had to take her the way she wanted to give. We went housekeeping together. Then I found another woman and we lived in sin. There were a lot of women. Father, I want to confess and forsake my sins."

Henry's confession gave him a real sense of relief. Followers at the table seemed to know how he felt and smiled encouragement. After the banquet, they talked to Henry helpfully, now that they knew he had been blessed by Father to confess. They talked of places where he could get a job. All businesses, they said, operated by followers "in the name and spirit of Father Divine" gave the preference to followers and sympathizers when they needed to hire help.

A follower who operated a shoe-repair place offered Henry a shoeshine box with "Peace" printed in white on the sides. Though the proceeds were small, they were ample to pay for a bed in one of the extension heavens, at a dollar a week, and two meals a day for ten cents apiece. Henry was humbly thankful.

After he had worked with the shoebox for a while, even though Henry was not a full-fledged follower, since he still could not understand how Father Divine could be God, he got a job delivering coal for a coal business owned by followers. He was kept very busy there and his income increased.

More and more every day, Henry began to think about Father. Whenever he recalled the time when he had had no place to sleep except park benches, his love for Father grew more powerful. How mysterious it had been that he should have been drawn to follow Father Divine on that day near Easter, into a heaven he had never known about! To Henry there was something mysterious about Father Divine too. Father just didn't act like any human man Henry had ever heard of.

Henry did not wonder about the mystery any more after the night, at the banquet table, when looking lovingly at Father, he saw just what he had heard many others tell they had seen . . . He has often told of it himself, but he still pales a little at the memory of such a thing happening.

"I saw a light in Father Divine's throat and goin' up into his face. That was when I knowed he was God."

About ten years ago, Henry—to learn a trade—began working for a follower who ran a contracting painting business. For the past six years, he has been a self-respecting, able workman, earning sixteen dollars a day doing exterior paint work. He lives in an extension heaven and runs a Buick car. He has been taught to read and write by volunteer teacher-followers, at a free Peace Mission night school. He knows that everything he is, he owes to Father Divine.

"There's not enough money in the universe to turn me against Father Divine," he says.

Perhaps Mr. Henry Lee and Miss Jonathan Matthew reveal, more clearly than any theorizing can do, the real reasons behind Father's success as a depression leader. Illogical, illiterate, naïve, he succeeded so well in his communal system that his Peace Mission movement promised to solve the economic needs of many Negroes whose problems seemed insoluble to responsible public and private agencies.

And it was the Jonathan Matthewses and the Henry Lees, the great bulk of the fanatically faithful, who spearheaded his success. Because of everything Father Divine had given to them, they considered it little enough, after they themselves became independent earners, to turn all the money they made above living expenses back into the movement. It was they, more than the few wealthy white followers who joined the movement in the thirties, who were most responsible for Father's success.

By 1935, they had contributed so much money and so many services that Father had become a figure to be reckoned with. He received publicity throughout the country. His followers took advantage of that publicity; some because they were asked by Father, some because they figured this to be the most adequate contribution they could render, left New York and began to recruit followers in other cities throughout the country. Peace Mission movements were organized not only in New York environs like Newark and Bridgeport but also in Chicago and Detroit. Recruiters went as far west as California, and a great number of new followers, most of them white and wealthy, were obtained there.

Then Father was faced with a new problem. New followers from all over the country who had never laid eyes on him began to clamor for a sight of their God.

Father could not satisfy the followers, both in and out of New York, who required personal contact with him. They became a terrible drain on his energy. And there was no one to whom he could delegate responsibility. Sister Penny, in spite of her healthy, strapping look, had grown delicate since he had made her his wife. She was ill more often than she was well, and followers became used to seeing her reserved banquet seat beside Father's vacant for months at a time. Sometimes they asked about her. More often, sensing that Father was not happy in discussing her with them, they didn't ask at all and, absorbed as they were by Father himself, practically forgot he had a wife. Father didn't forget, though. He needed someone to be as she should have been, dependable. And there was nobody like that.

So, seeing himself as a man without a lieutenant and with too many demands upon him, Father creatively set out first to alleviate the demands and second to find a lieutenant.

Consciously, he weaned his followers away from their deeply inculcated recognition of him as a completely personal God to a new recognition of him as a half-personal, half-impersonal one. He persuaded them that it was not necessary for people to be close to him in his "personal body" to achieve the benefits he could grant them. In order to meet their needs, for instance, he did not have to be personally informed of what those needs were. He knew followers' needs, even before they knew them themselves. Everywhere the followers were, that's where Father's spirit was. He said:

"Your prayers are answered without literary correspondence. It is not necessary for me to go by feet. I am in your workshop. I am in your cook kitchen. I am even in your bedroom at night. I don't need to go there by feet."

After he sold the followers his new concept of "impersonality," Father found it comparatively simple to persuade them of his need for a lieutenant, preferably a woman, who would always remain secondary to him but would nevertheless be recognized as an authority figure in his absence.

He told the followers that he needed an assistant to take care of routine matters which were preventing him from being as effective as he might be, and he implied that he himself, through "the cosmic forces of nature" which always worked "in harmony" with him, would produce exactly the assistant he might need.

In 1935, those very "forces of nature" miraculously produced this assistant. What further proof was needed that Father Divine was God than that there should be drawn to him the lowliest one of all, one who was a living proof that Father Divine and only Father Divine could raise people from the dregs of destitution and disease into a state of health and happiness and such ability that she could become his second in command?

Father Divine exhibited surpassing powers when he raised this lowly convert into the sovereign seat beside him, the very seat that had previously been occupied by Sister Penny.

The woman whom the "forces of nature" chose for this honor was Faithful Mary.

6

"GOD! HE'S JUST A NATURAL MAN!"

Faithful Mary first came to Father Divine in 1933. Her name was Viola Wilson then. She was a prostitute and an alcoholic who foraged in garbage cans for her food. She had been in and out of courts, hospitals, jails, and mental institutions.

According to her own testimony, before she came to Father Divine she'd been "roaming the streets drunk, bent over, wearing clothes I didn't know who put on me. I was not fit for a dog to come to me. I was out in the cold and didn't have a place to sleep. I didn't know when the body was in a bathtub last, for it was full of lice, filthy and rusty."

She weighed ninety pounds and was tubercular.

"The X-ray showed one lung was gone," she said, "and just a piece of the other one was there."

There are many followers in the movement today who still remember the early days of Faithful Mary's residence in heaven. She was everything she'd said, they tell, sick in body and heart and mind.

"Father cured her," sweet-faced white follower Happy Love reports feelingly. "He put his spirit in her body and cured her of tuberculosis. After she'd been with him for several months, she increased her ninety pounds to two hundred and thirty. Father cured her of drinking and of all her other bad habits. He made her fat and merry and happy."

It is literally true that Father Divine took the human wreck that was Viola Wilson and made a new woman of her. He saw to it that she was fed and clothed and certain of a place to sleep every night. He gave her hope. He treated her affectionately. She blossomed under his attention. She became womanly and attractive despite her overweight.

Father Divine blessed Faithful Mary materially as well as spiritually. He helped her open a Peace restaurant in Newark. Then he helped her open a larger one.

"I praised Father," Faithful Mary told about this period of her life, "more and more, and the more I praised him, the more blessings he showered on me. I asked Father to bless me to feed the poor, the drunken people who were like I used to be, who had nowhere to go, who had doors shut in their faces and had to walk the streets, hungry."

Father did bless her.

During 1933, Father Divine claims to have fed 96,000 people in Newark through Faithful Mary.

In 1934, after she had proved her business acumen in Newark, Father Divine brought Faithful Mary to New York and put her in charge of his Faithful Mary Kingdom at 152 West 126th Street. Here, Faithful Mary was so successful that outsiders always asked her secret. When they questioned her, she gave them a stock Divine answer.

"Don't ever have limitations in your consciousness. The flour is almost out, I see the barrel full. And it will materialize. It is indeed wonderful."

Before she had been two years with Father, Faithful Mary was presented to all the other followers as Father's "sample and example of my supernatural powers." Father showed her off to outsiders, too. He used to say, "See her now, fat and healthy, lively and prosperous in every joint, sinew, limb, and bone of her body. Think of what she was before she came to me—a bad, abandoned woman, the lowliest of the low. It is indeed a miracle what I've accomplished in her."

Faithful came to be known in the movement as "God's Exhibit Number One." She wore the most expensive clothes. She had her own cars and chauffeuresses. Her apartment at the 126th Street Mission was sumptuous.

It was at the Faithful Mary Kingdom that the most tremendous banquets were held. And always, the seat at Father's right, the seat which should have been reserved for Sister Penny, was kept for Faithful Mary. This was public recognition that she had supplanted Penny in God's heart. Followers began to honor her as a goddess is honored. Father Divine loved Faithful Mary best of all his children. Every day he openly avowed his love. That meant the followers must love her, too. They began to vie with each other to express their love for her.

The other followers thought that the flame of God's love for his Angel Number One would last forever. It didn't, though. The "California incident" served to cool it.

In 1936, California followers wrote eager letters requesting that Father Divine show his holy body there. Father did not want to leave the East. On the other hand, he could not offend California. The wealthy white followers there would not like it if he refused to come to them. What to do? Divine's dilemma did not last long. With great regret he turned down California's request for himself. But he sent Faithful Mary to represent him there.

The California children were happy under Father's emissary. They showered her with wonderful presents—dresses, furs, furniture. They gave her money with which to feed the hungry back East. And they obviously worshiped her.

Why should the compliments the California children made Faithful have gone to her head more than the compliments she'd always received back East? Why, when before her trip to California she'd been modest and sweetly grateful for her Angel Number One status, did Faithful return home from California feeling the complete peer of God himself? Up to today, followers don't know the whys and wherefores, they say.

Faithful Mary returned from California with "a swelled head." She behaved, to the other followers, and even to Father himself, as though she and God were equals. Naturally, Father would not tolerate that. A coldness developed between him and Faithful that grew more and more intense until, in the spring of 1937, when she gave him a reason for open anger, it resulted in a complete break.

The ultimate break between God and Faithful Mary was precipitated by a white follower, William Gottlieb. He came from Ohio with a tremendous enthusiasm and his entire fortune, $9,995. He wanted, as any good follower does, to invest all of his money in the Peace Mission movement.

Father, though, seemed indifferent to William Gottlieb and to his money, which is typical of the apathetic way in which he still handles those who have money to invest in the movement. He would not grant William Gottlieb an interview. Day after dragging day, Gottlieb held his money and waited in Father's outer office to discuss his investment. Father remained out to him. It was nerve-wracking.

One day, sitting in the outer office as usual, William Gottlieb met Faithful Mary. It was inevitable that he should explain his problem to her. Here he was with the money. It wasn't much, he knew that, but it was all he had, and he wanted to give it to Father. If only Father Divine would see him . . .

Faithful Mary, grown greedy for money since her trip to California, persuaded William Gottlieb to invest his money with her.

Father learned of Faithful's perfidy. He was furious. He ordered her to return the money. She refused to do so. Father insisted. Finally, under protest, claiming that Gottlieb had made her take his money, Faithful did as Father asked. William Gottlieb denied he'd forced the money on Faithful. His money was no good to him, he said, except as it might be utilized in God's service.

Everybody waited to see whether God's one-time favorite angel could make her way out of this difficulty. The movement's masses, who had learned to love Mary, hoped that Father would forgive her. Those who aspired to her status, though, wanted to see her punished.

On April 18, 1937, Faithful Mary was summoned to headquarters at 20 West 115th Street. She has since told about this, in effect her last interview before excommunication.

"Divine came up to where I was. When he entered the door he said to me, 'Peace, Faithful.'"

"I replied to him, 'Peace, Father.'"

"'Faithful,' he said, 'I have decided to punish you for

getting out of line. I am going to take everything away from you because I am having a lot of complaints about you. I am going to send you out to work in the kitchen.'"

Work in the kitchen? Give up all the material things which she had come to accept as her due? Faithful Mary refused.

"Even God," she said, "can't do that to me."

Father Divine could do that, though, or anything else, he told Mary. God could treat his children exactly how he chose to treat them.

"I made you," the tone of his voice was a whiplash, "and I can break you by withdrawing my spirit out of you. Remember when you were a bad, abandoned woman, rotten to the bone? Yet you were not too low-down for me to feel compassion for you. You were sick and evil, but I put my spirit in you and healed you. I made you lively and well, peaceful, successful, prosperous, fat and healthy in every joint, sinew, limb, bone, vein, and cell of your soul and body. You will go to the kitchen to scrub floors for your sins."

Faithful Mary weighed the pros and cons. Then she concluded that she would never scrub floors. She would leave the kingdom first.

Before Faithful Mary could vacate heaven, however, Father Divine was forced to. On April 20, 1937, a process server, accompanied by another man, came to the kingdom with a summons. Father was in the very midst of orating his Holy Message when the process server tried to reach him.

This was insult. The followers resented it. They hit the process server. Someone stabbed his companion. The stabbing appeared to be serious and resulted in an accusation against Father Divine of assault and battery.

To avoid facing the charges, Father went into hiding in Milford, Connecticut. Authorities found him there behind a coalbin. Newspapers ridiculed him. To Faithful Mary, the entire incident seemed a sure negation of Father's immortality.

"God," she smirked, "should have been able to hide without being found."

She publicly divorced herself from Father and disclaimed his divinity to the newspapers. With what seems to those who know Father Divine today to be motivated by prejudice, she declared that Father was not God but that he was a "devil of a man." He blackmailed rich followers for money. He had a cruel and vicious temper. And he treated his wife dreadfully. She said that Father was telling the truth when he denied that there was any sexual relationship between him and Sister Penny, but that was not because of his purity. On the contrary.

"It is a known fact," she said, "that there is one of his secretaries who acts the part of a wife to Divine . . . Mother Divine, being an old woman and sick, humbly accepts her position and tries to make the best of it."

Faithful Mary cited incidents to illustrate how cruelly Father treated his wife. She told of a time when a Newark follower gave Penny two hundred dollars to be divided equally between Father and herself. Sister Penny, according to Faithful, then attended a Divine meeting and grew very excited at it. When she got home, she discovered she'd lost her purse containing the money.

"Divine was furious," said Faithful Mary, "and acted like a madman. The next morning he made her get up at five o'clock to go down to the hall to look for the money. She did not find it there, he acted like a madman again."

One of the most shocking statements Faithful Mary made in regard to Father's relationship with his wife was that, when she needed medical attention, he made her enter Kingston Hospital in Kingston, New York, as a charity patient under an assumed name.

"I tried to get him to place her in another hospital when I heard of it, but he refused," she said. "He told me that he didn't want any of the followers to know that his wife was sick. If they found out, what would they think of his miracles?"

The most publicized of Faithful's accusations concerned Father's sex life.

"Up in the chambers of Divine at night, with the lights low," Mary told, "Divine can be seen going through strange movements, while upon the floor lay several angels moving their bodies in sexual spasmodic jerks, disrobing themselves and some completely nude. They are hysterically crying out to him, and you can see that they are burning up and that the evangelical life is not in them. Many parents would be shocked, whose daughters have deserted them and gone into Father Divine's kingdom, if they could see their daughters lying in the bedroom of this beast, under the spell of hypnotism, their breaths rising and falling while the hands of Divine are caressing every curve of their bodies, and in this act of seduction he whispers, 'Your body belongs to God. And now you are being blessed by giving your body to God.'

"On leaving the quarters of Divine, these angels can be heard saying, 'Thank you, Father,' and he replies, 'It's truly wonderful.' In telling this story I am not saying that this is true among all of his angels. There are, I believe, the majority leading the evangelical life. Many of these angels who were claimed in body as well as the spirit dropped out of the kingdom when they found out how Divine actually was."

The newspapers rushed to print Faithful Mary's "exposé." This was the man who preached purity, they moralized, this was the man who called marriage a defilement. They quoted Faithful Mary regarding the relationship between Quiet Devotion, her white secretary, and Father Divine:

One day, as Quiet Devotion sat at her desk, Divine walked in. He stood at the door, gazing into the eyes of this young girl. She was an attractive young woman and ordinarily would attract the attention of men. The girl stopped her work and was staring back at Divine. Suddenly she stood up, fell to the floor and laid on the floor. She turned upon her stomach and began to crawl toward Divine as a snake would crawl to a forest and, coming to the feet of Divine, she pulled herself up to a kneeling position and, encircling her arms around Divine's legs, she cried out to him, saying, "Father, you are wonderful. My body and soul are yours, God."

The truth of Faithful's accusation has never been proven, but it is a fact that Quiet Devotion became a favorite secretary to Father Divine and that, after Mary left the movement, she inherited her seat at the table. It is a fact that Quiet Devotion remained in a privileged position until 1946, when Father took his second wife, Sweet

Angel, and when she left the movement because she was so jealous of Sweet Angel she could not stand to see her.

Almost from the very hour that Faithful Mary threw up the protection of the Divine kingdom and began to hurl accusations against her former God, circumstances changed for her. She ceased to "the fortunate one."

When she attempted to rival the Divine cult with her own creation, "The Universal Light Movement," she could find no recruits.

When she attempted to personally administer her hotel in High Falls, she found that all her clients had left and that non-Divinites did not wish to board there.

When she went to California, where she had been so beloved, Divinites, once they had made certain that she would not repent and confess her sins to God, ostentatiously washed their hands of her.

Nothing Faithful Mary did worked out. She kept losing money in one unsuccessful venture after another. She began to drink again and could not stop. She decided to try matrimony. The man she wanted to marry didn't want to marry her. She was almost killed in an automobile accident. Divine angels came to see her—to shout "Retribution!" at her.

In the very midst of Mary's trouble came the death of Sufi Abdul Hamid—a superb lesson to Mary on what God, Father Divine, could do to those who stood in his way. When Sufi's plane crashed to earth and when Father explained the crash, Faithful Mary was one of the first to be informed of the explanation. Gloating followers came to her home and repeated the story.

Miss Light-o'-love told Mary, "Sufi Hamid was crazy. He thought he could drive Father out of New York City. He bought a airplane to show he could go higher than God. Father showed nobody could go higher. He brought Sufi lower than low. He made that plane crash and all the breath went out of Sufi Hamid's body."

Light-o'-love and the droves of other faithful followers who accompanied her to Faithful Mary's home asked— hadn't Mary been taught her lesson yet? Didn't she understand the significance of Sufi Hamid's death? Was she too

stupid to realize that Father Divine had killed Sufi as a
warning to herself? If she didn't realize that, it must be
that she had gone completely crazy since the day she'd
"walked out on God." Certainly if she were in her normal
mind, she would realize that God's retribution was directed against all his enemies, and just as Sufi had lost his
body, so Faithful Mary could lose hers.

Faithful grew more terrified. Sufi preyed on her mind.
So did her own misfortunes. She began to drink more
heavily. Alcohol wasn't any good, though. It offered forgetfulness of a sort. But alcoholic forgetfulness was far
too temporary.

There was only one thing for Faithful to do. Somehow,
she must induce Father Divine to take her back into the
fold. She wrote to him. "Dear God! Please, God!" Her
letters remained unanswered. She telephoned and could
not get through to Father. She stationed herself in front of
his office door and waited for a glimpse of him. When he
came out, she knelt in front of him.

It took a long time before God accepted Mary back.
Nobody knows exactly when he did. It is known, though,
that Faithful was back in the kingdom long before her
return was publicized.

On New Year's Eve, 1939, Faithful Mary appeared at
Rockland Palace in New York. Thousands of followers
and sympathizers were there to see her. They sang to her.
Their voices rang out strong and happy.

> *Father drew me safe back home,*
> *Father drew me safe back home,*
> *I have never seen such happy days,*
> *Till Father drew me safe back home.*

Faithful Mary came out onto the platform. She was
dressed in white satin. Her hands were held supplicatingly
together and her eyes never left Father's face.

"I lied," she said and kept repeating the words. "I lied. I
lied and lied. Everything I said, it was all lies."

She told the followers that reporters had plied her with
liquor and made her crazy with it just to get her to tell
untruths about Father. "I lied and lied." She'd signed
papers which they'd asked her to sign. She didn't know

what had entered into her when she'd signed those papers.
She'd been drunk, she guessed, and "conflicted." She'd
had no rest since she'd left the kingdom, though. The
children needn't think she had.

The children hadn't thought any such thing. "Hallelujah!" they cried. "Beautiful God Almighty!" And
clapped their hands. And stamped their feet.

Faithful Mary told how Father had been with her all
the time she'd been away from heaven. When she'd been
awake, she'd had visions. When she'd been asleep, she'd
had nightmares.

"I was running through a barbed-wire fence," she
screamed, "and my dress caught and before I could snatch
it from the wire, Father came through the fence with his
head looking right at me. And when I went to bring my
arms down, Father had come suddenly under my arms—
now, truly, the hour has come—oh, I am a prisoner of the
Lord and today, at the judgment bar, I confess. I want to
thank Father for allowing me to come back to the fold!"

Faithful Mary returned to the fold, but never to her
original position there. Father commanded her to go back
to Newark. There she ran a humble place of Peace with
no help. She did her best with it, but she could not combat physical circumstances.

She tried in every way she knew to make her way again
into God's good graces. But nothing she did helped her
with him.

The other children reacted to her as Father did. Every
time she looked into their eyes, she read their accusations
there. How could she have denied God?

She was unhappy after her return to the kingdom. Obviously, the rewards of heaven were not for her. She had
forfeited them.

Shortly after her triumphant return, Faithful Mary
again left the mission. This time she went quietly, though,
knowing full well that she was beaten.

Father's children paid little mind to Faithful's second
departure. They knew that she stayed in the East for a
short time and that she returned to her old habits. They
knew that what property was left to her was sold from
under her. They knew that she left the East and went

back to California again and that there she went from bad to worse. After they had learned these circumstances, which were just what they'd expected for a woman who had been foolish enough to dare to defy God, they dismissed Faithful Mary from their minds.

It was not until April 3, 1949, that the children who had forgotten were reminded of Faithful Mary. God read them a letter that had come from W. M. Poise, a Los Angeles follower:

Peace, my sweet loving Father:

This will inform you that Faithful Mary passed out of the body on March 28, 1949. I know you know because you are God Almighty, but you always say you want us to tell you those things.

She got a heart attack, had the flu, pneumonia, double pneumonia; her sister got her the dr. He gave her some pills to take and in three days she had eaten all the pills. I guess the dope in them affected her. The sister says she crawled around the floor like a dog and went crazy. The nurses and doctors had to restrain her or tie her to the bed and she hollered at the top of her voice day and night, they took her to General Hospital where she passed.

Father interpreted Faithful's death. "So you see," he spoke cheerfully to the gathered group, "retribution has long since come to Faithful Mary—she would not live according to my teaching—and then, when my spirit left her, seven other spirits more wicked than the ones I cast out of her entered into her and she returned like a dog to his vomit and like a pig to its sty."

7

ROOT OF ALL EVIL

Father's wrath against Faithful Mary is still a burning thing. As long as he lives, he will remember her with acrimony. It is not only because she was the one whom he'd once loved best and therefore he has now to hate her most. It is not even because she had dared to set herself up as his rival once. The basic reason for Father's hatred for Mary is a practical one. It is because Faithful Mary, collaborating with Verinda Brown, another disgruntled angel, and with Verinda's husband, Thomas, was responsible for forcing God, in 1941 Anno Domini Father Divine, to flee, in disgrace, from his New York heaven.

Since 1941, Father's Empire State followers can glimpse him on Sundays and not on any other day, because on any other day but Sunday summonses can be served in New York. The city, for the past twelve years, has been awaiting an opportunity to serve him with a summons.

Father Divine says that Faithful Mary is in large measure responsible for this indignity against him . . . "she and those two other former followers, Thomas and Verinda Brown."

He says that for their actions, they have "gotten what they deserved." Faithful Mary is dead. As for Verinda Brown, although she is still alive today, she is bound to "walk the same path" as did Faithful Mary. She is already, Father tells, on the relief rolls of New York, because of her "treachery" against him—and only twenty-five years ago she had been, as are all of his faithful followers today, "healthy, happy, loving, faithful, and very, very prosperous."

Verinda Brown met Father Divine in 1929. She was tall, brown-skinned, and voluptuous. In her middle thir-

ties, she worked as a cook and children's nurse for a
Forest Hills, New York, family. Her husband, Thomas,
was their butler and houseman. Between them, Verinda
and Thomas earned two hundred dollars a month, an
excellent wage for that hard year. They had insurance
policies and two savings accounts. Verinda dressed almost
as expensively as her "boss lady." She and Thomas were
very much in love.

What did two people who were seemingly normal in
every respect, who were financially secure and in love
with each other, want with Father Divine? Verinda and
Thomas had an excellent physical relationship. Why did
they want to give that up? What did Father offer them?
These are questions that cannot be easily answered.
Verinda Brown, herself, disillusioned with Father today,
cannot answer these questions even though she would like
to.

"It's just—well, I guess I don't know," she says.

None of Father Divine's other ex-followers can find
adequate reasons for their fascination with Divine. Some,
unlike the Browns, have attempted explanations.

"He's a hypnotist," some have said.

Others have called him "a magician."

Some, slightly versed in psychiatry, have said that he
has advanced his position with the practical use of psychiatric theory.

A few psychiatrists have concurred in this feeling.
Mostly, however, even the psychiatrists have found Divine
too much of a challenge. None of them has attempted or
been able to pigeonhole his effectiveness any more than the
Browns themselves have been . . . and any more than
other disillusioned followers have.

When the record is examined, as a matter of fact, it
becomes obvious how much farther the Browns have gone
than any other ex-followers have. It took great courage
and some intellectualizing to overcome fear of Father's
retribution which has forced as many ex-followers, even
those of high educational and intellectual attainment, to
an uncomfortable sort of silence. It took great courage for
Verinda and Thomas Brown, unversed in legalities as they
were and, having functioned as they had under Father's

iron-bound tutelage, to make public accusations which Father Divine would, for the rest of his natural life, regard as the utmost in treachery.

Father Divine came into the lives of the Browns at a time when they would have been in the midst of hunting for something. Their minds and hearts were ready to accept the message which he gave them.

Fate, in the guise of a quite ordinary laundryman, first brought Verinda and Thomas into contact with Divine. The laundryman mistakenly left a package in Verinda's kitchen that was meant for a house up the street. Thomas returned the package to its rightful owners and gave it to their cook, Divine disciple Priscilla Paul. Miss Paul explained Father Divine to Thomas, and later, when she met her, to Verinda. She invited them both to a banquet at Sayville headquarters.

Father Divine was kind to the Browns at that first banquet they attended. Because they came before his wealthy, white followers and because the permanence and type of their jobs placed them an economic cut above his general membership, he was eager to involve them in his movement. He gave them banquet seats close beside his own.

Verinda and Thomas went on going to banquets. Father kept honoring them. His notice was a wonderful thing to Thomas and, more especially, to Verinda. It made them feel like people of note.

Father Divine recognized no difference either.

"It was truly wonderful," Verinda recollects today. On the occasion of their seventh banquet with Father Divine, Verinda and Thomas both, at almost the selfsame moment, saw a golden halo over Father's head. Then they knew that he was God and that they, to whom he had chosen to reveal his divinity, were important people.

After that seventh banquet, happy days began for the Browns. Heaven became their real world. Their jobs were nothing, merely difficult days to be gotten through before the wonderful nights when they could be with Father.

Of course, Verinda and Thomas were bound to encounter some difficulties in heaven. Any married couple who, for all the years of their married life, had lived happily together would be bound to encounter difficulties in Father's heaven.

"If ye live after the flesh ye shall die," Father decreed, "but if ye do mortify the deeds of the body ye shall live."

All of Father's happily-married followers tried to mortify the deeds of the body. Most times, they were successful in carrying out Father Divine's decree. Sometimes, though, they were not successful at all. And then, how ashamed the happily-married followers were. They felt like sinners on those nights. There were other nights when the happily-married followers seemed to be right, but when they knew in their hearts that they weren't. These were the nights when things could easily have happened, "but nothing happened that shouldn't have." There were the nights when women came into men's dreams and men came into women's. They didn't discuss those dreams with one another. They tried not to admit they happened even to themselves. Until the night when Brother Ezekiel Light, confessing his own sins to Father, brought into words what so many people had been feeling.

"You stopped me from sinning with the woman. But, oh, Father, even after you stopped us, she still keeps coming into my dreams. Oh, Father, when she comes into my dreams, come like a bolt of lightning between us."

After Brother Ezekiel's confession and their realization that their problems were not unique in the movement, happily-married men and women felt somewhat better about themselves. Every time physical desire would have its way with one or the other of them, Father came "like a bolt of lightning" to the other one, and the virtue of both was maintained.

A most difficult tenet for the Browns to observe was that dealing with a philosophy Father strongly preached in those days, that money was the source of all evil.

"Lay not up for yourselves treasures upon earth where moth and rust doth corrupt, and where thieves break through and steal, but lay up for yourselves treasures in heaven."

Father maintained that insurance policies and bank accounts were the wickedest of earthly treasures.

The Browns agreed with Father but some small seed of mortality caused them to continue maintaining theirs.

One night, Father spoke more vehemently than he ever had before on the evils of insurance. He presented the followers with a superb case in point. A woman named Ruth Snyder and her lover, Judd Gray, had murdered the woman's husband, Albert Snyder, to secure his insurance.

"Look at the Snyder-Gray case," Father admonished those followers who possessed bank accounts and insurance policies. "If Albert Snyder had not been insured, he would never have been killed. He was putting temptation in the way of the iniquitous. He who insures his life and property is of little faith." And a murderer and an arsonist at heart, he implied.

The Browns felt guilty about their small insurance policies just as they did about their bank accounts. They talked things over and decided that free consciences were more important than savings. They set about disposing of their assets.

First, they cashed their life insurance policies. Then Verinda drew all of her savings out of the Railroad Cooperative Building and Loan Association. Today, she tells that she and Thomas took the money and bought a dining-room suite, a bedroom suite, and a few other pieces of furniture which heaven could use, and presented them to Father. After Father accepted the gifts, Verinda says he told her that she and Thomas must be alert to further blessings which he might bestow upon them. He might, for example, be tempted to give them spiritual names.

"If and when you are blessed by inspiration to have new names you will tend to materialize what you visualize yourselves to be," he said.

Verinda and Thomas knew that those who had taken spiritual names, Miss Buncha Love, Mr. Wisdom Smiling, Mr. Sincere Satisfying, Miss Victory Dove, would live forever. They discussed Father's promise about granting spiritual names to them and told each other that they would be alert every moment to receive them.

A few nights after the gift of the furniture, a light

flashed before Verinda's eyes. Simultaneously, one flashed before Thomas'.

Verinda clutched Thomas' arm tight. "Father's spirit," she whispered. "I see it."

Thomas saw it too.

The spirit revealed that Verinda's name was to be Rebecca Grace and Thomas' was to be Onward Universe.

When Rebecca Grace and Onward Universe discussed their new names with Father Divine, he warned them that now, of all times, they'd better "put on the new mind and put off the old man, Adam, with all the mortal versions." He said that now, since they were known to be his chosen, they were committed to heavenly precepts. They must not hold on to evil money. They must not desire each other physically, not even in their dreams. Above all, their only loyalty was to be to him.

Onward and Rebecca felt their new names committed them completely to be angels and assume angelship responsibilities. Onward Universe took deeds to some Florida lots, worth about $350, and signed them over to Father Divine. Rebecca Grace tells that she surrendered her savings of $995 to Father. Onward Universe, who, in his mortal life, had been something of a fashion plate, turned over fifteen of his sixteen suits of clothes to Father.

After they had given up all their worldly possessions, Verinda and Thomas took the ultimate step. They decided that Rebecca Grace would keep her old job as cook, donating most of her wages to Father Divine, but that Onward Universe would cut himself off from lustful temptation by giving up his job and the bedroom he shared with his wife and moving into heaven to live only for Father.

Onward Universe was put to work doing carpentry and repair work around the Macon Street house. When there was nothing for him to put his hand to, he obtained odd jobs in the village and turned over his wages to Father in return for his board. When he saw Rebecca Grace at banquets, he would pass by with "Peace" and she would say "Peace" to him.

Once, though, Onward Universe yielded to mortal weakness. He confided to Rebecca, in secret, that he would appreciate a little pocket money. She slipped him some cash. A keen-eyed angel was quick to report it to Father who scolded Rebecca Grace. She was still tied to the lusts of the flesh, he said. Otherwise she would treat Onward Universe like a total stranger. Until she could live the life of Jesus, he said, she need not bother to consider herself a true angel.

Trying to mend her mistake, Rebecca gave Father a present. She bought him some beautiful blue serge material which she hoped he would make into a suit for himself. Father did not consider the giver or the gift good enough, for he handed it to Sister Penny, who showed it to Rebecca Grace after she had it made into a dress. This hurt Rebecca's pride but she could swallow that. Father Divine was more important than hurt pride after all.

After the blue serge incident, Father treated Onward and Rebecca more coolly than he had. Day by day, he grew more obviously disapproving of them. They were heartbroken. They tried to understand him and to figure out what had happened, but they could not do it. True, they had disobeyed an important tenet. True, they had revealed themselves bound, to some extent, by lusts of the flesh. But these lusts were not nearly as strong as the others had been when Rebecca and Onward had shared that double bed together, and in those days Father had approved of them. Now, merely because Rebecca had committed a small indiscretion by giving Onward Universe a little money, she and he were being so badly punished. It didn't make sense. Verinda felt there must be a reason behind Father's coldness.

One day, suddenly, like an inspiration, she realized what it was. It wasn't that Father objected so much to the Browns' small lapse into mortality. It was rather that he had an opportunistic reason for behaving as he had. Why hadn't she seen that before? She felt sure that now she and Thomas and the little they could give Father were no longer important to him. For now Father had more important kinds of followers newly recruited. They were white and they were wealthy. They could give him automobiles and jewelry and huge cash gifts. These were the sort of people who now occupied the chairs beside Father Divine that had formerly been reserved for the Browns.

And their relapse into mortality had nothing to do with their fall from favor.

Watching the white followers being courted by Father night after night, just as she and Thomas had been, Verinda grew bitter and resentful. She wanted to love Father Divine just as he had directed her to. But she couldn't do that. Sometimes, she sat in her seat, farther and farther from Father's, and let the malevolence inside her take full sway. . . . Now that she had given Father Divine her life savings, she was being cast aside in favor of people who had more money to give. If Father Divine was really God, he would never act that way. Deliberately, she called to mind characteristics about him that should have showed her he was not God in the first place. She stopped attending banquets, and when her employers advised her to leave the movement, she did.

Onward Universe remained at Macon Street. He had always been influenced by Verinda, and he was shaken by her leaving, but he had loved Father so much that he could not yet question his deity.

It was not long, however, before Onward Universe, probably because his Rebecca Grace had left the movement and later criticized Father to anyone who would listen, was banished to a small Harlem extension. He was assigned to a janitor's duties, and found himself sharing a bed with a follower who was dying of tuberculosis.

Verinda got in touch with him there and reminded him of some of Father's ungodlike behavior. She reminded him how Father had in the past sometimes dropped in on her, in her kitchen at Forest Hills on Sunday mornings. If Father was God, she pointed out to her husband, he would have never said he would like a snack of her fine cooking to bolster him, even while his angels awaited his coming to bless the banquet food. No god, she told Thomas, could have such a keen appetite as Father displayed on those occasions.

"Pancakes, sausage, fried potatoes and eggs—why, I never cooked less than six for him."

She finally won her husband away from Father and back to her and his former job.

After Onward Universe became simple Thomas Brown

again, he wanted nothing further to do with Father. He wanted to forget Father had ever existed. Verinda didn't feel at all that way though. She wanted to get back at Father. Revenge would be sweet, she told Thomas. Besides, she tells today, "I did not want that fake racketeer to use all the money I gave him. I wanted to get back every dime." She engaged a white laywer, William W. Lowell, to help her collect on her claim.

In the court of trial Judge McCook, Verinda Brown charged that the money and property she had given Father Divine added up to $4476. She charged that although Father Divine had assured her that the money she gave him would be put in the "heavenly treasury" where it would be safe and separate, it had actually been placed into a common fund. Through her lawyer, the plaintiff alleged that "the greater part was concealed and misappropriated by Father Divine, and large sums expended for real estate in Ulster County. The deeds were taken in the names of other followers who furnished little or no part of the purchase money, for they had no money which would enable them to buy property."

Father Divine denied Verinda Brown's statement. He said she was a perjurer so greedy for money to spend on fine clothes that she was suing him for funds she never gave him. All she ever did give him, he swore to the Court, was "a bunch of flowers for the dining-room table." He told the Court he had no money of his own and never had had any. In a one-hundred-page affidavit, he and numerous followers attempted to persuade the Court of the fact that no follower had ever, in his whole career, given Father money.

It was Faithful Mary who most harshly negated Father's allegations when she took the stand in behalf of the Browns. Her testimony rocked heaven with a bombshell.

She described herself as a former trusted first lieutenant familiar with every detail of the inner workings of Father's finances. Father was a liar, she said, when he told the Court he had no money. Every week during the time she'd been with him, favored angels brought him fifteen to twenty thousand dollars collected from other faithfuls in the rooming houses and restaurants. Even after he paid maintenance and other charges, he cleared ten thousand dollars a week for himself. She claimed to have seen money packed in candy boxes in his "forbidden office" in the main kingdom, "stacked so high that it would make Rockefeller jealous. He handles all that money and he keeps it for his own purposes."

Judge McCook, on motion for execution, stated that Father Divine had taken the $4476 as claimed by Verinda Brown. He entered a judgment against Divine for the full amount plus court costs.

The angels were indignant. Six hundred of them in white robes picketed Judge McCook's courtroom.

Father, himself, was outraged. Faithful Mary and Verinda Brown had told "malicious lies."

"Every knock is a boost," he assured his followers. "Every stonecast is a shove-up. Here I stand. I will not budge."

And Father has not budged. He never paid the judgment as ordered by Judge McCook. He merely appealed the case. It came up again in a court of Equity before Judge Benedict J. Dineen. Again the verdict went against Father. Again he was ordered to pay. Again he expressed his indignation.

Emerging from the courthouse, accompanied by six secretaries and two bodyguards, entering his expensively outfitted Rolls Royce limousine, he denounced "the outrage." Indicating that, with admirable self-control, he was able to hold his powers of retribution in check, he stated:

"If that judge—with his holy robes on—if he could live after that!"

Just as he had ignored Judge McCook's judgment, Father ignored Judge Dineen's. He reiterated he would never pay Verinda Brown a penny.

The case came up for the third time before Judge Charles B. McLaughlin. Judge McLaughlin directed that Father Divine pay Verinda Brown her $4476 in installments of $100 a week.

Again Father denounced a judge. He said he would not pay a penny of such an unfair judgment; he would go to jail first. And he held to what he said. He refused to permit wealthier followers, who begged to be allowed to assume the payments for him, to do so. After nine weeks of non-payment, he was held in contempt of court and his arrest was ordered.

Father did not go to jail. Neither did he pay the debt. He had made a vow and he would not budge from keeping it forever. It is typical of the personality of the man that, to avoid meeting a payment of what, after all, must have amounted to a man of his assets as a *mere* four thousand dollars, he moved from New York to Philadelphia. That move cost Father many times four thousand dollars. And, for the rest of the life of Father and his movement, it will go on doing so. For Father will never pay the judgment. Which means that he will never be able to return to New York.

Father maintains that New York needs him far more than he has ever needed New York. Soon after he left for Philadelphia he began to say that. He wrote a letter to Governor Dewey. First, he listed all the benefits he had conferred on the world in general. These were numerous. Then he listed all the benefits he had conferred upon New York in particular. These were even more numerous. Then, in detail, he described the Brown case as an example of a case where "a constitutional right is involved and which warrants your investigation and action." He told the Governor that, if only New York knew what was beneficial for itself, it would beg him to return.

Today, Father still says that. In 1952, he granted an interview to William Lowell, former attorney for Verinda Brown. Lowell opened the interview by explaining that Verinda Brown, being on relief now, had been required to transfer her judgment against Father to the city of New York. He suggested that, now that she would no longer have the satisfaction of collecting from Father, Divine would be wise to pay his debt. Then he could return to his important work in New York.

Father is consistent. He reminded Mr. Lowell that "New York needs me more than I need New York." He said that if New York had belatedly discovered what was best for itself and was really interested in his return— which would be bound to result in lifting the people, saving the city fathers three millions a year in relief money—"the city officials and the courts that were responsible for this outrage against me should confess and forsake their sins in sackcloth and ashes . . . and remove this outrage from the record. Otherwise, it can go down just like Sodom and Gomorrah did."

One of Father's favorite secretaries, present at his interview with the lawyer, challenged Mr. Lowell and, through him, the entire city of New York:

"Bring the mayor to Father's private office and get New York to beg for Father."

Since New York's mayor doubtless does not intend to come to Philadelphia to beg for Father Divine, Father probably will not ever return to New York. In his more practical moments, he knows as well as anyone does that New York is his only logical headquarters. He remembers how it was for him in New York, where his position as one of the more important Negro leaders of the thirties was recognized by white and colored people alike. Politicians sought him out, and his influence over them might have been significant. When he moved to Philadelphia in 1942, he sacrificed that political power.

Nobody knows better than Father Divine that these facts are so. Austin Norris, the attorney in whom he has implicit faith, keeps telling him that he ought to pay the judgment "under objection" and return to New York to extend his movement.

In 1951, according to Mr. Norris, he was ready and willing to pay two hundred thousand dollars for a swimming pool, a bad property investment, because it discriminated against Negroes. Yet, he will go on for the rest of his life refusing to pay the small sum of four thousand dollars, which would enable him to expand his movement freely in the place that is its only logical headquarters . . . this is Father Divine, a man who highly prides himself on having no compromise in his soul.

8

SEX AND SEGREGATION

Verinda Brown is Father Divine's "magnificent obsession." Through her, he has been enabled to prove to a doubting world that, in his eyes, righteousness is more important than self-aggrandizement.

"I would go to jail to rot but not yield to such unfairness. There are those who call me stubborn, who talk about the stubbornness of God as though he was man, but God is not men. Isn't it wonderful, wonderful, wonderful! And God won't never compromise with men."

Father Divine has compromised with men, though. Around a mixture of selfish practicality and true idealism, he has compromised no less a thing than the sex lives of all of his followers.

While he envisioned his movement, and long before he established it, the practical part of Father Divine's labyrinthian mind took account of certain realities. He knew that he could not ever hope to institute, in one and the same headquarters, a place where white and colored people could really live together as equals, eating at the same tables and sleeping in the same beds, and where they could also maintain their lives as men and women. Along with every other American who asks equal opportunities for Negroes and whites, Father Divine is aware of the fear which white people experience when they think of equal rights. He has heard this fear voiced.

"Negroes are okay, in their place. If you give them job opportunities without regard to their race, however, if you give them equal school opportunities, they will soon begin to feel your social equals. Then, they'll want to marry white women. How would you like the white women in your family to marry Negroes?"

Father Divine has heard that argument as often as any Negro has heard it. He knows, the way he knows everything—from emotional rather than intellectual realization—that if he encourages intermingling of the races and does not at the same time vigorously outlaw sex, the church, the press, the business interests, and white people generally would not permit his missions to endure very long. He knows that if he permits racial equality and sex simultaneously, he will be handing his critics a prime weapon for his own destruction. They will say that heaven encourages intermarriage. That is all they would need to say. And an indignant public would take minor infractions or even non-existent ones and would utilize law and the power of the police to magnify them into major attacks which could easily mean his end.

Knowing these facts about white and colored people in America as clearly as he has ever known anything, Father Divine, the god who never compromises with men, weighed all of the pros and all of the cons when he first conceived his movement as something big—complete interracial equality in his establishments against the sex lives of his followers, past, present, and future. For him, the scales balanced overwhelmingly in favor of complete racial equality.

That is the way the scales would always be balanced where Father Divine is concerned. For his passion for social justice is his most sincere characteristic. Nobody can doubt that. Some outsiders to the movement have doubted Father's sincerity on other scores. They have called him a rank opportunist. And a "fake" and a "phony." They have questioned his every motivation—except one. No one who has spoken to Father Divine one time, no one who has read a single speech that he has had recorded in the *New Day*, his movement's newspaper, no one who has once heard him speak in public can ever doubt the intensity of his desire to eliminate racial discrimination.

Which is certainly not to say that the only base, or even the prime base, of Father's no-sex tenet is a striving for positive race relations. The prime base is today, as it always has been, Father's overwhelming need to be not only supreme with all of his followers but also "the one and only" with them. It rests in Father's recognition that if he did permit his followers to have normal sex lives, their lovers would be bound to gain some of the affection he wants to keep entirely to himself.

Father's motivations in imposing his tenet are comprehensible enough. What is not understandable, right off, is the reason why the followers are able to accept it. You sit and you look at them and you talk to them and you find yourself categorizing them. There are those who are unattractive. There are also those, however, who are most attractive, who must have been extremely sought after.

There are those who must have been brought up to regard sex exactly as Father characterizes it "a dirty thing" and who are pleased to be able to retire from any need for physical relationship. There are also those, however, who had had vigorous sex lives. And there are the young men and the young women who have never known sex and who, you would think, would be curious at the very least.

You sit and you watch all of Father's followers, and you wonder about their ability to discipline themselves. You talk to them. At first, the things they say don't make sense to you. Then, suddenly, not gradually, but suddenly, you are hit by the impact of what you are hearing, and you realize that, among the great bulk of Negro followers, men and women both, the indignity of living as a Negro and the economics of it make the Divine no-sex tenet realistically possible of acceptance. It is a horrible conclusion you are coming to—that the treatment accorded one-tenth of our nation is such that, with some of them, even an instinct as strong as sex cannot remain normal in the face of it. You don't want to conclude this. You try to avoid concluding it. But if you are honest and if you keep talking to Father's Negro followers, one after another for days and days, you cannot help but conclude it.

"Any physical relationship between men and women is a black sin," Father Divine says.

All his followers echo him. "Amen, Father dear."

"To think," Father states dramatically, "of how there are thousands of people today, under the guise of man and wife, binding young women. Many men are putting them into what you might term to be white slavery, getting behind the legal procedures of legal authority to commit the crimes they are committing. It is enough to reach the heart of an elephant when you think of men at times marrying women behind the law of man which should be the law of God to put them into prostitution."

Father's followers see married women, as Father does, through pitying eyes. Father has made them know that physical relations between men and women "is such a dirty thing" that wives who have intercourse with their husbands are sinners in exactly the same way that prostitutes are.

Miss Beautiful, who is thirty-seven years old and has "lived in the truth of Father Divine" for twelve years, sees marriage as Father does. She has not known a man during any of those years she has been with Divine. She has had no desire to know one. If you were to ask her how she was able to carry out Father's rigid no-sex order, she would regard you as a person with peculiar standards. She would shrug her shoulders and laugh in your face and tell you that, thank Father Divine, she had never found it hard to "do what's only right."

"If you usedta live like I usedta live . . ." she would tell you.

Miss Beautiful was born on an Alabama cotton plantation. Her mother and five older sisters and brothers, ranging in age from six years old to fourteen, were pickers. Marylee, Miss Beautiful's favorite sister, was eight years old when she was born. After Miss Beautiful grew old enough to understand, Marylee told her the story of her own birth.

"You were borned right out in the middle of the field. A load of folks was watching you get borned."

Miss Beautiful had never seen her father. After she, the sixth child, had been conceived, the burden of his family had become too much for him to keep assuming. He had just picked up one day, when his wife was in the seventh month of her pregnancy, and taken his belongings and left the dirty shack.

"I was fourteen years old," Miss Beautiful tells today, "when I got married. At seventeen, I had two children and a husband who was like my pa had been, not the proper kind to take care. For seven years I acted in night clubs and I worked for two white ladies and I did everything else that I could do, until I lost my health.

"I got to the place where I didn't have a place to lay my head. I went to gin mills but they wouldn't let me come in any more. I didn't have my health and couldn't do what they wanted me to do—buy whiskey. I was no good for their business. It was prohibition. They would never even let me in. I didn't know nothing about God being in the land, but he had mercy on me. It was wonderful. The places where I sat down, there I slept.

"I had only the clothes on my back.

"When my child was fifteen years old, she did what I did. At thirty-two I was a grandmother. I did not have a penny, didn't have a home. Father's spirit drew me to him.

"I never seen him right after the spirit drew me because I thought I was too bad for Father to have anything to do with. Then I was hungry and nobody cared. I *had* to come to Father. And when I got there, Father smiled. I said, 'Take me in.' Seemed like everybody was waiting for me that day. Mother smiled. I said, oh, heaven, somebody cares. There was those two little children, they never spoken a word. I took up with this man and had two children. When I took the children there, to Father, I was scared. The little boy said God four times and pointed to Father.

"That was Father's way of convincing me. It is wonderful. I weighed about 109 pounds. Praise his Holy Name. The flesh began to come on the bones. Father gave me a job working for a lady, three hours' work to open and shut the door when the lady had company.

"I don't know nobody but Father and Mother. Everybody here knows I am telling the truth. He has made me independent, blessed me with homes, jewelry, so much in the world. He took the cigarettes and liquor out of our mouths.

"I am getting happier. My heart started beating so fast, I always have to say something. We love him more and more every time.

"We don't have to ask anybody for anything. I thought

I could not go two days without committing adultery. That's why I live this holy, clean life!"

Father Divine has given Miss Beautiful a feeling of being loved and cared for that the husband whom she'd married at fourteen and the father whom she'd never seen and the man who fathered her two children never tried to give her. Father Divine took responsibility for the two children, even though he was not their legal father, and for Miss Beautiful, even though he was not her legal husband.

"It was the first time anybody ever cares what happens to me," she says today. "Those men I know while I'm livin' the mortal life, all they ever did was drink and make me buy the gin. That man was the father of my two little children, he could really put that gin away. And he couldn't never get a job nohow. The little money I made before I got sick in the night clubs and later workin' as a cook for two white ladies, I had to give some of it to that evil man. What I need him for when he can't get a job and I'm getting all the money? 'Suppose I get sick?' I ask myself then, 'Who'll take care of me? Will he? He sure won't.' Besides, after I knowed him awhile, I didn't like him no more.

"He used to be a weakling, that's why. I make all the money, so I tells him what to do. He does like I say because he wants me to go on giving him a slice of that money I works plenty hard for. It ain't he likes me and if something happened, he'd be good and take care. Even if he wants to take care, he can't. Sometimes, he acts like a woman should act. I tell him what to do. He answers, 'Yeah, baby!' I make him do the cooking and wash the dishes. Why not, when I'm the one bringing in the money?"

Miss Charmed Life reports basically the same kind of relationship with her two husbands, three lovers, and her own father that Miss Beautiful does. She reports, basically, the same kind of relationship with Father Divine.

So does Miss Smile All the While.

And Miss Sweet Soul.

The story Miss Sweetness Love tells you differs only in detail from that which Miss Beautiful and Miss Charmed

Life and Miss Smile All the While and Miss Sweet Soul have told.

Father Divine has given Miss Beautiful and the other Negro followers of the lower economic groups a security they'd never envisioned before. You talk to them and, as they unburden themselves, you learn how it is that their ability to observe a no-sex tenet lies buried deep in the roots of their oppression. It lies in the peculiar fact that in lower-class Negro society it is the women who control the purse strings, that, while domestic jobs for women are always available, the jobs that men can do are dirtier, less desirable, and, more important, far less available. So that the men must yield many of their male prerogatives to the women who often support the homes. In a sense, they must become unmasculine while the women grow unfeminine.

As you talk to Father's Negro followers, they make you see how it is that Negro women resent playing the role that white society has decreed for men. Men resent it too. Daniel in the Lion's Den, a twelve-year follower, is typical of this resentment.

"What's women?" he asked. "Nothin'!" He answers his own question. "Bosses tryin' to tell me what to do alla time. My so-called mother th' same as my so-called wife. Then, when she gets to be big enough, th' so-called daughter doin' the same thing. Preachin' on me. Lordin' it all over jus' cause they got jobs'n I can't."

When Daniel in the Lion's Den entered the Peace Mission movement, he gave up all thought of wife, daughter, and mother. He had done that, however, before he'd entered heaven.

"I left them three womin," he said. "Always pickin' they was'n I couldn't stand it. I used to go to Newark or Baltimore or some other town and find a young, attractive girl. I brung her back to New York and taken all her clothes away from her, locking her ina room and hiring her out to other men. I was a terrible mean man. I like bein' mean to womin then. And I drink a lot of liquor, all I can get my hands on. And them womins pays. I make womins pay for everything they done to me."

Daniel in the Lion's Den is only one extreme example of the type of Father's male followers.

You talk to Father Divine's Negro men, and their stories, like the stories of the Negro women, are heartbreakingly alike. They all illustrate, one more clearly than the other, what tragic ends economic ineffectuality can drive men to.

Mr. Righteous Government tells you that he married four times before he met Father Divine and left all four of his wives because they were too demanding of him. He left three "lil' ol' so-called girl friends" for the same reason too.

Mr. Cheerfulness Good says that his wife and daughters and mother drove him to drink. He says that, just because he was never able to get a job that paid as well as their jobs did, they treated him "like dirt." You listen, and, in his own simple way, he explains to you that he feels himself to have been emasculated and that he considers the women in his family responsible.

Father Divine's Negro men tell you how it has been with them, the same as it is today with so many other Negro men. You look at them, you listen to their stories, you think to yourself—in one way, how fortunate that they have found the outlet of Divinism. You look at them and you see in them all the depressed Negro men you've ever known, those who have not affiliated with Father as well as those who have. You see them as many of them are, often so dominated by the women in their lives that, compulsively, they must prove that, even though they're down, they're never out. By drinking the most liquor. By playing the number that just came short of winning. By making up to enough women so that people will know they count for something after all. Or by giving up the fight to preserve their male prerogatives and renouncing their wives and mothers and sweethearts for Father Divine.

The men who join Father's movement have stopped worrying about being men and earning money to care for their wives and children. Father's fantasy world, where the kind of a job a man does or the amount of money he makes just don't matter, understandably becomes an ideal world to them. Certainly, they can give up their wives and sweethearts who reminded them every hour of every day that their dark skins were badges of inferiority, preventing them from being good providers and whole men. Certainly they can give up "the lustful life" which demanded far too much ego-payment from them who could not approve themselves, because they could not hope to support the wives and sweethearts to whom they made love and the children who would result from that love. Most of these men, when they came to Father Divine, were half-men in their own minds. Father gave them a chance to grow whole again. That is why they love him so. That is why they can so successfully down their lustful feelings.

Perhaps Vernon Jones, who joined Father Divine at a difficult time, when, unemployed, he had *almost* to yield his male prerogatives of supporting his household to his wife Dorrie and who left Father Divine when times changed and he could "begin to wear the pants" once more, is as indicative as anyone of what motivates a great many lower-class Negro men who join the Peace Mission movement.

In 1932, when Father Divine first came into his life, Vernon was in his middle thirties. His wife Dorrie was a few years younger. Vernon and Dorrie had a marriage built on warm companionship begun 'way back when Vernon was in his middle teens and Dorrie had only just passed her fourteenth birthday.

Soon after Vernon and Dorrie were married in the small town outside Miami, Florida, where they had both been born, they migrated North to Newark, New Jersey, where Vernon secured a job as a member of a construction gang. He was physically very stong in those early years of his marriage, and willing and able to outwork any two other men put together. His bosses were pleased with him and rewarded his strength by paying him a good salary. For a while, Vernon was the most highly paid member of his construction gang. He provided adequately for Dorrie and for the ten children who came during the first eleven years of his marriage.

Up until 1932, Vernon Jones was a satisfied man. He was proud of his children. He loved his wife. He enjoyed his home. He was pleased with his job. Then tragedy struck him and his family. While removing a heavy rock on his job, he strained himself and hurt his spine so badly that it invalided him. Every time he moved his back, it hurt him. The only time he felt comfortable was when he was sitting upright with his back resting against a chair's hard back. When he tried to walk, he felt intense pain. Naturally, any kind of physical work was out of the question after his accident.

What to do about taking care of the family? Compensation laws were inadequate and Vernon received little money as a result of his accident. The construction bosses were kind, as kind as Vernon could have expected them to be. They made some small cash gifts to the family at the beginning of his illness. Their wives came and visited sometimes and brought food packages and clothes which their children didn't need any more for Vernon's children to wear. It made Vernon mad when they brought those gifts. He was almost happy when their interest ceased and the gifts stopped coming. Even though his family needed them.

In 1932, much against his will, Vernon Jones placed his family on relief. "That wasn't much better than if we gotten no money," he tells today. The food allowances were small and little money was allowed for the special needs of the children.

Finally, there was nothing for it. Dorrie had to leave her children and Vernon at home and do by-the-day housecleaning. Vernon hated to see her do that. Dorrie was a fine wife and a good mother. She wasn't dictatorial and nagging like other women he knew. She'd never bossed him around. If she began to work, however, if it was her money that supported the family . . .

Dorrie assured Vernon that it was all right for her to take a job, that she would never become, like those other wives they both knew, "boss ladies." Vernon had always been the boss of their family, and he would always remain the boss.

Today, Vernon thinks Dorrie's intentions were probably exactly what she had said they were. But her intentions and actions just didn't tally. After a hard day at work, when she came home and saw Vernon sitting in his usual chair, "she kept looking at me like I was lazy and too bad to wipe her feet on," he tells today. "I began to think she couldn't like me any more. So I didn't like her neither. 'You don't like me, woman,' I said. 'I don't like you too.'"

Vernon still tells with feeling how much he hated the nights when Dorrie came home, her feet sore and swollen, and took her shoes off and rubbed her feet. "I seen her rub her feet and I thought she does that only to make me feel bad because she's working and I can't." Everything Dorrie did became a source of discomfiture to Vernon. He had daydreams about her. If only he could be well and never have to see Dorrie again. He began to dislike the children, too. They were noisy and disrespectful to him. He felt that they treated him exactly as their mother did "like a no-good." He conceived himself a burden to them just as he was to Dorrie. Every time he looked at his children and his wife, he felt guilty and miserable.

Then conditions changed for Vernon. He made a friend of Mr. Honest Disciple, who had lived in the apartment upstairs from him until six months ago, when he'd suddenly picked up and left his wife and four children to join the Peace movement.

"Father Divine," Mr. Disciple told Vernon, "he's as fulla love as a rubber ball. He loves his chillun so much, his love makes him bounce up and down."

Mr. Disciple was a different man from the one he had been when Vernon knew him. Then, he had been harassed. Then, he had been temperamental. Then, he had drunk gin by the quart. Then, he had beaten his wife up regularly, and the four children had been bruised more often than not. Now, though, he was never drunk. He was one of the happiest men Vernon had ever seen.

"It's all Father Divine," he said, "it ain't me at all. I'm feeling good. It's Father's spirit making me like that."

Mr. Disciple never worried about his wife or four children any more after he joined Father. And he had used to worry plenty. "I done sinned when I had 'em kids but now I done quit sinning. That's how come I'm happy."

By the time Vernon accompanied Mr. Disciple to his first Divine banquet, he knew all about what Father had done for other men in predicaments like his. Father had

cured men of worse ailments than his hurt spine. He had
gotten jobs for them. He had given them back all the good
feeling about themselves which their wives, "nasty women"
like Dorrie had become, had taken away from them. And
all he asked in return from these men to whom he was
giving so much was that they love him and nobody else
and that they cease "living lustful."

After a time, Vernon was fortunate enough to secure
an interview with Father Divine. Yes, Father said, of
course he would cure his lame back. He gave Vernon a
picture of himself and told him to paste it on his back and
keep it there until the lameness was better. He enjoined
him to live a good life, free from lust.

Vernon kept coming to Divine banquets. It was good in
Father's headquarters, warm and happy, and with Father's great love permeating every place. The companionship of the men whom he met there seemed a beneficial thing to Vernon. Most of them had left their wives
completely. Some, like Vernon, had left them only partially, continuing to live at home but having ceased all
physical relationship and having their true lives at Peace
Mission headquarters.

"You don't have lust with no woman," Mr. Disciple
said happily. "She don't think you need to take care of
her. It's wonderful, wonderful, wonderful!"

Vernon thought it was wonderful, too. He put Dorrie in
her place. Boss him around, would she? Not for long!
After she learned that the lust that was in most men was
not in him, Dorrie would stop bossing him, all right.

From the time Father Divine granted him his first personal interview, Vernon Jones refused to make love to his
wife Dorrie. Every night before they went to sleep, instead
of even kissing her good night, he would sit up in bed and
face her. Then, in a loud, clear, monotonous voice, he
would sing her a song:

> Father, oh, Father, give me the victory,
> I can't live without you,
> So many people doubt you,
> I know you is God, God, God.

At the conclusion of his song, he would tell her a
cursory good night and turn his back on her. Always, the

picture of Father Divine, real as life, was pasted on his back.

Dorrie began to hate that picture of Father Divine. It became an obsession with her. She begged Vernon to remove it or else, if he could not do that, to sleep facing her. Vernon only smiled and repeated his lullaby song:

> *Father, oh, Father, give me the victory,*
> *I can't live without you,*
> *So many people doubt you,*
> *I know you is God, God, God.*

He never removed the picture, and he went on sleeping with his back to his wife.

Dorrie didn't know what to do. She was a strong, healthy woman, accustomed since her girlhood to a virile sex life. She needed her husband's physical attentions perhaps more now than she ever had before. She began to beg Vernon to make love to her. Vernon wouldn't.

In the bed, she moved close beside him. "Ain't you loving me no more?" she asked.

Vernon only smiled sweetly.

"I'm loving you," she said.

Vernon only went on smiling.

She put her hand on his face, brought it down caressingly to his neck and his shoulder. "I'm loving you, Vernon," she repeated.

All the answer Vernon made was to sing his usual goodnight song: "Father, oh, Father, give me the victory." Then, with infuriating placidity, he turned his back on her. Naturally, Father's picture appeared on it.

Dorrie couldn't help herself. That night when she tried to induce Vernon to make love to her, the sight of Father's picture made her violent. She put her arms around her husband's neck, tight like a bracelet, and shook him until he pleaded with her to stop.

"Listen," she said, "you and that Father Divine you're so full of, how do you think I'm feeling anyway? For seven months you never even touched me. I'm waiting here and feelin' so bad every night and you go leave me going to meetings."

Vernon did not answer. He only hummed a song to himself, and when Dorrie recognized the tune, she wanted to kill him. "Father, oh, Father, give me the victory . . ."

It was after that difficult night, when she thought she could happily kill her husband, that Dorrie Jones went to see Mrs. Raskins, a social worker for the Newark Department of Welfare. She told Mrs. Raskins all about Vernon and Father Divine's picture on the sore back which had been turned to her every single night for seven months.

"What'm I gonna do?" she asked.

Mrs. Raskins advised her to tempt her husband with feminine wiles.

Dorrie rejected the suggestion. "I done tried that one time. Stood up smack in front of him, stark, starin' naked like the day I was borned. What do you think he done?"

Mrs. Raskins asked, "What?"

"He taken that picture of Father Divine right off'n his back and put it on his front. Then, 'stead of lookin' on me, he turns and looks down on that homely little man."

Mrs. Raskins decided that it might be well for her to see Vernon. She came to call on him one morning. He was very cordial and all through the interview kept smiling sweetly at her.

"You have a nice home, Mr. Jones," said Mrs. Raskins.

Vernon smiled his agreement.

"Your wife is a wonderful woman."

Vernon went on smiling.

Mrs. Raskins made her voice threatening. "But you're forcing your wife to put up with more than any woman can logically be expected to take. If you want to keep your home and your wife, you'll have to change your attitude. You know what I mean, don't you, Mr. Jones?"

Vernon smiled again. He nodded at the social worker and began to sing to her as he always sang to his wife:

> *Father, oh, Father, give me the victory,*
> *I can't live without you . . .*

Mrs. Raskins left before he finished the song. She did not give up, though. She called Dorrie into her office for an interview and instructed her as to what feminine wiles really were. Her naked body was all right in its place but obviously it had ceased being effective with Vernon. Dorrie would have to do other things to win him away from Father.

Maintaining that actions were more important than words, Mrs. Raskins took Dorrie to a drugstore and bought her a can of April Showers talcum powder and a bottle of April Showers toilet water. Dorrie had never used powder or perfume before. Mrs. Raskins showed her how. Then she evolved a campaign for winning Vernon back. She told Dorrie exactly what to do when she and Vernon retired that night.

"You've got to do things Vernon doesn't expect from you," she said.

Dorrie followed Mrs. Raskins' instructions to the letter. The night after her interview with the social worker, she grew coy with her husband.

"I think I'm gonna take me a bath."

Vernon was not interested in the idea.

Dorrie didn't let his disinterest faze her. She set about making preparations for her bath. There was no bathroom in the apartment, and when any member of the family wanted a bath, he merely climbed into the kitchen washtub. That's what Dorrie had always done during the years she and Vernon had lived in Newark. Now she didn't just climb in, though. She took a sheet and hung it modestly surrounding the washtub. She took a long bath and stirred the water so that Vernon could hear it. Then, after she had dried herself well, she sprinkled the enticing April Showers, toilet water as well as talcum, all over her body. She began to feel confident of her ability to win Vernon away from Father Divine, for surely never since he had become a man had he been exposed to such feminine wiles.

The next day, Dorrie reported her husband's reactions to Mrs. Raskins.

"He kinda fidgeted in bed, moved and twitched—but he never oncet turned his face to me."

The second night, Dorrie repeated her April Showers ritual.

"He turned to me and got real fidgetin'." Disappointedly, she told the social worker that she might have triumphed that second night if only she had continued to practice her feminine wiles. But she'd grown "too anxious" and placed her hand on Vernon's arm. Her over-anxiety had, she was certain, "stopped what mighta happened."

The third night Dorrie disciplined herself to stay calm-seeming and her discipline paid off.

"Vernon got loose," she triumphantly told Mrs. Raskins, "and from now on, I think he's gonna stay that way."

At first, Vernon Jones was upset by his lapse into lustful living. But Mrs. Raskins helped him through his difficult moment. She came to see him on his "morning after." When she came into the apartment, Vernon looked conscience-stricken. He could not even sing "Father, oh, Father, give me the victory." The social worker addressed him gently. She told him that his wife was a happy woman now, because she needed his love more than she needed anything in the world. She kept stressing that, no matter what happened, he would remain the boss in his house because that was what Dorrie needed him to be. She said that Dorrie was not like other women he knew. If she had really wanted to "wear pants," would she then have tried so hard to please her husband by spending her hard-earned money to purchase perfume and powder just because she thought he'd like to smell it on her? With that proof, she was able to dispel Vernon's antagonism toward the wife whom he really desired now. Then she gave him a piece of good news. The Acme Chemical Company had called and asked her to recommend a night watchman. She had recommended Vernon. He could start working that night, and, if he wanted her to, Dorrie could give up her job.

Today, Vernon Jones thinks Father Divine is a good man but a mistaken one where sex is concerned. Ten months after his wife and her social worker weaned him away from Father Divine, he became the father of twins.

The case of Vernon Jones, while it points up the devastating economic forces which are at work among lower-class Negro men, is basically an atypical one. For most men, unlike Vernon Jones, once they join the movement, do not leave it again for their wives and families. Most of them are not lucky in the way that Vernon was when his wife Dorrie discovered her social worker. Nor can most lower-class Negro men command the respect from their wives that Dorrie had for Vernon. For most of them have never had the opportunity that Vernon had at the beginning of his marriage, for persuading their women that they really want to protect them and provide for them and their children.

Too many lower-class Negro women, judging from their own experience rather than from the larger economic picture which they are not equipped to understand, think of their men as natural-born liars and selfish thieves who will use women for their own advantage and then throw them aside when they can't be used any longer.

Naturally, women with these feelings and opinions cannot respect their mates. How can they trust men when they expect nothing from them except children and trouble? How can they accept the exploitation and the irresponsibility? It is no wonder that so many lower-class Negro women can take on the no-sex tenet of the Peace Mission movement and absorb it into their very beings. Father Divine, who has decreed physical purity for them, is, after all, a more satisfying husband than their men can ever be. Is he not the father who will provide for them, the kind of father they've never known in all their hard lives? Is he not the husband who will protect them?

Father Divine, in his role of protector-provider, is the kind of lover his followers have always dreamed of but never found. He is good and kind and completely concerned with them. For what Father gives his lower-class Negro followers, the sacrifice of sex—which, without mutual respect between man and woman, must sometimes have been very unsatisfying anyhow—is, according to a vocal follower, "no trouble at all to step right over."

Miss Holy Light is a typical lower-class Negro woman follower. Her life story is so like the stories of numerous Divinites that they might as well be, as she terms them, her sisters.

"Sex?" she laughs. "Men? What I want with men when I got Father now?"

Miss Holy Light was born in Miami, Florida. From the

time she was a tiny child, she'd known what it meant to
be a Negro in a Southern city. It meant that, when she
was seven years old, she began to work on a chicken farm
with her parents and six other brothers and sisters. It
meant that, in all the time she was growing up, she'd
never owned a pair of shoes that were especially bought
for her or a new "store-bought" dress.

Miss Holy Light matured early. At fourteen, she had
her first affair and her first baby. Shortly before her eldest
son was born, his father disappeared. The next year, she
had an another baby. By the time Holy Light was twenty-
seven years old, she'd known five men and had twelve
children.

"I never been in love, though," she laughs easily, when
anybody asks her that question about, "Did you ever love
any of your children's fathers?"

Sex had been an outlet for Holy Light, a diversion
from the long, hard working day. She'd never trusted the
men she'd known, not even during the periods when she'd
lived with them. Though they'd fathered her children, "I
didn't like none of 'em so much," she says now.

By the time Father Divine came into Holy Light's life,
she was more than ready to love him.

She tells her own story:

"I was there in Miami, Florida. That was before Father
Divine came. My kids was there, too, all twelve of them. I
got so lowdown, so naked, so hungry, no home, no
clothes, no shoes. God Almighty, I prayed and I cried all
night askin' for God."

Holy Light's God, though, hadn't helped her to care for
herself and twelve children any more than their five fathers had.

"I used to go to church good. But I didn't get shoes to
go to church with."

Then the voice of a new God spoke to Holy Light.

A Divine follower came to Miami from New York,
Father's headquarters then. She came to Holy Light's
church and preached about Father Divine, who was God
on earth. He wasn't like preachers who talked about religion on Sunday, she said, and spent the rest of the week
trying to get people's money out of them. Father Divine

really loved his people. The follower said, "He feeds them when they're hungry. He shelters them when they haven't any home."

It was Holy Light alone whom the sister talked further to. "Give Father a chance," she pleaded. "Open up your heart and let him step inside. Just wait and see what he'll do for you then."

Holy Light opened her heart to Father and he stepped inside, just as the sister had said he would do. He came to Holy Light in a vision.

"I will always protect you," he told her. "Now that you have me, you'll never starve again."

Then Holy Light knew—Father Divine was the answer for which she'd prayed to God who her minister claimed was in heaven. Father Divine *was* God.

Father Divine soon rewarded Holy's faith. She said, "I been goin' from pillar to post draggin' them chillun around. Nothin' good happenin' for nobody. Till God come to me, Father Divine. He done everythin' I wanted 'im to do. When government made fabricated houses in Miami, Father Divine made me hear about them houses. I was livin' in sin with that so-called what-you-call-'im brother (meaning her lover of the moment) —it did got so bad, I couldn't stay with him and I wanted to get into them fabricated houses.

"People tole me, 'You can't get this home because you got to be married.' I said, 'I know to who I'm married to. He can give me a house and I don't have to have no man.' "

Because of her faith in Father Divine, Holy Light did something that, in the days B.F.D. (Before Father Divine), she would never have had the courage to do. She made application to the white tenant-selector for the Negro housing project. There was one question the tenant-selector asked. Did Holy Light have a job that could be considered permanent? Could the authorities be certain of her ability to meet her rental obligations?

Wrapped tight in the security of Father's love, Holy Light went to the lady for whom she worked (it was Father Divine, of course, who had blessed her with the job, which she'd found soon after she'd come to him) and asked for some guarantee of permanency. The lady signed a paper. "She has a lifetime job," she wrote.

Another problem arose to test Father Divine. What about furniture? the white tenant-selector asked. Well, what about it? Holy Light had the furniture that had been in the old shack she and the children had shared with the so-called brother—couldn't that be carried into the project?

The tenant-selector minced no words. "Suppose there are bugs?" she asked.

Holy Light was comfortable. "I'll get me some furniture. Jus' see if I don't."

Father Divine guided her to the nursery school where she'd once worked. He caused her to ask the supervisor whether there was any furniture the nursery could spare her. He made the nursery-school supervisor tell her that, coincidentally, the school was vacating its premises and that Holy Light could take anything she wanted—chairs, beds, bureaus.

Life in Miami went on improving. Holy Light maintained Father's spirit, which kept her on the right track. After the twelfth child, she had no more children. She took no more lovers either. Now that she had Father's spirit, what did she want with men?

"Men never done nothin' for me or mine. Only kep' me makin' children in sin and shame."

When she'd needed it, she'd never been able to afford "one of them things to keep th' kids from comin'." Now she didn't need one. For hadn't God, through the medium of the *New Day*, decreed that "Self-control is birth control"?

Whenever she had a problem, Holy Light turned to Father. Nothing was too small for him to deal with for her. No problem was too great.

One day, Holy Light had another vision. For the second time since she'd learned about Father, he came to her in the body. He beckoned. "Come to New York. Come to my headquarters."

After the vision, she worked hard, harder than she ever had before. She denied herself and the children food and clothing. She saved her money. In one year, she had saved sufficient for the trip to New York.

"I told them children, 'All you got to do, you follow me.' "

Part of the way, Holy Light and the children rode on the bus. They walked part of the way. And, one time, a driver whose truck had an open back asked them, through the kindly intervention of Father's spirit, to ride with him.

The trip was wonderful. Holy Light and her children were protected throughout by Father's spirit. As soon as she arrived in New York, she gave her twelve children to God.

"Out of all the children I had," she said, and danced with the joy of her freedom, "I done got none now. I is free, free, free. As for a man, I don't need no man. I ain't got no lustful feeling now."

Holy Light has not overcome her lustful feelings as completely as she thinks she has. Neither have Father's other followers. They have learned, however, to direct those lustful feelings into channels that are socially approved in the Peace Mission movement.

Holy Light, for instance, while she no longer needs to live in sin with her "so-called brother" does need a physical outlet for the sexual feeling she had once given him. There is a physical outlet in the Peace Mission movement, and it is known as "vibrating." It is highly regarded, not merely as a vent for repressed sexual feeling, but rather as a tremendous way in which followers, men as well as women, can display their love for God.

Since Holy Light came to Father Divine, she has attained the distinction of being one of the movement's most effective vibrators. It is often she who sparks the vibrations in which other followers join. Her leadership in this respect provides her with a real creative satisfaction.

Holy's vibrations follow this pattern: She looks at Father and jerks her hips. She looks for a long moment with the love shining out of her eyes. The she starts to speak. Her voice sounds low and rich. She says, "From the very first moment I saw that precious, holy body of your'n, I fell in love head over heels. Oh, I love you. Gee, I love you."

The adoration shines out of her so that, momentarily at least, her plain face seems beautiful. "I love you so much.

You is my mate. You is beautiful, Father. You is so pretty, Father. Oh, Father Divine, how cute you is."

Father glances at Miss Holy Light. His face is imperturbable.

She begins to walk toward him. "You is my husband, my one and only, Father!" she says. "God!"

The other followers echo her. "God! God! God!"

Tears come to her eyes. She screams, "You is my lover. You is my everything." She reaches Father's seat. She falls on the floor in front of him. She falls hard but does not hurt herself. She bangs her head against the floor with utmost deliberation. She lifts one leg into the air and beats the floor with her other one.

"You is all that I need, Father dear." She rises and stands rigid. She gives Father a loving look. Then she closes her eyes and dances away. She jerks her hips again, and her breasts. She takes her head in her hands. She holds it as though penitently.

"Hallelujah!" she screams out. "I love you—love, love, love you."

She releases her head and drops her right hand onto her bosom. She holds it there caressingly. "Love, love you."

She stops moving and sits down with a happy look on her face. Her vibration has finished. It is apparent that, in her testimony to Father Divine, she has reached a sublime climax of fulfilment. That is apparent in the way she holds her fists clenched and her eyes tight shut as though she cannot bear to open them, and in the harsh breathing she could not stop if she wanted to. You look at Holy Light in her naked happiness and you know, beyond a doubt, that what she has told you before is true. For the rest of her whole life long, she will never need a man other than Father Divine, her God, her husband, and her most desirable lover.

9

"LET THE DEAD
BURY THE DEAD!"

Outsiders to the movement often wonder how Father Divine expects the continuation of his heavens when he has outlawed sex. Without having new babies born, they ask, how can the movement go on? Is Father only interested in maintaining the cult through his own lifetime and the lifetime of those who are presently affiliated, or does he wish to extend his influence beyond his present generation? If he does wish to extend his influence, how can he hope to?

Father always answers these questions with the same bland assurance. He generally counters the curiosity of outsiders by asking a question of his own. "Why should we go on increasing and multiplying and replenishing the earth with more misery?"

When outsiders try to answer Father by citing the need for human reproduction and the practicality of it, he interrupts them.

"I feel," he says, "that if we will clean or cleanse those who are now living and purify them—I think we are about a greater work than self-indulgence."

When outsiders return to their argument of "unless babies are born," Father interrupts. He might be talking about the weather for all the emotion in his voice when he says, "Well, of course, when we learn to live, we unlearn to die."

With this idea of unlearning to die, Father Divine, in his own mind, effectively dismisses the need for sex and babies. If people know they are going to live forever, he explains easily, they have no need to reproduce themselves.

And Father's followers know that if they behave as good followers should, they are going to live forever.

"A person cannot die," Father says, "unless they give up the ghost ... Not a suggestion of death or any expression a man could suggest that would bring death upon you could overcome you if you be substantiated in Faith and refuse to believe the suggestion that may be made concerning such an expression——"

For the thirty-five-odd years that Father Divine has been functioning, there have, of course, been deaths in his movement. Followers have had no trouble in rationalizing them, however. They explain that anyone who has an ounce of sense can, as Father would say, "see the mystery." Followers who die are offending angels. They divorce themselves from God in some way. After that, they cannot expect to live. No one can offend God and go on living.

Father maintains that heaven has no room for dead angels. In an interview with a non-follower, an Illinois teacher and writer named Charles Braden, he speaks for the record on this score.

"What about those who die?" Dr. Braden asked.

Father replied, "My true followers do not die."

Dr. Braden persisted, "But surely people who have been in your movement have died. I am certain I have read of such cases."

Father only repeated his statement, "My true followers do not die."

"Do you mean to say," Dr. Braden asked, "that the death of a follower is *prima facie* evidence that he was not a follower?"

Father Divine nodded his head in assent.

Back in 1935, while Father was in Sayville, he openly disavowed his first dead angel. Her name was Tessie Bowan. She was seventy-five years old and had lived in heaven for some two and a half years.

Hearing about the death of Miss Bowan, the local undertaker phoned Father Divine. Did Father want him to dispose of the body? What were the burial instructions?

Father had no burial instructions for the undertaker. The welfare authorities could bury Miss Bowan.

"Let the dead bury the dead!" he stated.

The welfare officer refused to accept responsibility for

the death of a woman who was obviously a Divine follower and therefore a Divine responsibility. He said that Miss Bowan was Father's angel. Father disowned Miss Bowan. Tessie Bowan was no angel of his. If she had been, the welfare officer might know, she would still be alive.

The battle over Miss Bowan raged for several days. Neither side would give in. Twenty angels who were lodged in the house with the dead body moved out. Finally, the welfare officer yielded. He ordered a pauper's burial at the county's expense.

In September, 1936, a follower named Charles Jenkins who had been with Divine since 1933 had a hemorrhage of the lungs. Immediately this happened to him, he was removed to an apartment on 129th Street that was not officially known as part of the Peace Mission. He was taken from this apartment to Harlem Hospital, where he died on October 7. No one claimed his body, and he was buried in Potter's Field on Riker's Island.

According to Faithful Mary, these incidents were hardly unusual. After she left the movement, she claimed that she had taken an important part in many arrangements for disposal of the inconvenient dead.

She said, "During the time I was there [in heaven], I believe that at least two hundred persons have died. Whenever a person dies, we notify Divine. He tells us to close the room of death and keep all the other angels in their rooms. Then the police are notified and the body is removed at night to the morgue and eventually buried in a Potter's Field. The angels are told to stay in their rooms when the body of a deceased is being removed, so that they will not know that anyone has died. Divine always claims to the officials that he doesn't know the party who died. He says that the person just came in, even though the angel may have been with him for years. The sad part is that many people die in the kingdom and their loved ones do not know anything about it, many thinking that their loved ones were alive and they may have been dead for some time."

Father tells true followers that, just as they must not die, so they should not become ill. If an angel does allow himself to grow sick despite Father's negation of illness, he must seek Father's spirit for a cure. If he does not find a cure with Father, it means one thing—he does not truly trust in God.

At the inception of the movement and for many years thereafter, Father Divine outlawed doctors. He said that they were all thieves, out to get the people's money. Either a follower grew better by calling on Father's spirit or he didn't grow better at all. Today, he is not so rigid.

Two years ago, he issued a new regulation to sick believers. He told them:

"If you get out from under my jurisdiction mentally and spiritually, and bring sickness and affliction upon yourself, then my spirit cannot reach your affliction in matters not whatsoever reasoned. It may be justifiable for you to have a physician under that premise or statement."

When you talk to Father's followers, they make it clear to you how little faith they have in doctors.

"If I get better," a very sick follower will say, "it will be Father who made me that way."

When you talk to them, they explain to you that Father is the real doctor. Then they sing you a song to illustrate it.

> Father is the doctor,
> Father is the doctor,
> Father is the doctor,
> He'll cure us of anything.

Unlike the great bulk of his followers, Father Divine, himself, has recently begun to recognize some few members of the medical profession. About a year ago, he stooped to say:

"Most of the metaphysicians and the healers by faith and the like, they would think of discarding the physical science; but I work through physical science just as effectively, sympathetically, and harmoniously if they will work through me accordingly. And therefore, they leave the results with me from a mental and spiritual point of view and I allow them to perform their scientific and skillful duty from a professional point of view, and we two work together systematically and can bring anyone back to life, matters not what their ailments may be."

Often, in spite of his offer to work co-operatively with them, when doctors give orders to his sick followers, Father Divine disregards them in favor of his own theories. Naturally, the followers believe Father and not their mortal doctors. Often, they reject their doctors' orders in favor of Father's theories. As Miss Lovely Best did when her doctor ordered hospitalization for her.

A follower of many years, Miss Lovely Best, during the 1951 Christmas season, had gotten a bad case of pneumonia. Her doctor said she required hospitalization. Miss Lovely refused to go to a hospital. She was living in a Divine hotel in Philadelphia when she became ill, and that, she told her doctor, was where she proposed to stay. "I ain't takin' this body one lil' step out of this here hotel," Lovely said. "Here, Father maybe can stop in and see me. He can't never do that so easy if I go to some ol' hospital."

The day after Christmas, Lovely Best knew that her stubbornness with the doctor had been more than justifiable. For at close to one o'clock in the morning of December 26, after she had fallen into a fitful sleep, Father Divine came and caused her nurse to waken her.

At first, Miss Lovely thought he was a vision. When she found out he was real, she could not contain her happiness.

"Oh, Father," she said. "Oh, Father, you really did come. It's so wonderful. Oh, Father——" Her eyes filled with tears.

Father considerately waited for Lovely Best to regain her composure. Then he asked, "How are you feeling?"

Miss Lovely hated to admit her illness, but she could not lie to God. "I am just not myself."

Father was amazingly tolerant. He did not accuse Miss Lovely of having become ill because she had renounced him. He was not even angry with her. When he spoke to her, his voice was the epitome of gentle kindliness.

"Well, I came, so you will be yourself from now on."

Lovely tried to keep the tears from pouring down her face. But she could not. It was so wonderful—Father having come to see her and not disapproving of her because she had been "bad enough" to contract pneumonia.

"Well, I know I will be myself now," she finally brought the words out. "I am just trusting and I know there is nothing else to do. Oh, I trust you, Father."

Father said, "Well, you should." Then, in the tone of someone asking about the opinion of an unfavored inferior, he inquired, "And what does the doctor say is the matter with you?"

Miss Lovely Best told Father about her discussion with the doctor, his diagnosis of pneumonia, and his suggestion that she should be hospitalized.

Father thought a moment, evidently considering the medical diagnosis and finding it lacking.

"I see. Maybe you need another doctor. Maybe you need another doctor because improvements must take place if the doctor is in harmony with me and things work systematically and harmoniously. You must get all right. Remember, I said if the doctor is in harmony with me and things work systematically and you are in harmony with me and your nurse and those with whom you are concerned be in harmony with me, I can help you through them and you can be restored to your health completely. But all obstructions must be moved out of their places, anything that would tend to hinder you, I mean, like as if anyone would think conflictingly or antagonistically; they must contact me sympathetically and harmoniously."

Lovely Best told Father that she was certainly in harmony and she knew her nurse was too. But she was not sure of her doctor's sympathy for Father. She would test him the next time he came to see her. If she found that he did not "harmonize" with Father, she would dismiss him from her case.

"Fine, fine," Father answered. "If he is an obstruction he would be hindering you."

As it happened, Miss Lovely's doctor passed the test she gave him (she engaged him in a discussion about Father's divinity and he reacted favorably) and was permitted to see her through the pneumonia. After her recovery, she smilingly testified at a banquet.

"Y'all see me now, healthy in every limb and sinew of my body. Just a few weeks ago, I was not healthy but sick. The pneumonia had me wracked with pain. The doctor came to see me. He done what he could. He couldn't do it, though, he couldn't drive the pneumonia out. There was only one doctor could do that. He is the real doctor, Father Divine, the main doctor. Thank you, Father, for pulling me through."

Father acknowledged Lovely Best's gratitude. "O.K.," he said. "You follow my orders, you'll always be well."

Father's Newark followers tried to follow his orders about doctors and medicine and almost got him into trouble with their trying. As Father had ordered, they refused to permit their young children to receive diphtheria injections. The health authorities threatened and cajoled them to no avail. Didn't they love their children, the doctors asked the parents, and want the best possible health for them? The parents answered that yes, they loved their children just as they loved any other children of God— but that these children did not belong to them any more than they belonged to the doctors. These were God's children, and, whether the doctors believed it or not, God would keep them well.

The doctors argued. The followers remained sweetly stubborn. There was no need to inject the children with foreign substances which could not be expected to help them anyhow and which were against the practices of their religion.

Finally, as a last attempt, Dr. Charles V. Craster, director of the Newark Health Department, wrote a letter to Father Divine. The followers were breaking the law by not allowing their youngsters to be inoculated. He could have Father held legally. If Father would come to his office, however, the matter could be talked over and no doubt settled to everyone's satisfaction.

Father Divine came to see Dr. Craster. He wore a blue suit and a red tie and he had a carnation in his lapel. He walked dignifiedly, head up, looking neither to right nor left. He was attended by three secretaries, a curiously small company for him, and by Philip Light, his chauffeur. He was smiling and relaxed. He said he never wished to break the law and neither did his followers. They prided themselves on being good, real, true Americans.

Dr. Craster told Father about a Christian Scientist

whose young daughter had died of diphtheria because her father had refused to have her treated. He said that the father had been held for manslaughter.

Father Divine did not seem to hold the case of the Christian Scientist applicable to himself. He remained friendly but imperturbable. He repeated his first statement to Dr. Craster. His followers were real, true Americans and had no desire to break the law. He did not indicate once during the interview whether or not he intended to permit inoculation.

Some days after he had been in to see Dr. Craster, however, all the delinquent followers brought their children to be inoculated.

Public health and social agencies do not generally have as easy a time with Father Divine as Dr. Craster did. Usually, their representatives who have dealings with him go away from their interviews with the feeling that they do not understand him, and that he certainly does not understand them.

Mrs. Lorraine West is a social worker in Rehabilitation. She went to see Father in June of 1952 about a follower of his, who had become a patient in her hospital. Her name was Sweet Music.

After Mrs. West had partaken of a sumptuous banquet and waited six hours for the chance to speak with Father, she was ushered into his office.

"Peace," Father said.

Mrs. West said, "Peace."

Father said he had many missions in Australia. Mrs. West said she thought it was wonderful that his fine work should have spread so far. She had come to talk, she said, about . . .

Father said he had missions in England, too.

Mrs. West voiced her approval of Father's English missions too, but it was late and if he did not mind, she said, she would like to talk about Sweet Music.

Father said, no, he didn't mind at all, but would Mrs. West be interested in seeing a true-to-life recorded picture of one of his missions in Russian-occupied Germany, and did she know that, whatever her business, she'd better get it over with rapidly because there were millions of followers waiting to see him and all he could spare for an ordinary interview was five seconds.

Mrs. West thanked Father for granting her even five seconds of his time and launched, before she could be stopped, into her story about Sweet Music. She said that Miss Music had recently had a leg amputated. The operation had been successful and she was recovering nicely.

"And now," Mrs. West said, "we are at a point where we don't just exactly know what she is going to do for the rest of her life. She has no place to go and has no family. All of her friends were your followers and they don't want to do anything that would not be right . . . That is why I thought that, by coming to see you, you might be able to help Miss Sweet Music."

There was no way Father could help Miss Sweet Music. He wished Mrs. West to know she was no follower of his. He said:

"A good many think that, because we do everything so freely—because we feed thousands of people daily for almost nothing and been doing it for many years—many people even those in the hospitals and different places, if anyone comes around and says they are acquainted with Father Divine and they have been to his place—they have eaten at his places and the like, the same as Miss Sweet Music—whether they have ever done any work or not, some of the representatives of the different hospitals and places think I should be responsible for them for the rest of their lives."

Mrs. West agreed with Father that social agencies might have taken advantage of his beneficence and that many of the disassociated might have claimed to be followers so that they might profit.

"But," she said, "in all the years that I have been working as a social worker, I have never seen anybody show such faith as Miss Sweet Music shows in you."

Mrs. West told Father that she had mentioned to Sweet Music that perhaps assistance might be secured for her, and that Sweet Music had answered, "I believe in Father Divine and Father doesn't believe in assistances. I can get to help myself."

Mrs. West felt that eventually Sweet Music could, as she earnestly wanted to, get to help herself.

"Until she can get around to doing something for herself," Mrs. West said, "and since she is minus that leg, her health is better than it has ever been—and, if we can somehow get her an artificial leg and a place to eat and sleep temporarily until she can get back on her feet and earning money that would be quite a help."

Whether Sweet Music secured an artificial leg or whether she didn't was not Father's concern, he told Mrs. West. He reminded her that, as he had said before, not all who took his name were true followers. Sweet Music could not be a true follower. If she were and had always been, she would never have needed to undergo any such wickedness as a leg amputation.

He said, "Many people bring upon themselves such conditions as they experience and such as she has been experiencing by disobedience to both the laws of God and of man, and when they put themselves into such a predicament or condition, they should know that the assistance should come from someone or some concern who is set apart for that purpose." Emphatically he explained, *"She should know that I do not believe in people getting sick and getting old and decrepit."*

Mrs. West gave up. Father's logic was beyond her.

Father Divine's logic is not beyond his followers, though. They heartily approve his rejection of the old and the sick and the dead.

"When people grow old," an intelligent white follower who came to Divinism via Christian Science said, "when they grow sick or when they die, they are disobeying Father's order. They are not exemplifying the positive."

Visualization of the positive is the philosophical basis of the Peace Mission movement. The followers see God, themselves, and each other in the most positive terms. God is perfect. The angels are nearly so. True, the outside world is a problem world. It shan't be for long, however. God is here to change the world.

Father Divine often tells his followers about a young girl whose lover left her when she was nineteen years old, and who became insane with grief. Her family had been forced to commit her to a mental hospital where she'd lived until she was eighty-some-odd. In all the years between her commitment and her death she never changed her physical appearance.

"She never changed her physical appearance," Father repeats, "because she held in her mind the identical thing she first conceived concerning her lover. If such could be true of the thought of a lover who had forsaken her and could keep her in such a perfect state of expression, think of how it could be for you. So vividly visualizing the perfect, the real, the pure, and the true, it should be more true for you than that of the so-called insane girl visualizing her lover as an individual—the individual that was imperfect, the one that forsook her. I repeat, think of how it could be for you."

The followers do think how it could be for them. Mary Bird Tree, formerly Mrs. John Hunt, widow of the Cleveland milk millionaire, says she knows well how it is for her. Even though in the world outside, she would be considered to be seventy years old or nearly that, it is a different story here.

Recently, Miss Tree made a public testimonial. "I thank Father to say that I have always visualized myself as young. I remember Warner [her son] asking me one time how old I was, and I said, 'How old do you think I am?' He said, 'Twenty-two!' and I have always kept that in my consciousness."

Because the followers embrace Father's tenet of the positive, they report numerous healings.

Father Divine healed one woman of a "leaky heart." Another woman was healed of chronic indigestion. Nothing helped her overcome this unpleasant condition until the day when she looked on Father's beautiful body.

Miss Uni-Presence is a white Texan. She is convinced that Father healed her of a "twisted spine."

Father Divine is giving Mr. Joseph, who claims to be one hundred and one years old, a brand-new set of "natural, not false teeth." Mr. Joseph smiles a toothless grin and talks about his "miracle" to anyone who will listen.

And there is Miss Saint John Sincere of Philadelphia. Father is proud of what he, with the slight aid of a good doctor who believed in him, did for her. He often tells about the miracle of Miss St. John.

"She had such faith in me, even though the doctors just thought she could not live, but she knew that her health could be restored as long as she trusted in me. And I told her that this time she must trust in me through the physicians; giving them the right of franchise, you see; giving them immunity to treat her according to medical skill. But they were to think with her and with me, sympathetically, harmoniously, and the like, and my spirit could work through them. And, you know, Miss Sincere had an operation. The doctors said she was cancerous. Her whole system was eaten up with cancer. He said when he opened her up, he said if it had not been for his faith in me as well as she, he would have sewed her up again and let her pass on. But, because of her faith she was healed."

Father's tenet of the positive is a basic reason why many Negroes have flocked to him. Its whole concept denies the reality of what it means to be a Negro in America.

Father tells his white and Negro followers, his Negro ones especially, that there "really is no race" and "there really is no color." These two words, "color" and "race," are mere bug-bears formulated by bad Americans, he says, who have thrown God out of their hearts in favor of the devil.

Father states, "There is no such nation nor race of people as 'Negro,' as you may call them. Such an expression was a liar from the beginning—calling yourselves intelligent and allowing yourselves to be abused and robbed by the abuses of men; by calling you such vulgar names. The very name 'colored' is a curse. Those who impose it upon you, if you allow them to do it, they are cursing you. They are not only cursing you but they are robbing you—the very name is a robber in itself. I came to eradicate these curses and abuses and to dispel them."

In the Peace Mission movement, Negroes are referred to as "people of the darker complexion." Whites are called "people of the lighter complexion."

Father tells his followers, "Your belief will cause you to be just as you see yourselves to be."

Miss Uni-Presence and Mr. Joseph and Miss Saint John Sincere and even the Negro followers who no longer believe in the color of their skins are only slight examples of Father's philosophy of the positive. The best example of all is, he says, "I, myself exhibiting every desirable attribute."

He does exhibit desirable attributes!

At least in his late seventies today, Father Divine does not appear a day older than forty-five. He lives an excruciatingly demanding life. He often interviews from early morning until early morning. He keeps twenty-six secretaries harassed with the details of a most voluminous correspondence. He seldom sleeps more than four hours out of twenty-four. And he is never ill. In the twenty-five years since he has become a public figure, he has not had even a slight cold.

Since Father's condition is understood by the followers to be the result of his adherence to the positive, they all strive to achieve his state of mind.

Throughout the movement, negatives are rejected. The Divine vocabulary has become a striking example of rejection of the negative and embracing of the positive.

In heaven, the word "hell" is never mentioned. It is known simply as "the other place." "Hell" cannot be used as part of a word either. A Divinite, for example, would rather be laughed at than to say "Hello." His usual greeting to outsiders, as well as to other followers, is "Peace." If an outsider does not respond to "Peace," the follower might say, "How do you do?" If he had to say "Hello," however, he would be most likely to say, "Other-place-o."

Nobody ever mentions the devil in heaven either. If the devil must be spoken of, angels speak of him as "the other fellow."

The word "damn" is eliminated from angels' vocabularies. Here, the positive operates to its straining point with angels substituting "bless" every time "damn" is indicated.

Patience Budd, a very well-contained lady, is a "sample and example to the world at large" of the positiveness of the Divine vocabulary.

Speaking to a group of followers recently about a racial

incident that took place on the Amsterdam Avenue bus in New York, Miss Budd said, "Yesterday, I was riding on the Amsterbless Avenue bus——" Her substitution of the word "bless" for "damn" was instinctive.

Father's followers try to be as positive as he is in more important ways than their vocabularies. They try to be as positive as he is in every detail of living.

Mr. Robert Right, white, former publicity man, says "Many of us were bad before Father's tenet of the positive made us good. That is why we say 'hurray for the positive.' It has made former murderers become law-abiding and former scarlet women become 'pure as the driven snow.' The magical power of Divine positiveness changed them."

10

"JUST TO HEAR YOU TAP YOUR BEAUTIFUL FEET"

Mary Loveheart is a follower who has been magically changed by the irresistible power of Father's doctrine of the positive. She says she was "a hereditary thief" before he "entered my soul." Before the day that Father Divine came into her life, she had never held an honest job.

Mary Loveheart was born in St. Thomas in the Virgin Islands, while her mother was serving on a prison chain gang for the murder of a lover. Until she was eight years old, Mary lived right inside the prison where her mother was held. A prison matron took care of her during the day while her mother worked as a member of a street-sweeping gang. At night, her mother cared for her. Her only contacts were the matrons and the other women prisoners. There were no children for her to play with in the prison.

On her eighth birthday, Mary was sent to live with her maternal grandmother. It was her first experience outside the gates of the prison, and she was thrilled by everything. The green grass. The sunshine. The other children. The wonderful freedom of knowing she could come and go without issuing reports to matrons. She didn't get along well with her grandmother, but that didn't matter compared to her freedom. At eight, she already knew that freedom was a valuable possession and one worth making compromises for. If the grandmother had an evil temper and slapped her hard across the face at the slightest provocation or even without any provocation at all, she could take that without showing how the slap hurt her.

Today, Mary Loveheart says that she never cried like other children when she was a little girl.

"That must come from what I knew when I was a little

girl. Nobody would care if I cried, so why cry? It didn't matter what I did."

She was an amazingly mature, self-sufficient little girl. Today, she says she does not think she was unhappy with her grandmother—or happy, either. She "just was" and "that's the best thing I can say about those days.

"I was glad when my grandmother gave me food to eat. Most of the time there wasn't enough food, though. Sometimes there was plenty, and we both ate and Grandmother said, 'Go on, enjoy your eats. Eat all you want.' A lot of times there was no food for anyone. Most of the time there was some food but not a lot. Then Grandmother ate it all herself. When I was very little I begged her for some. She never gave it to me, said, 'You want food, go get your own. Hard enough for me to get eats for me and keep this house. You can't expect me to get it for you too.'"

There were few jobs in the Virign Islands for an old lady like Mary's grandmother. And even if there had been, Mary tells today, her grandmother would not have wanted to work.

"She liked to take the easy way. She used to go out stealing every night. She was good at it, too. When I was little, I was proud of how good my grandmother was at stealing. I wanted to be the same way. But the grandmother didn't think I had it in me to be as good as she was."

When Mary was eleven years old, her grandmother was caught trying to break into the home of an American widow. She was arrested.

Today, Mary comments calmly on this crisis in her life. "When I found out the grandmother was arrested, I didn't feel bad. I just thought, 'What am I going to do now? No house to sleep in.' I thought I might as well start sleeping in the streets. I could support myself by stealing."

Mary had to sleep in the streets for three weeks or thereabouts. Then a police officer picked her up and took her to the jail where her mother and grandmother were.

"I was only in that jail a little while and then a lady came and got me out of it. I don't know who told her about me or why she wanted to come and get me but she did. I used to ask her, 'Why did you want me?' She never answered me why. She said she came to the jail and got me and that was all I needed to know, except I was to be very good and pay her back for everything she was doing by taking me out of the prison. She was a United States lady named Mrs. Anderson."

Mrs. Anderson had five children, ranging in age from one to six. She had a nurse who took care of the children, and Mary was supposed to assist the nurse. She was with the children and their nurse from the time they all got up in the morning at seven o'clock until the time they went to bed. After the children's bedtime, she did little things Mrs. Anderson asked her to. "Sometimes I washed stockings for her and dusted books—she sure had more books than anybody I ever knew except Father—and did all like that she asked me to."

Mrs. Anderson gave Mary all of her meals "just as much eats as I ever wanted" and half of a small bedroom which she shared with the children's nurse.

Telling about it today, Mary does not know why it was that she was unhappy with Mrs. Anderson, "but I was, though." She used to lie awake at night and long vaguely for another kind of life which she was never able to define for herself. She didn't want to be an assistant to Mrs. Anderson's children's nurse forever. She wanted to be something else that would allow her to be the "boss" of her own time. She wanted to be something that would give her the freedom to do whatever she wanted, even though she didn't know what it was she wanted.

One night, after the children were in bed and after her small tasks for Mrs. Anderson were accomplished, she tried to talk to the nurse about her vague longings.

"I don't know what——" she said. "I don't know why——"

The nurse didn't listen to Mary. She didn't try to understand what she was saying. All she did was laugh at her.

This attempt to communicate herself to the nurse was Mary Loveheart's first trial at becoming involved with another human being. The laughter made her feel that the attempt was a failure. She had been smarter when she'd been a very little girl in the prison with her mother and later in the house with her grandmother. She had known, back then, that she could not cry and expect other people to cry with her. Now that she was older, she had forgotten that important fact. Look what happened when she trusted people and tried to grow closer to them. They laughed at her the way the children's nurse had laughed. She didn't like to be laughed at. No one would ever laugh at her again. She would see to that. She would never talk to people any more unless they asked her questions she could not avoid answering.

After Mary's conversation with the children's nurse, the nurse tried to talk to her. In her own way, she gleaned how she had hurt Mary by laughing at her, and she wanted, somehow, to make up for it. But Mary would not permit her to. She answered the nurse's questions about her life and her future monosyllabically. The nurse became angry with her. The anger didn't bother Mary, though. She had closed her heart again, as she had when she was a little girl.

One night when they were alone together in their little room, the nurse made a desperate last attempt to communicate with Mary.

"Mrs. Anderson told me all about you," she said. "You and your mother and all your relatives. Your whole family were thieves. You're a thief, too. You're what they call a hereditary thief."

Mary asked, "What's a hereditary thief?"

"A hereditary thief," the children's nurse explained, "is somebody who steals because she can't help herself. It's because stealing runs in her family like it does in yours. Your grandmother couldn't help stealing. Your mother couldn't help stealing, and when you get to be older, you'll see that you can't either. Stealing's in your blood."

Mary did not answer the children's nurse, but she found herself affected by her information. It kept churning around in her mind . . . a hereditary thief, a hereditary thief. The children's nurse must be right. It must be that she was a hereditary thief, and that, therefore, now, living with Mrs. Anderson, having enough food for the first time in her life and a real roof over her head, she was not happy as she should have been. She wanted to steal, that must be why, stealing was in her blood.

One night, after it was late and she had heard the children's nurse snoring for hours in the bed beside hers, Mary quietly rose from her bed and dressed herself. She left the Anderson house and walked for blocks until she came to another house. Some baby clothes were hanging on the line of this house. She removed them all and ran home with them. Today, she still recalls the thrill of that experience.

"I didn't need those clothes. What could I do with baby clothes? I wasn't a baby who could wear them, and I didn't have one. I never wanted to give them to Mrs. Anderson's babies. But I felt good when I took those. I hid them in a drawer, and sometimes I used to take them out and look at them. It made me smile."

This experience convinced Mary that the nurse was right in her analysis, that being born to thieves had made a thief of her. And life at the Andersons' grew exciting. The days were dull as always, but the nights were to be looked forward to. Every night, when the children's nurse was asleep, Mary dressed and went looking for things to steal. Most often, she stole washed clothes which Mrs. Anderson's neighbors allowed to hang on their lines overnight.

"Most of them weren't even nice things," she says. "Some were just rags, that's all."

Finally, the inevitable happened. A neighbor was awake one night when Mary tried to steal from her clothesline. She caught her and reported her to Mrs. Anderson. Mrs. Anderson found the other things which Mary had stolen and hidden away. She said that she was humiliated, that she could not have a thief around her children. She threatened to return Mary to the prison.

Mary ran away from the Anderson house before Mrs. Anderson could carry out her threat. For a while, she did as she had done when she was younger—supported herself by stealing and lived in the streets. Then, somehow, she managed to get to Puerto Rico.

"How I got there," she tells today, "I don't know, but I did. I stole there, too." She was arrested. "The judge let me off because I was only sixteen. I went back to St. Thomas and was arrested there for stealing."

Mary's mother was still in the St. Thomas prison when

her daughter was brought in. Coincidentally, her mother was one of the first inmates Mary met.

The mother told Mary, "You follow in my footsteps!"

"Who else's steps am I going to follow in?" Mary asked.

When Mary was released from prison, she went right on stealing and saving her money for fare to New York City. She had heard a lot about New York and envisioned it a paradise of opportunity for a "hereditary thief" like herself.

In New York, she discovered Klein's Fourteenth Street department store. "This sure was paradise," she says. It was always crowded and understaffed, so that an expert thief like Mary could steal with little fear of detection. Although she discovered all the other New York department stores, Klein's remained her favorite. For many years, she took care of herself by appropriating their merchandise.

Mary made no friends in New York. She lived in a small Harlem room, ate her meals in "a greasy spoon" on 128th Street, never went out with men, and secured "all the excitement I needed" by dodging department store detectives.

One night, Mary's landlady knocked at her door. Did Mary want to go some place? she asked. No, Mary didn't want to go any place. The landlady persisted. Did Mary want to go some place where she could see God in a human body? Mary laughed at the idea of God in a human body. She was lonely, though, and the landlady was friendlier than anybody had ever been to her. She agreed to go where this personal God resided.

When she first entered heaven with her landlady, Mary was fearful. She knew that these were righteous people, and she was a "hereditary thief."

Fortunately, her landlady stayed by her side all evening. She introduced her to many of the other followers. All of them treated her kindly. It was a wonderful atmosphere. Since Mary's face was a new one, and since she was here with the landlady, who was close to Father, the followers hovered around her. This was Mary's first social experience, and she found herself enjoying it.

At the banquet held that night, Mary saw Father Divine for the first time. It is still, today, a living experience for her. She was wearing a dress she had stolen from Klein's and a pearl necklace she'd stolen from one of the smaller Fourteenth Street shops. As Father's eye caught hers and her landlady whispered, "Beautiful God is lookin' straight on you 'n can see in your soul!" she felt impelled to remove the pearls from around her neck and place them in her handbag. Father looked at Mary, then glanced down at her purse.

"I knew Father knew I stole those pearls," she tells today. She looked down and away from Father, trying to avoid his eyes.

Father went on staring at her, though. No matter how she looked away, she could feel him staring.

A follower rose from her chair. She began to sing a song:

> *Just to hear you tap your beautiful feet,*
> *Just to hear you tap your beautiful feet,*
> *I wish I was in heaven ten thousand years,*
> *Just to hear you tap your beautiful feet.*

The other followers joined in. Mary says that, without consciously wanting to, she felt herself singing too.

After the singing was finished, an elderly woman rose from her chair. While she stood, she kept holding tight to the chair.

"I usedta take fits," she said. All of her friends had steered away from her because they were afraid she might embarrass them by "takin' a fit in public." Recently, even her son had said he wanted nothing to do with her. This had nearly broken her heart. Then she'd found Father. She was living in a mission now and had been for three weeks. All the followers were her friends, and Father was her lover and her God. Since she'd been in heaven, she'd never "taken a single fit. Father cured me, praise his holy name."

A male follower talked. He had robbed a filling station in the Midwest. For years, he said, the police had looked for him there while he'd been in New York "laughing up my sleeve." Then he'd met up with Father Divine and goodness and justice and truth. Father had made it clear to him that he had no choice, that he had to go back and confess his crime and take the consequences. Well, he'd done as Father had commanded, he'd confessed his crime and gone to prison for two years. Now he was a happy man with, thank Father, the freest of consciences.

After the man took his seat, there was applause. It was loud and approving. Then there was quiet for a while.

Mary's landlady broke the stillness. She began to clap her hands together. She stamped her feet hard on the floor. She sang:

> *Listen, world, we want you to know*
> *That Father Divine is the God we adore,*
> *He is the one that created the heaven and earth,*
> *He is the one that brought this spiritual birth.*

The other followers joined Mary's landlady. The singing grew loud and frenzied:

> *So why stand by and criticize*
> *The one who can open your blinded eyes?*
> *Listen! Stop and realize*
> *That your God is here and not in the skies.*

Mary kept looking down the table at Father. She could not stop herself. Father looked back at Mary. Hardly knowing what she was doing. Mary rose from her seat . . .

"I'm a thief," she said. "My mother stole and my grandmother. I steal because I can't help it—and it's a habit. Sometimes, I'd like to die instead of steal."

Father kept looking at Mary long after she took her seat.

The landlady was ecstatic. "Look at Father look at you," she said. "Amen. He'll cure you, sweet God!"

A white lady sitting on the other side of Mary grabbed hold of her arm. She held it tightly. "Oh," she said, "how Father condescends to you. Just see how sweetly he smiles in your direction."

Mary Loveheart requested an interview with Father Divine after the banquet. He granted her request.

Sitting aside of Father's desk, Mary repeated her story. "I wish I could die," she said.

Father told Mary she did not need to die. All she needed to do was to open her mind and her heart to make room for his spirit. He would do his best to inject that spirit into her. After the injection occurred, she would have one other task. She would have to visualize the positive. He told Mary, as he always tells his new or potential followers, to "vividly visualize the perfect, the real, the good, and the true. And that is what it will be for you. When you have me, you have victory in your soul."

Father told Mary that she could be pure. God loved her and did not condemn her. All she needed to do now to be accepted into his heaven was to repent of her wicked past. She should make restitution for the things she had stolen. Those objects which were returnable must be returned. Those things which she had stolen and could not return, she must pay for.

In 1938, Mary formally entered heaven. Since she had returned every piece of returnable stolen property, she wore clothes provided by sisters who were sympathetic to her reform. She did not have money enough to pay her room rent for one week.

Today, Mary Loveheart is a domestic. The family for whom she has worked for the past twelve years and who knew her history when they hired her on recommendations of the Divine Employment Service don't just like her. They really love her.

On August 1, 1952, Mrs. Mildred Reiss, Mary Loveheart's employer, wrote this letter to Father Divine.

Dear Father:

I want to take this opportunity to thank you for the privilege of having Mary Loveheart working with me for 12 years. She has been a great part of my life during this period of time. Mary possesses the finer qualities of honesty, dependability and faithfulness.

Now the time has come when I can no longer afford to employ Mary. The thought of our separation sickens me. The room and bath which has been hers will remain hers. She may come here to live with me as long as I live. I will always be happy to share with her.

Father Divine is accustomed to having his followers highly praised for their honesty and trustworthiness. He answered Mary Loveheart's employer: ". . . Mary is a living witness of what I have done for millions and what I could do for millions more."

Father has helped many former criminals to new lives and realizations just as he helped Mary Loveheart. Anybody who has talked to Father's followers knows how very much he has helped them. There are former murderers and gangsters and prostitutes and pimps who today live law-abiding lives as members of the Peace Mission movement. Joe Patience is one. Mr. Patience was a gangster before he came to heaven. Father's spirit influenced him to throw his gun into the river.

Sunbeam Willing ran a house of prostitution.

Determination Charm was a confidence man.

Nicey Love was a gambler who traded on her sex appeal.

Young Jack Mays who has not yet acquired a spiritual name was a dope fiend. To get his own "stuff" he'd become a pusher.

Good Truth had helped her daughter to prostitute herself, sometimes serving as procurer for her.

Lovely Thought had done away with her illegitimate baby.

And there is Charles M. Cheerfulness. Charles tells his own story. It is difficult to believe. Still, it might have happened.

"I lived in the deep South with a brother. We used to work on a farm and drink hard liquor. One day a white young man of about our age was drinking with us and he took away a quart of whiskey. We tried to get it back. He refused. Some days after, I took my shotgun and said, 'I'm agoin' after my whiskey.' I went over to his place and demanded my liquor. He refused to return it, so I shot him dead. Then I had to git out and I got. After some fifteen years in the North, one day I met Father Divine and I was converted. But I had killed a man. How could I make that right? I went to Father and told him and said, 'Father, what can I do?' He said, 'Go back and give yourself up to the sheriff.' "

Charles Cheerfulness had spent all of his early life as a Negro in the deep South. He knew how criminals "of the darker complexion" were handled there. He knew how innocent people of the darker complexion were handled. He'd seen his uncle beaten almost dead because he'd pushed ahead of a white woman one day. In view of the things he knew, the fact that Charles Cheerfulness did return South was the ultimate test of his faith in Father.

"So I went back," he said, "and I hunted up the sheriff of the county and I said, 'Sheriff, I killed so-and-so seventeen years ago and I've come to give myself up.'

"The sheriff, he looked at me hard as though he couldn't believe what he'd heard.

" 'You killed a white man?'

" 'Yes, sah.'

" 'And you are giving yourself up?'

" 'Yes, sah.'

" 'Well, what makes you do that?'

"And I said, 'I met Father Divine and I was converted and he told me I must come back and give myself up.'

"The sheriff didn't say nothin' for a while and then he said, 'If Father Divine can make a man do what you just done, then you go along back up North and stay with him. You're free—go.' "

Today, Charles Cheerfulness is law-abiding, far beyond the concept of ordinary men.

Whether or not Charles Cheerfulness' testimony is true, its idea of reformation is typical. Police officials know that the majority of testimonies made by reformed criminal angels are completely true. They must admit that some former hardened criminals, their "hardest nuts to crack," are presently living lives of purity.

In heaven, the standards of morality are set in sharp blacks and whites and with no allowance whatever for the in-between grays of the world outside.

"You're either honest," Father tells his followers, "or else you're dishonest. Keeping even a straight pin that does not belong to you is dishonest."

The scrupulous honesty of Divinites must be seen to be believed. Only a heavenly newspaper could list these and other similar losses: a gold watch; a streetcar token; a blue leather pocketbook with red trim containing $6.84; a rubber band; 10¢; a silver ring set with a ruby; a hairpin; 2¢; four safety pins on a card; another hairpin.

Father's followers are as conscientious about paying past debts as they are about returning lost articles. It does not matter how long an obligation has been outstanding, how long a bill has remained unpaid—once a person affiliates with Father, he will become fanatic about seeking out past debtors.

A letter received some time ago by George Haas and Company of San Francisco is typical of letters received by business firms throughout the country from former ordinary employees who later became Divine followers.

Dear Sirs:
Inclosed you will find a money order for $3.00. This am't. I am returning to you because 16 years ago, I worked for your ferm, Store No. 5, and while there I took candy and ice cream and ate it and no doubt some small change and I knew in my heart it was stealing as it was not mine. Am sure the $3.00 will cover what I took.
To be honest I had no intentions of ever paying for these things but since God, Father Divine, has entered my heart, not only mine but 22,000,000 of us, He has absolutely changed our hearts and bodies—I know Father Divine is God, for no man could make me pay this.
—Father brought to my memory that I had taken a salt and pepper shaker, if you will please let me know what the price of them were, I will also send the amount.
                              Yours truly,
                              Ethel Caldwell

Father's followers, in paying off their debts, have been known, in the 1950's, to report to relief offices which helped them in the thirties and to insist upon paying "my just debts." Social workers have been embarrassed. Old records of relief cases were either lost or stored away.

"But I owe it," Divinites always answered these arguments in the same fashion, "and I got to pay it back. It's a just debt."

The strict honesty with which Father has affected his followers is most apparent in their job relationships. Employers of Divine followers are fortunate.

Father tells his followers, "You must give a fair day's work for a fair day's pay."

Divinites would never, no matter what, shirk on a moment of their work time. All the way from Miss Hopeful, domestic employee, to John Germaine, architectural engineer, from Good John, packing-house worker, to Anne Sterrit, schoolteacher, Father Divine's followers scrupulously carry out "the fair day" tenet. They hold completely to what is doubtless the most unpliant ethical code that workers anywhere have ever been required to submit to.

In a New Year's speech at the beginning of 1953, which Father made to many of his followers who are engaged in domestic work, he said in regard to their ethical code:

"One of the children said to me that since they had embraced my teaching, they will not even taste anything in cooking, at the absence of the employer, they would not do in their presence! Honesty is the keynote to salvation, and those who adhere to my teaching, they will reproduce honesty and bring it to fruition to an extent that you will be able to express honesty as a reality and no longer something as mythological and as imaginary!"

Miss Lovely Rose of Sharon was one of those who confessed to Father that she had been guilty of tasting food in her employer's absence.

"Oh, Father, I done just that what you said. I used to take a spoon, stirring food in a pot, and taste the food and put the spoon right back. It was a mistake of my head, Lord. Now I got some sense in me. You shown me how to live pure on my job. I ain't gonna sin no more."

Miss Rose of Sharon's employer can be certain that the spoon that goes into her pot will never have been in her employee's mouth.

Father Divine instructs his followers as to what their personal behavior patterns are to be with their employers. They are always to maintain the employer-employee relationship on a dignified level. One thing they must realize, that, although their employers have more money than they do and can therefore afford to pay their salaries, they are in no way better people.

"You are as good," Father tells his followers, "as anybody you work for is good, and don't let anybody tell you no. Do what is right on your job and get what is right in return."

To preserve the dignity of his follower-workers, Father Divine goes to extremes. One of the most widely known of these is his refusal to permit followers to accept gifts, tips, or bonuses.

Around Christmastime, Father's voluminous correspondence is often aimed toward answering the letters of troubled employers, who write to tell him that their firms have been accustomed to giving Christmas bonuses or gifts and that it is disconcerting to have Father's followers, as they invariably do, refuse these offers of good will.

Within the last two years, Father received so many letters from employers regarding his followers and gifts that he prepared a form answer. It is significant because it clearly outlines Father's ideal for his follower-workers. It reads in part:

To whom it may concern:

A true follower of mine does not want or desire to receive a gift or present or anything of that type for Christmas or any holiday, and considers it to be unevangelical, unconstitutional, and not according to the Scripture otherwise; especially so long as they are earning an independent living and expressing a real citizenry of independence individually, even as our country declared her independence as a nation. When a person earns a salary sufficient to meet the high cost of living and pays all of their past obligations, such as may be imposed upon them, they would not and will not seek tips or presents, for the system of tip taking is trying to get something for nothing that is not justly due them.

For this cause, MY true followers, as long as they receive just compensation for their labor, business, service and trade and their merchandise, will not accept of tips, gifts or presents, for such is in violation to the teaching of the Scripture and they feel and are sure they are not living evangelical if they break any of the rules and regulations, especially when they are receiving just compensation for the service they are giving.

Many commands of God, laws, rules, and regulations of men have been violated for the lack of understanding and for the lack of receiving just compensation for the service, labor and merchandise and personal help they are giving.

At times such has been forced upon them by panics, famines, and depressions through the different political administrations which are responsible, but yet MY true followers have been for many years making good for that which they received through the depression when they were not allowed to earn a livelihood. But since they can earn a livelihood now, they will abstain from the violations of tip taking, receiving gifts and presents, donations, love offerings or any such things that are in violation to the Declaration of Independence, for individuals should express their independence individually even as our country declared it as a nation.

The following quotations of the Scripture I add for your consideration and for the consideration of all humanity:

EXODUS 23:8 And thou shalt take no gift: for the gift blindeth the wise, and perverteth the words of the righteous.

DEUTERONOMY 16:19 Thou shalt not wrest judgment; thou shalt not respect persons, neither take a gift: for a gift doth blind the eyes of the wise, and pervert the words of the righteous.

If an employer persists in offering a gift to a Divine employee, he is likely to receive a form answer which will be bound to put a crimp in his insistence:

"If you really think I am a good worker," the employee will say, "good enough to deserve a bonus or a gift or a tip, then you must think I am good enough to deserve more money. Increase my salary."

Only an employee who can feel the equal of his employer could possibly speak in such a manner.

"It is wonderful," Thunder Territo, domestic worker says, "truly wonderful. Before I came to Father, I used to be laid out like a floor so's people I worked for could step all over me. Now I ain't laid that way no more because now I knows me to be good I can be what Father tells me, *independent*."

11

DO NOT LOVE
ANYONE . . .

"Independence" is one of the most preached-about tenets of the Peace Mission movement. It is not in the followers' attitudes toward their employers only that Father preaches it. He preaches it for every phase of living and in regard to every person whom followers know or expect to meet in the future . . . except himself.

"Individual independence is something wonderful to strive for," he thunders out, "because only then can you be close to God. Be independent, God's vision and nobody else's forever."

The followers are zealous about carrying out father's "independence tenet." They would rather die than disobey it. Many of them have given up good jobs and taken lesser ones because the jobs impinged on their peculiar standards of independence. Most of them who work in the world outside or go to school in it refuse more than a cursory acquaintance with their co-workers and co-students, because friendships with outsiders must result in some social exchange, which might threaten their "independence." And, most important, for this reason they have given up any contact with their families in the world outside.

It is amazing, the ease with which the Divine followers have been able to renounce all thought of their husbands, wives, mothers, fathers, sisters, brothers, sons, and daughters for as long as any of them shall live.

"It is an easy thing to do." If you asked sixty-three-year-old white schoolteacher Dancing Soul how she was enabled to give up three sons, two daughters, and seven adorable grandchildren, she would attempt to give you an explanation. "I just put my mind to driving out thought of all of them I formerly loved. Father told me that is what I must do, and so I did it. Once you recognize Father's divinity, you can do anything he instructs you to."

Dancing Soul wanted her "independence" more than she wanted her sons or daughters or grandchidren. She knew that only through its complete attainment could she attain her "union with Father Divine, which was more important to me than a million mortal families."

It is fascinating in a morbid kind of a way to listen to true followers talk about their "mortal families." Not that it is easy to get them to talk in such a vein. For followers only talk about their families if they are forced to talk, and they have evolved a vocabulary to indicate, just as though their manners didn't, how entirely they reject them. They never mention their husbands or sons or daughters. They speak only about *so-called* husbands and *so-called* sons and *so-called* daughters.

"My so-called son," a second white schoolteacher of advanced years, Miss Rapid Integration, told in tones of saccharine sweetness, "just didn't approve when I joined the movement. We separated, of course. I haven't seen him for twenty years. He was never a well man. I do not know whether he is living or not. I could find out, of course, by looking up his name in the telephone directory. I shan't ever do that, though."

This is the stuff of which "individual independence" is composed in Father Divine's Peace Mission movement.

"If you are willing to follow me by self-denial and be independent," Father tells his followers, "that is, being willing to say, even as Jesus said, 'Who is my mother and who are my brethren and who are my sisters, who are my sons and who are my daughters . . . I have nothing to do with none other but those who do the will of my father,' . . . why then, you would be expressing love for me O.K."

All of Father's followers with the rarest of exceptions have expressed their love, "O.K."

"God is your father," Father Divine says, "your mother, your sister, and your brother and you never had another. But God shapes and fashions bodies to be to you a father, mother, sister, and brother. But God is the real one that has always been your father, your mother, your sister, and your brother and all others."

Schoolteachers Dancing Soul and Rapid Integration say

that when followers accept Father Divine as their only relative, they must cease longing for the others whom they have left behind.

Dancing Soul tells, "I don't want to own any relatives other than my God. In truth, I know I never had them. So why should I own them in truth?"

Rapid Integration echoes Dancing Soul. "What Miss Soul said expresses my own feelings exactly. Her interpretation is only logical, you see. If I accepted a family other than Father Divine, it would mean that I was rejecting God. If I rejected God, I would bring all sorts of punishments onto my head and also onto the heads of the so-called family I thought I was accepting. See the mystery?"

Outsiders seldom do understand the mystery of the Divine logic of family rejection, and Divinites seldom understand how outsiders can accept their families, mere husbands or children, in place of Father Divine.

"So," Dancing Soul says in an attempt at mortal humor, "we're even. You can't understand us. We can't understand you. You think we're bad when we say we no longer belong to our so-called families. We know you're bad when you go on living in mortal lust, husbands and wives together, and producing children, reminders of your lusts and your sins. We who know God would not do that. We would not live in lust and produce children of sin. If I had known this truth earlier, I would never have given birth to the so-called sons and daughters. They are my regrets and my blackest sins."

When she talks about her so-called children, Miss Dancing Soul, who once loved young people well enough so that she trained to be able to teach them, is only echoing Father Divine. From the beginning of his movement, birth and babies came in for the lion's share of his disapproval of mortal things. For this reason, followers from earliest days on until now reject their children almost more completely than they do other members of their families.

"The mother of sin is the mother of death. The mother of birth is the mother of sin. Then, I say, in multiplying propagation, we shall bring a complete limitation to such expression."

Father first said this back in the early thirties. He is still saying it in 1953. Doubtless, he will continue to say it as long as he lives. He does an effective job of reaching his women with that message.

Mary Lena, a long-time follower, proves how effective a job he does. She voices the point of view of all the other women followers who happen also to be mothers. She says:

"Before I had Father Divine, I lived in Adam's sin. The children is proof that I sinned."

In the 1930's, large numbers of self-righteous Divinite parents were often haled into court by indignant neighbors and relatives for neglect or complete abandonment of minor children. The name of Father Divine became a familiar one in domestic and children's courts. This, more than anything else about him and his movement, aroused public wrath.

"My wife done left me for that black magician," complained Robert Jones of Harlem, who had eight children ranging from two to ten and no woman to care for them since his wife had left him for Father. "I been to see her, begged her to come back, tole her anything she wanted me to do, I'd do. It wasn't me wants her. I tole her that it wasn't me wants you. It's them chillun needs you! The chillun don' faze her none though. Since she run in the life of that black magician she don' like her chillun no more. Her own chillun too."

There was a man named Tinsley whose wife joined Father's Sayville, Long Island, heaven. He went with a policeman to 72 Macon Street where she lived with Father Divine and asked her to return to him and the four children. She ordered him out of heaven. He went back a second time and brought the children with him. She ordered them all out.

Eleven-year-old Roger Smith testified in Children's Court, "Sure, I need my ma. But I ain't got 'er, though. Father Divine's got *her*."

Newspapers in the thirties report many cases of Divine mothers who abandoned their husbands and their minor children, ranging in age from two years to sixteen and in number from one child to eleven children.

Judges who were concerned with the abandoned children of Divine followers issued scathing denunciations of Father. Hon. Richard Hartshorne of the Common Pleas Court in New Jersey called him "responsible for the promotion of family disorganization." Hon. Jacob Panken of New York's Children's Court called him "a destroyer of children." He ranked him along with communism as one of Harlem's "two worst evils."

Public sentiment in the late thirties was so much against him in regard to the children that Father Divine had to evolve a practical method of counteracting it. He issued an ultimatum to parents of young children and had it publicized. Mothers and fathers, he stated, must support their children until they reached the age of eighteen.

"Clothe your children," he told the parents, "feed them and house them."

Under the circumstances, this was a step in the right direction from the point of view of the children's welfare. It certainly was not enough of a step, however. For never once did Father Divine enjoin his followers to love their children.

On the contrary, he told them that, even though they had to support the children till they reached the age of eighteen, it was a disgrace to show love for them or even to own them at all. Today, he still tells followers that. As late as January of 1952, he told a follower, Mrs. Amelia Johnson, that the word "mother," within heaven's holy precincts, was a "dirty word."

Mrs. Amelia Johnson lived in a Harlem heaven. She had first seen Father twenty years before in Sayville, when her nineteen-year-old daughter Jean had joined the movement and when she had gone there to try to persuade Jean to come home with her. Jean, however, had become Beautiful Peace and made it very clear that she wanted nothing to do with her.

Mrs. Johnson had, ever since Jean's early teen years, respected her intellect. Their relationship had been a peculiar one. From the time Jean had been about fifteen, it had not been her mother who had guided Jean but Jean who had guided her weak-willed mother. When Jean joined Father, Mrs. Johnson felt drawn herself to investigate the movement.

Two years after Jean Johnson became Beautiful Peace, her mother Amelia joined Father Divine's corps.

Even after she herself joined the fold, Amelia Johnson never saw her daughter. They resided in different missions and their paths didn't cross. The few letters Amelia wrote Jean were returned unopened. Now, Amelia Johnson came to Philadelphia headquarters, Jean's residence.

She entered freely, as anyone may, and began to talk to some of the other followers who were friendly—at first.

"Almost twenty years ago," Amelia Johnson told the followers, "my daughter came to Father——"

"Don't say that!" sweet-looking Miss Peace, her soft voice become strident, said. "Don't ever talk about *your daughter* here."

"I didn't mean——" Amelia was apologetic, "I really didn't mean——"

The other followers turned from her, though. It was obvious they didn't want to hear any more.

It didn't take five minutes before Amelia's "dirty conversation" was reported to Father Divine, who was so disturbed that he interrupted his other duties to send for her immediately.

Quaking inside, Amelia Johnson entered Father's personal office. A secretary seated her at a large table directly across from Father himself. Ten of the twenty-five other secretaries sat around the table. Their notebooks were opened up in front of them, and their pencils were poised.

Father Divine looked at Amelia. She could not bear to look back at him, so she looked down at her lap and up at the ceiling. Then she looked at each one of the secretaries in turn. They all studiously avoided looking back at her. Father spoke, finally. His voice was harsh punishment for her effrontery.

"Now," he said, "you have said, even since you have been in this house last night, that you were someone's mother and *you are no mother here.* You are no one's mother. I just want to let you know you should not say it. Yes, unless you deny yourself completely and that means deny yourself even speaking of such a dirty thing . . . God is the father and mother and brother and sister of all of his own and no one else has anything to do with it."

Amelia Johnson was frightened. She told Father that she was so sorry. "I didn't want to do wrong," she said. She hadn't meant to be offensive. For twenty years she'd stayed away from Jean. Hastily, she amended herself. For twenty years she'd stayed away from Beautiful Peace. Father Divine hadn't ever been disturbed by her before, had he? Well, now he could take her word for it, he would never be disturbed again. Her voice trembled. "I know I sinned," she said.

Father's voice was hurt rather than angry. He told Amelia, "I came to save the people, to save you and to save all others, even those or that one or someone you might want to claim as your own. If they would have been living in the flesh, they would have been dead no doubt before now, but I lifted them, and I don't want any mortal feeling conveyed or any mortal thought whatever."

Most true followers need no such chiding as Amelia received. They have learned to treat their children with more impersonality than they treat anyone else. And the pitiful effect of the lack of parental love has always been apparent, as it is today, in the personalities of the children in the movement.

What happened to Jim Slaughter, nine years old, whose mother brought him to Children's Court, has happened in one form or another to many other youngsters whose parents are Peace Mission members.

Jim's mother Leila, known as Buncha Sweetness in the movement, joined Father's fold in 1934. She went to live in the Divine kingdom at 66 West 128th Street, taking Jim and his two younger sisters with her. The two girls, who were amenable youngsters, adjusted easily to the rigid demands. Jim, though, was a problem from the first.

Bitterly, Buncha Sweetness attacked her son in Children's Court. She told the social worker that he was absolutely unmanageable. She said he lied. He was a habitual thief, and he made a practice of staying away from home till far into the night. He had a record of exceptionally poor school attendance, and, on more than one occasion, he and another boy had been caught exploring each other sexually.

The Court examined Jim Slaughter.

The Court asked Jim, "Do you steal?" Jim admitted that, yes, he did steal money. It was because he liked movies, and Father Divine did not approve of movies, and he'd had to steal money in order to get to go.

Under the kindly questioning and obvious interest in him, Jim admitted all his mother's other accusations. Yes, he did stay out late at night. That was because he didn't like the atmosphere of the kingdom. There were so many old people there and so few boys and girls of his age. His mother's statement in regard to his poor school attendance was also true. There was a reason for that, too, though. Jim happened to be at the head of his class in school and for the five days of his last nonattendance, the teacher had been reviewing material which he understood perfectly.

"Now," Jim was asked, "what about you and the other boy?"

Jim freely admitted his sexual irregularity. "This is Father Divine's way," he said, and told of Father's preachings against relationships between men and women.

"Who is Father Divine?"

Unhesitatingly, Jim answered, "He is God. He has the world in his hand. He can contact anyone's spirit through space."

Asked whether he did not feel bad because he had no father, Jim answered, "I have one—Father Divine." And professed himself quite satisfied, even though "in the mortal world," he had neither a father nor a mother.

"Not a mother?"

Jim, like a parrot, glibly echoed what he heard in heaven. When parents and children joined the movement, it was with a complete understanding of the Divine tenet applying to relationships of mortality.

"I am Father's child," he said. "I have nobody else but him."

The moment Jim Slaughter entered the gates of heaven, he stopped using the word mother. His mother became his "sister" then (today she would be called his "guardian"), and the relationship between them had to be completely impersonal.

"My mother'll never have another child," Jim said in a

matter-of-fact fashion. "She knows babies come from committing adultery."

Jim was asked, "Don't you want your mother to love you as others mothers love their children?"

He answered, a bit too vehemently, that no, he did not need the kind of mother other children had. He had Father Divine.

He went on reiterating, Father Divine *was* more important to him than a mortal mother ever could be, he was, he was.

Then, strangely, he broke down. It wasn't true that he didn't care about his mother. He did care, dreadfully. It hurt him when she called him her brother. He wanted, more than anything in the world, to have his mother own him as other mothers owned their children.

"Mothers love their children more than anything else in the world," Jim said. "But my mother loves Father Divine more than anything else in the world."

Is Father Divine responsible for the difficulties of Jim Slaughter and the hundreds of other children who, for the past twenty-five years, have spent their developmental time behind the uncompromising walls of the Peace Mission movement? As with every other question involving the paradoxical Father, it is impossible to answer an unequivocal yes or no to this one.

Jim's aunt and uncle, interviewed by Dr. Bender, stated adamantly that Father Divine was responsible for the breakup of the Slaughter home.

Jim's mother just as adamantly declared that Father Divine was most certainly not responsible. She said her home had been broken up years before she'd come to Father, when her husband, so-called, had beaten her and walked out of the house and left her to support the three children.

Jim's mother told the truth insofar as it was possible for her to detect it. Her husband had "walked out" as she said he had. Only he'd "walked out" emotionally long before he'd done it physically. He'd "walked out" emotionally soon after the youngsters had been born, when it became increasingly apparent that, no matter how he tried, he'd never be able to find a job that would enable him to support them. From the very first, Jim and the two little girls had represented an unbeatable problem to him. They'd pointed up his ineffectuality with horribly frustrating clarity. A Negro, an unskilled laborer in a time of depression when skilled white men were starving, what did he want with a wife and children? Yokes around his neck they were.

In the realization of the economic difficulties faced by many men like Jim's father, the fair observer is enabled to see both sides of the Divine coin, where family organization and children are concerned.

It is true, as Judges Hartshorne and Panken declared, that Father Divine was and is today "a destroyer of children." It is true that he was and is today responsible for family disorganization. It is equally true, however, that, in lower-class Negro families, family cohesion is low to begin with. Can Father Divine then be blamed for being a destroyer of what does not exist in the first place?

It is true that Father Divine has influenced many women to leave their homes and families. It is just as true that many wives who are presently in the movement had been abandoned by their husbands. And many children who might have had to live on the streets are cared for in heavens while their mothers work.

Great Love is one of these. Today she lives at the Philadelphia headquarters. She has a fine job as a court reporter. She is a pretty, charming girl. Of course, she never has a date with a man. And she has no friends outside the Peace Mission movement. But she is happy in the kind of life she leads. She earns sixty dollars a week and invests most of it in Peace Mission properties. Which means that she is a person to be reckoned with, as all Peace Mission property-owners are.

Great Love's mother Mary Mason (Miss Beautiful in the kingdom) had desperately wanted to hold on to her marriage to Great Love's father, Arthur. Arthur, like Jim Slaughter's father, had been beaten down by no money and many obligations. He'd abandoned his wife and daughter without any explanation. It was just that one night he had been in the dreary Harlem furnished room they all three slept in, and the next morning Great Love and her mother awakened to find he had walked out of their lives.

Mary Mason was an uninformed woman. She didn't know what to do without her husband or where to turn. A friend advised her to contact the Welfare Department for help in raising Great Love, but she didn't want to do that. She'd heard too many stories about people who'd been put in jail because the Welfare had learned they couldn't support themselves. She refused to risk her freedom for food for her child and herself. So she and Great Love starved together.

Great Love was seven years old when her father deserted her and her mother. She was nine when her mother entered the Divine fold and took her along. Today, she is approaching her twenty-first birthday.

"I *know* Father Divine is God!" Great Love glows when she talks of Father. "He took me, a child who had seen so much bad in the street, and cared for me. He made me good and pure. That is why I thank him every minute of every day."

What Father Divine did for Great Love he did for many children who came to the Peace Mission with their mothers when they had no other place to go. These, amenable from childhood on, make up the bulk of his present young adult group, which is still amenable and very happy and self-satisfied. To these amenable children, he gave affection and even love. He made them feel important and virtuous. In a sense, he courted them.

He never courted Jim Slaughter, though, and other boys and girls like him. Father Divine has never liked problems or challenges, and he holds no more brief for child problems than he does for adult ones. As a matter of fact, he judges children more harshly than he judges their parents and, as the Bible has done before him, even goes so far as to hold them responsible for the sins of their parents. That is why one of his favorite songs is addressed to children of parents who doubt his divinity rather than to the parents themselves. It is called, "Woe, Children of Sinful and Perverse Parents."

> *It is better to be a little puppy dog,*

(Father's followers sing happily to children of unaffiliated parents),

> *Than to be the child of one who hates*
>   *the body of God,*
> *For the sins of the fathers are being visited*
>   *on them,*
> *Unto the third and fourth generations of*
>   *the children of men,*
> *Causing misery and woe, causing grief and pain*
> *And complete annihilation to some.*
> *It is better to be a little puppy dog*
> *Than to be a child of one who hates God.*

Since he holds no brief for children's problems or for children either, Father Divine told his followers that he used his power of retribution to have a six-year-old burned to death because her "wicked old grandmother" had been overheard by a follower referring to him, Father Divine, as "nothing but a man. He is just taking the people's money."

Father admitted that there might have been some followers in his movement deluded enough to "suppose that the grandmother should have reaped the retribution and the child, simply because it was a child, should have gone scot-free." This was a foolish opinion, however.

"Just because she was a child," Father explained, "did not spare her or lessen her punishment, not any more than the children was spared in the time of Elisha. Infants and little children reap retribution. It may seem tragic to you, but the sins of the parents are visited on them. If they are nipped in the bud, so to speak, they are not given access for expression to further encase the globe with the bonds of limitations."

If children who are already within the movement wish to avoid Father's retribution, they must always be good and show their love for him. Those children whose parents have brought them into the Peace Mission must reveal dedication as completely as anyone does. There are as many regulations and more that they must obey as there are for adults. There are regulations for behavior within the Peace Mission "homes" and also outside them. There are regulations for behavior with neighborhood children and with their mothers and fathers. There are regulations for behavior in school. In February of 1951, at the beginning of a school semester, these were issued through the impersonal medium of the *New Day*.

BACK TO SCHOOL

It is almost time for school to begin. Your first day should make a lasting impression on your teacher, so brush up on a few points that she will notice about you.

1. See that your clothes are fresh and the right kind to wear to school.
2. See that your shoes are polished and clean.
3. See that your hair is well-groomed and neat.
4. See that your fingernails are clean.
5. Carrie a hankie, some pencils, and a notebook with you; you may need them and you don't want to borrow. It doesn't look nice.
6. Speak courteously to your teacher and fellow classmates.
7. Use correct grammar.
8. Do not take anything to eat in school at the wrong time. There is a lunch period for that purpose.
9. When school is out, wait until you get outside to shout and play.

If you remember to do all these things, your teacher will know you are a Rosebud or Crusader of Father Divine because your deportment will be excellent.

It is a fact that in all the public schools, elementary as well as high school, the conduct of the children of Father Divine is considered excellent. For the children dare not do anything else than obey Father's orders. Already at six years old and seven and eight, they show the molding of their world. They are frightened little personalities but, according to the Divine ideal, they are also independent ones. Even the littlest children, so long as they are able to manipulate themselves, are responsible for their own clothes and baths and meals under the supervision of one person in each kingdom whose special assignment the children are.

Through the past twenty-five years, at least five hundred children have entered the Peace Mission movement with their mothers or their fathers or with both. Even those who came as babes in arms were relinquished by their own parents to Father's spiritual care and to the physical care of whatever person was assigned by Father. The parents were convinced that they were doing their children the greatest good.

In 1950, white musician Kenneth Daire, who joined the movement with his wife Anita and his two young sons, Robert, nine years old, and Kenneth, Jr., four, thanked Father for assuming the care of the boys.

"I appreciate the privilege," he said, "of being able to have the little brothers brought up under your jurisdiction, because I know that you will be to them what no other one could be." His wife Anita, who is today one of Father's favorite secretaries, echoed that statement.

In the two years since Robert and little Kenny, Jr., have been with Father Divine, Father has indeed been the only one for them. When he was five, Kenneth injured his finger. It bled. He did not run to his mother with it, for he knew she would be unconcerned as she is about everything that happens to him. He did not run to his father, for he knew that his father would not care either. He did not go to the woman who had been assigned to care for him, Miss Justice, a secretary to Father Divine and a former nurse. For Kenneth knew, after a whole year behind the Peace Mission gates, that Miss Justice was all right about some things; she was good about looking in his ears on Sundays, for instance, to make sure they were clean, and sometimes, when he was hungry for snacks and would ask her to, she might be good about giving him an apple to eat . . . but for the important things, like an injured finger, Miss Justice was not good at all. There was only one in the whole world who could be of use to him—Father Divine.

So Kenny took himself and his finger to Father Divine. He knocked at the door of Father's office, which was opened by a secretary. Coincidentally, the secretary was Anita, Kenneth's mother in the mortal world.

"Peace, Miss Anita," Kenneth said.

Anita said, "Peace, Kenneth."

"I have to see Father," Kenneth said.

"I will put your name on the list."

"Thank Father," Kenneth said. He did not tell his mother about his injured finger nor show her where it was bleeding. He sat on the bench outside the doorway of Father's office and waited four hours for his turn to be "interviewed"....

To a person who is not a Divine follower, perhaps the most pathetic people in the movement—for they are people here, grown up even at five or six years old—are the very littlest children. Today, there are only six of them in the Philadelphia headquarters, and, despite the differences in their coloring and in their features, there is something about their expressions that makes them look horribly alike. They are so mature, from the little ones on up; and so consciously, devastatingly self-sufficient. There is no spontaneity about them. Looking at them, you feel that if you were to offer to play a children's game with them or to tell them a story, as you might to an ordinary youngster, they would only look at you and mock. What do they need games and stories for when they have Father Divine?

All of the children's spare time away from school and lessons is spent in thinking about Father Divine and about how to be worthy of his great love. Some of the most approved testimonials and songs to Father's divinity are evolved by young children who have no other creative outlet.

On May 12, 1951, Father granted his usual five-second interview to a group of white followers from California, who had never seen him before and had flown in for a day. Among them was an eleven-year-old boy who went by the name of Loving Jeremiah.

Loving Jeremiah opened the California followers' interview. "Peace, Father," he said.

Father answered, "Peace."

"I thank you, Father," Loving Jeremiah said, "for helping me in my schoolwork. May I sing a little song?"

Father considered. "Well——" He looked at the enthusiastic little face. "All right. If it's not too long. I said I was going to give you all five seconds. It would have been nice if you could all have been here long enough to be free to testify in the meetings and at the banquet tables and have a real nice time and not to have been cramped and pushed from the greatest to the least. So if Mr.—what's your name——?"

The eleven-year-old revealed no surprise at having Father address him as "Mr." If he felt any, he was, as all Divine youngsters are, poised enough to control it. He told Father Divine his name: "Loving Jeremiah."

Father continued in his formal fashion. "So, if Mr. Jeremiah desires to sing a little song, he could have sung it and would not be pushed or cramped to do so, but if you want to sing a little song, you may sing a few seconds."

Loving Jeremiah was grateful for Father's condescension to him. "Thank you, Father," he said. "Thank you, thank you, Father." Then, in a piping, almost-soprano voice, he sang a song of his own composing:

Father is on the mountain, Father is in the sea,
Father is down in the valley, saving humanity.
Father is ever-present, Father is sublime,
Father is God Almighty, Father-Mother Divine.
Thank you, Father.

Father received Loving Jeremiah's song with no more appreciation than if he had been an adult from whom such testimonials might be expected. He coolly said, "That is very nice, Mr. Jeremiah. O.K., I will not detain you any longer."

In recent years, there has been one child who received Father's special recognition. Her name was Martha Green, and she came to see Father in August of 1952 of her own volition. Martha's father is a Long Island eye specialist. He holds no brief for Father Divine. Martha's mother is not sympathetic to Father either. Martha's sympathy for Father Divine came via a maid in the home, Miss Beautiful Heart.

Miss Beautiful Heart had been with Martha's family since Martha had been a tiny baby. The mother and father were both busy people, and most of Martha's home contact had been with Beautiful Heart. Naturally, Miss Heart had influenced her. It wasn't conscious proselyting that Miss Heart had done with Martha. It was just that she, dedicated body and soul to Father Divine, could as soon have stopped breathing as talking about her God. From the time

Martha could understand language, she had known about the existence of Father Divine, God Almighty. From the time she'd been a tiny girl, she, along with Miss Heart, had believed in Father's divinity.

Her mother and father had not taken her baby prattlings about Father very seriously. When she'd grown older, however, and continued to talk about Father Divine as God, her parents had treated her belief with irritation at first and later with anger. Every time she talked about Divine, her father lost his temper with her, made it clear that he just did not want to hear such nonsense. Her mother, while she never said anything to Martha about her beliefs, did talk to the maid.

One day, three weeks after Martha's tenth birthday, Mrs. Green called Beautiful Heart into her bedroom for a "heart-to-heart talk."

"I am worried about Martha."

"Ain't nothin' to worry about that child," Miss Heart answered.

Mrs. Green was tactful with Miss Heart. "Listen, Beautiful," she said, "you have your own beliefs. We have ours. Martha is our child; we want her growing up our way."

Miss Heart regarded Mrs. Green somewhat contemptuously. There were many things mingled in her look. There was the idea that Martha, who understood the truth about Father, was more Miss Heart's child than her mother's, and also pity for Mrs. Green, who didn't know how well off her daughter really was to have been guided, since babyhood, by one of God's high priestesses.

"We don't want you talking about Father in this house any more. We particularly don't want you talking to Martha about him."

Miss Heart said, "I don't talk to her, Mrs. Green, unless'n she talks to me." She didn't say it to Martha's mother, but she implied that the order to stop talking about Father had come a couple of years too late.

Mrs. Green talked over the problem of Martha and Miss Heart with her husband. Miss Heart's conviction was so real, she said, nothing she could say would put a dent in it. And Martha was so attached to Miss Heart that, if she asked Miss Heart to leave . . . Besides, she was sure she

could never find such an efficient maid as Miss Heart wa
so honest and trustworthy. Dr. Green interrupted his wif
She was really making a big fuss over nothing. Martha w
a good, bright, sensible child and, in a year or so, would b
bound to have outgrown the maid's silliness. He was .
sure about that, he hardly felt the subject warranted fu
ther attention.

If Dr. Green had seen his daugher at a Divine banqu
on August 20, 1952, he might have felt differently. For, a
the banquet, the child's complete dedication to Father D
vine was obvious to everyone around her.

Martha and Beautiful Heart came to the afternoon ba
quet and stood among the side-line throngs watching F
ther come down to serve. Miss Heart looked at Father wi
all the love in the world shining out of her eyes, and Marth
looked at him the same way, too. Father caught Martha
eye. He smiled at her. She smiled back. Then, withou
being asked, she began to testify:

"Peace, Father dear. I am so happy . . . I waited for s
long . . . three whole years to lay eyes on your beautifu
body and now I see you . . . and I'm so happy. Oh, Fathe
oh, Father——" Her emotion was too much for her. Sh
buried her head in Beautiful Heart's lap and kept it ther
For the three hours of the banquet, after she had onc
stopped crying, she stood looking at Father, never takin
her eyes from him.

Martha Green is the kind of a child Father Divine wan
for his movement. That is why he gave her special notic
during her visit to Philadelphia. While several importar
visitors cooled their heels for hours waiting to see hin
Father granted an interview to Martha and Beautifu
Heart, making them wait hardly any time at all.

"Peace, Father," Martha said.

Father smiled warmly at the child, courting her as con
pletely as he ever courted anyone. "Peace, dear."

Martha said, "Father, would you give me a blessing?
want my father and mother to come to you. My father
an eye doctor and he listens to all the stories his patien
tell him and the things they have and all their troubles an
it makes him quick-tempered and I wish you would giv
him a blessing so he won't be so quick-tempered."

Father reached out and took Martha's hand in hi

"O.K. No doubt, he will be blessed." Then he dismissed Martha's father. He looked deep into her eyes and told her he knew she had another, more troubling problem. "What else did you want to see me about?" he asked, never even implying to Martha, as he does to the more typical young people who come to see him, that he could only spare five seconds for her interview. "What else did you want to see me about?"

Feeling warmed by Father's sympathy and entirely secure with him, as few young people have ever been "blessed" by Father to feel, Martha blurted out her problem.

"This has been on my mind so long! You see, I was going to Sunday school the first two weeks of my vacation this summer, and, you see, it was Catholic school and I am Jewish, but all the children in the neighborhood were going, so Mother let me go. It was a teacher there and she was talking about Jesus Christ and I was learning about it, and I happened to mention to her, 'Do you know Father Divine?' And she said, 'Yes, I do.' And she was talking about Jesus coming back and all of that, and then she said——"

Martha paused a moment and said, "I wish I didn't have to say this. It is all prejudice."

Father smiled at Martha. "That's all right, *you* are not saying it from your heart. *You* are not saying it. You are just saying what *she* said."

Martha blurted out her next sentence. She said, "The teacher said, 'Father Divine is no good. He is just a lot of foolishness,' and everything. I—I hated to say that, Father."

Miss Heart entered the conversation. She turned to Martha. "Tell Father how it stayed in your mind."

Martha brought her finger to her mouth. She said, "It stayed on my mind, and every time I thought of you and how beautiful you are, I just went blank and something made me think something against you."

Miss Heart spoke again. "She would never tell me what the teacher said. She said, 'I will tell Father and Father alone.' She said, 'I won't tell him in public,' she said, 'because those bad things shouldn't be said in public.'"

Father was touched by small Martha's sweetness and

loyalty to him. He explained to her that she did not need to worry about the teacher in the Catholic school or anyone else who maligned him. He told her he knew how to take care of God's maligners and always had. Even though she was only eleven years old, he discussed with her, just as though she were an adult, how he wreaked havoc and retribution against those who disagreed with him.

He said, "This reminds me—I gave a lady an interview today and she was telling me how she told me some time ago that her employer said some time back—said I had the heart trouble because he read it in the paper. *None* of it was true. And she said he said that, and now he has been in the hospital for so many weeks with a cyst or something, and they said the doctor didn't know what's the matter with him, and they can't do him any good—just what he said about me.

"So, when a person has those prejudiced minds, ideas and opinions and fancies and tendencies through preconceived ideas and opinions, they bring conditions upon themselves; but you *do not have to feel bad* because you heard her say it!"

"Well, I did feel very bad," Martha said.

It wasn't only that she was unhappy because she found herself thinking "bad thoughts against God." She'd also been worried because she thought Father might wreak retribution against her for those evil thoughts and make her or other members of her family die or become crippled or blind or tubercular. Now, sitting here in a chair directly across from God's, she wanted to say something else to Father. She hoped, she really hoped, that he would wreak retribution on the Catholic teacher, exactly as he had on the man he'd been talking about. She truly hoped he would; the teacher who had almost made her doubt God deserved retribution. And, much as she hated to admit it, she, Martha, also deserved it. After all, it was she who had allowed the teacher's bad words to lodge in her mind.

Father smiled and took the responsibility off her shoulders. He said, "You are not responsible for what she says so long as you know you do not say anything derogatorily or criticizingly! It reminds me, as you spoke, you said about you being Jewish. You know Abraham was Jewish.

He was a Jew and so was Moses; but Moses married an Ethiopian woman—what the people would call someone like myself—of dark complexion, and Miriam and Aaron spoke against Moses because he had married an Ethiopian woman and she was stricken with leprosy and turned white as snow. So the thought of it is, *whatsoever a person sows through maliciousness and prejudice, they have to reap the same!*"

Martha listened, wide-eyed. "Yes, Father dear," she said. And told God how grateful she was that his retribution would be directed against the Catholic teacher and not at all against her and her family.

Her eyes shining with the thought of the terrible things that could happen to the teacher, Martha rose from her chair. She was sensitive enough to know, before he told her, that Father wished the interview concluded.

"Peace, Father dear," she said.

Father answered, "Peace, dear."

Many hours after her interview with Father, Martha sat with Beautiful Heart and four other elderly women angels, Miss Stark Happiness, Miss Jacob Jeremiah, Miss Charity Love, and Miss Bright Light. All five of the ladies admired Martha profusely.

Bright Light said, "Thank Father, the testimony you done give this afternoon you done give to th' banquet is one of the prettiest I heard in all my time with Father."

Charity Love agreed with Bright Love. She said, "Amen. A-a-a-men."

Jacob Jeremiah said, "Yeah. Young as you is, your sweet little heart recognized your God and you come flying right into his arms."

Charity Love agreed with Jacob Jeremiah. "Amen. A-a-men."

Martha Green lapped up the praise. It made her feel good and took out of her mind the fear that had been there—even after she'd spoken to God and been reassured by him—of Father's directing retribution at her because of the thoughts the teacher had put into her mind. She told the women what their praise meant to her.

"I'm glad everybody knows how I feel about Father. I thought maybe Father's retribution——"

Miss Heart put her arm around Martha's shoulder and pulled the child close to her. "This little 'un sure does think a whole lot about retribution," she said. "Ain't it so, honey?"

Martha nodded. "I think about retribution almost every night."

"She reads about all the cases in the *New Day,*" Miss Heart told the other ladies. "It's what she likes to read about best, don't ya, honey?"

Martha nodded again. It was true that the record of Father's retribution against his enemies fascinated her more than almost anything else about the movement. It was more exciting than the fairy tales her mother had persisted in buying her when she'd been a very little girl—and true besides.

"I believe," she looked around at the five faces surrounding her, "I believe that retribution shows how much Father Divine is God. It shows it more than anything."

Charity Love agreed with Martha. "Amen. A-a-a-men."

12

"HAPPY AS THE RAMBLING PIANO KEYS ON EASTER MORNING"

Martha Greene's theory that retribution serves as Father's most imposing example of divinity is deeply inculcated. It goes back to the years when she was two and three years old, and when Beautiful Heart, who'd been in charge of her bedtime ritual more often than her mother and father had been, had told her stories of Divine retribution in place of the fairy tales other children hear at bedtime.

While most children were learning stories about dwarfs and giants, Martha had learned about the cataclysms which Father ordered nature's forces to perform for him. She had learned about floods and fires and famines and deaths by illness which could overcome people or whole nations that were critical of Father Divine.

"She made fun of Father," Beautiful Heart used to tell Martha, "and you know what happened to 'er, Honey, don't you?"

"Yes," Martha used to answer. "She died."

Young Martha Green, filled since babyhood with the idea of retribution, is, however, no more steeped in it than Father's older followers are. To all of them, regardless of age or intellectual background, retribution is one of the most important realities of the Peace Mission movement in exactly the way it is to Martha.

"The cosmic forces of nature," Father asserts flatly, "they obey me and work harmoniously for all who are conscious of my actual presence on the earth among men but they work havocly and destructively against those who think wickedly and choose to ignore my presence and lightly esteem me. Those who rise against me should take cognizance of it for that which a man soweth he shall reap. Retribution is sure and retribution is assured."

Actor Will Rogers is dead. At one time he made a flippant remark about Father Divine.

Louisiana Senator Huey Long was assassinated. He once turned his back on a Peace Mission delegation.

Adolph Ochs died. The New York *Times* publisher used to print unfair editorials about Father.

"It does not pay to criticize Father Divine," gentle-voiced Quiet Dove whispers, "because he is a live wire."

Quiet Dove was acquainted with a rich doctor who once lived in Chicago. She says he didn't live long, though, after he once ridiculed Father Divine.

"It was woe, woe, woe to the little Dr. Rosenberg. He fell with two strokes in one week and is in bad shape if not dead."

Quiet Dove knew another rich man who made fun of Father.

"He went down from two hundred pounds to almost a hundred. He cannot get up. He cannot walk, has a stroke and heart trouble. He is hooked. He is doomed. He starts crying every time he sees me, but it is woe to that rich man who thought he was making fun of Father."

Father's followers vie with each other to report to him occurrences which may be interpreted as retributive. Hunting for proof in coincidence, they use every auxiliary event to which they can trace a thread, however thin, to prove Divine's power. Many of them need no thread at all to connect Divine retribution with true situations.

Mr. Uni-Presence of Dayton, Ohio, visited Father's Philadelphia headquarters in early 1952. He testified at a banquet there:

"I have flower boxes in all of my front windows. An electrical storm came up one evening filling the two inches between the flower boxes and the window sill with water, which was overflowing into the room. I had a 6-inch chisel in my hand, trying to make a passageway beneath the box, so the water could go back the other way. I had the window up during the storm, working in the water with one hand. My next-door neighbor also had a chisel working on the window. A loud burst of thunder, then the flash of lightning came through the window. It seemed as though the chisel were on fire, I said, Peace, Father, Almighty

God! My next-door neighbor, Brother Miller, said God was up in the sky. Now, Father, I thank you, here is what happened. The flash of lightning that came through the window struck him on the side of his face, knocking a hole in his face and scorched or burned his face all over, knocked his voice out. He lay as a dead man on the floor. Everybody thought he was dead. The same lightning just seemed to me like nice warm sunshine. I thank you, Father. I thank you, Father."

Mr. Anna Dearone also thanked Father to report some case of retribution. Mr. Anna was a school bus driver in Pine Brook, New Jersey. Sometimes, he had trouble with the girls and boys who rode his bus, and, sometimes, he had trouble with their parents or with other men and women of the community. He "blessed Father's holy heart" to take care of the children as well as the grownups who gave him trouble, and Father's holy heart did just that.

Pridefully, Mr. Anna reports, "Father killed the police commissioner in our town and also a girl by the name of Vera."

Mr. Anna testified to Father's divinity through retribution at a banquet held on March 28, 1950, at the Divine hotel in Pine Brook.

"I thank you, Father," he said, "to report two acts of retribution that have reacted on two of the townspeople of the village of Pine Brook, New Jersey. I thank you first to report the death of Police Commissioner Sharkey of Parsippany-Troy Hills Township."

Father acknowledged Commissioner Sharkey's death with a beaming smile. It seemed to him that he had heard someplace that Commissioner Sharkey had not believed in his divinity.

Indeed, Commissioner Sharkey had not believed. He had, Mr. Anna said, been so stupid as to ridicule Father.

"One day in January, my employer Mr. Kevah Konner, called me into his office. In the office were two of his brothers and the late Mr. C. J. Sharkey. Mr. Sharkey started questioning me as to how I was getting along with the ladies. What he said I dare not repeat, but this is the thought of it. I told him that you had converted me from those things back in 1932 and that I did not give them a thought any more. He then said that 'that is where Father Divine and I fall out. I realize he is doing a lot of good for the people, but when it comes to women, that was what he was made for.'

"Then this Mr. Sharkey went on to speak critically and slanderously about your holy purity. This was the finish and I told him that he would pay and pay dearly for what he had said about you. I walked out of the office and as I glanced back he and the Konners were just a-smiling, as they thought they were having a good time at our expense. I smiled too, but to myself as I felt and knew that he would be taken care of from there on in.

"Father, you rewarded him for his blasphemies."

Father smiled at Mr. Anna. "Things do not just happen," he commented in a kindly tone, "they happen just."

The followers who were gathered, some two hundred and eighty of them, wildly applauded Father's statement. They yelled and screamed and kicked their applause until the floors and ceilings shook with the sound of it.

Mr. Anna continued his report:

"The second case of retribution happened Friday, March 24, to a young high-school girl of the senior class.

"Every day at the close of school I go to Caldwell High School and bring home students who live in Pine Brook. These Pine Brookers have been vulgar, with cursing, smoking, and swearing, even in the presence of teachers. They got to the place they would throw snowballs and rivets and other things at me when I was driving.

"I reported them a few times and they checked up for a while. When they found they could not do anything to me, they started to destroy the bus, by breaking the seats, and partitions, and other destructive things. The bus was overcrowded, and the girls would stand up in front and cover the ones that were doing the dirt, so I couldn't tell which ones were doing the damage. After another report the school supervisors then decided to make all the students pay two dollars apiece, since they would not tell on one another. Since that time they have been acting pretty civil, and not showing antagonism outwardly like they used to do.

"Many of them since then have reaped retribution in one way or another with broken arms, broken legs, and sicknesses of every kind. Friday, coming home, some of the girls were about to tell me of the misfortune one of them had, when some said not to tell. I said I didn't care since they didn't want to tell, and wasn't interested. Then they said that this girl by the name of Vera had taken sick Wednesday and was sent home from school, and taken to the hospital and died Thursday night. They said she had taken a cold and it went to her heart and she died. The girl, to my knowledge, never said anything outwardly and had seemed so unconcerned about everything, but, Father dear, you do know and did know her inner thoughts. She was buried Monday, March 27, and when I went to school to bring the children home I had only four students to bring. They said the rest had gotten off half a day and had gone to the funeral.

"Then again in the little schoolhouse on the corner in Pine Brook the attendance has been very poor, and they had to close the school for two days extra over the weekend, on account of the epidemics that have been spreading. The cemetery has been, in the last two months, just overrun with bodies being laid away."

Father acknowledged Mr. Anna's second case of retribution in the same way as he had the first one. "Things do not just happen. They happen just."

Again, the followers applauded, even more wildly enthusiastic after the death of the young girl Vera than they had been about the police commissioner's death.

In chorus, voices deep, some of them recited the movement's retribution poem. Its title is "Retribution."

I am the grim reaper, Retribution,
Whom all men should terribly fear!
I seek the godless in sure visitation
And destroy the wicked both far and near.

I am the law of retributive justice.
Who now shall escape my command?
I hold the destiny of my critics
In the hollow of my mighty hand.

I am vengeance, the rewarder of crime,
Punishing the blasphemers against God's Name.
I curse them to the very end of time,
For not believing in the Lord's Holy Reign.

I am the administrator of equity,
The accuser of men's polluted lives;
I am the judge of their iniquity,
The persecutor without compromise.

With my deadly sickle in hand,
I am reaping on the left and the right.
Righteousness shall rule in every man
Or Retribution shall destroy his birthright!

Executions, fire and loss,
Beatings and murders appointed to be,
Cosmic disasters and death are the costs
Of retributive justice on land, air and sea.

Moses and Jude and the prophets of old
Wrote of hate and strife and ungodly crimes;
Of Justice and Judgment they all foretold
And revealed the curses in those olden times.

Thus treachery and strife and irreligious hate
Mark the reaping of all my critics the same;
Not one has escaped his retributional fate,
For the grim reaper, God, Father Divine, compensates!

Father's most ardent recorder of retribution is Miss Beautiful Love of Newark, New Jersey. She carries on an involved correspondence to inform him at regular intervals of all the Newark men, women, and children who have been killed and injured. Her letters always begin in similar fashion.

"I thank You for Your world at large, and Your beautiful, sweet Peace that You have given to all of the children."

On May 13, 1951, she wrote this letter:

Peace, my dearest Father:
I thank You for allowing me to write as it is my deepest desire to try to please You more each minute. I thank You for Your

world at large and Your beautiful, sweet Peace that You have given to all of the children. . . .

I thank You to report some cases of retribution, Father.

Father, there was a man who used to live at this address, 28 Vanderpool Street. His name was John. He had a very dirty mouth. He tried to class You with himself. It was a little later his sister-in-law's baby drank kerosene and died.

There is one whose name is Yaddy, who also tried to class You with himself. He used dirty words. He stated You were a little bigger sport than he was. His wife has given birth to a baby who has never closed its mouth, according to their statements. I saw the baby when it was about 9 months old and its mouth hung open very wide.

Father, there was one who lived here, whose name is James Nickerson. I reported him once before. He said he knew where You came from. Father, his wife has given birth to a strange unknown baby. He left home at first. The cop went out on his job and got him and told him he would have to support them or else go to jail. I saw the baby, and all evidence proves that the baby is not his.

There was one whose name is Mr. James Barr, who also thinks he is cursing You. He and his truck fell 20 feet below the level, according to their statements. He was sent to the hospital; according to their statements, now he is going blind.

There was a Mrs. Scrap, she has a very dirty mouth. She also said dirty things about You. She got in a fight. She told me someone bit her finger; it looked to me like a dog had been chewing it. According to her statements, she can't use her arm.

There was a Mrs. Harman, for whom I had been employed for more than a year. She knew my belief in You. I told her so she would not make a mistake. She still tried to insist on my taking a present and what not. She said she believed giving was the right thing. Father, she had something in her, I don't know what. All I know, she was not like You. She was operated on and was doing fine; then she tried to give me something and passed her belief about it. Five days later she had a heart attack and died.

Father, there was a man who used to live here. He said he was employed by a woman more than 10 years—chauffeur and butler. He said in the A.M. she would not even show courtesy enough to speak to her servants when they spoke. He said 10 years ago she had a stroke and has been in bed now more than 10 years. She can't walk, can't talk, can't sit up, can't use her hands, can't hear. She has been this way in bed more than 10 years. I thank You, Father.

Father, I will try to please You each day. I will try to make You as happy as the rambling piano keys on Easter Sunday morning, or a happy angel when she does a holy dance.

Father answered Miss Beautiful Love.

My dear Miss Love:

Your letter of the 13th has come to hand and I am replying to say concerning the cases of retribution you wrote about: you can see in every instance that those who tried to measure Me with the measure of a man received the reward meted out to finite man, for it is written in Samuel's ministry:

"If one man sin against another, the judge shall judge him: but if a man sin against the Lord, who shall intreat for him?" (I Samuel 2:25)

In the case of the man, who you say, classed Me with himself, retribution came to him, if what you say is true, for it was retribution when his child was born with its mouth wide open and it cannot close it. What says the Word in the Ten Commandments?

"Thou shalt not bow down thyself to them, nor serve them: for I the Lord thy God am a jealous God, visiting the iniquity of the fathers upon the children unto the third and fourth generation of them that hate me." (Exodus 20:5)

The man, who you say thought he could curse Me, if what you say is true, suffered retribution when he and his truck fell 20 feet below level and he was hospitalized and is going blind. Things don't just happen, but they happen just! Anybody can see that the critic himself was cursed, for his own cursings returned to him, even as they never left him. What he intended for Me came to him heaped up, pressed down, and running over.

The lady, Mrs. Hardman, who you say tried to give you a present over and above your conviction of not receiving gifts and presents, if what you say is true, she suffered a heart attack and passed on because she tried to destroy your faith and belief in My Word. She just touched a live wire and destroyed her own life. Such is the reward of those who think they can go up against My Commandments.

Although you did not say that the lady who suffered a stroke had said anything about Me, the very fact that she refused to show courtesy to speak to her servants, deeming them lower than herself, if what you say is true, such was against the law of the Spirit of life, for if prejudice ruled in her heart and she divided herself against and from others racially, prejudice afflicted her and the law of retribution brought justice and judgment against her accordingly.

The lady is in a terrible state, if what you say is true, not being able to walk, not being able to talk, not being able to sit up, not being able to use her hands, and not being able to even hear. Had the lady truly prayed as Jesus taught men to pray:

"And forgive us our debts, as we forgive our debtors," She would have found Mercy from her affliction. But what said the Word following the Lord's Prayer:

"For if ye will forgive men their trespasses, your heavenly Father will also forgive you: But if ye forgive not men their trespasses neither will your Father forgive your trespasses." (Matt. 6:14, 15)

And so, the lady has remained for ten years in her pitiable condition; but retribution is sure and retribution is assured, for truly has the Word declared:

"God is no respecter of persons."

Thus, retribution rolls on, striking here and there at those who think they can criticize and slander Me, but none can reach Me to destroy the Fundamental Principle of My Life and of My Teaching, but they are destroyed who run against the Universal Law of Life; hence, it does not pay to defy My Name, for this leaves Me, as I am ever Well, Healthy, Joyful, Peaceful, Lively, Loving, Successful, Prosperous, and Happy in Spirit, Body, and Mind and in every organ, muscle, sinew, joint, limb, vein, and bone and even in every atom, fibre, and cell of my bodily form.

Respectfully and Sincere, I am
Rev. M. J. Divine, MsD., D.D.
(Better known as Father Divine)

Father's letter made Miss Beautiful so happy. "Oh," she tells, "you can't know how good it is to be under the protection of God who can move mountains." She knows that just as Father has punished all the enemies whom she wrote him about, so he will always protect his good children. She says that she is wealthier than Rockefeller, for, "look you," she says, "Rockefeller gets sick and he dies. I will live forever, though." She says that other millionaires not so rich as Rockefeller also get sick and die and are subject to the visitation of plagues ordered by Father.

"Father ordered a plague on Newport one time," she sweetly says.

Father was forced to order a plague on Newport. He had no choice. For Newport had the effrontery to challenge him. When, in the middle 1930's, Mrs. Angela Kaufman, a wealthy socialite, offered to donate her mansion to the Peace Mission movement, her neighbors would not let her. They banded together and stated that they would never permit God to enter Newport.

Father Divine did not remain silent.

"What do they want?" he meaningfully asked about the residents of that town. "Do they want a tornado with a ball of fire going through, consuming houses as a bombshell? Do they want the flu and other contagions such as man has not heard of? Do they want the beaches to be contagionized by all sorts of contagion and disease germs?"

Miss Beautiful is pleased to report that Newport suffered as a result of Father's blasting. There were many who died there in the 1930's and more who became ill. Up until today, many more Newporters than other people "sicken and die out."

Rockaway Beach, according to Miss Beautiful, is another place which has received "its come-uppance" for denying Father's divinity. The Rockaway difficulty began away back in 1917 when Father and Sister Penny attempted to rent bathhouses there. The prejudicial beach authorities refused to accommodate them.

"That was at a public beach," Father said, "but they thought the water was too good for me to go into. However, I said, 'If we cannot go in, nobody else will go in.' Shortly after that, tar came up in the water at Rockaway Beach as never before and spoiled the whole season."

"Just as Newport and Rockaway used to be places accursed," Miss Beautiful explains, "that's how it is in New York today. Father's real angry at New York. It may be he's angrier at New York than he was at Newport and Rockaway Beach."

Ever since Father left New York in preference to paying the judgment of Verinda Brown, that city has been at the very top of his detailed blacklist. In 1950, New York suffered a severe water shortage and Father told the reason. In an open letter to all residents of New York, he threatened:

If you do not love me and keep my commandments, I will curse your going out and I will curse your coming in and I will curse you in your storehouses and in your bread baskets. I said I will dry up your rivers and I will dry up your streams. This water shortage has been just a slight sketch and reflection of what I will do . . .

Miss Beautiful says that Father's threats are not ever made in vain. She advises wise New Yorkers to leave that wicked city as she, herself, left it in 1942.

"If you own property in New York, sell it," she says. "If you can't sell it, give it away or just walk out leaving it abandoned."

She cautions New Yorkers who persist in continuing to live in New York to heed the plight of the Mikado of Japan. On May 7, 1945, Father Divine deigned to write him a letter.

"Surrender or be totally annihilated and become extinct."

Miss Beautiful says that nobody is required to take her word for what happened after the Mikado received Father's letter. It is a matter of public record. The atom bomb was dropped on Hiroshima on August 5, less than two months after God's warning had been issued. Sixty per cent of the population was annihilated exactly as Father had predicted it would be.

Nobody can say Father didn't try to help Benito Mussolini either. On the very day that the Italian dictator invaded Ethiopia, Father wired him orders to return it to the Ethiopians. Mussolini ignored Father's wire. He died.

"Mussolini," Father beamingly commented, "might have been alive today had he taken cognizance of my message."

Miss Beautiful says that is certainly true.

Today, according to Miss Beautiful, there is a whole group of people aside from New Yorkers headed for the fate of Mussolini and the Mikado of Japan. This is the working press. Father Divine despises all newspapermen, and photographers head his blacklist.

"Father will make it for newspaper people so that they will kill their offsprings and land up in jail," Miss Beautiful recently told a visiting social worker.

The social worker asked, "Why?"

Miss Beautiful pursed her lips and half shut her eyes. "Those pictures coming out of Father, did you ever see any?" she asked.

The social worker said, yes, she had seen many pictures of Father Divine.

"Well, then," Miss Beautiful spoke bitterly, "you ought

to know why us, who love God, hate the photographe[r]
who took those pictures."

The social worker struggled to recall what could ha[ve]
been so offensive in magazine and newspaper photograp[hs.]
True, they did not portray Father as a handsome ma[n.]
How could they have been expected to? Nevertheless, [it]
must be this, she figured, that the followers found so obje[c-]
tionable, the fact that the camera did not flatter Fath[er.]
She told Miss Beautiful that.

"Flatter?" Miss Beautiful's voice grew hysterical. "Fla[t-]
ter? We are not asking for flattery. All we want is justice[.]"
She hesitated for a tense moment. "All we want those ph[o-]
tographers to do is to take pictures of Father and not ma[ke]
him look like he is of the darker complexion."

"But," the social worker said, allowing her confusion [to]
show, "Father is a Negro. Do you people think the ca[m-]
eras ought to make him look like a white man?"

That was exactly what Miss Beautiful did think. [It]
wasn't that she expected the cameras to do something th[at]
was not honest. It was just that she resented having t[he]
cameras lie when the truth was right in Philadelphia, avai[l-]
able to anyone who had the eyes to see. What was wro[ng]
with the social worker, calling Father Divine a Negr[o?]
Didn't she know that that word, N-e-g-r-o, was a dir[ty]
word, that it was a curse word never to be used by an[y]
person of good will? Besides, what was wrong with the s[o-]
called social worker's eyes anyway? Was she, who, eve[n]
though she was an outsider, had been blessed by Father [to]
move in his very presence and in the very midst of all h[is]
holiest angels, too blind to see that Father was not real[ly]
dark-brown colored at all but that "his beautiful little face["]
was white, yellow, and, well, somewhat on the brown sid[e]
also?

Miss Beautiful's illusion about Father's color, shared b[y]
all his other followers, white as well as colored, is ju[st]
another one of the Peace Mission illusions which no im[-]
pingement from the outside world can take from Father['s]
followers.

Father Divine maintains, "I am not of the darker com[-]
plexion."

His followers say, "No, no, Lord."

Father's own photographers dedicate themselves to making pictures that Father could approve. Joe Patience, former gangster, and Kenneth Daire, a white man, former musician, are in charge of Father's personal photographs. They spend their days turning the brown face white and utilize every known photographic technique to do so.

Father uses the pictures made by his personal photographers to prove how grossly unfair ordinary photographers are to him. He says that if Kenneth Daire and Joe Patience can make him look "of the lighter complexion," other photographers can do the same thing.

"If they are real photographers," he explains about non-follower cameramen, "they could make the picture the same as my amateur photographers can make of me. If they don't it is based on prejudice of the lowest order. Let newspaper photographers use Mr. Patience and Mr. Daire as 'samples and examples' of how to take my picture."

Since photographers refuse to use Joe Patience and Kenneth Daire as examples of the only men in the world who know how to photograph God and since they have persisted, through the many years Father has been a press subject, in photographing him as a Negro, he has fought them in two ways. In the last five years he has refused to allow any but his personal photographers to take his picture, and he has issued the sternest warnings regarding retribution for the working press.

In 1949, he told representatives of the Associated Press and the Associated Negro Press:

"I hope you are co-operative. It does not give the paper and those who represent it a very good protection if you are not. People come to me from all parts of the world, many of whom were absolutely decrepit and invalids, having been healed automatically by thinking sympathetically and harmoniously and talking the same. Those who have thought antagonistically, critically, and try to accuse and slander and ridicule, many of them have been cut off the stage of action and gone to see if there is a reality in another world other than this one. Planes go down!"

"Plenty of them do," commented a laconic reporter.

The reporter who dared answer God mockingly was a brave man. A number of followers could cheerfully have killed him if it hadn't been for the fact that they were depending on Father's power of retribution to do it.

Father promised them that he would take care not alone of the laconic reporter but also of all the other "bad, perverting members of newspapers."

In a statement of retribution that rather exceeded in its scope any other he had made to date, Father Divine addressed his followers regarding the working press:

"Because of prejudice, because of inequality and division, because of racism, color, and every other abomination, they try to pervert the likeness of the individuals—and they doing their work in making the pictures—their photographers! And the same like manner in the publications—what they write in the copy; they try to pervert the minds of the people! They are perverting their offsprings! —they are perverting and making decrepit and deforming your offsprings that shall come after you!

"How would they like to have a child born in their family, though they may be caucasians, as they may be termed; and even may say, they may be blondes, both of them, and yet their offspring may be the same complexion of my patent-leather shoes! Then they may want to kill it—but if they kill it they shall pay the penalty according to the law! I thank you! I thank you! I thank you!"

Outsiders to the Peace Mission movement who have written about Father's retribution have dealt mostly with its more amusing aspects and told about it with an understandable tongue-in-cheek technique. But anyone who has actually lived within the Peace Mission gates for any length of time and who has had fairly close contact with Father Divine and with his followers cannot be funny about retribution and let it go at that. It is too vital a part of the character of Divine and of the Peace Mission movement to be dismissed with a facetious pen. For, because of retribution, some followers, only a few fortunately, are almost eaten up alive by their fear of Father.

In an appalling kind of a way, retribution is the weapon of a stern despot, consciously wielded by Father Divine as the most certain means he has been able to evolve for keeping his followers entirely submissive. There are a few followers in the movement today who would wish to return to the outside world but who dare not attempt to divorce themselves. It takes more courage than they have been gifted with to tangle with the "terrible cosmic forces." They stay in heaven and keep wondering whether Father has seen through them yet and when he intends to mete out their just punishments. They go to bed at night and are not at all sure that they will wake up well the next morning. You see them, moving like automatons instead of people with the fear written boldly on their faces, and you try to help them, you try to talk to them, you try to explain to them, that Father's vaunted retribution is nothing more than a series of coincidences. They look at you and the shock of what you are making them listen to shows in their look, and you know, too well, that you have not helped them at all; that, on the contrary, they are watching you and waiting for retribution to strike you, for you to fall down dead because of the blasphemies you are uttering against God. And when you don't fall down dead they are surprised but never really convinced. They know that you will die as soon as God gets ready to have you do so. And—Father Divine help them—so will they.

Retribution, despite its devastating effects on some followers, is not Father's big stick alone. Nothing is ever one thing only where Divine is concerned. While it is true that retribution represents a medium of effective intimidation to him, it represents also a medium for self-security which he will always need more than most people. For Father Divine, retribution is, at one and the same time, his big stick and his particular and, it must be admitted, pitiful, form of whistling in the dark. It is the knife that he who is, in the last analysis, George Baker, can use against a hostile white world. It is his most vital mechanism for denial of the true status of the Negro in America. It is the force by which God-Negro-Baker can throw off the dark-brown skin which could have kept him subordinated for the rest of his life and can become whiter than his whitest oppressors. To date (one must always talk about "to date" when one talks about a Divine conception, for no one can know what novelty will be conceived tomorrow)—to date, retribution is the sweetest fantasy of Father's intricate mind for improving the life not only of George Baker, black man, but also of all of America's Negroes.

That is why he aims his most vigorous retributive

denunciation not only against those who defy his divinity,
but also against those whom he terms "segregators and
discriminators." There is a song in the movement which
tells the punishment that Father will mete out to them. It
is called "The Mills of God Are Grinding On."

The song's chorus is:

> *The mills of God grind slowly*
> *But they grind exceedingly fine,*
> *And sometime, somewhere, the Judgment of God*
> *Will be your portion and mine.*

It has twenty-six verses, of which fourteen inform white
people that God is on earth now and that he has come to
avenge his own, the ones who are humble as he, himself,
might look to be. It warns those who discriminate:

> *You must repent! You must seek mercy,*
> *From one you thought too meek and humble,*
> *Because everything in this dark world,*
> *Is turning to ashes and going to crumble.*

When Father's Negro followers sing "The Mills of God
Are Grinding On," they express, in a strongly realistic
fashion, the plaint of their people not alone for justice, but
also for vengeance.

> *Let them come in "dust and ashes,"*
> *Let them moan and seek GOD's Face;*
> *Let them feel the bitter lashes,*
> *And of their own evil, get just a taste.*
>
> *Let their blood help pay the price*
> *Of centuries of sorrow and blinding pain*
> *They dealt to others in their arrogance;*
> *Let them feel GOD's cold disdain.*

In bitterness and in righteous indignation they ask white
people:

> *Did you think you could go on forever and ever*
> *And never reap your harvests in "blood and tears"?*
> *Did you think GOD forgot and turned aside?*
> *Didn't you care—or—didn't you fear?*

What of the weary one who had to walk
Because he wasn't allowed to ride beside YOU?
What of the thirsty one who couldn't drink
Because he couldn't use YOUR fountain?

What of the one who had no learning
Because he couldn't go with you to school?
What of the ones who learned to hate you
Because all you left them was hate and despair?

They tell white people:
"All of these you owe a debt."
And ask them:
"Think you not to pay it now?"
And they dictate how white men are to behave toward
Negroes from now on. They sing:

If you live on the face of this earth from now on,
You are going to enact the Bill of Rights;
You are going to sit side by side with the one
You spurned in your arrogance and selfish might.

You will see that each has the same hopes and desires,
The same ambitions, the same thoughts—the same prayers
as you;
You will see each living soul has a heart just like yours—
That is, if GOD lets you live to see it through.

Anyone who knows Father Divine knows how thoroughly
he believes in his song. He really does believe, just as his
followers do, that he can "wipe discriminators off the face
of the earth."

"Look," he tells, "see what I did to Miami Beach discriminators."

In 1950, Miami Beach authorities tried to prevent dark-
complected Divinites from using beach facilities. Father
fought the authorities.

Unlike more practical fighters for civil rights, he did not
sue the Beach in the name of his followers. He did not
sponsor an educational program which would work to
eradicate prejudice there. All he did was to call on his

fantasy powers and to cause tons of dead fish to come up in the water and be washed onto the beaches.

"There was such a stench, the people could not stand it and the beaches were deserted," he tells today. "Bathing was impossible. Millions of dollars were lost by resort owners and the cost of digging ditches to bury the dead fish was tremendous. They called it 'The Red Tide,' but, whatsoever the scientific cause, the real mental and spiritual cause was prejudice, segregation, and discrimination."

Atlanta, Georgia, was another city that suffered for its discriminatory patterns. Father caused a fire in the Winecoff Hotel and 121 persons "lost their bodies."

In Texas and Oklahoma, he caused tornadoes.

Father's Negro followers received great gratification from the Atlanta fire and the Texas tornado and the Miami Red Tide.

"It goes to show you," Mr. Equality Smart says, "how equal dark- and light-complected is in the only eyes that means something—God's."

You talk to Mr. Smart and to Father's other Negro followers, not to those who are frightened by retribution, but rather to the many who bask in it. They laud it as a design for achieving civil rights. You listen to their praises and keep looking at their faces and you start knowing for a fact what you have only half believed before—that Father Divine's Negro followers get more immediate satisfaction from the way their leader attacks discriminatory patterns than the followers of more down-to-earth Negro leaders can ever get from theirs.

"All them dark-complected leaders," asks Equality Smart, "what do they do for other dark-complected folks?" He answers his own question. "Not a one thing. All they does is talk, talk, talk. Father Divine ain't the one to talk, though. He acts just like he done in Stuyvesant Town."

Stuyvesant Town is a housing development in New York City. Before it opened and for some years afterward, it refused to accept Negro residents. Practical leaders of civil rights agencies fought the ban. So did Father Divine.

The fight began in 1943 when New York City and the Metropolitan Life Insurance Company first entered into an agreement to construct Stuyvesant Town which was to be a moderate-rent housing development for 25,000 people. Among other advantages, the city provided for tax exemptions of two million dollars a year for a period of twenty-five years.

Before the project was officially opened, and when the contract came up for approval before the city's Board of Estimate, Metropolitan officials adamantly asserted that Negroes would not be admitted.

"Negroes and whites don't mix," said Frederick H. Ecker, then chairman of the board.

The down-to-earth leaders started immediately to work to change Metropolitan's policy. They made contact within the Board of Estimate and asked members to disapprove the contract because of the threatened discrimination. While five members disapproved, a majority of eleven effected the passage.

In 1947, Stuyvesant Town opened its doors—for white residents only.

Two weeks later, three national civil rights organizations—the National Association for the Advancement of Colored People, the American Civil Liberties Union, and the American Jewish Congress—started legal suit against the discriminating company.

They pointed out that the United States Constitution and the New York State Constitution forbid racial discrimination and that, since tax exemption and other powers are held by the city for the benefit of all the people, they must not be distributed, on a basis of favoritism, only to white people.

Everyone concerned freely admitted the right of the plaintiff's arguments. Still, the case of Stuyvesant Town dragged on for three years.

Father rejected the procedure of the practical agencies. No headaches of long, drawn-out legal battles for him. No subtle wrangling. God could afford to be direct. He merely wrote a letter to Leroy Lincoln, president of the Metropolitan Life Insurance Company.

I am writing to you as an organization father that those under you and affiliated with you might escape the disasters that follow in the wake of prejudice, discrimination, bigotry, and segregation. When you segregate in the Northern Middle Atlantic States and in a state that has passed the Fair Employment Practices Committee Bill and the Civil Rights Bill, all evidences reflect as if though you desire to endorse segregation and discrimination, which bring on such disasters as have claimed the lives of millions in recent years.

Father listed the most recent disasters to his credit. A Canadian Pacific DC-3 had crashed and killed all of its twenty-three passengers and crew. A raging thunderstorm off Nantucket Island had drowned nine persons who were sailing in a yacht. A boat had caught fire at a pier in Toronto, Canada.

It may work out the same with the enterprise with which the Metropolitan is connected," Father warned, "if you and other officials do not immediately bring to an end your policy of segregation. The law of God is above the laws of men and if men fail to obey God, they may think that God is, indeed, Public Enemy #1.

To Mr. Leroy Lincoln, this letter seemed a persiflage, no doubt. But to the great bulk of Father's followers, it seemed the greatest social document that had ever been penned.

"Father showed them," Mr. Smart still triumphantly tells today.

You talk to Equality Smart, who "never had no decent room before I come to Father," and see, as he can see it, the tortuous process by which the Metropolitan Life Insurance Company had to be forced to accept Negro residents. You talk to Mr. Smart, and even though you are not a Negro waiting three years to get a chance at good housing, you almost feel like you are, for a moment, and in that momentary feeling, you cannot fail to comprehend Divine's appeal to the Negro mass.

It is this. Of all the Negro mass leaders, Father Divine is the only one who does not try to meet the fact of discrimination head-on. He is the only one who flees from it. Mercifully, he brings his followers along on the flight.

They, who have been unable to find homes and jobs and food enough for their children to eat, can't be bothered with the long-range planning of practical race relations agencies—which must take three miserable years to force the Metropolitan Life Insurance Company to open its doors to

Negroes. They can't wait three years. They want housing and food—and dignity—today. Of what matter to them the important fact that Father's tenet of retribution is in a real sense the turning of his other cheek to the oppressors of the Negro people? What do they care that, every time Father rejects legal and educational means for attaining civil rights in favor of his retribution, he is opposing the final goal of the Negro in America—complete and equal integration? That final goal for tomorrow is too far off to make sense today. It is like the "sky-God"—of no use to depressed and earth-bound Negroes. With the same intensity that they have rejected their sky-God for Father, they have given up thought of integration for Negroes in some distant future. They would rather have Father's fantasy today.

13

"EVERY TONGUE
CONFESS!"

Father's fantasy elected a President.

The followers who accept floods and deaths and famines as Father's normal retribution against those who do not love him accept victory as his normal reward to those who do. They say that Father, being God, can, if he wishes, bring victory to non-followers as well as angels, so long as the non-followers are sensible enough to reveal their good intentions. President Dwight D. Eisenhower was.

If Father Divine had not willed it so, Ike would not today be holding "the highest position of all in America underneath God himself."

White teacher Beautiful Peace calmly explains that, "The general's victory was meant to be. Father, you know, was on his side."

Father says that he elevated Ike to the presidency because Ike alone, of all who sought political office from the city assembly right on up to the presidency, was the individual who had proven himself to be least ashamed to take God's name. Ike Eisenhower actually owned Father Divine as his God at a conference of newsmen from all over the country.

"Peace, it's wonderful," he said. Then, displaying true courage of his convictions, he admitted God to be the fount from which that thrilling phrase had sprung. "Borrowing a phrase from the Reverend Major J. (Father) Divine, 'Peace, it's wonderful.' "

"Peace, it *is* wonderful," Father beamingly told his followers. "General Eisenhower wasn't ashamed to say it. He is tired of the people making so much fun of me and of 'Peace, it's wonderful.' He did not just say it, but he even heard the soldiers in the army under his jurisdiction mak-

ing fun of me. He didn't say it but he heard it. That is what
stirred him up so, because he knows what I stand for."

Father prefers not to talk about a somewhat unpleasant
fact in relation to the presidential election of 1952, but
under severe questioning he admits that there was a time
when his followers miscalculated the issues of the election
and actually conceived themselves to be in favor of Adlai
Stevenson. He also admits that this peculiar state of mis-
understanding lasted from the day the presidential campaign began to the day it ended. What prompted the followers' partiality to Stevenson? Well, that's a very difficult
question to answer with customary Divine honesty. Father
really doesn't know what prompted it unless, perhaps, it
was because, throughout the campaign, pictures of Stevenson, not Eisenhower, lined the lobbies and meeting rooms
of all Peace Mission headquarters.

Who had hung the Stevenson pictures in Peace Mission
headquarters? The Peace Mission housekeepers had hung
them, no doubt. Who had authorized the Peace Mission
housekeepers? What difference did it make who had authorized them? Father Divine never quite admitted to any questioner what everybody interested in his movement knew for
a fact during election time—that he had, up until Eisenhower's election, been a passionate Stevenson m-a-n. He
forgot, when he talked to questioners, all the statements he
had made for the record, on the positiveness of the civil
rights program which Adlai Stevenson had advocated.

Immediately after election results were announced, Father revealed that he had been, as he always was and
expected to be forever, on the winning side. In a long
"election victory speech to my followers," he discussed the
"true reasons" behind Stevenson's defeat and Eisenhower's
victory.

The reasons behind Stevenson's defeat were simple but
vital. Never once during the course of the campaign had
Adlai Stevenson been religious enough to take the name of
Father Divine. Father told his followers that what had
happened to Stevenson could as easily have happened to
any other person who would not call on him.

"Insignificant as I may apparently be," he admonished,
"everybody better mention me in business, profession,

labor, and trade, and they better not be ashamed nor afraid to mention me. Matters not how they stand in profession or classification. For the name of God is a strong tower, and everyone knows this, meaning myself, is God's name. If they don't know it is God and even if they don't believe it is God, they know it is God's name. So Mr. Eisenhower was elected. Because the followers did not even know it. The majority of the followers were for Stevenson. They thought he would be elected."

Father Divine said that, with the bulk of Divine followers against him, Ike's chances of becoming President were slim indeed until God entered the battle for him. He knows that Ike appreciates that intervention, but it is perfectly all right and the President must consider himself a debtor to no one, not even to Father Divine. He must merely do his job and go on, through his whole term as President, standing for the things he stands for now, "democracy, Christianity, Americanism, civil rights." And Father Divine. Then God will have "no kick" against him.

John Germaine, college-educated executive secretary of the Peace Mission movement, says that Eisenhower's election is "typical of what has been for nineteen hundred years. Sometimes evil triumphed but not for long in the world of men, for then Father entered the battle and virtue won, as President Eisenhower won for President. Father made George Washington become the first President, and he was on the side of Abraham Lincoln, helping him win the Civil War, also when it looked like Harry S. Truman didn't have a chance of becoming elected President, Father saw to it that he would, and you know he won. Father was always active in politics, as far back as the beginning of our country, and he is just as active today."

Father's political activity today, although Mr. Germaine and the other Peace Mission devotees could not be persuaded of it, consists of taking credit for the election of every successful candidate for public office and of disowning every unsuccessful one with the loudest of declamations. It consists of taking credit for every progressive piece of legislation and of assuring followers that all legislation will soon be progressive. It is composed of the most loving pats on the back granted by Father Divine and the doting followers to Father Divine in recognition of his political astuteness.

Father and all his followers, from the greatest of them to the least, are convinced that the Peace Mission movement is God's gift to American politicians today. Nothing can dissuade them from this delusion. The younger followers believe it on faith alone. The older followers believe it by faith and also by their recollections of the days when Father Divine, despite his peculiarities, really was an important political figure.

For throughout the dark days of the depression, when politicians began to seek the Negro vote they reckoned a great deal with Father Divine. Father's potential of political strength first exhibited itself in the early thirties. That was when nearly every Negro newspaper in the country and every agency working for Negroes had embarked on an ambitious campaign to urge Negroes to utilize their votes for improving their circumstances. That was the exciting period when Northern Negroes, strengthened by the hordes of incoming Southerners, began fully to recognize the power of a properly utilized ballot and began to vote pretty much as a self-conscious bloc. That was the period when, in New York City—Father's headquarters then—350,000 Negro voters began, race-consciously, to bargain with the politicians who sought them out. That was the period when New York's Negroes stopped being absolute affiliates of either one of the political parties, even during national elections, and shifted their votes from the Republican party to the Democratic as wise bargaining procedure dictated. That was the period during which New York Negroes supported independent candidates locally and contributed vitally to the election of one of their best friends—Reform Mayor Fiorello La Guardia.

During the 1933 New York City mayoral election, Mayor O'Brien, seeking to be re-elected, came to Divine headquarters.

"Peace," he said, in a voice brimming over with emotion, "come what may, adversity, joy, or sorrow, you can meet it by reason of your leadership under Father Divine."

An observer not connected with the movement made a cryptic comment about the mayor's speech.

"It looks sometimes," he said, "as if a good many people besides Father Divine think maybe he is God."

Fiorello La Guardia, reform candiate against O'Brien, also sought help from Divine in 1933. He also came to the Harlem Peace Mission.

"Peace, Father Divine," he greeted Father, and the followers. "Peace be with you all, I say . . . I say, Father Divine, no matter what you want, I will support you."

The followers cheered wildly, not for La Guardia but for Father Divine, who was nodding his holy head, accepting the tendered support as merely God's due.

Small Fiorello La Guardia, "the little flower" to loyal white voters and nicknamed "Shorty George" by his Harlem supporters, who in three elections voted ten to one for him, jumped about on the Peace Mission platform.

"I am going to clean up this city," he shouted, "and I came here to ask Father Divine's help and counsel."

Father did not offer his help to La Guardia. He did not offer his help to any of the politicians who sought it and who offered to pay for it. He refused to make bargains or to form combines with any of the political leaders. It is indicative of the personality of Father Divine that, being given every opportunity for political self-advancement, he would reject practicality in favor of his own peculiar idea of good politics.

Instead of aiding La Guardia or O'Brien, instead of helping the senatorial candidates or the other political aspirants and requesting their patronage in return, Father Divine, believing even then that he, God, needed no human help in politics, undertook a campaign to accomplish righteous government not only in America but also throughout the world. It was doubtless the most ambitious political undertaking of the century. He called a three-day conference of followers and world leaders, including Pope Pius XI and President Franklin Delano Roosevelt, to formulate a new and righteous code of government for "the entire world at large."

Father Divine's Righteous Government Convention was held on January 10, 11, and 12, 1936, at three New York headquarters—at Rockland Palace, 155th Street and Eighth

Avenue, at the New Star Casino, 167th Street near Park Avenue, and at St. Nicholas Palace, 69 West 66th Street.

St. Nicholas Palace, the headquarters at which Father Divine himself appeared most often, was decorated in various combinations of intense orange and deep purple. On the platform, there was a silver backdrop, slightly tinged with purple and having an open orange center. The two colors were representative, according to Father, of the Eastern and Western hemispheres. The speakers' chairs were decorated in alternate oranges and purples, and the throne chair, reserved for Father even when he was not there to sit in it, was covered with the purple-silver of the backdrop.

In the audience, Negro and white followers sat, one white, one colored, self-conscious examples to the visitors present of how white and colored people could really live together. When they were not listening to speakers, they were singing songs. A popular convention song was "Not Only Equal but the Same":

> *We shall have the same rights,*
> *Not only equal but the same,*
> *Side by side we shall ride*
> *The same car, bus or train.*
> *We shall play in the same parks,*
> *Study our lessons in the same schools,*
> *There shall be the same equal rights*
> *For you and you and you.*

Arthur A. Madison, Father's trusted attorney, was chairman of the convention.

Father himself made the opening speech and set the keynote.

"Peace, everyone, righteousness, justice, and truth, with hearts filled with merriment, your bodies exuding enthusiasm, for the recognition and the realization of God's presence is a living reality. This has been established and individually and collectively in millions, but it shall be established universally through legality that all must realize the legitimacy of God as well as the illegitimacy of unrighteousness, debauchery, and falsehood. Because of this I came and for this very purpose I stand to bring about the righteous government, not only in the hearts and lives but in the affairs of the children of men, that we might fulfill that of which we sung just a while ago."

"So true, Lord," the excited audience responded.

An old man sprang out of his seat. He leaned one hand upon a cane. He waved the other hand wildly to gain Chairman Madison's attention.

Mr. Madison recognized the old man. "Universal Cheerfulness wishes to speak."

Mr. Cheerfulness cleared his throat. He looked round at his audience, waiting for absolute quiet.

"I move that Father Divine is God," he said.

Mr. Cheerfulness' motion was noisily applauded and unanimously accepted.

A second motion was made. Rita Gans, schoolteacher, moved that the Constitution of the United States be endorsed by the Divine convention. This was also vigorously approved.

It was the Constitution of the United States, as a matter of fact, which was suggested as a keynote for world government, Divine fashion.

"There will be one language, English, one speech and one flag, American," Father promised, "when the government which I have exemplified and brought to fruition shall have been established in all of the people. For, I say, all of the nations of the earth politically must be brought into subjection of the government universally for the people, by the people, and through the people, shall perish from the earth without me."

As is everything else in the Peace Mission movement, Father's Righteous Government meeting was a blending of the sensible and the ridiculous. Its more practical platforms were specifically aimed at the abolition of racial discrimination.

The convention ordered lynching abolished and lynch mobs outlawed.

"Everyone who is known to participate in a mob violence," Father stated emphatically, "should be classed and found guilty as a murderer." He added, "Whatsoever that means."

The convention demanded immediate abolition of all

segregated neighborhoods, schools, and colleges. There was to be no more segregation in theaters or in public conveyances or in churches.

Legislation was to be enacted to "make it a crime for newspapers to use segregated or slang words referring to any race, creed, or color."

Different wage scales for "what they term to be different races, creeds, or colors" were to be abolished.

The convention directed "the immediate repeal of all laws in the United States and elsewhere that have been passed contrary to the spirit and meaning of the Constitution of the United States."

After a long discussion of racial discrimination, the convention directed its attention to other matters.

All laws providing for any form of compulsory insurance were to be repealed. Father himself took the floor on this point:

"As far as taking out insurances, we will not tolerate it and I would tell the President so." Father said that true followers would far rather break the law than to take out "insurances to mistrust God and visualize disappointments, failures, accidents, and disasters."

Capital punishment was to be abolished in all states of the union and countries of the world.

Physicians who treated ill patients were to be forced by law to guarantee complete cures and to be liable for damages in cases of death.

Employment agencies were to be prohibited from collecting fees or other forms of remuneration from employees.

The rule requiring persons who applied for work on relief projects to be on relief was to be abolished.

There was to be abolition of tariff schedules and other obstacles to free trade.

Any person who spent money except for the necessities of life while owing a just debt to another person was to be held as a criminal.

The word "hello" was to be abolished as the conventional form of greeting in America. The word "Peace" was to take its place, so that "a generation with Peace on its lips instead of what war has been said to be hell-o may

come into being." The convention requested the co-operation of the telephone companies in this regard.

Counterfeit money was ordered to be immediately destroyed at the expense of those who held it.

The United States government, as an example to "the
world at large," was to redeem all its bonded debts immediately.

At the conclusion of the conference, Father and his
lieutenants, modest as always, admitted that "the recommendations contained in this platform will not solve every
problem of the world at large." "But," they added, "the
fundamental principle will."

For the sake of those world leaders who had been
unable to attend, Father composed a form letter about the
convention and its significance.

On January 21, 1936, Anno Domini Father Divine, His
Eminence Pope Pius XI was blessed to receive a special
delivery registered letter with a return receipt requested.

Father advised first that the Righteous Government platform, enclosed in his letter, was the platform on which he
himself would always stand. Then he explained his motivations to the Pope.

We are not seeking to form another party, neither to run
in collision with partisan parties that are in operation, but to
release to them and to all that are in authority the high ideals
for true partisanism that all parties might take the fundamentals
in the text of my Righteous Government platform to serious
consideration and act upon them as a significant legislation.

Father instructed the Pope on how to utilize the platform.

Please kindly endorse it to be handed down to your Congregations as a significant legislation and to be recommended
by all of the Catholic people and in all countries under your
Advisory.

Senator Wagner of New York, blessed to receive a similar letter, advised Father that Vice President Garner would
have the Divine platform read into the Congressional
Record.

Although Pope Pius remained in Italy throughout the
convention and President Roosevelt remained in Washing-

ton, there were many non-followers who did faithfully attend and enthusiastically participate in all the sessions for Righteous Government. The most faithful and enthusiastic of all of these were men and women, both Negro and white, who openly identified themselves as members of the Communist party. They were obviously impressed by Father and his outline for world government, and he was just as obviously impressed by them. The communists said Father Divine was "wonderful, wonderful, wonderful," and Father returned their compliments. When anti-communist critics attacked him for inviting communists to his convention and for permitting them to take an active role in it, Father vigorously defended communism in an answer as clear and sharp as any he has ever given in his life. He said:

"I stand for anything that will deal justly between man and man. The communists stand for social equality and for justice in every issue and this is the principle for which I stand. I am not especially representing religion. I am representing God on earth among men and I will co-operate with an organization that will stand for the right and will deal justly."

Thus was inaugurated the flirtation between Father Divine and the Communist party, which would last on and off, with differing degrees of coyness on both sides, for some eight years. The Communist party was certain that it was utilizing Father Divine, and Father Divine was just as certain that it was he who was using the communists.

Perhaps the eight years of Father's co-operation with the communists were the only years during the existence of the movement when he could be identified as engaging in any program which other Negro mass leaders also engaged in. For during the 1930's Father Divine was not the only Negro leader to respond to communist courting. In the very midst of the depression, groping Negroes could not help but pull at any string that was dangled before them, and communism, seeming to offer equality and a sense of dignity no organized fighting group had ever offered before, seemed not just a string to be groped for but rather a strong rope to be tightly held to. It seemed to be a sort of last-shot answer. Many ministers co-operated with the communists to some extent during depression days. The plight of their congregations forced them to.

The terrible days of the thirties were no days for honeyed words. They were the days for plain, straight-from-the-shoulder talking. Most of the Negro ministers talked plain. And Father Divine, he with his twenty-syllable words, imitated their plain talk to the best of his ability. Sometimes the ministers' plain talk and even Father's talk sounded like what people have been accustomed to think of as communist talk. But the sound of the words could not be helped. It was the effect of them alone that had to be reckoned.

Reverend J. C. Austin, still today the highly respected pastor of Pilgrim Baptist Church in Chicago, is not a communist and certainly never was. But he had seen too many men and women of his congregation charged enormous rentals for filthy, rat-ridden apartments, and he was indignant. He had a huge sign hung out on the very front of his church.

"What must we do to be saved?" it asked. And answered its own question, not by exhorting for salvation through godliness but by stating the earthly conditions from which salvation was necessary. "Beset by rent hogs, overcrowded in hovels, come to the housing mass meeting Wednesday."

Negro churches throughout the country offered their pulpits in the 1930's to James W. Ford, many times candidate for Vice President on the Communist party ticket. Cleveland's Ebenezer Baptist Church was not peculiar when, in 1934, it brought two thousand people out to hear him one night.

The Scottsboro boys, openly sponsored by the Communist party, were also offered pulpits in Negro churches throughout the country.

None of the Negro ministers who so freely offered their pulpits were communists, and amazingly few members of their congregations were. It was just that, as they tell today, they were tired to death of seeing their congregations the coldest and hungriest of all cold and hungry Americans. It was just that the overwhelming majority of Negroes—and Negro ministers—agreed wholeheartedly with the young minister who, in 1934, told a world with ears too closed to hear him right, "We are tired of the gospel of 'dem golden slippers.' What we want are some thick-soled shoes."

To the tune of "thick-soled shoes," Negro ministers called meetings against high rentals and bad relief administration. To the tune of "thick-soled shoes," they organized marches on City Halls in city after city to dramatize and publicize their plight. To the tune of "thick-soled shoes," they undertook aggressive "Jobs-for-Negroes" campaigns.

And Father Divine—also to the tune of "thick-soled shoes"—embarked on the strange sea of communist co-operation.

An editorial in the *New Day* in 1933 defined Father's idea of the relative positions of the two co-operators.

"It is plain to see the extent to which Father Divine has co-operated with the communists insofar as their actions have been in harmony with his teachings, and it is gratifying to see to what extent communists co-operate with him; yet they do not participate or co-operate in the activities of any other religious movement. They recognize Father Divine and his principles as absolutely honest, sincere, and of constructive benefit to the people and even write constructive editorials concerning the movement."

In the usual switch-about inherent in Father's fantasy world, followers believed that all communists had already, or would shortly be forced to "throw away" their attitudes of anti-godliness in the recognition of Divine.

A story to illustrate this went the rounds of the heavens.

A man from the Republican party came, followers told each other, to speak at a Peace Mission meeting. Appearing on the same platform with a communist representative, he vigorously denounced the latter's party.

"In Russia churches have been destroyed," he said. "They have been bombed. They have been burned down. They have been razed to the ground. The communists are a godless people."

The communist representative answered his Republican attacker. It was true that some churches in Russia had suffered destruction. They had not been burned or razed by the government, however.

He said, "The people themselves, realizing that it was the

church which had for generations kept them in darkness and subjection, destroyed the symbols of their subjection. They could not be stopped." He turned to smile at Father Divine—significantly. "But we know there is a God!"

"Hallelujah!" the followers clapped loudly for the communist representative who knew God's face when he saw it.

The most publicized co-operation between the communists and Father Divine took place in 1934. It was at a huge parade organized by the Communist party, under the slogan "Fight War and Fascism." From the inception, differences between Father and the party were apparent. During the planning stages, the communists publicized it as a workers' parade of all racial and nationality groups. Their publicity claimed that thousands and thousands of workers would march under the banners of the countries of their origins. There would be Chinese workers, Japanese workers, Ukrainian workers, Turkish workers, Italian workers, Greek workers, and Father Divine Negro-American workers.

Father's representative explained the parade quite differently.

"Officially, it is known as the parade of the communists, and its slogan is 'Fight War and Fascism,' but this very readily co-operates with Father's Mission of Peace in a measure, since, stated more positively, it means 'Peace on earth and the brotherhood of all mankind.' It may be called the communist parade, but it is another of the mighty deeds of Father for New York City and all the world to see that God is reigning in the affairs of all men, whether they are conscious of it or not."

Apparently, the misled communists were not nearly so conscious of God's reign as they were interpreted to have been. For, on the day of the parade, even their banners revealed their lack of understanding. They marched under such ungodly heads as: "Workers of the World, Unite!" and "Down with Capitalist Imperialism!" Naturally, Father's signs sweetly counteracted the harshness of the communist ones. Their banners bore slogans like this: "Every Knee Shall Bow and Every Tongue Confess, Father Divine is God, God, God."

At ten-thirty on the morning of April 6, the parade

began. About twenty thousand marchers, one-third Divinite and two-thirds communist, participated. Divinites, led by God himself, who rode, especially for this occasion, in his most proletarian Packard car, started from headquarters at 20 West 115th Street and wended their way down Madison Avenue to Madison Square Park at Twenty-third Street.

As soon as he reached Madison Square Park, communist leaders pompously came to escort Father to his reserved seat on the platform. The communist leaders did not get to escort Father, though. The followers would not let them. Why should communist leaders who, even if they did unconsciously recognize Father's divinity, certainly did not completely admit it, be so close to God's body while true followers were to be pushed farther away? The communists were not entitled to such an honor. The followers saccharinely but stubbornly refused to give it to them. They kept their God surrounded. Where Father Divine went, there they would also go.

The way the ceremonious escort turned out, the communist leaders acted as buffers not only for God but also for his followers. They humbly went first and broke a path. Father walked mightily along the path, head held high, looking neither to left nor right. All the followers came directly behind him. When Divine finally was comfortably ensconced on the platform it was surrounded by followers; and the communists who had arrived first in order to secure desirable places found themselves pushed into the background.

Father's representative, reporting the parade to those followers who had been unfortunate enough to be unable to attend, stated unself-consciously:

"From the speakers' stand, it was an inspiring sight to look over the masses solidly filling the street for four blocks stretching into the park with every eye fixed on Father. Near at hand were the banners and placards declaring 'Father Divine is God,' while in the distance were those of the communists, depicting war and starvation."

After Father's arrival, the speeches began. Communists spoke first. They discussed "imperialist wars" waged by the United States and other capitalistic countries with but a single aim—to make rich men richer. They said, "In America and in England, life is cheap and money is precious." They enjoined their listeners to look at the millions of people who died every year of starvation. They said that thousands of children in New York City alone did not even know what milk tasted like.

On that note, Father Divine was introduced. Benignly, as God should, he surveyed the audience. Then, in the inimitable Divine fashion, he broke the gloom engendered by the communist speeches. He placed his hand on his breast. He smiled slightly. He said:

"Peace, everybody. Good health, good will, and good appetite for all the inhabitants of the world the same as it is for the inhabitants of New York. For this cause I came and for this purpose I stand advocating peace among the children of men and good will and love for all mankind."

While the communists bit their fingernails, the followers wildly applauded Father as the brightest star of the event.

After the parade, the communists did not malign Father. On the contrary, for many weeks they kept rationalizing his behavior as just one more example of what capitalist oppression did to poor Negroes. A *Daily Worker* editorial explained away the movement's "strange and foolish placards." It stated, "Father Divine is a true representative of the underprivileged black folk and as such must be worked with."

The "true representative" went on speaking at every communist meeting he was asked to speak at. Instead of pointing up the miserable fates of other unhappy black folk like himself, however, he enjoined his audience to have "good appetites." The communists became disgusted with him as a star speaker. They requested his attendance at fewer and fewer of their meetings.

Father was unperturbed by their rejection. He said, "Even though they have not or may not or do not know it, I work through the communists as through anybody."

"Amen," his followers said.

In 1941, when the depression was over and the Communist party's impact on Harlem was considerably reduced, Father Divine rejected it too. Whereas, in 1934, when an observer at the Madison Square Parade had accused him of being paid in Moscow gold for his co-operation, he had explained with grave calmness, "No, I never got any money from Moscow. It's the other way around in fact. I don't altogether agree with them, but I've helped them some," by 1941, he spoke in an entirely different vein. By 1941, he called the communists ungodly and cruel and un-American. And, by early 1950, he had declared himself, for the record, a "righteous fighter against the forces of communism."

Even though Father fights communism today, he does not worry about it. There are so many new and overwhelming improvements in government, he says, that the people have no reason for listening to communist propaganda.

Take this matter of segregation. Father Divine maintains that the South itself, the very same deep South which lynched him thirty-two times, that same South is today so impregnated with the Father Divine ideology that they want to run him for *the presidency of the United States.* Father is not one to publicize himself or to cry race relations improvements from the rooftops. He had not even told most of the followers about the South's offer to run him for President. It was just that he happened one day to be engaged in a conversation about conditions in the South with a visiting minister, Reverend E. A. Mays of Baton Rouge, Louisiana, and, since the Reverend had told him of some advancement in Louisiana race relations, he had told the Reverend how real the advancement was, and cited, as just one more little example of it, the South's desire to make him President.

The Reverend started the conversation. He told Father that, in Louisiana, "we have some one, a Negro, to be elected on the school board and another for council. So there are two Negroes to run, and there is a transformation taking place."

It was then Father gave out with his news. "Oh, sure, there is a transformation taking place. As soon as the people will allow me to extract that stigma of racism and the phrase that tends to low-rate out of them, we will be ready for the establishment of democracy effectively as I have it jurisdictionally." Quite unconcernedly, as though he did not know he was throwing the Reverend a bombshell, he added, "Sure. I do not recall now exactly what year it was they spoke of I running, of running me for the presidency down there."

"You?" Rev. Mays asked, "for President?"

"Yes. Sure. They did say the time was or should be right now."

"Oh? Yes?" Reverend Mays was beginning to regain his lost composure.

"But, of course," Father emphasized. He modestly added, "Personally, I am not seeking any office."

"I know you are not!" the Reverend said adamantly.

Father explained, "I have my office."

Reverend Mays knew Father had his office. "Yes, sir."

Father repeated that he did not seek the presidency. But he said that he was glad for this final proof of the fact that the South was so rapidly becoming inculcated with his ideal for true democracy. It proved that the thirty-two times he'd permitted himself to be lynched had not been in vain.

Father's followers believe, as Father himself does, that the South's offer to run him for President is very indicative of the good condition the world is in presently.

"Even though Father will never accept the presidency," Beautiful Peace says, "it makes me for one feel wonderful to know that the South offered it to him."

14

MISS HOLY GETS
"BOOK-L'ARNED"

If Father Divine should ever decide to run for the presidency of the United States, all of his followers, from the men and women who hold Doctor of Philosophy degrees right on down to the lowliest of them all, Miss Holy Grace, ninety-seven years old, former Kentucky slave child, would be able to vote for him and to influence other people to vote by talking about Father's virtues, and even, praise his holy name, by writing about them.

"If Father ever did runned for President," Miss Holy smiles a toothless grin at the absurdity of the idea of Father ever wanting to limit himself to the presidency of a single country, "I could help good's Miss Fern, she's the head of my school. Because now, ever since I come to Father I could read or write or work around with numbers, adding and taking away all like that." She shakes her head at herself, almost catching herself in a tiny white lie. "That is, I could read or write. I ain't so good for numbers. That is, I ain't so good for taking away big numbers from other big numbers, saying you want me to take away a big number 20,000 from another big number 69,000. I ain't so sure I can give the answer to it."

She smiles again to catch herself getting away from the idea of the original subject, Father's presidency, and returns to it to tell you that, since she can read today and since she can write and with Father inculcating her with his spirit, she could certainly be helpful in an election campaign for him. She stops smiling and laughs out loud.

"But you is silly to ask a question if Father wants to be President, could I be helpin'? You is silly. If Father wants to be President, nobody needs to be helpin'. If Father wants to be President, he just goes on and be's it. I don' need to be helpin' God."

She stops laughing and smiles once more. "If need be he wants me helpin', though, I could be helpin'. Account of even if I don't know numbers good, I sure knows readin' and writin' fine."

It may be that Miss Holy Grace, who lives at a Peace Mission headquarters in Harlem, is the oldest elementary school student on record in this country. In 1948, when she was ninety-three years old, she first applied for admission to the Peace School of New York at 128th Street. For the four years that she had been in attendance there, her record was excellent. Her effort's been tremendous and her conduct fine. Although her arithmetic is still poor and her penmanship can stand improvement, she is turning out to be a prize pupil in the class called U.S.A. Sometimes, she is discouraged because she does not progress fast enough to suit her perfectionist standards. Most times, though, she is delighted with herself.

"I'm about to bust with joy," she says. "Who'd think I'd know readin' and writin'?"

Back in South Carolina on Massa John's cotton plantation, none of the slave men and women would ever have thought that Holy Grace would learn reading and writing.

Today, she says, "What a shiverin'-scared little 'un I used to be. Never could learn nothin', not only readin' nor writin'." She smiles to think of herself in the days of her early childhood and to think how it was that she, such a happy angel today, could never smile at all in those days. She thinks back, remembering, and shudders to remember.

When Miss Holy Grace was five years old, "lil' Massa William, he was the lil' ol' boy belongin' to big Massa John, pulled my pigtail."

Today, ninety-two years after the incident, Miss Grace recalls it with tears in her voice. She tells:

"I go on up to Aunt Eliza was my so-called ma. 'Massa William pulled my pigtail,' I tell her."

Aunt Eliza held Miss Grace close to her large bosom. "Poor lil' ol' girl," she muttered, "gotta learn your lesson, honey. Might's well learn soon's late. Lil' nigger child expect to have her pigtails pulled."

Aunt Eliza's words seared deep.

"That wasn't the onliest time," Miss Grace tells, "my so-called ma told me that 'lil' nigger child expect, lil' nigger child expect.' I keep thinking nothing good could happen to me, only bad things, 'cause I was a little child of the darker complexion."

When Miss Grace was seven years old, something good did happen to her even though she thought it never could. President Abraham Lincoln signed the Emancipation Proclamation that made her and the other slaves free.

"That was way back long ago," she says. "Us'n of the darker complexion called it the hallelujah year. All the time then, the so-called ma says, 'Honey, we's free. We's free!' I don't know what that means though, free!"

After the hallelujah year, Miss Grace and Aunt Eliza and the other former slaves had continued to work around Massa John's plantation. It was not far different than it had been before except for the fact that Massa John and the Mistress and little Massa William had packed up and gone away, just gone away to nobody knew where, and the former slaves had stayed on the plantation, working it without supervision. Instead of planting cotton, they'd planted food that they could live on in the spring and in the summer and that they could put away for winter eating. The crops never had grown "lush" for the ex-slaves, though, never had grown the way they'd used to grow for Massa John.

Miss Grace recalls great hunger when the crops didn't grow in the early years after the Proclamation.

"I seen me to be a skinny little 'un," she says. "In them days I keep thinking, 'Just the way it gotta be. Lil' ol' dark-complected child got to expect big hunger.'"

Miss Grace, in her earliest years, accepted everything that happened to her with the stoicism induced by her slave psychology. The Emancipation Proclamation never did succeed in blotting out or making less important the experiences of her first seven years. "Lil' nigger child," she thought, and was enabled to survive because of that thinking. When her mother died shortly after Holy Grace's twelfth birthday, she did not cry or carry on. She merely accepted the death, despite her sadness, as her just due.

When a job was found for her in the home of a family named Haislip who lived just outside Charleston, and when she was assigned long arduous workdays by Mrs. Haislip with no time for play, she accepted that as her just due too. She even learned to love the people who made her work so hard.

"I never thought they done me wrong," she says today, knowing full well how much wrong they did do her then. "I just never did think it a little bit. It used to look right to me in them days—light-complected young 'uns plays, dark-complected young 'uns work, all day, sometimes in the nighttime too."

The Haislips gave Holy Grace a room in their house. They fed her, not too well, but better than she'd eaten at Massa John's. Sometimes they bought clothes for her. Aside from the cooking and cleaning, she was assigned partial care of their twin boys, Barty and Roddy, who were not quite a year old when she came there.

Twenty-five years after she had first come to the Haislip home, when Barty and Roddy were grown men and married, Miss Grace left the household. She left because Mr. and Mrs. Haislip gave up their house after the boys married and went East to live in an apartment. More than anything Miss Grace wanted to go with them. The Haislips said they were sorry, but there would be no room for her in the small apartment. She had been a good servant and a loyal one and they would always feel some sense of responsibility for her. But . . .

Miss Grace was panic-stricken. Living with the Haislips had become a habit with her. The Haislips were her only family. She loved them because she had no one else to love. She depended on Mrs. Haislip to tell her how to behave and what to wear. She catered to Mr. Haislip. And she adored the boys, feeling possessive about them as she might have felt about her own children if she had had any. Now, with the Haislips going out of her life, where would she turn, what would she do? Whom would she love?

"I was still thinkin' about me the way slaves thinks," she says. "I was worryin' about me 'cause I didn't know who would take care."

Then one day Holy Grace's problem solved itself. Her

"baby," Mr. Barty, and his brand-new wife, Miss Jean, said they would take her into their home.

In addition to supplying her room and board and clothes, Mr. Barty said he and Miss Jean would pay Miss Grace $2.00 a week which would be all hers to use just as she saw fit.

"I don't know what to tell y'all," she said, "exceptin' you're sure 'nuff makin' me happy."

Miss Grace stayed with Mr. Barty and Miss Jean for twenty-nine years, four years longer than she'd been with the older Haislips. They moved from Charleston to New York, and Miss Grace moved with them. She took care of their three boys and their girl, Miss Patty Ann, and saw all four of them married. She thought she was set forever in the Haislip home. Miss Jean was satisfied with her, and she was certainly satisfied with Miss Jean and Mr. Barty. Then, suddenly, without warning, for he had hardly been ill a day in his life, Mr. Barty died.

Miss Grace's first overwhelming insecurity since she had joined the older Haislips' household came with Mr. Barty's death. She felt it keenly. In one way, it was like seeing her own baby die. That was sorrow enough. Mr. Barty's death was something else to Miss Grace too, though. It was the bleak fact of being sixty-seven years old with no family, no friends, no money, and no place to turn.

At first, Miss Grace was sure she could count on Miss Jean. But then, she knew she couldn't. For Miss Jean was too broken up over her husband's death to care about anything else. She was moving to her sister's apartment in Philadelphia. Her sister had her own maid and the apartment was small and, of course, much as Miss Jean regretted it, there would be no room for Miss Grace.

After Miss Jean left for Philadelphia, Miss Grace found another job with a family named Collins. The Collinses were born and bred New Yorkers, and they did not understand Miss Grace's need to identify herself with them. They did not like her possessiveness about them. Her abject devotion made them laugh sometimes. It often made them angry.

"I want a servant," Mrs. Collins told her husband, "not a damned old slavey."

The climax of Miss Grace's difficulties with the Collinses came one day when she'd been with them for some six months. Damy, the baby, had a cold, and Miss Grace, instead of treating him as his mother ordered, gave him a camphor plaster which she'd always used when Mr. Barty was a baby. When Mrs. Collins remonstrated with her, Miss Grace said, "I love my baby, ma'am, and I knows this——"

Mrs. Collins never gave Miss Grace a change to finish her justification. "Damy is my baby," she said, "and I'd appreciate it if you'd leave this house before tomorrow morning. You'll get a week's discharge pay, of course."

After her job with the Collinses, Holy Grace could not find a permanent job. New York employers did not understand her. The psychology of the Southern slave servant was foreign to them, and they had little sympathy for it. They wanted Miss Grace to do her work, collect her pay, and mind her business. How were they to know that, all her life, Miss Grace's only business had centered around "her families"? Even if they had known it, could they possibly have been able to like it? And Miss Grace was old and feeble by the time she left Mr. Barty's house. Certainly, she was not the most efficient worker available.

Anyone who condemns Father Divine and his Peace Mission movement wholesale ought to talk for an hour with Miss Holy Grace.

Miss Grace says, "I know Father 'n God's one. I know 'cause of what he done for me. Sometimes, I wake up in the night, thinkin', 'Father, you're a dream.' Ain't no dream, though. I see him every day with my own two eyes."

After she had failed at all the live-in jobs she'd tried to get and been refused day's-work jobs because of her age and delicacy, Miss Grace had come to Father Divine. A Negro social worker in the Department of Welfare had told her about him. She'd hardly known what she was doing, the day she'd found herself inside the door of the 128th Street heaven.

A woman sitting on a bench in the lobby stood up when she saw Miss Holy Grace.

"Peace, sister."

Miss Holy Grace repeated, "Peace." The welfare worker had instructed her about the salutation.

The woman got Miss Grace a seat. She asked her about herself and what had brought her to the mission. She talked about Father Divine and the whole heavenly family. It was good, warm, companionable talk.

"I know you is God!" Today, Miss Holy Grace says that when she saw Father at the first Divine banquet she ever attended, the recognition of who he was hit her, the inferiority feeling that had been with her all her life left her, and she rose from her chair and yelled out, loud and clear, so everyone could hear her, "Father Divine, I know you is God!"

For Miss Holy Grace, life began at eighty-six. In the Divine Peace Mission movement, she found warmth and attention and self-respect.

"Ain't no slaves," she says today, "ain't no massas. Complexions don't make differences."

In the Peace Mission movement, Holy Grace found a family.

"Sure 'nuff Father Divine been a father to me. All the lady angels been sisters. The men been brothers."

She found a job. Working as a cleaning woman in Father's mission, she knows that she is paying for the benefits she is receiving.

No one can doubt the value of what Father Divine did for Holy Grace. Now, six years after she came to him, he is making her another important gift. He is allowing her to attend the Divine Peace Mission school. She is learning to read and to write and to be a patriotic American. She can recite the Declaration of Independence word for word, and is being taught the meaning of the Constitution of the United States.

"I'm learnin' writin'," she proudly reports. "I'm learnin' readin' too. It's all that good God, Father Divine, is puttin' his spirit right on in my lil' ol' slowpoke brain and makin' me learn so fast can't hardly believe it."

It was a strong drive that forced Miss Holy Grace to seek an education at her age. It was a desire to read, for herself, the words uttered by her Lord. From the day she'd first become a follower, she had been buying the *New*

Day religiously. She'd been taking the papers as she acquired them and placing them on the floor beside her bed. A lovely woolen stole which she had knit during her spare time in the twenty-nine years she'd worked for her "last family" protected them from the bare floor. Now, she owned a stack as tall as herself.

"I wanted to know to read them *New Days* so bad," she tells today. "I wanted to come and be sittin' in my chair and them beautiful words of Father Divine just belonging to me like they can belong to anybody knows how to read them."

The other followers had always been kind to Miss Holy Grace before she'd learned to read for herself. Whenever she had attempted to press one or the other of the angels into duty to read the *New Day* to her, the angel had always been happy to oblige. But Miss Holy Grace felt a yearning to make herself independent of other followers.

"Used to be I thought me to be dumb," she says. "Them days with Massa John and then later and then me with them families I worked for in New York didn' want nothin' to do with me. Father put the wonderful spirit in this old temple and showed me. 'You ain't dumb, Holy Grace, but you is smarter than them light-complected peoples, Massa John 'n all them, because you is one of my chosen, sure enough.' "

Father Divine came in a vision to Holy Grace. He wasn't bald in the picture she saw. He had smooth, silky hair. And a gold crown topped the silky hair.

"You got to go to school," Father admonished. "Now you is free 'n one of the chosen, you got to learn to be smart also."

At first, Miss Holy Grace was afraid to go to school. Then, one Sunday, Father Divine came to New York and to Miss Grace's mission. She requested and received an interview with him.

She said, "I know you is God an' you can put your spirit workin' an' learn me to read." She told Father how desperate she was to be able to read the *New Day* and how, if only she could do that, she would consider her life fulfilled.

Father took her shaking hand. He held it for a while in his own. Holy Grace will always remember what he told her.

"You *will* be able to read, my sweetheart," Father said.

Then, Miss Grace felt unafraid.

On the Monday following her interview with Father Divine, she requested discussion with Miss Fern, head teacher of the New York Peace Mission school.

"We are happy to have you with us," Miss Fern assured Miss Grace.

Miss Holy Grace is one of only two ex-slaves who attend the Peace Mission school. But her needs are considered in curriculum planning.

"If we can teach Holy Grace," Miss Fern says, "then we can certainly teach the others." The job with them is not always far easier than it is with Miss Grace either. After all, most of them were born and bred in Southern rural areas. They are products of the South's separate school systems still maintained today.

Miss Fern knows that, today, at least 15 per cent of Southern Negro school-age youngsters have never set foot inside a schoolroom, and at least 60 per cent have never gone beyond fifth grade. She knows that, in the South, there are few rural areas with enough Negro schools to meet the needs of their populations, and that there are many rural areas with large Negro populations that have no schools at all. Miss Fern knows that, today, while white rural students have individual desks and are provided with supplies, paper, ink, chalk, and books, Negro students, six or eight of them together, are required to share tables and are not provided with supplies. She knows that, today, Negro teachers are inferior to white ones because they receive salaries that are sometimes less than half what white teachers receive and because there are no educational requirements imposed upon them as there are upon white teachers, and because most of them work as the only teachers in one-room schoolhouses containing all ages and grades of students, and because after they have finished teaching every subject in their curricula, Negro teachers are then required to render janitorial services in their buildings. She knows that, today, truancy laws for Negro students are not enforced and that Negro schools have no real time schedules but are dependent on the schedules of the surrounding plantation owners.

"I know these terrible things," Miss Fern says, "partly by reading about them and also from my experiences with my own students."

Miss Fern has a student in her eighth grade called Lovely Life. Miss Life is twenty-nine years old. She grew up on a farm in North Carolina. "There wasn't no school in my place," she says. "Oh yeah, there used to be one just about twelve miles from the farm me 'n the so-called family lived on. How's I gonna get to it, though, in the wintertime. Walk? No. I ain't never had no learnin' before I come to Father."

There is a student named Sweet Peace in Miss Fern's seventh grade. She is twenty-five years old and had spent all of her life before she came to Father on a Florida cotton plantation. "I gone to school," she said, "right on through to class four. Then, I didn't go no more. I didn't like that school. My teacher, Miss Robertson, didn't know how to learn us kids. And there used to be blackboards in the school but never no chalk to write on them with. Miss Robertson used to have five pencils sometimes when I used to be in class, and us forty-five kids used to fight over who was going to get to use them."

Miss Sweet Devotion, who is twenty-seven and also grew up, as Sweet Peace did, on a cotton plantation in Florida and is also, as Miss Sweet Peace is today, a Divine seventh-grader, did want to go to school when she was young. The sessions, though, were too short to do her any good.

"School'd just be getting started nice," she tells. "You'd be learning something. All of a sudden in comes the boss-man. He looks around us chillun and talks to the teacher. 'I need these here chillun for pickin',' he says. Next thing you knows, they don't even tell you nothing about closing down. It's only you come to school that morning the same's any other morning, and you can't get in the door. It's locked up too tight. No teacher's in the class. So you do like the other chillun. You get down in the fields and you start in picking. First off, you care because you want to go to school and they won't let you. Then, you don't care no more."

Father Divine's Peace Mission school curriculum, being aimed around the needs of Sweet Devotion, who does admit now that she cares about securing an education, and around Sweet Peace and Lovely Life—and Miss Holy Grace is unique.

Miss Grace, Miss Peace, Miss Life, and their co-students are being informed about practical things. They are shown how to dial telephones and how to travel on the subway. They are instructed how to read street signs and how to ask for directions. They are taught how to talk.

Like in the most progressive children's schools, Divinites learn by doing.

Spelling is learned by the handling of familiar household articles which have their names printed on them with large letters. Thus, students have learned how to spell "soap" and "cleanser" and "detergent" and "insecticide" and "pot" and "kettle." It is learned by the reading of familiar signs. Lenox Avenue. 128th Street. Subway Station. From the spelling of the familiar, the teachers bring their students on to the spelling of the unfamiliar. And always there is the lodestar in view—"Soon, soon, you yourself will be able to read the *New Day*. Father's words will be your possessions, your very own, never to be taken away from you."

Reading is taught the same way as spelling is. Students are brought from consideration of the familiar to the unfamiliar. Arithmetic is taught in that way, too. Students learn to distinguish between different pieces of money. They count a hundred cents to make a dollar. And ten dimes. And nine dimes and two nickels. From these simple problems, they go on to more difficult ones.

Music is taught in all its phases. Singing is simple, since there are all the devotional songs to be sung. Piano is also taught. And if a student has a genuine desire to learn any other instrument, that is generally encouraged.

Simple facts about astronomy are learned by watching morning, day, and night merge into one another or by considering the effects of the various seasons of the year. From the easy knowledge that winter is cold and summer is hot, students learn the whys and wherefores of natural phenomena.

English and enunciation are learned by listening to the radio commentators and absorbing and discussing their techniques.

There is little formal organization in the Divine schools. Aside from the requirements which, being unwavering from year to year, are listed on report cards as Arithmetic, English, U.S.A. Class, Reading, Spelling, Penmanship, and Music, subject matter is variable and dependent on the needs of the pupils. If there is something a student wishes to learn and a teacher can be found to instruct in it, a class is set up and it becomes incorporated into the curriculum for at least one semester.

The requirements for teachers are also informal. Those who feel the call may volunteer to Father to become schoolteachers, and if he recognizes their spiritual validity for that calling, he will appoint them. They work without salary. Fortunately, there are a sufficient number of trained and experienced and even highly trained and highly experienced schoolteachers, so that it is they who staff most of the classrooms.

Typical of these dedicated people are Miss Fern, responsible for a great number of the techniques, white, University of California educated; Miss Gladys, who took her M.A. training at the University of Chicago and taught for a great many years before she joined Father; Miss Anne Sterrit, who is presently teaching and very effectively in a New York public school; and Chester and LaVere Belstrom, white, education majors and Ph.D.s, who taught in Minneapolis public schools and in Montclair, New Jersey, for many years.

None of the schools has a principal, since, according to Miss Fern, "Father's mind and spirit eliminate the need." She adds, in true Divine fashion, "If only the whole world would conduct its schools the way we do, no school would need a principal. At the present time, of course, that is too much to expect, even though Father has gone to great trouble in instructing them how to proceed. The reason we need no principal is because we aren't paid for our work and are therefore performing for the love of it."

The dedication and the idealism of the teachers, which Miss Fern always points out, is unquestionable. One must wonder, however, how it is that, on the whole, their program is such a basically effective and even practical one.

Only after a long time in a Divine Peace Mission school

does the answer to the practicality appear. It lies in the true love these teachers have for their students and in the strong identification they feel with them. That is why they instinctively know how best to help them. That is why they are able to utilize the informal instructional methods, which are admittedly more difficult for teachers to use than the formal methods are. Divine teachers have all the patience in the world, and place no limits on the time required to teach one student.

Strangely, despite the teaching informality, Father Divine's schools have more rigid scholastic requirements than ordinary schools do. From his elderly students, just as much as from the younger ones who attend public school on the outside, Father demands perfection.

"One hundred per cent won't do," he said meaningfully. "Pupils who are learning in the schools must make one hundred per cent plus."

Father has instituted a new kind of grading. Significances of marks are defined on the students' end-term report cards:

> AA—200
> A—95—100
> B—85—95
> C—75—85
> D—65—75
> F—Below 65—Failing

Last semester, the one ending in February, 1952, Miss Holy Grace was inconsolable. That was the semester when she tried to make the required 200 per cent—but couldn't. Although she received her teacher's distinctly unqualified AA in conduct and in effort, her difficulty in grasping even the rudiments of arithmetic brought her average down so badly that AA was out of the question and the attainment of even a plain A was impossible. She received a mere B. If she hadn't been so brilliant in the class called U.S.A., her grade might have been lower still.

U.S.A. Class is the most important course in the Peace Mission curriculum from Father Divine's viewpoint. It teaches about Americanism and citizenship and government. It teaches the Declaration of Independence, and the

Constitution, word for word. Miss Holy Grace can recite, without having to stop to think, many clauses of the Declaration and of the Constitution. Two years ago, when she was ninety-five, she was chosen by the U.S.A. teacher to star in the class's dramatic presentation of "The Boston Tea Party."

Dressed in the costume of the period, she hobbled out onto the auditorium stage.

"I want to have liberty," she screamed into the loudspeaker, "or else I will die."

Some of her friends dumped tea into Boston Harbor.

Miss Fern tells that there are some students who attend the U.S.A. class who do not need to attend other classes. These are the ones who, while they attended Negro Southern schools and learned the rudiments of reading and writing and arithmetic, never did learn citizenship.

Twenty-two-year-old Sweet Dove, who went through the eighth grade of a school in Georgia, explains this: "The light-complected school had a course called 'civics.' We didn't, though. We had one called 'character building.' While the children of the lighter complexion learned about the Constitution and all, we learned what they called 'courtesy' and 'humility.'"

Father Divine, while he strives for courtesy among his followers, has renounced humility and made the Divine Peace Mission schools his idea of a slap at segregation. In his own fashion, he describes them that way.

"You have been taught in your schools," he tells Negroes, "but you have been fooled. You thought many things you were taught in school were just and right, even your cursed, vulgar names by which they called you . . . Every school that teaches segregation is in violation of the Constitution and its amendments and is undermining the foundations of the government . . . Let them see our schools in operation and learn from us."

Father Divine is correct in his assumption that outside educators could learn a race relations lesson from Peace Mission schools. They could, as a matter of fact, learn more than a race relations lesson. For, from a practical point of view, the Divine Peace Mission adult schools have accomplished more than some other adult schools which receive due recognition from Boards of Education. They are exactly what Father calls them, "living samples and examples" of the fact that sometimes faith and loving-kindness can achieve more, where human beings are concerned, than practical brilliance can.

"Faith and loving-kindness accomplish miracles in our schools as elsewhere," Father smiles. "It can move mountains."

15

ONE LITTLE NAY?

Faith and loving-kindness moved mountains and made Father Divine and his Peace Mission movement wealthier than a great many more brilliant, more practical men and movements. Faith and loving-kindness transformed Father Divine from a somewhat ridiculous itinerant preacher to a real estate tycoon whose holdings today are valued, in New York, Newark, and Philadelphia alone, at over six million dollars. Faith and loving-kindness, more than brains and practicality, made it possible for Father Divine, today and in all the years he has been functioning as God, to provide many thousands of followers and numerous outsiders with excellent meals and fine residences at what he calls "evangelical rates."

"It is wonderful, wonderful, wonderful," Father says.

It is wonderful.

In the Divine Peace Mission movement, a person can secure a good meal consisting of meat, vegetables, bread, and butter for twenty cents. Up until recently, the same meal would have cost him fifteen cents. A person can attend a Divine banquet of thirty courses or more for a minimum cost of thirty cents. Until not too long ago, he could have attended free.

A person can live at the Divine Riviera Hotel in one of Newark's fine residential neighborhoods, exceptionally convenient to downtown, for two dollars per week. Before the Peace Mission movement acquired the Divine Riviera, the rate was the prevalent minimum of five dollars a day. It is the same at the Philadelphia hotels, Divine Lorraine and Divine Tracy.

A person in need of a week in the country can go to Pine Brook Hotel, twenty miles out of Newark among the pleasant New Jersey hills, and secure lodging for two dollars per week and more than adequate meals for thirty cents each. The recreational facilities, swimming pool, croquet, etc., come without charge.

Despite the expenditures that must come with maintaining heavenly hotels at weekly rates that are lower than mortal hotels charge daily and serving appetizing, even elaborate, meals at less money than the raw foods would ordinarily cost, Father himself lives in luxury. How does he do it?

Austin Norris is the outsider who is closest to Divine business manipulations. He says, "Father Divine's success can be explained with one simple word—co-operation. The Peace Mission movement is doubtless the most successful example of co-operation in the world today. It is organized as a combine of small co-operatives, groups of men and women banded together to purchase real estate or to buy businesses. It is organized on principles of honesty and justice taught by Father, and is effectively held together by the love and trust all the members feel toward him. Most important, all the co-operators have no interest in the profit motive. They really don't wish to make money for themselves. They are in business for one reason and one reason only—advancement of the cause of their God."

Attorney Norris is not exaggerating Father's followers' business motivations. The followers, themselves, explain these.

"Money is nothing to me," says Mr. Sober Living, part-owner of a successful Divine restaurant. "I am not a businessman, but an angel. God is all that matters."

Miss Lovely Life, a large investor in a Divine apartment house, echoes Mr. Sober Living.

"Why do I need money," she asks, "when I got Father?"

Attorney Norris says, "You cannot probe the Divine financial mystery unless you do two things. First you must realize that Divine co-operators are completely unlike worldly ones in that they just do not recognize the existence of the profit motive. Then you must compare Divine business investment and maintenance with worldly business investment and maintenance. Take a restaurant, for example, that has been bought by a group of worldly owners and compare its owners' principles with the principles of Divine restaurant owners. . . ."

If a restaurant has been bought by a group of worldly owners, they have each made capital investments. They have maintenance expenses. They must pay for whatever labor they employ, for their cooks and waitresses and hosts. They must buy raw foods. Their operating costs are considerable. Then, naturally, as businessmen, they demand returns on their capital investments. The very idea of serving meals, as Divine restaurants do, at fifteen to thirty cents a meal, would be laughable to them.

To Divine restaurant owners, however, the fifteen- to thirty-cent meals are not only realities but also, as Mr. Norris points out, their reason for being in business. Unlike mortal restaurateurs, Divine restaurant owners want no return from the capital investments Father Divine has "blessed" them to make. They don't want to earn from their restaurants any more money than exactly what they absolutely need to live on. Few mortal restaurant owners would be satisfied with a maximum take-home of fifteen dollars per week. Divine owners are more than satisfied. Fifteen dollars provides them with board and lodging in approved hotels and kingdoms and with pocket money for approved outside expenses.

Divine restaurant owners are also enabled to effect other more conspicuous savings than take-home money. They save a lot on rent, for instance. Their restaurants, like all Divine businesses, are operated in co-operatively owned buildings whose owners' motives are similar to these of the restaurant owners . . . advancement of Father Divine. The rent charges are low. Therefore, while they are comfortably furnished, these restaurants, not having to depend on "atmosphere" to attract clientele, are enabled to dispense with expensive, luxurious equipment.

On raw food very striking savings are made. It comes, generally, from co-operative farms operated without profit motives, or from co-operative stores and markets also operating for the good of the cause.

It is, however, on the cost of service that Divine restaurants practice their most overwhelming economies. For the managers and the cooks and the waitresses contribute their labor for subsistence return, as their service to God. Instead of money wages, they receive maintenance in hotels and kingdoms which are run on the same principles as the restaurants and get their food in the restaurants they work for.

The co-operative hotels and rooming houses, which can afford to offer comfortable lodgings at $1.50 to $2.00 per week, are run as the restaurants are. The "mystery" of how these hotels and rooming houses function is no more real than the restaurant "mystery" when adequate analysis is made.

A typical Philadelphia rooming house for sisters has several floors. Comfortably furnished lounge-rooms, dining rooms, and kitchens are on the first floor. The upper floors contain sleeping rooms, a few of them single, most furnished dormitory style. In the smallest room is one double bed for the accommodation of two sisters. In the largest room are twelve beds for the accommodation of twenty-four. Bathroom facilities are adequate, with a division of baths and showers.

Because the price is low, occupancy of this rooming house is practically 100 per cent the year 'round. The sacrifice of privacy in the living is reckoned as unimportant by the followers and has no influence in creating vacancies.

"Privacy?" Miss Sweetness Love laughs when you ask her if she misses her privacy. "That's silly. I'm living here with five sisters in spirit. We all know God. We get along good and there's only one bedmate with me. Back when I was young, up on 134th Street right off Seventh Avenue, there was still three of us families having to pool our money for to rent a five-room apartment."

The room of Sweetness Love and her five roommates is attractive. It, like every room in a Divine house or hotel, is scrupulously clean and attractively furnished. There are pink candlewick spreads on the beds. The curtains on the wide windows are also pink and blend well with the light-gray walls.

Sweetness Love and her housemates are satisfied guests. The forty-odd owners of the rooming house for sisters are satisfied landlords. They are helping to maintain God's work and, just incidentally, they are not losing money.

At the present prevailing rate of $2.00 per week per person, this rooming house for 100 young women takes in $10,400 a year. Five full-time maintenance people service the building. Their work is a labor of love. They put in long, arduous hours. They never watch clocks. And instead of payment for their services, they receive maintenance. Rooms are provided for them at the regular $2.00 weekly rate. A maximum of $.75 pays for their three daily meals. Even with the provision of a little pocket cash, their weekly expenses can be easily met by an output of $10.00 per week for each of them. The cost of providing their service for a year comes to $2600 for all five. Perhaps the rooming-house owners spend another $2600 for annual maintenance and repair—perhaps not. For repair work, like other service, is rendered on a maintenance basis.

Total annual expenses for administration of this 100-person rooming house are about $5200. If $2000, a generous figure, is added for other maintenance items, total expenses become $7200. At the end of a year, the rooming-house co-operators are left with an actual $3000 profit. To Divine investors, this is a more than ample return on their capital.

Other businesses operate exactly as the restaurants and residences do. There are hundreds of them. Small co-operatives—garages, meat markets, painters, grocers, building contractors, tailors, furriers, photographers—are scattered about New York, Newark, and Philadelphia. There are also Divine co-operative businesses in Detroit, Cleveland, Chicago, and Baltimore, and as far west as Seattle, San Francisco, and Los Angeles. Although the individual businesses operate independently of one another, they are mutually friendly and help each other out whenever they can. The mutual help is inspired by two facts, first that there are many followers who hold some interest in several businesses, and, more important, that they feel thoroughly united by their universal loyalty to "Father's principles."

What are "Father's principles"?

The most important of "Father's principles" naturally concerns his followers' faith. Business co-operators must recognize Divine as their entire security, present and future. They do recognize him that way.

"Father Divine serves as the followers' rock of security,"

comments an attorney who is handling some of Father's legal work. "Their naïveté is unbelievable. You would have to see it to believe it." He describes one way in which Father guarantees the success of any business under his jurisdiction. He says that followers always set up what is called "Father's office."

"Father's office," furnished with his desk and chair, is located in a separate part of the business premises.

When they need to consult Father about a business problem, businessmen sit in his chair and "converse" with him.

"He is here, there, and everywhere—impersonally," they say.

What Father's spirit tells the followers to do guarantees the success of their businesses.

Father's second most important principle concerns the financing of Peace Mission businesses. He insists that his followers pay cash for every purchase.

"If you pay a million dollars for an hotel," he says, "or ten cents for an item in F. W. Woolworth and Company, you must pay cash."

Father tells his followers that credit is "lowering to your prestige" and not consistent with truly honest behavior. No Divinite has ever applied for or accepted credit in any business transaction. When Father's followers purchase properties, they always bring their payments in cash.

In 1948, when they purchased Newark's Riviera Hotel for $500,000, they sent a purchase delegation from Philadelphia to Newark lugging heavy suitcases crammed chockfull of one-, five-, ten-, and twenty-dollar bills wrapped in brown paper. The sanctimonious group arrived, smiling. They came without a guard and went immediately to the Federal Trust Company, where it took ten tellers two hours to count the money.

When they were questioned about their fearlessness in carrying so much money unguarded, Executive Secretary John Germaine, speaking for the group, matter-of-factly declared, "We trusted in the Lord, as always."

Questioned about their reasons for paying in cash instead of by check, Mr. Germaine replied, "Cash payment is God's principle."

Father's third important principle is practical and clearly aimed at preventing outsiders to the movement, relatives of any of his co-operators who may be foolish enough to die instead of living forever, from acquiring any kind of a hold on Peace Mission properties. Even though he does not approve admitting the reality of death, he relishes even less being involved in legal disputes wherein dead co-operators' legal heirs may ask for their property shares. He insures that, on the death of any one of the co-operators, his property shares, instead of being subject to claims by his mortal family, will revert to the surviving Divine co-operators. He tells his followers:

"It should be distinctly understood that such [co-operative] business is to be owned and operated by those in charge as joint tenants, not as tenants in common but as joint tenants, with right of survivorship, each business being an individual independent enterprise or being an individual independent unit."

Father Divine says, and the followers verify his statement, that his chief relationship with the co-operatives is that of adviser. It works this way. A group of followers evolve an idea for a co-operative business, or property. They consult Father as to the efficacy. Or, sometimes, Father himself suggests to a group of followers that they form a co-operative to purchase a specific property which has been offered to him.

Father's followers own thirteen incorporated home and church training schools in this country. They own fourteen residence clubs for women and nine for men. They own eighteen tremendous and expensive country mansions. They own twenty-nine apartment houses. They own eight small hotels and four large ones. They own, in addition, eleven properties in seven foreign countries: England, Australia, West Germany, Austria, Canada, Panama, and Switzerland.

Until recently, co-operating purchasers bought properties under the Divine names by which they identify themselves. Thus, the deed to a Divine mansion in Newark's Forest Hill section lists all of its twenty-five owners: Snow White, Honey Bee Love, Holy Ivy, Keep On Smiling, Joy Love, Perfect Love, Perfect May Love, Meekness Love,

Beautiful Smiles Love . . . Newark's Divine Riviera Hotel lists about two hundred such names on its deed. Philadelphia's Hotel Divine Lorraine lists about five hundred.

Attorney Norris, ever since he began to work with Father Divine, has been urging him to change his property-buying methods. He says, "I kept telling him how impractical it was, pointing out that properties containing so many of such names would be very difficult to sell. I told him that few prospective buyers would undertake to search deeds with so many names in them. Father was stubborn, though. For years he rejected my advice. Whenever I talked to him about deed-searching and so forth, he answered me the same way, 'The followers who put up money for a property or the ones who work it are the real owners, so why not put it in their names?'"

Very recently, Father yielded to his attorney's opinion. Most followers who co-operate to make property purchases today make them in the name of the Father Divine Peace Mission movement through its four branch churches, the Palace Mission Church, the Circle Mission Church, the Unity Mission Church, and the Nazareth Mission Church. Although these are incorporated individual religious corporations, they are defined also as branches of the mother church.

"The branch churches are incorporated under the mother church, the Peace Mission movement," Father says, "of which I am the founder, bishop, and pastor."

Branch churches are supported by their members. Members who work outside the Peace Mission can contribute to their branch churches as they feel "volitionally moved to do so." Most members are very volitionally generous. If branch church properties yield profits, these are utilized in the maintenance of the branch churches.

Branch churches render services both to the Peace Mission members and to outsiders, which have been calculated to increase membership and to gain for Father Divine the respect of the unassociated. They conduct banquets where Father's speeches are the main items on the agenda. They maintain chapels for preaching and meditation and conduct Bible classes. They operate schools and employment agencies. They hold Righteous Government meetings. They sponsor educational movies, which are open to the public, and in some cases open their buildings as recreation centers "for the underprivileged." They maintain rooming house and apartment house and hotel accommodations at "evangelical rates."

The churches, and their properties, are administered by boards of trustees, answerable of course to Father Divine. According to format, trustees are elected at annual meetings of the church groups. Actually, they are appointed by Father Divine and approved by his adoring congregations. The number of trustees varies from one election to another. It is more dependent on Father Divine's whim than it is on any specific need.

On Sunday morning, February 12, 1950, the Circle Mission Home, School, and Training School of New York held its annual meeting at 2064 Boston Road in the Bronx, with Father Divine presiding. After the president's and treasurer's reports, and eulogies to Father Divine were read, Father asked for the roll call of the fifteen-man trustee board and the names of those who were to be "either reelected or replaced." There were five, including the president, Saint Mary Bloom; the vice president, True Sincerity; the secretary, Marguerite Bell; the assistant secretary, True Love; and the treasurer, Peaceful Rachel. Father asked them all to join him on the platform.

"In the board of trustees," he told the gathered church group, "we have five here whose term expires at this annual meeting and here they are and there they stand. If anyone here has any nominee to nominate for the replacement of either one of these trustees, you may present them. If not, you may pass on each one by motion. It may be that someone has some nominee they would like to have replaced; by that I mean, to replace the ones that are now going out on this term; or it may be that you may desire to have these replaced or succeed themselves for the next term."

Only one trustee was recommended for replacement. A young girl, Miss Faithful Heart, was nominated for the open job. The qualifications which Father sets for his trustee-property-administrators, so different from the requisites of the outside world, are brought out clearly in Father's interview with the prospective trustee. She was nineteen years old, her business experience was admittedly nil, and she was not even an actual member of the church on whose board she would soon be sitting.

"Miss Faithful Heart," Father requested, "will you come forward?"

Miss Faithful came.

Father asked, "Are you a member of this church?"

"Well," Miss Faithful unself-consciously replied, "I am not a member of any church at this moment."

Father asked, "Do you desire to be a draftee in the membership of this church?"

"Yes," Miss Heart answered, "I do."

"And elected as a trustee?" Father asked.

"Father dear, I do," Miss Faithful said.

Father knew Miss Faithful well. She had been in the movement since she'd been a very little girl. Although she was not a member of any specific church, she lived in one of the mission rooming houses and attended banquets and services at any of the churches whose programs interested her at particular times.

"You reside in one of the missions, do you?" Father asked, just as though he did not know it.

"Yes, I do."

"And you live according to the faith and order of this church?"

"Yes, I do."

"And I understand you are living a life of virginity?"

"That's right."

"Then I understand," Father commented kindly, "that you must be pure. Are you?"

Miss Faithful answered, "Yes, Father dear."

Father spoke on the qualifications of Miss Heart. His voice and manner indicated that he, for one, was impressed with her equipment for the job.

"All right." He turned from Miss Faithful Heart to the congregation. "You all have heard the statement of the nominee, and evidences show, to a certain extent, that she must be living according to my teaching, an evangelical life—a life of virginity and holiness. Since it has been moved and seconded that Miss Faithful Heart become a trustee, all in favor of the drafting, electing, selecting and electing Miss Faithful Heart as to this church a trustee let it be known by raising your hand and by the usual sign aye."

The ayes almost shook the walls. Miss Faithful Heart was elected.

"You have been elected," Father addressed the new trustee in a serious tone, "as a trustee to this church and to carry out the duties of a trustee and as one in whom the church has entrusted you with, to a certain extent, the duty and cares of the church from a material point of view, while God is the care and the protection of all, mentally and spiritually."

Miss Margaret Faith, another young girl, was nominated and seconded for the job of assistant treasurer. All in favor, the entire congregation, let their approval be known by the usual sign, aye, and her election was secure.

Father Divine addressed Miss Margaret Faith. "Miss Margaret," Father said, "you have been elected as assistant treasurer of the Circle Mission Home and Training School. No doubt you understand the requirements of a trustee and officer in this church. You understand what is required to accomplish what you are carrying out. If you are living a virgin's life, I believe you would be eligible to carry out official duty in the church by carrying your virginity in business and in profession as well as in the spiritual activity of all your duty."

Father's assistant pastor at the Circle Mission church, who preaches in his absence, is Reverend Paul Selfless. Father, who had first appointed him, wished the appointment renewed. He modestly requested the congregation to do so.

"Peace, everyone. I would like to say at this instance, the Assistant Pastor, Reverend Paul Selfless, stands at my left here as the Assistant Pastor of this Church, and has been placed by appointment. It is understood that he stands still, as an appointee, and if desired to be, it could be a confirmation of the appointment at this annual meeting, or it could be a withdrawal of the appointment by this Church, if you desire to do so. Therefore, it is up to the Board of Trustees and Officers of the Church and the Members in general to make the confirmation as Assistant Pastor to continue, or to make a move for his discontinuance as the Assistant Pastor. It is your privilege to make such a motion or move as you see fit, and as you deem eligible and justifiable and essential for the good of humanity generally! I thank you."

One of Father's Philadelphia secretaries rose. "Peace, Father, and peace, everyone. I would like to confirm Mr. Selfless' appointment."

Mr. Selfless was unanimously approved.

Only once in the entire history of the Peace Mission movement did Father support a candidate who was even slightly questioned. The year was 1945, and the office seeker concerned was Mr. Jonathan Good Heart. It happened that his virginity was clearly established.

"I know that you are living," Father told Mr. Good Heart, in the presence of the gathered group, "a life of virginity and holiness."

Mr. Good Heart assured Father that he was living such a life.

"All in favor of Mr. Good Heart," Father asked in exactly the same tone he always uses, "say aye."

"Aye," came the resounding answer.

Purely as a formality, Father asked, "Any nays?"

From somewhere in the back of the huge auditorium, a small voice piped, "Nay."

Father stared in astonishment. Doubtless, this was the first nay he had ever heard and the last one he would ever expect to hear.

"Only one small little nay?" he remarked jocularly. And added seriously, "Let me hear that nay again."

The nay was not repeated.

The election of property-administering trustees on the basis of whether or not they are holy virgins proves once again, if any proof be needed, how utterly the followers trust their God. Property owners know that if their trustees are virginal, Father's spirit will make them wise. They do not know, and would reject the knowledge if they had it, that the trustee movement is actually organized to take advantage of very astute leadership. No trustee is elected unless he is close to the throne of God. No trustee would dream of engaging in property administration without consulting Father. Father would never offer advice without consultation with his legal staff. Thus, Austin Norris today and Arthur Madison previously are the true church trustees.

Attorney Norris is very wise about movement properties. Father Divine and his followers never build new buildings. They watch the market for real estate bargains and buy properties at advantageous prices. Since they always pay cash, they can be assured of further advantages with those who need lump-sum monies. Often, the buildings are in bad condition and need repair when Father buys them. If current prices had to be paid for everything, the cost of this procedure would be prohibitive. For Father Divine, however, with all the free service he has access to, it is more than practical.

Robert Denny is only one of the followers who has offered his money and his services to Divine. He lives in New York at a rooming house for men. He pays fifty cents a day for his room and sixty cents a day for his food. He owns a car but its maintenance does not cost much. He buys his gas and oil at co-operatives which are dedicated to making no more than one cent a gallon profit. He lives, as well as he wants to, on thirteen dollars a week.

Robert Denny is an artisan who, when he works, makes at least twelve dollars a day. At the end of a six-day work week, he has at least seventy-two. What does he do with the sixty dollars a week which he does not need to live on?

"Two years ago," Mr. Denny tells, "I saved three thousand dollars. I put it into Peace Mission properties."

Last year, Robert Denny made a better than financial contribution to Father Divine. He gave his services.

"I worked three months," he says, "and made $864. Then I stopped working for outsiders except maybe one day a week. Now I am working for Father. I do maintenance work, keep up the repair for any building that needs me. I'm so fortunate I need to give only one day a week to take care of myself. Then I have six days I can give to God."

It is all the Robert Dennys who make the Peace Mission movement's prosperity a reality. Whenever an advantageous property offers itself, there are more voluntary investors than are necessary and more free maintenance workers. When, in April, 1942, Atlantic City's million-dollar Brigantine Hotel was offered for sale at $500,000, there were numerous followers who begged to invest in it. It was the same with Newark's Riviera Hotel, and Philadelphia's Hotel Tracy which was purchased in 1949 for $485,000.

The large city hotels are Father's favorite investments. They are his "demonstrators of democracy in action." In them, for the first time since the inception of the Peace Mission movement, Negro and white non-followers, attracted by the cheap rental rates, live together under one roof exactly as followers have always lived.

"I am proving in the hotels," Father claims, "that one human being is not better than another so long as they comply with human decency, democracy, and brotherhood."

Non-followers who seek residence at any of the three hotels are accepted on the same basis as followers are and are subject to the same regulations.

"Enact the Bill of Rights!" is the most important regulation. Its observance means that, in a Divine hotel, white and colored non-followers must sleep side by side just as followers do. Every double bed must be shared where proportions permit by one white and one colored person.

"I am defying segregation," Father says. "It is not in the hotels alone, it is all over the world. I am proving it will soon be the same all over as it is under my jurisdictional. By the places where I now own properties, formerly those of the darker complexion could not even enter in there."

Father is right. In Newark, New York, and Philadelphia, his followers own properties in the most exclusive and elegant white neighborhoods. Father says they have not bought there deliberately. The neighbors say they have. Father says that although they have not bought deliberately, they are happy to be examples of democracy. The neighbors say they have bought deliberately and that they are examples not of democracy but of nuisances who happen also to have some Negroes in their midst.

Within recent years, the knottiest of all Father's knotty neighbor problems occurred in Newark. It was reminiscent of Sayville.

In 1949, twenty-five angels purchased a three-story mansion, set in spacious landscaped grounds, at 60 East Abingdon Avenue in Forest Hill, one of Newark's more exclusive, residential sections. Shortly afterwards, ten of them, headed by a housekeeper, moved in.

Some time later, neighboring homeowners instituted a formal complaint in Newark's Municipal Court. They demanded that they be legally protected by the existing zoning law which prohibited the very thing being perpetrated by the Divinites—the running of a rooming house, a dangerous precedent.

The matter, at first, seemed a simple one. Zoning Enforcement Officer Fiverson handled the "alleged violation." He asked the angels, since they were obviously not members of one family, to leave their heaven.

Father Divine fought the ousting of his followers. He sent Austin Norris from Philadelphia to defend the Abingdon Avenue owners.

Mr. Norris, in his defending action, claimed that his clients actually were "a family group" under the definition of the existing zoning law. He said that they were all children of one Father, Father Divine.

The Zoning Enforcement Officer, faced with the "ambiguity" of the legal definition of family groups, effected a clearer wording of the restriction. The resulting new law defines a family group as "one or more persons related by blood, marriage or adoption."

Shortly after the new zoning law went into effect, an event occurred which effectively countered the action of the Forest Hill homeowners.

The ten follower-residents of the mansion moved out, and a large Negro family, consisting of Reverend Mr. Charles Boyer, his wife, thirteen children, and his father-in-law moved in.

Public reaction to Father Divine's action was strongly in sympathy with the Forest Hill homeowners. Newark reporters got in touch with Father's Philadelphia headquarters. Was his action motivated by prejudice in Forest Hill against the Peace movement or against the Negro people?

Whenever they tried to obtain an interview, Father was "in conference." However, he relayed a written statement through his secretaries.

He portrayed himself not as a crusader for civil rights but in the role of a benefactor of a needy family. The mansion, he said, had been offered to him as a private home by the follower-owners, but he had refused it. He and Mother Divine already had sufficient accommodations. He felt that "it would be more profitable, a service to humanity, if a large family needing many rooms for their progeny could have the use of the mansion."

The most extraordinary angle of the Abingdon Ave. case is that the Boyers were not followers, at the time when Father gave them the mansion. As a matter of fact, the Reverend Mr. Boyer had never laid eyes on Father, and Father had never seen the minister, before an interview which took place in June, 1952, when Reverend Boyer spoke his first words to Father: "I place myself at your mercy to instruct and guide me. My burden is large, so I came to you."

"I will help you," Father promised. "But only as a Principle—not as a Person. I will be with you."

Father has given that advice to practically all who have come to him asking aid. But, unwittingly, Mr. Boyer's visit occurred at the time when Father and his attorney were pondering what move to make in the Forest Hill controversy.

Five months later, in November, 1952, he gave the use of the Forest Hill mansion to the Boyer family, promising the minister that the follower-owners would assume tax payments.

"You see," he told his angels after the Boyers took possession of the Abingdon Avenue house, "it is always what I say that it shall be all over the wide, extended plane just as it is in my jurisdictional."

The followers applauded wildly, and the Abingdon Avenue owner-angels, Honey Bee Love, Snow White, and all of them, were gratified to know that their property would be utilized to advance God's work.

"What else is money for?" investor-angel Peaceful Love asks. "I mean, if you don't use your money as God would want you to——" She shrugs her shoulders and smiles.

"If you don't use your money as God would want you to——" That is the key toward the clearing up of the entire Peace Mission financial mystery, and particularly that part of it relating to: "What does Father get out of all this himself? How much money does he have salted away? And what property does he, not his followers but he alone, actually own?"

Father says he does not own anything. There are no bank accounts in his name. There are no insurance policies. There are no businesses. There are no properties. There are no stocks and no bonds. And if you requested him to, he says, and if he felt compelled to comply with a request that would seem to be doubting his divine word, he could empty his pockets—suit pocket, overcoat pocket, every pocket—and show you he does not own "a solitary penny of money."

Followers reiterate Father's statement. "He owns nothing. It is only us he has made rich by his condescension to the earth plane."

Non-followers doubt that. The United States Treasury Department also doubts it. From the days of the thirties, when Father Divine first blossomed out as an example of what the well-dressed God will wear, with custom-made suits and gray fedora hats, with four many-carat diamond rings on his fingers and a diamond stickpin in his tie, the Treasury Department did not believe his claim that he owned nothing—and tried to prove that it was false. They are still trying to prove it today. So far, despite their most expert sleuthing, they have been unsuccessful.

Why? Is it because Father Divine and Austin Norris and Arthur Madison are smarter than the Treasury Department? Is it because the Treasury Department, accustomed as it is to frauds and manipulators, has finally met such a fraud and such a manipulator that it is no match for him? Most people who do not know Father and his followers actually do believe that. The few non-followers who do know Father and his disciples do not believe it at all. They know that the true reason why Father's followers pay substantial annual income taxes while he pays none is exactly what Father and the disciples claim it to be—while they have incomes, he does not.

The key behind their assurance is not alone the efficiency of the Treasury Department but also, and more important, the words spoken by co-operative investor Peaceful Love and all her angelic brothers and sisters: "What else is money for? I mean, if you don't use your money as God would want you to——" The key behind their assurance is the fact that they have seen the followers with their God and that, once having seen that, they know indubitably that everything the followers own belongs, in effect, to Father.

Why does Father Divine need money? Without a dime in his pocket, he still possesses every luxury money can buy. And how joyfully it is provided for him! Anyone who believes that he must be pocketing money away for future use when the bubble of his movement will burst just does not know him and his confidence in himself and the faith of his followers. The Peace Mission movement is no bubble to Father Divine. He knows that, so long as his followers remain as devoted as they are—and he knows that the bulk of them will remain devoted forever—so long are all their possessions, in effect, his. The hotels, the restaurants, the rooming houses, everything held in the name of the Peace Mission church or the co-operating followers would, if he requested it today, be placed in the name of Father Divine tomorrow. He has sufficient security, so that he need not ever make that request.

In the meantime, without "a cent of money" in his pocket, he lives the life of a millionaire. In every mission, rooming house, apartment house, and hotel, exquisite, luxurious suites are set aside for Father and Mother Divine and for Father's personal staff. Sometimes, Father uses these suites frequently. Sometimes, he uses them only occasionally. And sometimes, loving followers know even while they are spending huge amounts of money to furnish "Father's suites" that they will never be used by "God in his personal body." That is the way it is with the kingdoms in California. Western followers know that Father will not ever come there. And in Switzerland and England and Panama and West Germany. Father has stated that he does not intend to bring his "precious little body" either "across the country or over the ocean." Still, California and European followers work hard to provide worthy suites, comforting themselves with the idea that Father's spiritual presence is as appreciative.

In Philadelphia, where Father's physical presence is a daily reality, followers provide him with the most elaborate suites of all. A typical one is in the Bible Institute. It is an old and most beautiful mansion dating back to the days when prosperous Philadelphians imported from France crystal chandeliers for their French rooms, and from China brightly colored wall tiles for their Chinese rooms. A tour through the Bible Institute, which Divinites have preserved in all its antique elegance, is an experience. A tour through Father's suite is even more so.

Father's suite in the Bible Institute is composed of a tremendous gray-walled bedroom with some ten ceiling-to-floor windows, draped in deep wine satin to match the bedspread, a smaller room which serves as his study, and a large blue-tiled bathroom that is marvelously equipped with personal accouterments supplied by the more imaginative sisters. The most striking of these is a towel rack on which are hung three hand-painted towels, pink with black mottoes reading: "Dis Towel Is For Youse to Use."

In the past seven years, Father has used the Bible Institute suite twice, but it is always spotlessly clean in preparation for his third use. And the large closet in which followers have hung clothes which might take Father's fancy is full of expensive, custom-made suits and overcoats and expensive lounging jackets and robes. The robes and jackets are mostly blue, because blue is Father's favorite color. There is a tremendous eight-drawer chiffonier which is full to bursting of shirts, mostly white but other colors, too: light pinks, blues, and grays. There is a small chiffonier containing Father's socks and underwear, which the lady followers point out coyly, and numerous pairs of expensive blue and deep red pajamas. There is a special hat and shoe closet with perhaps forty hats, mostly gray fedoras, and as many pairs of differently colored shoes, all spanking new.

The Bible Institute, as every other Peace Mission property, has a private dining room for the use of Father Divine, his personal staff, and especially favored visitors. A staff of waitresses and cooks is on special twenty-four-hour call, so that breakfasts, luncheons, dinners, or snacks may be provided Father at any time of the day or night he may grow hungry. There is a private kitchen with a pantry and double refrigerators always stocked with his favorite foods.

Loving followers provide Father and his staff with Cadillac cars, and Father does not have to pay for their upkeep.

Why does Father Divine need money in the bank or in his pocket?

There is a tremendous staff of workers, who, like the waitresses and cooks of his private dining room, are happy to do anything he requests at any time he wishes it done—and honored to be asked. Cultured young white man Philip Life considered it far more than he deserved when Father Divine chose him as his personal chauffeur. Pretty milk-and-strawberry-complexioned Miss Margaret, who is one of four personal waitresses to Father Divine and travels from mission to mission when he does, says with her blue eyes shining, "I feel so lucky to be on Father's personal waitress staff, and I try so hard to deserve his choice of me. I don't know what I would do if he ever dropped me off or felt I was undeserving." Miss Peace, who is a maid at Father's personal headquarters, is as dedicated to her job as Miss Margaret is to hers. "I could work all day and all night," she tells, "and never feel the work at all."

Perhaps Father Divine is right when he says, "So, here I sit and there I stand, with everybody lovin', lovin' me. So much love is more than two hundred million dollars. So much love is you cannot put a price on it."

16

GOD IN BEDLAM!

Much as Father's chauffeur, Philip Life, adores him, much as his personal waitress, Miss Margaret, does, much as his maid Miss Peace loves Father Divine, much as all his followers love him "more than two hundred million dollars so much love is, you cannot put a price on"—there are some followers who love him even more than all the others put together. These are Father's secretaries, twenty-six young girls, almost evenly divided between white and Negro, who think of themselves as "nuns dedicated to live for God and God alone."

Miss E. Ruth is one of Father's secretaries. She is small and slender and might, by mortal standards, be reckoned to be in her mid-thirties. She arises from her seat at the banquet table. She clasps her thin white hands together as if in prayer and turns to face her Lord. Tears flow from her eyes. Perhaps she is aware of their flow. Perhaps she is not. At any rate, you know when you look at her that, aware or not, she could not stop the flow of those tears.

"Peace, Father dear." Her voice is cultured but sounds broken with the strength of the feeling of her love for Divine. "Father, this is my birthday. I date the time I was born from the time I first saw your beautiful face. It was on a hot day in August and, honey, I'm telling you, that day I began to live."

Father smiles at Miss E. Ruth. It is not a full smile, only a half one, but it has a strange effect on Miss E. Ruth. She smiles fully, glowingly, and then she begins to shiver, palsiedly in every part of her slender body. She stands a few moments, just shivering, uninhibited, unashamed in the presence not of the followers alone but also of six outsiders, two of whom she knows to be there gathering material for a book.

She continues her testimony, looking at the other followers now and then, looking at her co-secretaries who sit
around her at the table, looking at the strangers, looking at
everybody and seeing only one.

"Father dear! The love you give us, Father! There never
was a love like this on earth! There never was love like this
and, as we love you more, our capacity for love increases
so we can see more of the majesty of your love. It is
something, Father, that you come in here and you don't
just come into possession of immediately because you don't
have the capacity for accepting the love of God. His love is
so infinite, so sweet, and so tender that you just can't say,
'Well, here I am, God! Love me!' Because you don't know
the love of God. The more you accept of Father's love, the
greater his love becomes, the more blessings you get and
the sweeter it is."

Miss E. Ruth and her co-secretaries have accepted of
Father's love more completely than any other followers
have, because Father has "blessed" them to do so. It is they
who are his very favorite angels.

There are twenty-six secretaries. They comprise what
Father calls his "inner cabinet." They are closer to him
than any other followers can ever hope to be. They spend
almost all of his and their waking hours in his presence.
They are his confidantes, who know the innermost secrets
of the movement. Divine secretaries are not typists and
stenographers alone. They are publicists and business managers and executive housekeepers and writers. They are
God's closest assistants.

They love Father so much that their overwhelming desire is to become anonymous and so enable themselves to
be seen and to be thought of, not as personalities separate
and distinct but rather as shadows of Father Divine.

Miss E. Ruth says, "I am nothing. God is everything."

Her twenty-five co-secretaries agree with her. There is a
poem which they always repeat to visitors. It is an inspira-
tional poem, composed by the all-time number-one secretary, blonde, voluptuous Sweet Angel whom Father Divine
lifted out of the ranks seven years ago and made his second
wife.

Sweet Angel said, and the other secretaries repeated:

You've got to make 100,
99½ won't do,
And if you make 100,
It will be Father who made it—not you.

The secretaries, more than Father's other followers, believe in their own nothingness; so that, striving for perfection, they can credit their achievements to Father. They are, most of them, quite young and very attractive. They are well educated. Of the twenty-six, six are college graduates and four have had some college training. The others have all been through high school. Their educational background, in their minds and in Father's, is unimportant, though. All of them stand equipped with what, according to Divine interpretation, is more vital than education for filling these most important Peace Mission posts—spiritual virginity. Most of them had always been physically virgins also. The few who had known men in the mortal world have been freed "of their lust" since coming to Father. All of them are privileged to wear the red jackets with large V's for virginity emblazoned on their pockets. They are all privileged to take the "Endeavor Pledge," the "Ten Commandments of the Sweets," who are recognized to be "the truest virgins" of Father's movement.

The Sweets' Endeavor reads:

To copy after Your Ways, being not different nor odd;
To prove it is truth when we say You are God,
To live pleasing to You is our hearts' desire,
To do only the things that You would admire;
To trust You in all things and never, never doubt, but
To know we'll always be cared for and never go without,
To follow diligently as You pave the way,
To never shrink, or even take a thought to go astray;
To uphold and stand with You, Father, no matter what may come,
To let Your Thoughts be our thoughts; yes, let all be one.
To speak only words we would want You to hear;
To think only thoughts we would say in Your ear;
To smile only smiles pleasing to You;
To touch only the clean things as You would want us;
To step where Your spirit has stepped before;

To give heart, mind, and body for they are all Yours,
To write not a word we want You not to see;
To breathe not a breath hidden from You in secrecy;
To take not an object, when to You would not show,
To read not a word we wouldn't want You to know.
To make over others neither admiration or fuss, but
To show appreciation only to You, for what's done for us;
To listen not to idle gossip, what others might say;
To take no thought, nor plan for the next day;
To taste not a crumb that has been hidden from Thee;
To be ever thankful of things already received;
To spend not a moment if You knew not where;
To make not a motion, made if Personally You weren't
*   there;*
To love, honor, and reverence You wherever we may be;
To let You bear record of our presence or our absentee;
To make every word we speak real and true;
To ask not of another, but ask only of You;
To let nothing ever break us apart;
To keep you forever, The Sweet of our hearts; and
To be by all these things, united forever
To You; this is the Sweets' sincerest endeavor!

From Your very own,
Sweet,
Sweet,
Sweet,
Sweet,
Sweet,
Sweet.

The ten commandments are:

1. The "Sweets" shall forever obey, cherish, respect, and praise their Lord and Saviour, FATHER DIVINE, above all else.
2. We shall always have a kind word and smile for others.
3. We shall keep guile from our lips.
4. We shall have one mind, one aim and one purpose— GOD, FATHER DIVINE.
5. We shall rejoice at the blessings of others.
6. We will endeavor to let our every deed and action express virginity.

7. We will deny ourselves and consecrate our heart, mind, soul, and body to the Cause.
8. We will stand by our Conviction to love GOD, even if all others oppose us.
9. We will never, no, never condemn or find fault with anything our Saviour may say or do.
10. We shall at all times recognize the all-seeing Eye of our Lord and be the same, knowing that He is always in the midst of us.

Aside from their "sweet virginity" and devotion to him, Father's secretaries hold little in common. They are of all types and backgrounds. There are even some few among them who are neither young nor attractive. These are the truly able ones, though.

Probably the least attractive of the secretaries, and also the brightest and most efficient of them, is Jane Shaneweiss. Miss Shaneweiss is in her fifties. She is tall and broad-boned and very plain. She has blue eyes which might be lovely if they ever looked alive, and white hair cut short and combed back from an intellectual forehead. She has a deep, cultured voice which could sound warm if she ever used it for more than monosyllabic answers to questions which she cannot avoid dealing with.

Jane Shaneweiss comes from a wealthy Chicago family. She has her M.A. degree from the University of Chicago. Why should such a woman ever have been attracted to such a Messiah as Divine? What inner drives forced her affiliation with the Peace Mission movement? Miss Shaneweiss won't tell. When questioned about herself, the most that she will answer is, "I am happy here." And looking at her, looking at the harshness of her and the deep repression that you know is no new thing, you give up trying to probe the reasons for her being in heaven. You accept her as just another Divine mystery that no outsider can solve. She is in charge of Father's business affairs.

Another secretary, outstanding in Father's group because she is not young and charming-looking, is Saint Mary Bloom. Saint Mary Bloom is also in her fifties. She is small and compactly built, with the sort of figure that seems to blend into her background, merging with walls and floors and draperies, never standing out as a figure at all. Her face stands out, though. It is a dark-brown, bitter, nervous face with small eyes that are always heavily ringed. Saint Mary Bloom has a certain dignity, and, looking at her, you have the feeling that, if ever you could reach inside her, you would find unexpected warmth. It is Saint Mary Bloom who is in charge of heaven's domestic affairs.

All of the housekeepers, cooks, and kitchen supervisors, not only in all the Philadelphia heavens but also in the New York and Newark ones, take their orders from Miss Saint Mary. She has also been delegated by Father to serve as a sort of a mother to the younger secretaries. She discusses their problems with them. She sees to it that they are physically comfortable. Their wardrobe needs, for example, are routed through her.

Saint Mary Bloom came to Father twenty years ago. It is said in the heavens that, in those early days of her affiliation with God, she was terribly crippled in both legs. She could not walk at all and sought help from Father only after she had been to doctors and specialists who told her, some kindly, some not so kindly, that she would never be able to walk. Father healed her "when the specialists couldn't." Today, when he discusses her healing, he says, "She could not walk and now she is the walking boss."

Saint Mary is a hard worker. Like Father and the great majority of other angels close to the throne, she works twelve-, sixteen-, and twenty-hour days. It is not unusual for her to work twenty-four straight hours, to sleep for three hours or four at most, and to begin another twenty-four-hour shift. How does she do it? Her explanation is very simple:

"Father has blessed me to contain his spirit inside me. There is nothing I cannot do."

Another secretary whose efficiency is unquestionable and who can work for twenty-four-hour stretches is Dorothy Darling. A freckle-faced, green-eyed redhead, small and slim, Miss Darling, until you talk to her confidentially, would seem to be the epitome of everything Divinites are not supposed to be. She has the look and the manner of a New York sophisticate. Not only does she look worldly; occasionally, she even sounds that way. She

goes so far as to "wisecrack" in the mortal fashion sometimes. But her complete dedication to Father Divine is
apparent every time she glances in his direction.

Miss Darling is a college graduate. She, her mother, her
father, her husband, her mother-in-law, and her father-in-
law came to Father ten years ago. Her advancement was
the most rapid of any of "the so-called family" who accompanied her. Father made her a secretary after she had
been with him for a short time and, in 1947, he formally
recognized her as his Secretary Number One, by assigning
to her the table seat at his left. It is Miss Darling who
greets visitors and serves as the intermediary between God
and the mortal world. She also serves as Father's main
contact person with his own attorney. Unless Austin Norris has important matters to discuss with God, he talks
with Dorothy Darling.

"She is one of the most able people I have ever met,"
Mr. Norris comments about Secretary Number One.

Father has one secretary who is not able at all in the
sense that Miss Darling and Miss Bloom and Miss Shaneweiss are able. On the contrary, Miss Darling and Miss
Bloom worry about her and attempt with all of the abilities
at their separate commands to keep her on the correct
path. Sometimes, both of them have got to admit defeat,
however.

For poor Sunshine Love, in spite of all the guidance she
receives, is always getting into trouble. She can generally
get herself out of it again, though, because she is always so
sorry to bring distress, so genuinely sorry, and because she
is so basically good and sweet and lovable. Sunshine Love
is nineteen years old, going on twenty. Her mother brought
her and her sister from California when Sunshine was less
than nine months old and gave both the girls to Father.

"I loved Father Divine since I was a little baby," Sunshine tells, "and I love him more every day. I love him so
much that, sometimes, I feel just as though my heart is
bursting with the love I feel. How is it possible to have so
much, much love?"

Her face shines when she talks with the wonderful love
she talks about. She is a warm, giving, happy person, and,
as you look at her, you cannot help but feel, more than

you feel about any of Father's other secretaries, even those who are as young and warm and charming as she is, what a pity it is that all that love must be wasted in Father's heaven. And you know, as you watch Sunshine Love and talk to her, that there will never be another love for Sunshine, not when she is twenty-one or thirty-one or fifty-one, not forever and ever as long as she lives. You know that, to her, Father Divine is indeed, what she tells you he is, her "one and only" forever.

Sunshine Love can be described in one word—"adorable." If she were any place but heaven, she would also be called "sexy." She is small and voluptuously built. Her legs are marvelously shaped, slim-ankled and slim-calved. She has a satin-smooth, café-au-lait complexion. Her black eyes are long-lashed. She wears her African hair smoothed into a jet-black bun on the top of her head. For anyone else, that kind of a hair-comb would be severe. For Sunshine Love, with her practically heart-shaped face, it couldn't be more right.

One of Sunshine's great handicaps is her sense of humor. She is ashamed to admit that it is almost mortal. She laughs too loud and too long and too often. Sometimes, she plays tricks on the other secretaries, hiding their clothes away, for example, or telling them stories in jest that are not at all in keeping with the dignity demanded by her position. Sunshine's second handicap is her temper. She often loses it when she shouldn't.

"Some day," she says, "Father will drive all mortality out of me."

Father's personal stenographer is Miss Great Love. Great Love is a quiet lady who has "breeding" written all over her. She is in her late-middle thirties, although she appears at least ten years younger than that. She has red hair, blue eyes, and a mediocre complexion.

"It was my complexion," she tells, "that brought me to Father. I used to be so dreadfully pimpled in high school."

She had tried all sorts of remedies to improve her complexion. She'd gone to doctors. She'd used commercial mixtures. She'd taken exercises and gone to Turkish baths. Nothing had helped her. Then, purely by accident, she'd heard of Father Divine and his miraculous healing. As a last hope, she'd written to Father. Three weeks after, she'd received a letter from him telling her to trust his spirit. She had. The pimples had disappeared. And Great Love had known Father Divine was God.

"Nothing in the world could make me doubt Father now," she says. "He is my world, all my world. If I didn't have him, if ever I unconsciously did anything against Father's principle, and Father said, 'Great Love, you can no longer stay with me,' I would——" Her voice trails away. "I would—well, if that happened, life would be worthless to me, that's all, just plain worthless." She smiles. "It is strange to be thinking like this. I never think like this unless——" She glances at you, a person from the mortal world, and she is too polite to tell you that it is you, you with all that worldliness, with that mortality you've not divorced yourself from, who have influenced her to think in this unpleasant vein. "Pardon me," she says, still sweetly, still politely. "Pardon me, I have a terrible amount of work to do. It's sinful to stand here chatting and all that work on my desk, Father's speeches yesterday and the day before just piled up, waiting on my desk. It's very nice talking to you but, but——" She rushes away, still polite, hoping she hasn't hurt your feelings, and you know that this is the last you'll ever see of Great Love, to talk with, that is.

Father has two schoolteacher secretaries. There is Anne Sterrit, who only works for him summers and weekends. She spends her winters teaching at a Harlem public school. In her early thirties, Miss Anne is small with a dark-beige complexion and soft, soft eyes. Her manner is modest and very sweet. And there is Miss Charity who is also dark beige and in her early thirties. Miss Charity is not modest, though. She is filled with a sense of her own importance. She came to Father more than ten years ago and gave up many advantages to affiliate with the movement. She gave up a husband and a small son and a beautiful home. She gave up a good teaching job.

"It was meant to be," she says. "I had been a hunter for truth all the years since I became a thinking person. I had been in Unity and in Christian Science and found them only preparations for Father Divine."

Miss Charity has the responsibility of proofreading Father's Messages to his followers and of reading them aloud.

"To think," she says, "that I am the one chosen to read Our Lord's messages and to interpret them. I'll never cease feeling honored. I love Father so." Her face, sulky in repose, shines when she talks about Father Divine.

Pretty Miss Sweet Heart, another of Father's secretaries, glows too. "I couldn't live without Father Divine," she tells you. Looking at her, you could never doubt she means what she says. Miss Sweet Heart has red, shining hair which she tries to keep in a straight page boy, but which forms into ringlets in spite of her best efforts. She has big blue eyes. She is always smiling, but shyly.

Miss Sweet Heart was converted to Father Divine before she was nine years old. Living in Montreal, Canada, and never having laid eyes on Father Divine "in the body," she was convinced, when she was not quite nine, and her two sisters, one somewhat younger than Sweet Heart, one somewhat older, were also convinced. Sweet Heart's mother, a truth-seeker, converted them. Incidentally, she herself had never seen Father Divine face to face either. She had acquired her conviction, Sweet Heart tells today, "through reading his sermons in the *New Day*." Sweet Heart sees nothing strange at all in the fact that her mother recognized her God through his newspaper. She says that that is a logical way to know him.

"His words are so beautiful," she explains in her soft, young voice, "so beautiful, so beautiful—— They are a fit company for his beautiful, precious, holy little face and body."

Miss Sweet Heart was twenty-one when she came from Montreal to take up residence in Philadelphia and become one of Father's inner circle of angels. She is twenty-eight today.

"These six years have been the happiest I've ever known," she tells. "Now, since I have Father, I have everything I'll ever need."

Father Divine is pretty Sweet Heart's father, mother, brother, husband, and lover—especially the latter.

It is said that God, in the early days of the movement, when Faithful Mary was still his trusted lieutenant, told her that he was able "to do more to the women in the movement by a single flick of his eye than their husbands could ever do."

All of Father's secretaries vehemently deny this statement of Faithful Mary's. It is ridiculous, they say, too stupid even to bother answering.

"Father loves us purely," they assert.

And again, "We love Father purely." Repeating their statement with such obvious sincerity and with such a through and through belief in their words that you must also believe what they are saying about the purity of their love.

Unless you had, at one time or another, been sitting exactly across the table from Father Divine during a banquet and had seen, with your own eyes, the way Father, generally imperturbable, glanced toward Sunshine Love. His eyes were narrowed. They were half closed. They were loving. It was only a split-second look he gave Sunshine. If you hadn't been watching Father very closely, you'd never have even discerned it. Sunshine Love, though, glanced back at Father. She sprang to her feet. She put her arms around her body. She screamed.

You must believe the secretaries' denials of lust in their love unless you had by chance observed the way Father turned from Sunshine Love and began to look at Great Love beside her. Great Love sprang up as Sunshine Love had, more quietly though because she is a quieter kind of girl. She caressed herself over and over again. If you had seen Great Love at that moment you would have had to recognize her expression. It was the same expression seen on many women followers' faces—pure physical orgasm rooted deep in spiritual ecstasy. It was something else, too. It was recognition of the marvelous status God afforded her when he glanced at her instead of at one of the other secretaries.

Status among Father's secretaries depends on one thing and one thing only—which one of them seems at a particular time to be closest to God. Heaven's secretaries are Father's harem. They go into favor with him for reasons which they do not generally comprehend and out of favor in the same fashion. Naturally there is intense jealousy among them. Every day is battle day in the secretaries' jockeying for position with Father.

"God," one intelligent follower tells, "lives in the midst of bedlam."

John Hunt, wealthy ex-follower, emphasizes the "bedlam" statement. He says, "It is the bitter rivalries among the secretaries which will cause the biggest cracks in the kingdom. Feuds are on and they are not giving Father too much peace of mind."

The most recent feud in the heavenly cabinet concerned the secretary known as Miss Anita. Her mortal name is Anita Nadler Daire and she stands out as one of Father Divine's "primest samples and examples to the world" of a true follower who has "beautifully" renounced all family attachments, including her husband and two young children, for Father Divine. Father truly loves Miss Anita. Those who know him best assert that, next to Mother Divine, it is Miss Anita who stands closest to the throne.

Anita Daire, unlike a great number of Father's followers, was not drawn to the movement because she was Negro and poor. On the contrary, she is white and Anglo-Saxon, and while she had not been wealthy before she joined Father, she had been in comfortable economic circumstances. She had been married to a man who loved her and who was, in fact, the kind of protector-provider that many of Father's followers seek in heaven's fictional world. She had had two sons.

What compulsions caused Anita Daire to give up her husband? What inner forces moved Anita Daire not only to renounce all fleshly love for her husband but also to reject Robert, her nine-year-old son, and her baby Kenneth who is not yet six today.

How is it that Anita Daire, walking through heaven, can meet her husband, who joined Father Divine when she did, and her two sons, and behave impersonally, as though she had never known them intimately?

"Peace," she can tell the husband and the sons and never inquire as to whether they are sick or well.

To Father's followers, Miss Anita's motivations are no mystery. Miss Peaceful, an intelligent white follower, says:

"Anita is one of the chosen. Father has permitted her to know 'who he is.' When a person finds God, she cannot allow a husband or children to influence her to turn her back on him."

Miss Anita herself says, "I always wanted to live the holy life. From the time I was a baby, I was trained for it."

Like Father's other followers, she sees no mystery in the fact that, in the year of her twenty-seventh birthday, she turned her back on normal living.

"Peace," she says, "what is there in the world outside except sin and death? What is marriage except a walk in the shadow that must finally lead to death?"

Miss Anita was born and lived all her life before she came to Philadelphia in Minneapolis. Since she recognizes no father except Divine, she will not speak about "the man who reared me." Her mother, Mrs. Nadler, also lives in heaven today.

When Anita was seven years old, the mother, having explored Christian Science and Unity, in a search for self-fulfillment had found Father Divine. Although she had not then moved into heaven, she had observed the tenets laid down by God.

Today, her mother does not own Anita openly. Still she is proud of her daughter. She says, "Father is honoring Anita so. In a way, I always knew this would be her fate."

Perhaps that was why her mother had been so disappointed when Anita, like any ordinary girl, had married at seventeen.

"Marriage is a sin," her mother had screamed at the bride. "It is walking in the shadow!"

Mrs. Nadler had not been happy with the birth of her first grandson either. "Marriage is a sin," she'd reminded the new mother.

Whether Anita's psychological unfitness for marriage was responsible for the fact that she was divorced after a few years of unhappy living with her first husband, is not known. It is a fact, though, that, on the day when her daughter's marriage was dissolved, Mrs. Nadler was a supremely happy woman.

After the divorce, she talked more fully to Anita about Father Divine. Father offered eternal life, she said. He offered goodness and happiness and all-enveloping love.

Miss Anita listened and absorbed and longed for Father Divine as her mother interpreted him—on the one hand. On the other hand, she continued to live "the lustful life." She dyed her light-brown hair a golden blond to emphasize her blue eyes and delicate complexion. She bought clothes especially designed to show off her voluptuous figure. Night after night she went to night clubs.

It was at a night club that Anita first met her second husband, Kenneth Daire. She married him three months after she met him.

"Anita's marriage to Kenneth was one of the saddest days of my life," her mother tells today.

After Miss Anita's marriage to Kenneth, and even after the birth of Kenneth, Jr., her mother continued to preach Father Divine to her. Father was the savior, and it was still not too late for Anita to be saved. Despite the sinfulness of her life with her husband and the two children who were living proof of her sins, she could come to Father. If she would but repent, if she would but give up the "filthiness" of conjugal living, Father would accept her into his fold.

Mrs. Nadler says, "Anita believed me all right, but the demands of mortality were too strong for her at first."

In early 1951, in response to her mother's urgings, Miss Anita was enabled to overcome the "demands of mortality." She left Kenneth and the sons in Minneapolis and came to Philadelphia. She could no longer resist Father's call. She had to see him for herself.

"I was a child of the flesh," Miss Anita told Father Divine, repeating exactly the words which her mother had said to her. "I made a mistake and I got married. I had a child. Then I was divorced. But I married again. I had another child."

Father listened to Miss Anita's testimony. She moved him as all repentant sinners do. He said she could be forgiven. She could forget the two husbands. She could forget the children she had had. If she wished, she could formally affiliate herself with God's kingdom.

Anita said, "So glad, Father." She told how it was that

she wanted to come to the movement, "while I'm young and not when I'm old." She said she wanted to offer God a young, healthy body.

For three weeks Miss Anita stayed at the heaven. In many ways, heaven proved to be exactly what she'd longed for. How right her mother had been when she'd urged the trip to Philadelphia.

Strangely though, something kept gnawing at her new happiness. Try as she would, she could not snuff out thought of her husband and of her two sons. How was the husband? How were the boys?

In the end, Miss Anita had to tell Father how it was with her.

"I want to live immortal life but there is too much of mortality in me."

Father remained kind to Anita. He told her she was not ready yet for the stringent demands of angelic living. She must return to the mortal attachments. At the same time, she must attempt to keep her mind turned to him. He would permit his spirit to remain with her after she returned home.

Back in Minneapolis, Father's spirit kept torturing Anita. Look at the way she was living with her husband, naturally, as any woman lived. Look at the way she yielded to demands of the flesh. It was impure. It was just as her mother had drummed into her . . . "walking in the shadow." It meant that she was denying the eternal life.

And her sons, the two poor little children whose mother knew of the existence of God on earth but did nothing about her knowledge. What would their fate be?

Desperately longing for Father, Anita knew she would have to return to heaven. She tried to persuade her husband to come with her.

"Think of the boys," she said. "In our world, what, after all, do we have to offer them? Only sin and death."

Kenneth countered, "I love you. I don't want to give you up."

Anita told Kenneth that she loved him too and that was exactly the reason why she could give him up.

Kenneth Daire, a well-educated only child of wealthy parents, was induced to join the Divine Peace Mission movement. Today, he lives in the Philadelphia heaven where Father Divine resides. He has given up all mortal thought of Anita, Robert, and Kenneth, Jr. He has dedicated himself to service to Father Divine.

How did Kenneth Daire come to Father? Why did he come? The reasons behind this strange conversion are not known. Unless Mr. Daire becomes disillusioned with Father at some future day, they never will be known.

When Kenneth and Anita Daire came to Philadelphia, they brought their boys with them. The two children are "little brothers" now.

Miss Anita does not experience the slightest conflict about having given up her "so-called family."

"The boys belong to God," she says smilingly.

From the day she first came to stay with him, Father Divine honored Miss Anita highly. Her rise in the movement was meteoric. First, she became a chauffeuress. He placed her in charge of a Cadillac car in his own private caravan. He gave her a room at his own Philadelphia headquarters. And then, as though this was not honor enough for a newcomer, after she had been with him a very short time he granted her the same freedom in the use of his private suite that the secretaries had. Although he did not formally make her a secretary, he did make it known, to her and to all of the secretaries from Dorothy Darling on down, that Miss Anita was to mingle as freely with them and to have as complete an access to him as any secretary did.

The secretaries became angry and resentful. They allowed their resentment to show. Why, they asked each other, should this woman, this worldly, evil woman, have obtained such distinction? When Father wasn't looking, they tried to punish Miss Anita for Father's notice of her. They grouped together as a clique of twenty-five. Those who had had previous grievances against each other swallowed them in the intensity of their common grievance against her. When she talked to them, they would not answer. When she entered a room, they stood together and tittered.

Miss Anita held her own. She was more sophisticated than many of the other secretaries. Besides, she knew what she wanted. Knowing how God felt about her, what did she care about the secretaries? She knew that their behavior toward her was really a compliment. One had to be important to arouse such a furor. So, although she was unwelcome in their office, she sat in it day after day. She told herself that everything they did to her would be returned to them triplefold. In questioning her, they were questioning Father's judgment. Hadn't Father made statements on numerous occasions about retribution for those who questioned his judgment?

Miss Anita's persistence in challenging the secretaries paid off. After only six months of the never-never state where she was neither an ordinary follower nor a secretary, Father rose at a banquet one day and announced formally that a new secretary had been added to his staff and that her name was Miss Anita.

Perhaps, after Miss Anita had finally become a secretary, the feeling of the others against her might have abated and finally died down entirely, if Father hadn't aroused the secretaries' feelings further by giving her a reserved seat at the banquet table which was within whispering distance of his own—only three places from where he sat. This was intolerable. There were some secretaries who had been with Father twenty years and more, and their seats were down the side of the table far away from Father's.

These long-time secretaries made the greatest fuss. They actually went to Father Divine and told him how they felt. They said that Anita was obnoxious and attempted to lord it over them. Besides, it wasn't fair to place her, a newcomer, over the tried and true old-timers.

Father warned the critical secretaries of retribution that could be used against them just as easily as it had been used against others in the past. "But I thought to let this be with you because then you get a foreknowledge of what brings afflictions, accidents, disappointments, and failure and hospitalization of every kind——"

In spite of Father's clearly expressed sentiments, some secretaries persisted in voicing their dissatisfactions aloud. These said that, as long as Miss Anita sat at the head table, they would not come to banquets.

Father characterized their attitudes as revolt and said he would not tolerate it. He made a public statement. "God will love whom he chooses!" His wrath was unmistakable. "Nobody can tell God whom to love." Then he mentioned Miss Anita. He would honor her because she deserved honor. Any secretary who disapproved of his feeling about Anita could, for all he cared, divorce herself from the movement. As a matter of fact, if this behavior continued, any secretary who disapproved would find herself divorced whether she wished it or not.

How dared secretaries defy their maker? What did they mean they would not come down to banquets? Let them try that one time, Father informed them, one time was all that was necessary. If, when he came down to a banquet, he noticed any secretarial reserved seats vacant, he would make a public announcement.

"I will announce to the public at large," he said, "that any seat that is vacant is for the use of the public at large."

The erring angels quieted down then. They did not dare defy Father further. Their secretarial reserved seats were their badges of status, and Father might well be expected to act on his statement. Of course, they would come down to banquets, they said. They hadn't meant anything. It was only because they loved him so that they behaved in such a mortal fashion. Father would have to forgive them. He would just have to. If he didn't, if he held their mortal jealousy against them and banished them from his heart— what use would their lives be to them then? Better to be dead, they said!

17

GOD TAKES A BRIDE

The jealousy over Miss Anita, resulting in practically open revolt among the secretarial staff, was a bagatelle when Father compared it to the bedlam heaven had experienced six years earlier, when he had made Sweet Angel his second wife. Then, it was not only the secretaries who had been indignant. The rank-and-file followers were also vexed. Some of them had actually expressed their criticism of God's act to his face, had questioned him about the godlike purity. Father's answer to these had been quick and harsh. Were they daring, were they, so-called angels, really venturing to question God's act? Weren't they aware of what happened to people who questioned God? Did they want "fires and floods and famines and other destructions"? Did they want "broken arms" and "sprained ankles"? He would not be at all averse to causing followers who censured him, as well as non-followers who did, to "lose their bodies all of a heap." The criticism stopped almost before it had begun.

Some of the followers did not criticize God at all. They only asked one question of him and of his inner cabinet and they asked that question humbly—what, just exactly what, had happened to Father's first wife Peninah? The followers were embarrassed to ask such a question of God, and, certainly, if Father Divine thought their question rash, they would withdraw it. It was not that they doubted at all that whatever had happened to Peninah was Father's will and therefore unquestionable and right. It was just that the last time any of them had seen Peninah or even heard any word about her had been six years ago reckoning by mortal standards, and . . .

Father did not rebuke the followers, either for their

admittedly mortal standards or for questioning him about Peninah. Instead, according to Miss Handsome Is As Handsome Does, "he just lifted his sweet, little head and let us look straight into his dove's eyes. Then he told us what had happened to the first Mother."

Peninah had "passed," Father said, some six years or thereabouts before he had legally married Sweet Angel. (She had died of cancer in Kingston, N. Y., but this was a fact that Father obviously deemed too unimportant to relate to the followers.)

"She passed," he told followers, "and I did not desire to see her do so."

The followers said, "Amen. Peace, sweet Savior."

Father said that before the followers could understand the "significance of Mother's passing," they would have to be informed of certain facts about her past relationship with God.

Sad-voiced, he informed the followers:

"Mother used to think she looked so much older than me in the which she did appear according to the mortal version. And she at times was apparently ashamed to be with me because people would think she was my natural mother."

But Father Divine had always been the most considerate of husbands. On more than one occasion he'd denied himself to please Peninah. Father told the followers that every time Peninah brought up her appearance of mortal old age, he sought to dissuade her from "sorrowing over it." One time, when she voiced her distress, Father felt so sorry for her that he told her: "That is all right. I will make my head bald and I will look a little older so that you won't have to worry about that."

Father is a man of his word. Anyone who sees him today knows that his head is exactly as he promised Peninah it would be.

Peninah, though, was a worrier. She went on being concerned over her appearance even after God became bald on her account, Father told the followers. She should have realized, he explained, how bored he, himself, had been with "all that worldly nonsense about wives who looked older and uglier than their husbands.

"I used to carry her everywhere I would go," he recounted benignly, "and there was no thought in me of being ashamed of her. But she would say—why is it that I would not take some of the virgins with me. She would say I should have some younger ones with me that could read or play the piano and do things for me that she was not gifted to do."

Even after he had obliged Peninah by displaying an interest in the younger, more attractive angels, Father said, she was still wretched. She used to ask him of what use her fat homely body was to him. She knew he counted on her spirit and needed that, but, she said, the temple in which the spirit was housed was a handicap to him and therefore to her.

God had grown bald on Peninah's account. He had surrounded himself with young virgins because she had requested him to. For these two favors, she heartily thanked him. Now she wanted one more boon. She wished him to take the spirit out of her homely old body and to place it in a young virgin body that would be attractive to his eyes.

Father told the followers how hard he'd tried to deny Peninah's request. If there was one body he certainly did not want "lost," hers was that body. Hadn't she traveled through the South with him while he offered his own body as a living sacrifice to abolish lynching? Hadn't she stood by thirty-two times while he was lynched in the South and brought himself back to life? Hadn't she been with him from the beginning of creation? Peninah must know that an angel who had shared with God all the experiences which she had must be precious—in body as well as in spirit.

"I am pleased with you," he said.

Peninah persisted, "Take me out of this body. Please."

In all the generations he'd known Peninah, Father had never been able to deny her anything. And, knowing that she was one of the most persistent of angels and would allow him no rest until he met this onerous supplication, he took the beautiful spirit and removed it intact from the homely body in which it had been lodged "for lo these many years." In one way, this was the most herculean task Father Divine has ever been called upon to accomplish.

"My thought was not that I desired to see the passing," he said.

In fact, Father hated the idea of Peninah's death so much that even after he'd caused her spirit to lose its body, he "never made any admission of it to anyone, not even to my immediate staff. I never admitted that she had deceased until the time and the season for this to happen."

The season for admitting Peninah's decease was also the season for providing her spirit with a bodily successor. God looked hard for a worthy virgin body of the kind Peninah had prescribed, "as incorruptible and undefiled as can be."

Sweet Angel was just such a body. She was twenty-one years old when Father married her and had never had a date with a man. Today, it is said in the heavens that, when she was fifteen years old and other girls of her age were thinking of dances and new gowns and dates, Sweet Angel had said stubbornly, "If I ever had to get married to a man, I would die. God is the only one I can marry."

The body of Peninah's spirit is a true, golden blonde. She has blue eyes and an alabaster complexion, which could look beautiful with just the tiniest dab of rouge and lipstick. She is "repelled," however, by the very thought of make-up. She would never touch her face with rouge and lipstick. Rouge and lipstick are, she says, "weaknesses and wickedness" and she, of course, being the "bodily temple" of a fine spirit like Peninah's, could never be either weak or wicked. Today's followers think of Sweet Angel as the most "beautiful body that ever breathed."

Miss Handsome Is As Handsome Does admiringly says, "Mother's body is so exquisite, such a beautiful, beautiful, beautiful temple. The reason it is so perfect, you know, it took Father thousands of years to create."

Actually, to those who do not see her with their unworldly eyes, Sweet Angel, while she is attractive enough, lacks the zest and expression and color that make for true beauty. She is about five feet, five inches tall and has a lovely figure. Her wardrobe is extensive. It contains mink wraps and chinchilla capes and evening gowns that are obviously expensive. Her street clothes, however, do not look expensive at all. They are certainly no designers' models. They seem to be haphazard, not chosen with her face and figure in mind.

"Mother just doesn't care about clothes or any mortal things like that," Handsome Is As Handsome Does comments. She tells a story about Sweet Angel that has gone the rounds of the heavens. She tells it with pride. "One day, Mother came into the secretaries' living room. One of the secretaries was sitting on the couch and reading over some *Vogue* magazines. She turned to a page with a beautiful dress on it. 'Oh, Mother,' she said, 'this dress would look lovely on you.' Mother just flinched. 'I would not be concerned with such mortal things as fashion magazines,' she said. 'I have too many more important things to do. And when my important duties are over, I tune my mind to Father. Looking at fashion magazines, if I ever did look at them, would lower my vibrations.' After Mother finished laying that secretary low, you can believe she was very much ashamed of herself."

Father's second wife was born Edna Rose Ritchings in Vancouver, Canada. Her father was a well-to-do florist. Neither her father nor her mother were followers of Father Divine. Neither were they very "spiritual" in Father's sense of the word. They were not sensitives or truth-seekers. They were good, kind, righteous people who believed in the "sky-God" that Edna Rose rejected.

Questioned shortly after his daughter's marriage to Father Divine, Mr. Ritchings was unable or unwilling to trace her interest in Father. All he would tell reporters who besieged him for information was, "Edna Rose was always a fine, healthy, normal girl. Everybody liked her."

Mrs. Ritchings was altogether unable to talk to anyone.

The neighbors said that Edna Rose had always been a pretty, bright girl, although different from the other children around her. How different? Well, they didn't know how, except that she was quieter, they guessed, and always thinking her own deep thoughts.

Sweet Angel does not like to talk about the days when she was Miss Ritchings. "My life began seven years ago when I married Father Divine. Anything that happened before that, I do not like to bear record of anything like that. For me, life began when I married Father."

The followers say that Sweet Angel knew about Father's divinity when she was "a tiny body" in Vancouver. They say that she knew one follower family there (they will not tell the mortal name because what do mortal names matter, after all?) and that, from talking to them, she recognized Father Divine when she was seven years old. They say that that year, when she was seven, she wrote Father a letter. They say that it was the most beautiful letter Father had ever received and that it touched him to his heart. They say that Father answered Sweet Angel's letter, and that a regular correspondence was begun between them which lasted until the time when Father's spirit brought Sweet Angel to his very own headquarters.

Handsome Is As Handsome Does asks, "Isn't it beautiful, beautiful, beautiful?" She tells that, by the time Sweet Angel had reached her seventeenth birthday, she was so much "a child of God" that she could no longer put up with her "so-called family." She left them behind in Vancouver and went, by herself, to Montreal, where she joined her "true sisters in this knowledge."

In Montreal, Sweet Angel, still Edna Rose Ritchings to people outside the movement, worked as a stenographer for a jewelry firm and lived in the home of a Divine-dedicated family—Father's secretary, Sweet Heart, Sweet Heart's mother, and her two sisters. All four of them read the *New Day* regularly and held Divine services with a few other Montreal sympathizers.

The followers say that, during her years in Montreal, Sweet Angel, despite her youth from a mortal point of view, served as president—and an able president she was— of the Divine Peace Mission movement there. They say that Sweet Heart, whose age, mortally speaking, was the same as Sweet Angel's, served as secretary.

Sweet Angel and Sweet Heart were twenty-one years old when they came, accompanied by Sweet Heart's mother, to Father's Philadelphia headquarters. Immediately, Father and all the followers took both girls to their hearts.

"They were both so sweet," recollects Handsome Is As Handsome Does. "They were both so pretty. Of course, Mother didn't have her present beauty then. She's grown into that since Father's injected the first Mother's spirit into her. But she was certainly pretty all right, so fresh.

Sweet Heart was pretty, too. Sometimes, some of us lady angels used to get together to talk about them, which one was prettier and which nicer, all that. Not that we didn't love them both very much."

Handsome Is As Handsome Does is proud to report that she had the tremendous perception to prefer Sweet Angel to Sweet Heart from the very beginning. Most followers, though, Miss Handsome must admit in all heavenly modesty, did not possess her insight. They did not immediately perceive Mother's more wonderful qualities. They, foolishly enough, preferred Sweet Heart to Sweet Angel.

"I guess they thought she was more sociable or something else mortal like that. Mother was always a more serious type than Sweet Heart."

Father's preference was, at first, evenly divided between the two young angels. First off, he did something that, until their advent, had been entirely unheard of in heaven. Without any tryout period at all, after they had been with him for no more than three weeks, he made them both members of his secretarial cabinet. Sweet Angel became his personal stenographer. Sweet Heart became Angel's immediate assistant. Then he did another unheard-of thing. Whenever he traveled anywhere in his personal car, he permitted Sweet Angel and Sweet Heart to ride right along with him and even went so far as to allow them both to ride in the "holy back seat which he himself sat upon."

"What an honor that was!" Handsome Is As Handsome Does smiles as she recalls how God honored Sweet Angel and Sweet Heart. As she talks, you can tell she is not jealous of the memories. "And Father honored both of them. He always did that, honored one whenever he did the other. We followers couldn't tell in those days, we just didn't know, which of them deserved his greatest love. We didn't find out for a fact which one did until we heard that Father had married Mother."

Father Divine and Sweet Angel were married on April 28, 1946. There were no marriage announcements or celebrations, and only three other secretaries, Dorothy Darling, Saint Mary Bloom, and Miss Charity, knew about Father's plans. Father and Sweet Angel did not share their secret with Sweet Heart.

At four o'clock in the morning, Dorothy Darling came

down the back stairs of Broad Street headquarters, walked
out the back door, and got behind the driver's wheel of the
Cadillac which she had waiting there. She turned on the
motor, preparatory to a quick getaway. Practically on Miss
Darling's heels came the bride. Sweet Angel was nervous.
Miss Bloom and Miss Charity accompanied her, each holding tight to one of her arms. Father came last. He ran
down heaven's back stairs, rushed out the back door and
into the waiting car. He took his seat beside Sweet
Angel.

Miss Darling headed for Washington, D. C., and the
home of the Reverend Albert E. Shadd, who had been
chosen to officiate at the marriage.

Still today, Rev. Shadd is overwhelmed by the honor
Father granted him. "Why?" he asks. "Why, why should I
be the one?"

Father answers, "It was meant to be so."

Up to the night before he married Father and Sweet
Angel, Rev. Shadd had not been a Divine follower. He was
a Baptist minister who had renounced his orthodox religion. He dabbled in the spiritual and sought honestly to
discover "what truth was, what my own truth was."

"Then, on April 27, 1946," he tells eagerly, "one day
before I was called upon to perform the holy ceremony,
someone brought me a *New Day*. I read it from cover to
cover and I knew this was truth. I knew another thing. The
one who spoke this truth spoke it authoritatively. Who was
he? What was he? I could not wait another moment to find
out. I had to see this seer immediately and to speak to
him."

That night, after his introduction to the *New Day*, he
went to Philadelphia to see Father. A miracle happened.
The moment he laid eyes on Father's face, he knew Divine
was God. "I wanted to talk. I wanted to say something, but
I could not. I felt entirely tongue-tied."

Father talked first. He said, "I have been waiting for
you, oh, servant of the Lord."

"Thank you, sir," Rev. Shadd answered.

"When you return to Washington from where you've
come," Father said, "some of my followers may wish to
discuss something important with you."

At eight o'clock on the morning of the wedding, Dorothy Darling phoned Rev. Shadd. "May I and a few of the other followers come up right away? We have something important to discuss with you."

Having arrived in Rev. Shadd's small, book-lined living room, Father, in his double role of God and bridegroom, sat down and stayed silent. It was Dorothy Darling who took charge of the proceedings and efficiently instructed the Reverend as to the circumstances.

Rev. Shadd started out to marry Father and Sweet Angel the Baptist way. Midway through the ceremony, "the spirit" interfered and prevented him. He could not read from the Scriptures as he had read for many hundreds of ceremonies before. When he tried, his mouth clamped shut and he could not speak at all, so that there were several moments of dead and terrible silence. Then, inadvertently, his hand closed the Bible and opened it again at the page of the "Marriage Supper of the Lamb." It was from here that he read.

Rev. Shadd never asked the groom to kiss the bride.

As soon as the ceremony was concluded, the wedding party returned home.

Dorothy Darling, Saint Mary Bloom, and Miss Charity kept Father's secret.

"We could not have released it," Saint Mary tells today. "If we had, there would have been no telling what might have happened. The marriage was such a world-shaking event, it might have made followers vibrate strongly enough to destroy themselves."

Miss Saint Mary says that it was not followers' vibrations alone which Father considered in his imposition of secrecy. "In his unselfish concern for all mankind, Father knew that there might be outsiders who would be critical about the marriage, maybe going so far as to criticize it out loud. Then he would have to cause them to lose their bodies. He did not want to do that, and the only way to avoid it was by saving the secret until the world was ready to receive it."

The dangerous secret was told before the world was ready to receive it, and it was told by Father himself, on the morning of August 27, 1946.

Father, Sweet Angel, and a few of the secretarial cabinet were driving. Father's Cadillac was chauffered by Philip Life. Mr. Life, who does not believe in death or accidents so long as Father is with him, was speeding. A policeman stopped him.

"What's the idea?" the policeman asked.

Philip Life was about to remonstrate with the officer when Father took the helm. He did not discuss the violation. Instead, he identified heaven's first lady.

"Mrs. Divine and I——" he said.

The officer seemed unmoved by the announcement. In the very face of it, he persisted in discussing the mundane traffic violation. Father brought himself down to the policeman's level, as he is well able to do on the occasions when he simply must deal with mortality. He took care of the violation.

The secretaries were thrilled by Father's announcement but somewhat perturbed. This was the first they had heard of any wedding. Yet Father had said that he was married and that his wife was riding right in the car with them. But Peninah wasn't in the car. Father was talking about "his wife" and no doubt meaning Sweet Angel, when all the time . . . where was Peninah?

It is indicative of the faith of Father Divine's followers that a God who, while married to one wife, takes unto himself a second, even while he vehemently orders sex off the face of the earth, was entirely acceptable. Lesser souls might have wondered. Father's angels didn't.

"Either Father must be married again," remarked Miss Lovely Best, who had never thought of him being unmarried before, "or Mother [meaning Peninah] must be reincarnated." Neither had she ever thought of Peninah as being dead before.

As soon as the news was official, heaven proceeded to celebrate the marriage. Thousands gathered at headquarters throughout the country to eat and to sing. At Broad Street, which has the smallest dining room of any, Father and Sweet Angel appeared at the noon banquet on August 28.

The dinner menu included twelve kinds of hors d'oeuvres, ten different varieties of cooked vegetables, eight salads of the vegetable, fruit, and jelly-mold types, and the following meats: bologna, tongue, sliced ham, sliced pork, sliced roast lamb with mint jelly, lamb chops, roast duck, roast chicken, roast turkey with dressing and cranberry sauce, and squabs with wild rice. There were six separate types of condiments, ten breads ranging from pumpernickel to sweet rolls, and desserts of: blueberry pie, lime parfait, assorted cookies, plum pudding, fruit doll wedding cake, cheese cake, nut cake, pineapple ice-box cake, jello, fruit salad, and molded ice cream. There were nuts and after-dinner mints.

"Hallelujah!" the followers cried. "Look at the beautiful bridegroom!"

The vibrations were more intense than they had ever been, with followers "falling out" and lying unmolested where they fell. Women sang and men shouted. The noise was deafening and did not stop until Father rose to speak.

"Peace," Father began, fingering the red rose firmly pinned to his jacket lapel.

"Peace, our beautiful bridegroom!" the followers replied.

Father talked about the significance of his marriage. He seemed self-conscious, because the hostile policeman had been permitted to share his secret before the anointed ones had. He went to great lengths to explain the circumstances that had prompted the revelation.

"These police officers, they thought I was a natural man riding around with a whole lot of women, no doubt, and that was my reason for wanting them to know that Mrs. Divine was with me, that it was not anything illegal or immoral about it. I wanted the authorities to know that this was not a representative of the group going around committing vices or crimes or anything. I had my wedding license right there with me and I could prove it, if necessary."

Father discussed the faith of those who had been in the car with him. He repeated Lovely Best's words for the followers' benefit: "Either Father must be married again or Mother must be reincarnated." Then he praised Lovely Best and the other secretaries who had been in the car for being able to renounce seeming fact. "I hadn't told them that Mother in the First Body had passed."

"Amen," the followers cried. "God Almighty!"

Father assured his followers that his second wife was a virgin when he married her.

"Amen!" the followers said.

Father told how it was that he had not married this second Mother out of physical lust any more than he had married the first one for that reason. He vowed to keep Sweet Angel virginal forever.

"Jot this down in your vocabularies," he thundered out. "God is not in lust and passion. God is not any more in self-indulgence today than he was fifty years ago. When Mother in the First Body seemingly deceased six or so years ago, her spirit was with me all the time. Her presence was just the same—but it is written, 'God giveth it a body as it pleases him.' The holy, virtuous, untouched body"— he pointed to his young wife—"is through which and by which the sacred matrimony was served and carried out to the letter.

"Through this marriage of which we are now speaking, it was marvelous because thousands have gone back and paid their old back bills. Can you not see it as a personal affair? It was not for me."

"So true, Lord!" sanctioned the congregation, grateful for the sacrifice Father had made for people who had money owing to them.

Outside heaven, Father's marriage was not received exactly as he had interpreted it inside. Many newspapers ran front-page stories about it. The Negro press in particular dealt with it in detail. Most of the reports ridiculed Father and Sweet Angel, and expressed very particular doubt about the virgin's virginity.

On September 7, the New York *Age* printed a poem about Father's marriage on page one. It read:

> *Last week the headlines big and black*
> *Almost convinced some angels God had slid back,*
> *For, staring at the people a sensational line,*
> *"Attractive blonde bride of Father Divine";*
> *The newsboys shouted and the customers raved,*
> *They wondered how the angels were gonna be saved.*
> *Hadn't the father often said separation was best?*
> *Hadn't he reacted in a manner vexed*

When he saw folks looking like they were oversexed?
Yet here was God, big as life,
Taking unto himself an attractive blonde wife.
The folks in Heaven couldn't understand.
Was the father slippin', they began to demand.
Bilbo called Talmadge on the wire,
Quoth Gene: "No, you must be a liar."
They called a meeting with Rankin down the way
And decided there'd be something hot to pay.
Meanwhile God began to explain,
The gossip of the people was giving him pain.
God issued a statement profound and wise,
Announcing he didn't marry for exercise,
His wife was pure as snow of a fleecy lamb,
And anyone who thought he was slippin' could scram.
He posed for pictures with his tall, blonde bride,
And his face shone with an extravagant pride.
He gave some banquets with all kinds of meat,
All the vegetables and delicious things one could eat.
God ate his fill and blessed everyone,
He said he was still God but would beget no son.
Some of the angels thought maybe God had been lonely,
And even though he said she was a wife in name only,
They noticed that God gazed with an extravagant pride
Upon his tall, blonde, attractive bride.

Father's followers were incensed at the press. They made it clear to Father that if only he would permit them to use their fists, the mockery could be quelled. Father made it clear to the reporters.

"Please be careful," he requested of a group of Negro press representatives. "Please do not insult millions of my followers in this country and other countries, my fame, my work, or my mission. Do not pervert these people. I do not want to turn my followers loose."

The reporters were not frightened. They went on printing stories about him. Father had always been good copy. Now, since his marriage to a white woman, he was excellent copy. For he had publicly defied the greatest fear whites hold in regard to Negroes.

When Father Divine married Sweet Angel, he attacked

the legal statutes of thirty states in this country which term marriages between whites and Negroes or mulattoes as offenses. Some statutes make intermarriages punishable by fine or imprisonment or both. Some, slightly more tolerant, while they do not penalize, do declare mixed marriages to be null and void. Eight states go so far as to prohibit cohabitation between the races.

When Father Divine married Sweet Angel, he attacked strong public sentiment against intermarriage in the Negro as well as the white community. While the white community's feelings on this score have been verbalized in print and from lecture platforms and church pulpits, the Negroes' resentments have not been publicized. They are no less intense however.

Anyone who doubts that Negroes are every bit as hostile toward intermarriage as white people are, has only to talk to some interracially married couples. Clara Jaynes, a white woman who has been married to a Negro for long enough years so that she has seventeen grandchildren, is a case in point.

"One time," she says, "I accompanied my husband to his church in Riverhead, Long Island. It was all colored. Everybody stared at me. I didn't mind that till one of the elders came up and asked me to leave, just said I wasn't welcome there on account of the color of my skin."

Any big city dweller who does not believe in Negro hostility toward intermarriage has only to tour his own city and search out clubs of interracially married couples who have banded together to avoid loneliness. New York has several. So has Chicago. And Detroit. And Cleveland. Los Angeles has one called "Club Miscegenation."

No, Negroes definitely do not approve intermarriage any more than white people do.

Why, then, did Father Divine, accustomed as he was to public censure, place himself in position to elicit new criticisms from whites and Negroes alike? Why, if he had to marry at all, did he have to go and choose a twenty-one-year-old white girl for a wife? As is always the case with the paradoxical Father, the answer that would seem to be the logical one does not apply here. It was not because he loved her and desired her physically to the point where any condemnation would be preferable to living without her. For Father's claims that he and his wife live chaste lives together must be believed by anyone who has been to heaven on a more or less intimate basis and seen the pair together.

Today, seven years after she married him, Sweet Angel worships Father Divine just as she did on the day she became his "spotless virgin bride"—as a God, not a husband. Her worship shows in her speech.

She says, "People say, 'Oh yes, the Lord will come, but He may not come in my day, He may come in your day.' But, just think, we are here in the day and time when the Lord God is here. The one that moved out upon the face of the deep and said, 'Let there be light and there was light.' The one that out of the blood that runs warm in his veins has created all nations of men that dwell upon the face of the earth—our Father. Oh, it is so wonderful!

"Father dear, we praise you! We thank you! We love you and adore you! We thank you for being with us in our hearts and in our minds and thank you for being with us in your beautiful bodily form that we love and adore and reverance more than we can say. I thank you, Father dear."

Sweet Angel demands from Father none of the things that ordinary wives demand from ordinary husbands—not even loyalty to her as the only woman in his life.

In a sweet voice, with shining eyes, she has a song which she sings to him practically every day at the banquet table.

I want the whole world to love you,
Just as I say I do.

Would a wife who considered her husband mortal be able to sing such a song?

Sometimes, after she finishes singing, Father makes a small quip at Sweet Angel's expense.

"You've heard Mother's song," he tells the banqueters. "She wants the whole world to love me just as she says she does. So love me, love me, love me as much as you will. You have my wife's permission."

Because Father is obviously jesting, Sweet Angel smiles.

But the song she has sung is no joke to her. She means it from the bottom of her heart.

She rises from her seat and makes a statement that she also means in the same way. "I rest secure in the knowledge of your allness and my nothingness."

The followers applaud the correctness of Mother's knowledge. "Hallelujah!"

It is only visitors who have not rejected mortality and acquired the higher understanding who see anything unusual about this supreme uxorial self-denial. In this respect, according to no less an authority than her husband, Sweet Angel has "no imitators in all the universe."

"No imitators is right!" Robert Dean, successful Baltimore businessman who attended a banquet for the first time and heard Mother make her usual expression, leaned across follower Marvelous Heart, who was sitting between him and his smart-looking wife, Betty. "I'd give a diamond bracelet," he told his wife, "to hear you talk one time like that blond Mother Divine."

Speaking for the great majority of independent American wives, Betty Dean fought the battle of the sexes. "You've got some case, brother."

Still leaning across Marvelous Heart, Robert Dean dropped his sarcasm. "I wonder," he pondered sincerely, "what that man has that I haven't to make a wife behave like that."

Numerous men who are not associated with the movement and who have seen Father and Sweet Angel together wonder the same thing.

"He must be hot stuff in bed," was the comment of Arthur Radler, another wondering male.

Nothing could be farther from the truth of the reason for Sweet Angel's worship of her husband. When she married Father Divine, it was with implicit belief in his divinity. Today, she maintains that same implicit belief. When she married him, it was with the acceptance of herself as a reincarnated body whose virginity would be preserved as a symbol for all eternity. Given Sweet Angel's particular naïveté, it is difficult to imagine her vaunting her virginity, if she were really, as critics are always implying, God's wife in fact as well as in name. If she and Father actually do have a physical relationship, then Sweet Angel is far and

away the best actress ever to perform on the stage or off of
it.

If Father's wife is herself not proof enough, there are
numerous physical confirmations to his chastity. First,
there is Miss Peaceful, a petite African-featured secretary
who serves as Sweet Angel's roommate and lady's maid
and is not ever, for one single moment of the day or night,
apart from her. Because she is always with Sweet Angel,
Miss Peaceful has come to be known as "Mother's twin."
Whenever Father sees Sweet Angel, he also sees her "twin."
Then, there is the fact that locked doors are prohibited in
heaven and that any of Father's twenty-six secretaries has
access to his suite or Angel's at any time of the day or night.
Incidentally, for whatever that is worth for proof, there is
the interesting fact that, from early morning to early morning, Father's activity is such that he seldom takes more than
four hours for sleeping.

If sex was not the reason for Father's marriage—what
was? Some who know Father say that, even though he and
Sweet Angel do not live together as man and wife, he was
sufficiently attracted by her physically so that he married
her in order to have her always by his side. This reasoning
is also fallacious. For Father spends as much time with any
of the other secretaries in current favor as he does with his
wife. Sweet Angel could have continued as her husband's
secretary for all the personal gain either of them have had
from their marriage.

If these obviously logical reasons are rejected, there is
only one reason that must be believed. Father married
Sweet Angel, because in his thinking, this marriage to a
white woman and one born outside the U.S.A. was a way
to achieve the amalgamation of the races which is his
prime ambition. When one recognizes Father as the most
fantastic personality of his whole fantastic world, one must
also admit the possibility of his own true belief in his
claim, "I married to propagate virtue and holiness and
move discrimination off the face of the earth."

Father's followers, women as well as men, Negro as well
as white, accept his marriage as exactly what he claims.
This acceptance may be the greatest example of Father's
assertion, "There is no prejudice in any of my followers."

Anyone who does not believe Father's assertion about

his followers' lack of prejudice just does not know the nature of intolerance where intermarriage is concerned, the strength and depth of it.

A devastating contrast between the angels' lack of prejudice and prejudice in the real world outside can be made by comparing the marriage of Father Divine to the marriages of other Negro leaders to white women.

In recent years, the marriage of a Negro leader and a white woman that elicited great but by no means atypical hostility was that of Walter White, brilliant executive of the National Association for the Advancement of Colored People, and Mrs. Poppy Cannon.

Mrs. Cannon, a writer and a home economist, had long been an active worker for civil rights. Over the years, her activities and statements had proven her to be a friend to the Negro people.

Friendship notwithstanding, however, from the moment the marriage became public, bedlam arose in the Negro community. The Negro press was adamant in its condemnation. A typical article appeared in the Norfolk *Journal and Guide*. It suggested that detractors of the National Association for the Advancement of the Colored People had used the marriage to prove that the entire program for Negro integration was a mask for the Negroes' basic yearning to marry whites.

"It is not likely," the *Journal* concluded about a leader whose sincerity had never before been questioned, "that the gentleman, prone as he is to serve his selfish interests, will feel overly concerned about what happens to the N.A.A.C.P., but an official resignaton is in order."

It took a white woman interested in minority problems, Mrs. Eleanor Roosevelt, to help Walter White over one of the most tumultuous times of his important career. She went before the controlling board of the N.A.A.C.P. and made them understand that if this marriage was used as a basis for firing White, the whole question of Negro rights would be compromised. She spoke to what might easily have seemed one of the most highly volatile trustee boards in history.

The tension in the Negro community, apparent as it was among the men, was, as always, most volubly expressed by the women.

"In the South," one woman scientist told, "plenty of white men still maintain two families, the legal white one and the always illicit Negro one. These white men don't worry about their Negro women. If the situation is ever reversed, though, Negro men worry plenty. Walter White worried about Poppy Cannon all right. He divorced a loyal colored wife who had stuck by him many years, the mother of his children, in order to legalize *her* position."

Therein lies the source of the greatest bitterness experienced by Negro women when their leaders cross racial lines in marriage. It is rooted deep in their racial oppression.

"If you are ever in the Congressional Library," the scientist said, "and care to take the trouble to investigate some facts about miscegenation, you'll find plenty about white men and their Negro mistresses. George Washington had a colored sweetheart named Mary Gibbon. Thomas Jefferson had colored children. Andrew Jackson was the father of three Negro children."

All the Negro women who expressed themselves about the white marriage revealed clearly that if Mr. White had taken Mrs. Cannon as a mistress instead of a wife, there would have been considerably less hostility against him. If he had done that, it might have been revenge in a way for the courtesan position Negro women have always occupied with white men and that they still do occupy today.

If Walter White had taken Poppy Cannon illicitly, it would have satisfied, in a sense, what sociologists Abram Kardiner and Lionel Oversey in their recent book, *The Mark of Oppression,* have characterized "the two most deeply suppressed tendencies of the Negro community— hostility and aggression." Therein lies the secret of the difference in reactions toward the marriage of Walter White and of Father Divine. . . .

In the real world, where Negro oppression is a clear fact, Negro women, in fighting to maintain themselves on a decent level, must resent intermarriages between colored leaders and white women which remind them once again of their positions as people and as women. In the fantasy world of Father Divine, where the frustrations of living in a white world are removed, so are hostility and aggression.

That is why, while Walter White was almost forced to the breaking point of his career because of his marriage, heaven's dark angels could herald Father's marriage as the beginning of a wonderful new amalgamation between Negroes and whites.

That is why Sweet Dove, whose complexion is deep brown, could write to blond Sweet Angel soon after she had become God's wife, "Since Father married you, he has become even more real to me."

That is why Negro domestic Sunny Side Up could say to her God, "Father dear, I've always loved you. Now, since you've married Mother, I love you even more. Because, when you married her, I felt like you also married me."

Only in the world of Father Divine can a Negro domestic identify herself with heaven's white queen. No wonder she can view an interracial marriage and say with positive emotion, "Peace! It's wonderful!"

Those Negro women, as well as the white women and the men of both races who really objected to Father's marriage, did so only because they viewed it for a while as a defection. They felt that Father should never have placed himself in the position of seeming to be faithless to his no-sex tenet. Once they had been convinced of his chastity, they accepted Father's wife exactly as he willed them to.

The only ones who did not accept Sweet Angel, who knew within their hearts that they could not ever accept her, who were passionately angry with Father when his marriage was announced, and who could cheerfully have murdered his wife, were white and close to Father. As a matter of fact, two of them who were least able to control their venom had, before Father's marriage, been "courted by him."

Father Divine's "courting" of Quiet Devotion, who was Dorothy Darling's predecessor as Secretary Number One, had been observed by the followers over a long period.

Having been secretary to Faithful Mary at one time, Quiet Devotion had been in the movement at least twenty years. Her real name was Rita Delap and she had come from an excellent family. At thirty-eight or thereabouts when Father married, Quiet Devotion was a really beautiful woman. She was recognized by the other followers as the ablest member of the secretarial staff. On many occasions, Father had announced publicly that he intended to extend his movement in Europe and that he would send Quiet Devotion to represent him there.

Then came the marriage! Quiet Devotion resented it bitterly. She tried not to. But the malevolence came through and showed every time she looked at Sweet Angel. The other followers saw it clearly.

"Maybe we just expected her to be sore," explains intelligent Life Longevity, "and looked for anger. Of course, when you look for a characteristic, you generally find it. I don't think that was the case with Quiet Devotion, though. She had always looked happy. Now she looked sad. You felt sorry every time you looked at her."

Soon after Father's marriage was announced, Quiet Devotion left the movement. She did not discuss her departure with Father or anybody. It was just that, one day, the banquet seat which was reserved for her, the one to the left of Father Divine, was vacant. It remained unoccupied until Father assigned it to Dorothy Darling. Then, the followers knew, once and for all, that Quiet Devotion was gone and that Dorothy Darling was Secretary Number One.

Life Longevity says, "It was a pity. All these years she'd worked for Father's blessings and then had to go and give them up. She couldn't help it, though. Jealousy rankled inside her soul and ate her up."

Jealousy also rankled inside of a pretty young redhead named Carole Sweet. Carole was not a secretary exactly, but Father had granted her the freedom of his suite and indicated that her secretaryship was basically assured and that it was only a matter of time before she achieved it.

"Father really courted Carole Sweet," Life Longevity reports disappointedly. "He really did. And then——" Her voice breaks. She loses her logical tone. She clasps and unclasps her hands. "And then, Carole—— Well, after Father married Mother, Carole went—she went crazy, that's all. You just should have heard her, yelling and screaming around."

It is still told in hushed tones around the Broad Street heaven that Carole "actually cursed. She did, really."

It is told that she maligned Mother in the Second Body.

"She stood in front of a mirror," Miss Longevity tells, "and she said, 'Look at me. I am more beautiful than Sweet Angel. I look like her but I am more beautiful. Father should have married me instead of her.' That's what she had the nerve to say. I saw her with my own eyes and I heard her with my own ears. Oh, jealousy really rankled in that one."

Jealousy festered so in Carole Sweet, say Father's followers, that it forced her to commit a horrible indiscretion for which she will pay the rest of her life. It forced her to leave heaven in the company of a man and go so far as to marry him. His name in the movement was the Prodigal Son, and he, like Carole, had been courted by God.

18

THE PRODIGAL SON!

When pretty Carole Sweet eloped with the Prodigal Son, the followers were surprised. A few said they weren't surprised at all. These said they were glad of what she had done. They felt that her life as a married woman would be "terrible." It would be punishment for her undisguised jealousy.

"Next year, when she looks back on this day," was the comment of Carole's erstwhile friend, Smile-a-While, "she'll wish she had been buried instead of married."

Universal Vocabulary, another friend, added, "So true!"

"She'll find out God ain't to be tangled with," emphasized Ready Love. "Father's a live wire!"

"So true!" the followers kept echoing each other. "So true, Father dear."

In the minds of all the followers gathered in the small "Sisters' Sitting Room" of the Broad Street headquarters was the same thought: in marrying the Prodigal Son, Carole was once and for all resigning her precious virginity. For the Prodigal Son was not one to be content with a marriage in name only. True, he had been wearing sheep's clothing for nine years, posing as a body in whom Father's spirit "held sway," but true followers knew now that, since his departure from heaven, the wolf had growled through the seemingly gentle exterior. In reality, the Prodigal Son was a "natural man" who had lost respect, if in reality he had ever had any, for angelic chastity. Stupid Carole Sweet. She would never, as Sweet Angel would forever, be a wife in name only. How could she be, having taken a husband who, by his own confession, had been, in the days before Father's spirit had entered him, "a depraved, diseased sex maniac."

The Prodigal Son was born John West Hunt in Cleveland, Ohio. His father, long dead, had made a fortune in the milk business. His mother had inherited most of it. There was a younger brother named Warner.

John Hunt had never been a well child physically and had showed the results of emotional difficulties from the time he was a very small boy.

His mother, today Mary Bird Tree, one of Father's most favored followers, had always been "spiritually inclined." She had exposed John, from his earliest boyhood, to Christian Science practitioners and also to spiritualist healers by the score. None of them had been able to help him attain physical or emotional health.

When young John was nine years old, he attempted to commit a sexual act with a five-year-old cousin.

"So what?" he asked the shocked adults who discovered him.

In school, young John Hunt was as much of a problem as he was at home. No school, public or private, would keep him for any length of time. Even the authorities of two military schools found him too hard to handle.

When John was seventeen years old, he ended the fruitless game of school attendance for a new and more demanding role; he married a girl for whom he had neither love nor respect, because he had made her pregnant.

This marriage interlude lasted three months. John's baby was born six months after he had left his wife to hobo his way around the country. Sleeping in boxcars, haystacks, and railroad stations and hobnobbing with road tramps and their women, John Hunt, at seventeen, contracted syphilis. This frightened him badly. How to deal with it? Discuss it with the family? That seemed impossible. Consult a medical doctor? John didn't like doctors. He placed himself in the hands of a Christian Science practitioner, followed the faith exactly as the practitioner laid it down, and waited hopefully for the miraculous cure which did not materialize.

Discouraged with his practitioner and certain that his syphilis was chronic, he determined to forget about it and went to California, where he hoped to start living a new kind of life. He sent for his wife and baby, and they lived together in a cat-and-dog relationship for a couple of months. Then Mrs. Hunt secured a divorce.

No sooner was John a free man again than he remarried. The second wife was many years older than he. After only a few months she, too, divorced him.

Marriage was beginning to daunt John somewhat, but he did attempt a third one. This one might have lasted with mutual affection for some time if the third Mrs. Hunt had not learned, soon after giving birth to John's baby, that she was syphilitic and that her husband was responsible. She had been so severely infected by him that the doctors suggested operation.

In an open confession to Father and the followers, made voluntarily in 1934 soon after John Hunt entered the Peace Mission movement, he talked freely about the life he led while his wife was in the hospital.

"I occupied my home with a well-known federal judge and a court reporter. Our time was spent in carousing about, drinking in company with many different women. On one occasion, we all three stopped at the hospital to visit my wife after a drunken party."

Understandably, this was one visit Mrs. Hunt could happily have done without.

John's wife returned home after her hospitalization. Practically at the moment she entered the door, he had a long, serious talk with her. He said he realized he was her legal husband and that his home, therefore, was her legal residence. But there were certain things she had to realize, too. First and foremost, he was a man who required a vigorous sex life. Being one single woman unable to give him "complete satisfaction," she must free him to live in his own way. If she would be adult enough to agree to this pattern, he would do his best to keep her uppermost in his consideration and would attempt to arrange all of his future contacts with women in such a way as to prove least embarrassing to her.

Evidently, John Hunt's wife entered into the bargain he demanded, for she continued to live with him all during the difficult years, the wildest period of his entire wild career. He described these times, with utter casualness, in his lurid confession to Father Divine.

"A prominent radio star with whom I had been living occasionally asked me to become the father of a child to which she desired to give birth. In spite of my conscientious cooperation, the experiment was a failure."

John Hunt had a friend, and the friend had a wife who was more fortunate than the prominent radio star—or unfortunate, considering later developments.

"She did become pregnant as a result of my association with her," he reported to Father Divine, "and it was with considerable difficulty that I arranged for a criminal abortion without arousing the suspicions of her husband."

John told Father about one of his mistresses who divorced her husband on his account. "Then I lost interest in her," he commented airily.

There was a man in California who tried to kill him because he didn't appreciate his involvement with his sweetheart.

John Hunt, during these roving days, had as little of the appearance of the stereotype Don Juan as Father has of the divine being he appears in his followers' eyes. Hunt was tall but somewhat pudgy. He had blue eyes, sandy-blond hair, and a girlish pink and white complexion. Obviously, the impression he made on women did not rest on the appearance of virility. Perhaps they sensed the satyr under the deceiving exterior.

"I maintained a lengthy list of women," he told Father. "Available on short notice."

The lengthy list included the wife and daughter of a retired president of a large insurance company with "both of whom I had all manner of illicit relations, one after the other."

John Hunt did not make special confessional note of an important fact regarding his third wife, but from her actions, as he repeated them to Father, it is logical to assume that whatever sexual scruples she'd had at the beginning of her marriage were successfully downed by her life with her husband. She and he and an architect friend and his wife had a party at the Hunt home which "resulted in the voluntary trading of wives in the same room with the lights turned on."

Strangely enough, this self-indulgent man ran an adver-

tising business, the John W. Hunt Co., Inc., which, during
its inceptive stages, revealed a fine success potential and
held a high rating with Dun and Bradstreet. Two of the
more prosperous Los Angeles women's clubs were enthusiastic clients. With his mother's consistent financial help
and his own flamboyant personality, the firm should have
realized its potential. Needless to say, it never did. For
whenever the business began to build up a financial re-
serve, its director withdrew it. When bills came due, he
could not meet them.

In early 1934, the Hunt creditors bore down as a group
and demanded payment of long-overdue bills. John declared himself bankrupt.

With nothing to do during the period following his
bankruptcy, he spent almost every night drinking himself
into a stupor. During his rare periods of sobriety, he attempted a job of self-analysis and was horrified by the
picture of himself that he had hitherto avoided facing.

"I was corrupt in body, mind, and soul, without reputation and despised," he admitted after he had come to lay
his burdens on Father's shoulders. "No mortal could ever
know the hopelessness and helplessness that gripped my
heart. Only you [Father Divine] who heard the forlorn cry
of my tortured soul have knowledge of the despair that had
become my bitter potion."

This was the time when, in his more lucid moments,
John began to think of himself as insane. He often felt
that, if he were a braver man, he would commit suicide.

In the midst of John Hunt's self-search, he was stricken
with acute appendicitis. Because of his state of mind, the
appendicitis attack assumed the hideous proportions of a
cancer to him. It was a punishment, no more dire than he
deserved, a rightful castigation from God for the corrup-
tion his entire life had been.

Inspired by a desire for revenge, his wife encouraged this
delusion of his stricken mind. She accompanied him to the
hospital for the appendectomy and, on the way over, kept
telling him, "You'll never come out alive."

John told Father Divine about the horror of those few
hours preceding his operation. He said:

"Within my soul, I faced what I believed to be the last,

hopeless hours of a miserable, feeble, sinful existence and delivered my broken body to the surgeons without help and not caring whether I lived or died."

When he found himself alive and recovering from the operation, John Hunt felt that "this recovery was more than I deserved." He determined to reform. He continued his self-searching and came to the conclusion that he needed an authority, someone stronger than himself, to guide him to a "purer life."

It was at this time, when he was frenziedly seeking a true authority-figure, that Father Divine first came to him.

John's brother Warner knew Father first. Sandy-blond, like John, with blue eyes and a charming baby face, Warner's personality had gentleness as its keynote. He was a university man with two degrees. Still, he'd found the competitive harshness of the world outside heaven's gates difficult to adjust to. Warner Hunt was always an idealist. Until his meeting with Father Divine, he'd seen "idealism consistently scoffed at."

Somewhat oversimply, he explains what first motivated him to accept Father's divinity.

"I wanted to see someone live the life of Christ. I never did, though. Lots of people talked about it in the world. Christian Scientists and other religionists talked. Nobody actually sank their teeth into doing the work, though. Only Father has ever done it."

Warner Hunt tells feelingly that in the advertising business, where he'd worked with John, people had been anything but Christlike. They'd smoked and drunk liquor and talked about their exploits with women until he had grown nauseous listening to them. Even in college, where he had had some relatively happy times in his enjoyment of group living in a fraternity house, he'd been perturbed by the vulgarity around him. It wasn't just the way the other boys had chased girls that had bothered him. It was also the way they'd boasted about their conquests.

Here, in the Peace Mission movement, Warner Hunt tells today, he is experiencing the very best of college living. The mission in which he lives is, in effect, a fraternity without vulgarity. Although he shares a room with three other men, he cannot disapprove of the behavior or the talk of any one of them.

Warner says that a little epileptic girl named Carole was overtly responsible for his "coming to God." Carole was seeking a cure for her epilepsy through a Christain Scientist practitioner who was one of Warner's good friends.

"She was getting no place," he tells. "The poor girl kept on 'falling out' in spite of the best efforts of the practitioner."

Then Father Divine took a hand and worked a miracle for the little girl. He put it into the mind of one of his loyal followers that she was to come to California. He put it into her mind that she was to visit her sister who lived on Carole's block—and into the sister's mind that she was to take her to visit poor little Carole.

"I heard about your condition," the follower told the girl. "I want to help you. I am an angel of God on earth. His name is Father Divine. He has a human body and he is a panacea for all the ills of every human who will accept his help."

Suddenly, in the midst of the follower's conversation, Warner Hunt says, Carole felt herself propelled out of her chair. With no seeming consciousness, she began singing spiritual songs. Warner says that she said, "I will never have an epileptic fit again." She didn't.

The miracle of Carole's story impressed Warner Hunt. This Father Divine had succeeded where a Christian Science practitioner had failed. It would be well to learn more about such a man. He secured the *New Day*. He read it from cover to cover.

"It was wonderful!" he remembers. "What a ring of authority it had, and what an idealistic life it prescribed!"

Soon after his introduction to Father's *New Day*, Warner Hunt set out for the East, to search for "the spiritual dream" the newspaper had described. He says, "I kept thinking even then—Father Divine can well be the embodiment of my dream."

Having arrived in Father's presence, he found himself spontaneously stirred. But his mind held back from full acceptance of the deity of this seemingly insignificant little man.

"I will test him," he determined. "I will see if he can read my thoughts." He forced his mind to dwell on the problems of his mother who had been troubled for many years with a weak heart and an invaliding rheumatic condition.

Father looked hard at Warner Hunt. "Your mother is sick!" he said.

Then Warner Hunt knew. Father Divine was who his followers claimed him to be. "I begged him to heal my beloved mother."

"My spirit will protect her," Father said, "if she will but think on me."

Warner returned home with the idea of Father Divine crowding out every other thought. Still today, he remembers the excitement in him when he told his mother:

"Father Divine is God! Father Divine can heal you!"

Mrs. Hunt pressed her son for details. Warner didn't give her many, except to describe the miracle of Carole and his own reaction to Divine.

"Keep your mind turned to him," he urged.

Mrs. Hunt promised to keep her mind on Father Divine even though she had never seen him. Having always regarded herself as psychic, she found it a simple matter to visualize Father from her son's description of him.

"The night of my return," Warner Hunt tells today, "my so-called mother went to bed an invalid. She woke up in the morning feeling well. Father had performed a miracle for her, just as he had for little Carole."

"I called on Father Divine," Mrs. Hunt told her son enthusiastically, "and it looked as if he was at the foot of the bed. I have been healed."

His mother's "cure" was all the substantiation Warner Hunt needed for his instinctive belief that Father was God. As for Mrs. Hunt, it was ample proof for her, too. She gave up her Christian Science practitioner and all her spiritual healers. Mother and son joined the movement together. Mrs. Hunt became Mary Bird Tree. Warner Hunt became John Devout. Naturally, they sought to bring John into the movement with them. They visited him in the hospital and talked Divine to him.

"In my darkest and most desolate hours," John Hunt told about his time in the hospital that became filled with thoughts of "this truth" his mother and brother were bringing to him, "Father's holy spirit ministered to my soul and brought the light of hope to my mind."

He spent the last four days of his hospitalization pondering on Father and reading the *New Day*. When he was discharged, he did not go home. He went straight to a Peace Mission meeting. Reformed sinners and recovered invalids testified at that meeting. John Hunt learned of broken lives that had been mended since Father's intervention. He saw people, some of them disadvantaged by worldly standards, possessed of more self-confidence than he had ever had.

"Father Divine is God Almighty in a bodily form," declared Mr. Strength Determination.

Watching Father's followers in their seeming security, John wished that he could believe as they did.

"I wanted so much," he said later, "to experience the blessings they had received."

Even though John Hunt's heart was more than eager to accept the ideal of Father's divinity, his mind kept refusing to. Until "one wonderful night" when, he says, "the mind found itself with no choice other than to accept the bidding of the heart." That was the night he went to his bed and was hardly in it five minutes before he felt his whole body reacting to a strange sensation he'd never experienced before.

"I was bathed in perspiration," he told the followers soon after his cataclysmic conversion had occurred, "and it seemed that every organ of my body was being twisted and torn. This continued for what seemed like . . . half an hour, and as quickly as it came upon me it left and I immediately fell asleep. When I awakened the next morning, I awakened to an entirely new sense of existence. I knew within myself that I had been healed by the power of God, Father Divine."

One week after he'd been converted, John Hunt was en route to see Father Divine. In Father's presence he began to feel happy, happier than he had ever been before in his life. He confessed his sinful life and felt eased by his confession.

"I was a living Jekyll and Hyde. I took advantage of every opportunity to watch women undress. Only God Almighty kept me out of the penitentiary. I had so many close calls, I cannot count them all. I abused myself every day for years. Every filthy, detestable thing the human mind can think of, I did. I acquired such a perverted sexual taste that ordinary intercourse was secondary."

Father was not shocked by John Hunt's lurid life story. He was glad that John had been such a sinner. He said that the very former evil, once it was cast out, could redound to the good of John's eternal soul. He said that, since John had opened his mind and his heart to the receipt of Divine guidance, since he was such "a repentant sinner instead of an unrepentant one," life could be beautiful for him.

John knew the truth of Father's statement.

"Every detestable mortal habit and characteristic has been cast out of this body," he told other followers after he had had several interviews with Father Divine. He said that now he knew what to do with the wreck of a body he'd never cared about before. He'd offer it as a "living sacrifice" for "God's use." He begged Father to grant a spiritual name to that body. Father did. He named John Hunt "the Prodigal Son" for the son in the Bible, and he promised to love and cherish him the way the son in the Bible was loved and cherished.

Father did love and cherish the Prodigal Son. He also respected him. From the very day he first confessed his sins to Father, Divine recognized the Prodigal Son as a member of his inner cabinet. He placed him in complete charge of his program of public relations.

The Prodigal Son embraced his public relations duties assiduously. He had many ideas for effectively relating God to his public. Sometimes these were utilizable. Sometimes they were so flamboyant that even Father's rather questionable modesty could not permit of their acceptance. One of these was a pet of the Prodigal Son's. He recommended that "a revolving throne for God" be installed in the rear of the Duesenberg in which Father rode in those days. He further recommended that a retractable gold halo which could be extended to the spot directly above Divine's head be placed above the throne. Regretfully, Father had to veto the recommendation as being perhaps not quite in good taste.

For two years, the Prodigal Son moved in Father's magnificent shadow. Just as Faithful Mary had been, he became another "sample and example" to followers and outsiders alike. He was a rich man's son, Father used to say dolefully, but his wealth and his position had done him no good. He had been sunk in deep mire until God had drawn him out. Now he was just as God himself was: healthy and happy in every limb, bone, and sinew in his body.

The Prodigal Son, after he had been with Divine for some three years, left the personal presence, with Father's full approval, to go West and spread the gospel there. He traveled between California and Colorado and recruited angels in every city he stopped in. He formed and led a movement in Denver that grew very important. He communicated almost daily with Father Divine.

"I am proud of the Prodigal Son," Father told the other followers.

Then, suddenly, after so many years of passionate self-denial, the Prodigal Son reverted to mortality and caused a huge chink in Father's pride. Mortality's name was Delight Jewett. When the Prodigal Son met her, she was not quite seventeen years old. She was blond and very pretty.

"I heard about the movement," Delight told, after she and the Son had disagreed, "and I decided to see what it was all about. The first time I went there, it was because I was curious. Everybody was nice, the singing was cheerful, the food terrific. I liked it there and came back a lot of nights. Prodigal Son talked to me, told me Divine was God. I didn't know was he or wasn't he. I couldn't make up my mind."

One night, Delight slept at the mission. That was the night the spirit of Divine happiness and good will entered into her once and for all, so that she felt sure of Father's divinity, and she wanted to remain in heaven forever. The Prodigal Son wanted her to remain forever, too. All night he talked Divinism to her:

"You are the Virgin Mary. I am Jesus Christ."

Late the next morning, he took her to a department store and purchased a wardrobe, including a nine-hundred-dollar fur coat, for her.

"Why is this?" Delight asked.

"Because," the Prodigal Son answered, "the Virgin Mary is the highest of all."

Delight spent more and more time at the Divine mission.

"I began to like the Prodigal Son," she says, "and to believe everything about he being Jesus, me being Mary, and Father Divine being God."

When, about three months after he had met her, Prodigal Son invited Delight and several Peace Mission angels to accompany him to his Los Angeles home, she happily accepted.

"I heard it was a beautiful nineteen-room house at 807 Roxbury Drive in Beverly Hills, right in the neighborhood where movie stars live."

The trip from Denver was uneventful. The Son's party stopped at hotels en route and registered for two suites, as "John the Baptist and Party." The Son and the other men occupied one suite. Delight and the ladies occupied the other.

Delight says, "The Son was very nice on the trip. I must say that."

Once arrived at his home, though, the Prodigal Son reverted to being the "natural man" he had been before Father's spirit was injected into him. Delight says that the first night they spent in his home, the Son undressed and came into her room in his pajamas. He said he had come to talk about Father.

"Then he didn't talk at all. He just got wild and attacked me. It was awful."

Delight claims her relationship with the Son was obnoxious to her. It must not have been as obnoxious as she tells, however, for, of her own volition, it was maintained for two months and in many places—including, in addition to Los Angeles and Denver, Cleveland, New York, and Colorado Springs.

It was not until she returned home to Denver in April of 1937 that Delight revealed "the obnoxiousness" of her physical relationship with the Son. That was when her father, Lee Jewett, ordered the Prodigal Son's arrest for having violated the Mann Act by having lived with his young daughter in many cities. Delight backed her father.

Speaking to Special F.B.I. Agent Rita Whittley, she claimed to have been "under a delusion" for the months she had lived with the Son. She said:

"I was told, and I believed for two months, that Father Divine was God and had brought a new heaven to this earth. I was told that John Hunt was Jesus Christ and I was the Virgin Mary. All I can say is, something happens to a person when he accepts Father Divine as God."

Father's followers jumped to the Son's defense. They said Delight was no better than she ought to have been. They never used the "negative word 'prostitute,'" but that, in politer language, was what they labeled Delight.

On April 22, the Prodigal Son was arraigned in Denver under his mortal name, John Hunt. He pleaded not guilty. In regard to Delight's accusations against him, he said:

"I can't control what she had to say. After all, she can say one thing; I can say another. After all, we'd both be talking. After all, Father Divine taught me to live in the spirit. That's what I've tried to do since I felt this great influence for good in my life." He was careful to free Father of any complicity. "Whatever were my actions, they in no way reflect upon Father Divine."

His actions did reflect, though. "This," ministers screamed out from their pulpits, "is an example of the virtue of Father Divine."

Negro newspapers wrote editorials about the Hunt case and directed their attacks against Father instead of the son. Reporters stormed heaven's doors. They wanted to know what Father thought of his Prodigal Son now. Father stood on his divine rights and refused to talk to reporters. His press secretary, John Lamb, talked for him, though.

"Father deplores sexual intercourse among his angels," Mr. Lamb gently explained, "and John Hunt used Father's name in vain to satisfy his vile lust."

Despite his seeming condemnation of the Prodigal Son, it was Father Divine who helped him to escape a jail sentence. He made contact with Lee Jewett and paid him money the Son gave him. He convinced Mr. Jewett not to press charges.

After his deplorable interlude, a thoroughly chastened Prodigal Son returned to Father Divine. He decided that he needed the inspiration of the daily sight of God's bodily form and so came back East. In New York, he continued where he had left off as Father's public relations adviser and became his private photographer. He also began to work with John Devout who was editing the *New Day*. All of the followers thought the Prodigal Son had slipped for the last time, and that this reformation would last forever. He seemed to be carrying out to the letter the sign that makes a Peace Mission room distinctive: "no drinking, no swearing, no smoking, no carnality, no fighting." Then carnality overcame him once again and he sinned—even worse than he had with Delight Jewett. Followers still can't understand how he could have become so interested in young Carole Sweet that he would desert God just in order to marry her.

When the Prodigal Son left heaven, he did not leave in the quiet fashion that some other dissatisfied members had left. His departure was in line with the flamboyance of his nature and resulted in "fireworks." He wrote an article for *Our World* magazine, which appeared in August of 1949 and purported to be a truthful exposé. It was titled, "Father Divine: Man or God?" The subhead read: "Here's the inside story of the fantastic goings-on in a million-dollar cult kingdom."

"Nobody knows better than Father Divine himself," the Prodigal Son wrote, "that his kingdom is falling to pieces. I lived with him thirteen years as a trusted lieutenant. I could see what was happening before I quit him cold."

He characterized Father as an "opportunist" and called the movement a "hoax."

He stated that Father's inner cabinet of secretaries was torn apart by bitter rivalries. "They know the innermost secrets. If any of them would spill the beans, Divine wouldn't have a leg to stand on."

He claimed Father had a bad heart.

The big thesis of the Prodigal Son's article dealt with Father and money. He said that Father had deprived many innocent people of their life's savings and mentioned the legal suits pending to force restitution. He talked about Verinda Brown.

"There are many more legal suits to follow," he wrote

emotionally. "One of them will be mine to make Divine explain what happened to a $200,000 fortune from my mother, now an invalid and a virtual prisoner at 41st and Westminster in Philly. Today, she cannot even buy herself a bottle of milk."

The article, discovered by Divinites two months before its scheduled appearance, created havoc in the movement. Followers were angry and disappointed. Above all, they were hurt by the duplicity of one whom Father had courted. The most violent reactions of all came from Mary Bird Tree and from John Devout. Both of them proved that God had indeed taken all mortality out of them.

Mary Bird Tree publicly called her son a "liar" and a "Judas." She issued a notarized answer to his accusations against Father:

"I have never given Father Divine any money, and Father Divine has never asked me for any money. Upon my own free will and volition, I came to Father Divine, because no doctor, no practitioner, or nobody else could heal me of my condition, but Father Divine did. Now, I would like to have paid Father if I could, because, for medical treatment, I have paid out thousands of dollars not only to Battle Creek Sanitarium to heal me but also to Christian Science practitioners."

Since Father Divine came to her as a free blessing, Mary Bird Tree stated that she desired to use her money to help others toward the same attainments and so had co-operated with other followers in the purchase of different Peace Mission properties. These purchases were investments, however, not gifts to Father. She had been happy to make them.

She asked, in regard to her son's designation of her as a virtual prisoner:

"How can I be a virtual prisoner among those whom I love and appreciate in an atmosphere of purity, holiness, love, and real Christ as Father Divine has produced it? This is the freedom and enjoyment and Divine family for which I have been seeking lo these many years."

She condemned her son for being an ingrate and an incompetent and regretted the many thousands of dollars she had once given him.

John Devout took up the cudgels against his brother. He wrote an indignant letter to John Davis, publisher, and David A. Hepburn, executive editor, of *Our World*:

"I should think you would first, as a publisher and an editor, make a little better analysis of the individuals who contribute articles to your publication before you take what they have to offer as authentic . . . Anyone in his [John Hunt's] frame of mind cannot give an accurate account of anything."

His brother, he said, was and always had been full of "bitter hatred, perversity, and destruction." He was "bad" and "dirty-minded."

19

"THERE IS ONLY
ONE FACT——"

John Devout and Mary Bird Tree, in their abject devotion
to Father Divine which caused them to relinquish all
mortal ties with their son and brother and to condemn the
former Prodigal Son in the same way they would condemn
any stranger who tried to harm their God, took the same
attitude that any one of Father's other white followers
would most assuredly have taken. For Father's white followers are no less lost to any world but his than the colored ones are. It may be that they are more lost. While
there is turnover among the colored followers, the white
ones remain a tradition. Most of them, driven to join Father by reasons of personality rather than by the comparatively weaker reasons of economic need, have more completely identified themselves with the God for whom they
have had to make considerable material sacrifice.

Most of Father's white followers were, before they came
to Father, at least of upper middle class. In the outside
world, many of them were professional men and women.
Some still hold professional responsibilities today. Father
Divine's Peace Mission movement contains white doctors,
dentists, lawyers, and architectural engineers. There are so
many schoolteachers and ex-schoolteachers that until recently the movement ran a large home outside Philadelphia
for those who had retired from school systems in New
York, New Jersey, and Pennsylvania. And so many registered nurses that a prime function of the Divine employment service is to secure proper placement for them.

People who are unacquainted with the movement are
always amazed to hear that the average educational background of white Divinites is rather above that of the gen-

eral average in this country. They are more amazed to hear
that the average income also compares more than favorably and that, throughout the years, white socialites have
become true followers. The three Hunts are typical of this
last group. So is Mrs. Mary Sheldon Lyon, of the Lyon
toothpaste family.

Mrs. Lyon is dead now. Her memory is revered in the
movement. In the early thirties, while Father was still in
Sayville and long before white followers became the almost-
commonplace they are today, she openly recognized Father
Divine as God and gave up the mortal name of Mary
Sheldon Lyon to become a new spiritual personality—
Peace Dove.

"Peace Dove was just like her name," white-haired Miss
Beautiful recalls today, "like a sweet white bird. Only she
was a sad soul before she found God. She must have been
sixty years old then. Reckoning by your mortal version."

Everyone in the movement who remembers Peace Dove
agrees that she was sad and lonely during her earliest days
with Father. Divorced from her husband, childless, and
with no family except for a brother, Dr. William Hill Sheldon, who spent most of his time abroad, and some cousins
named Latham who had active lives of their own in which
Peace Dove did not quite fit, she used to travel a great
deal.

"Her traveling was meaningless, though," Miss Beautiful
says. "There she was, all alone, nobody to care whether she
was coming or going or lived or died. She had nothing—
only money."

In her early sixties, Mary Sheldon Lyon began seeking
after "truth." In every city where she found herself, she
looked up spiritualists, those who were recommended by
other occult-minded acquaintances and those who were not
recommended at all but maintained listings in the city telephone directories.

"All those fakers did was fleece her of her money,"
according to Miss Beautiful. "It was all anyone ever did to
her. People paid her attention and tried to make friends
with her. All for her money. Nobody ever cared for her
until Father."

Father Divine sought Mary Lyon out and gave her and

all his followers the feeling that her money and prestige had nothing to do with the way he felt. What was money to him after all? He said that money was the root of all evil. Many a man as rich as Rockefeller and far richer than Mrs. Lyon had offered all his money to the movement and been rejected by a God who saw through his manners to the flaws of his character. Mary Lyon was different though. She had no character flaws. She was sweet goodness personified. That was why, when she attended banquets, she was always granted a holy seat at God's own table. That was why true followers made a fuss over her.

During her early acquaintance with him did Mary Sheldon Lyon accept Father's divinity or was she merely moved by the warmth of his hospitality? Since there is no testimony to indicate exactly when Mrs. Lyon's actual conversion occurred and since the objectivity of old-time followers who knew her can hardly be relied upon for accuracy, this question must remain unanswered. It is logical to assume, however, that the first appeal he made to her was on the basis of his recognition of her as a good person rather than as a wealthy one and that then the mood of the entire congregation began to influence her and that she responded to her environment and recognized Father as the rest of them did.

An outsider has only to spend a few hours in heaven to realize how completely even a strong, satisfied person can respond to its environment. You sit or you stand in the very middle of the hysterical devotees and you view them and their God with objective eyes—you think. You see Father, a short, bald man whose grammar is confused. You laugh to yourself at the ostentation of his preening. You recall all the musical comedies you've ever seen and think to yourself how it is that Father Divine is unconsciously more hilarious than the funniest musical comedy star. Then, suddenly, Father crooks a finger in your direction. He does not smile. He hardly even glances at you. He merely beckons his hand to let you know that you, of all people, have been invited to sit at his own table. You rise from your seat. You start walking to the one Father has pointed out. As you walk, you feel every follower's eyes directly on you.

"How Father condescends to you!" An old woman with

a throaty voice grabs hold of your arm. She keeps it tightly vised. She looks straight into your face so that you must see the envy written all over hers. You read on her face something besides the envy, too. You see how glad she is for you and how deeply she has come to respect you all of a sudden. "How Father condescends to you!"

Even if you are a completely stable person, you cannot help but become Alice in this Wonderland and respond, even if only for a moment, as though Father Divine is God indeed.

It is easy then to imagine what happened to Mary Lyon. Lonely, groping, somewhat unstable, and with a mind and heart already attuned to acceptance of the occult—she grew, eventually, to complete recognition of Father's divinity. And that recognition ended her loneliness. Although she continued to maintain her elegant New York apartment, she spent more time in heaven than she ever did there. She felt warm and wanted. She grew to the conviction that her feeble old body would be revivified by Father so that eventually it could serve as a fit temple for her young spirit. She took the spiritual name of Peace Dove and determined to live according to that name.

In heaven, Peace Dove met another devotee named Patience Budd. Patience was of the "darker complexion"; she was young and attractive and vital. She was a bright girl. Patience Budd and Peace Dove were attracted to each other early in their acquaintance. Peace Dove offered Patience Budd a job. She needed a maid and traveling companion. Miss Budd accepted the offer. The relationship, immediately it was initiated, was a mistress-maid one only ostensibly. Actually, Patience Budd became the daughter Peace Dove had always wanted.

"She loved me like a mother," Miss Budd feelingly recalls today. "It was the way she always treated me. And I loved her so much, too."

For eight years, from 1938 to 1946, Mary Lyon continued as heaven's Peace Dove. Then, despite Father's promises to make her younger and healthier, she found herself so upset by a large growth on her tongue that she entered New York's Park East Hospital for an operation. There, even though Father persistently kept on willing her well, she died of a coronary thrombosis.

"If Father could be grieved about anything," Patience Budd says today, "he would have grieved about that."

Peace Dove left a lot of money to the movement. That money never bothered Father, though, "not one way or another," according to Patience Budd. It did perplex Miss Dove's relatives and acquaintances, however.

To her cousins Janet, Lucy, Arthur, and Catherine Latham, Mary Lyon left one hundred dollars each. She left one hundred dollars to her cousin Margaret Latham Humphrey. To her brother, Dr. William Hill Sheldon, she left five hundred dollars as "a token of my esteem."

The Metropolitan Museum of Art received valuable pieces from her New York City and Kingston, New York, homes.

Patience Budd, written into the will as "my faithful and devoted friend who nursed and cared for me," received $2500, a Packard car, valuable household furnishings from both homes, linens, bedding, antiques, and jewelry.

The bulk of the estate, estimated at $600,000, was equally divided between two Divine churches—Palace Mission Church and Home, Inc., of Brigantine in Pine Brook, New Jersey; and Peace Mission, Inc., of New York, 280 West 155th Street.

Saint Mary Bloom and David Diamond, attorney, were named executors of the will, which had been dated and executed on December 28, 1943.

Dr. Sheldon and the Latham cousins challenged Mary Lyon's will. They stated in court that Father Divine and Patience Budd had hypnotized Mary Lyon into the notion that true belief in Father Divine could supply her with a new body, and that they had ordered her to submit to the operation which had caused her death. They said that when she had signed the strange will, she had not been "of sound mind."

Father Divine never set foot in court, but Patience Budd was ruthlessly grilled by the Latham lawyers. Every detail of her childhood and young adulthood was brought out. Today, she is still bitter about the unfair trial.

In spite of the testimony of Patience Budd and many other followers as to Mrs. Lyon's complete sanity, the Court ordered her will set aside on the ground that she was of unsound mind when she made it. It gave the Latham cousins $5000 to be divided between them. It gave $50,000 clear of taxes to each of the two churches named. And Dr. Sheldon received the residuary estate.

John Devout, the then-president of the New York church, expressed the indignation of all the followers at the Court's decision:

"Dr. Sheldon is unjustly enriched by one of the worst settlements on record because of racial identity of members of these churches."

Today, followers still burn at the "injustice." Attorney Norris repeats today, as he has for many years past, that the Lyon case, from beginning to end, was a most blatant example of racial discrimination and a travesty on justice.

"It is obvious," he comments cryptically, "to anyone who cares to see it that Mary Sheldon Lyon was perfectly aware of what she was doing when she left her money to the two churches. The Court's decision was discrimination against the living and disrespect for the dead."

The Court's decision was based in part upon the fact that Mary Lyon, advantaged as she was, had affiliated with the disadvantaged Divinites. Why had she done that? This question cannot be authoritatively answered by anyone who has not served for many years as Mrs. Lyon's psychiatrist, and Mrs. Lyon, secure in the belief that Father was her panacea and that the rest of the world was out of step, never sought psychiatric help. A total answer to that question of "why" cannot be given in the case of Mary Lyon any more than it can be given in the case of Father's other white followers. Loneliness? Yes. Ineffectuality in coping with her own environment? Yes. Coincidence in the fact that Father was available during a period when she needed a spiritual outlet? Certainly. But there were other facts about Mrs. Lyon's personal needs that are not known and that never will be known. It would be inaccurate, then, to seek a complete motivation for her conversion through the known facts alone.

That is the way it is with all the white followers. The surface reasons for their affiliation with Father, the reasons that are clear and analyzable, are only part of the picture.

"All white followers of Divine are psychotic personalities!" some observers have reported unfairly. It is easy to characterize those who do not fit an accepted norm as "psychotic." It is easy to find small facets of each personality to prove that point. But the fact remains that most white Divinites operate competently in heaven. They feel proud of themselves. People who can function adequately and pride themselves on doing so cannot be classified wholesale as "psychotics," even though their functioning takes place in an asylum of their own—the Peace Mission movement.

Recognizing the fact that most white men and women who have come to Father have come for highly individual reasons which must, at best, remain unclear, and that these are not necessarily of such a nature as to indicate psychoses, white followers' motivations can be nevertheless assigned to some extent. It is fair to maintain in the first place that all of them were somehow out of step with their previous environments. It is fair to say, second, that most of them, like Mary Lyon, were spiritual gypsies who sought ideal fulfilment which they had been unable to find in the churches of their traditions. And their categorization can be carried a step farther. The younger women of the movement have a few common reasons for their acceptance of the Divine world. So do the older men. And the younger men. And the older women.

The older white women, those who entered heaven after they were fifty, are almost all strong-looking and authoritative. Most of them were career women and successful ones. They are well read, well spoken, and not unsophisticated. They are dignified and efficient. They have a brisk air. Very few of them had been married. They are not feminine women.

These older, superior white women are pitiful in a way. A person can listen to them speak and lose the humor of what they are saying in consideration of the pathos of it.

Miss Lovely Best, sixty-three years old, unmarried, tosses her head into the air. She preens herself.

"Father says 'virginity is everything,' " she tells you. "I am proud to report that I came through the sins of the world and remained pure."

In heaven, Miss Best can carry her virginity as a badge
of pride instead of inferiority. She no longer sees herself, as
she did before she came here, as having missed out on an
important part of living. Father's no-sex restriction is important to her. It is equally important to the large majority
of elderly white women. It is one of the basic reasons for
their conversion to Father.

Most of them found conversion easy. They just fitted
into Divinism. For they were very "spiritually cultivated."
They came to Father by way of Buddhism or Unity or the
I Am movement. Many were ardent Christian Scientists
before they became Divinites. Rita Sanderson, today a
trusted lieutenant, was only one of a large number of mature women who came via the road of Christian Science.

She says, "Father has come to establish the kingdom of
heaven on earth. This is probably the last generation. All
sex will be ended with this generation."

Miss Sanderson is a calm, poised-looking woman in her
late fifties. She has blue eyes and naturally wavy white
hair. She is tall and raw-boned. She looks efficient.

Before Miss Sanderson came to Father, she had lived in
London, England. She was a free-lance writer there and
had done some editorial work. She had also served as a
Christian Science practitioner. She had never been married,
and she said she'd never wished to be. She'd lived in London "with a dear woman friend," a Christian Scientist also,
and they had been "beautifully attuned spiritually."

"My life was very full in London," she tells. "I held the
reputation of being one of the finest Science healers. All
the church people respected me. I had everything in life I
wanted."

In 1936, for the first time in four years, Miss Sanderson
came to New York for a vacation with her brother and
sister for whom she had, up until the time she joined the
movement, felt a great attachment. On the boat coming
over, a Christian Science friend who was acquainted with
Father Divine as "a man who was raising up the lowest of
the low and making decent, God-fearing people out of
them and performing marvelous healings without charge,"
gave Miss Sanderson several *New Days*. She read them
from cover to cover. She saw beneath Father's ungram-

matical sentence structure and was thrilled by his messages.

"A Christian Scientist must understand this," she repeated to herself, "even if no one else can."

Miss Sanderson's boat docked on a Friday. She spent two days with her family and then, on her first Sunday home, took another Christian Science friend to Father's Harlem headquarters.

It was hot there, and Miss Sanderson was somewhat shocked by the poverty-stricken appearance of the mass of actively swaying followers.

"Some were suddenly pulled off their feet in an ecstasy of what I recognized even then to be love."

The room was stifling. Miss Sanderson felt the perspiration, sticky-hot on her.

"The great mass of people were of a so-called race," she says today, "with skins a different color from mine."

Today, she will not permit herself to call colored people Negroes. Before she met Father Divine, however, she had all the racial prejudices of her social group. She even believed the old stereotype which uninformed white people still maintain today—that Negroes have body odors to distinguish them from other people.

"There were so many colored people," she wrote to a sister, "and yet there was no odor." She conceived Father Divine to be at the bottom of this miracle. "It must be that true followers have no odor," she said.

Miss Sanderson spent many hours in the Harlem heaven. She watched Father Divine carefully and came to the conclusion that "he must be the greatest metaphysician on earth." She still remembers clearly her every reaction at the first sight of Father. Her recollections are obviously honest and so are of some help in attaining insight into the minds of those spiritually dedicated before they met Father.

"I felt calm and above my body and completely untired, though in the morning I had felt very tired. I did not feel emotional but steady and farseeing. When my friend and I were ready to leave, someone beside me said, 'You can speak to Father on the way out if you want to.' We walked back to his chair and, without realizing what I was doing, I stopped, put out my hand, and said, 'Thank you.' He took my hand, and the kind, wide-set eyes looked at me gravely. He said, 'Peace.' I said, 'I know a little of what you are talking about, but you are living up to it more than I am.' He said, 'I thank you.' . . . I have said that I was not feeling emotional, and I wasn't, but to my surprise, the tears were rolling down my face and I felt young and happy. . . . My friend and I struggled through the crowds into a taxi and looked at each other. My friend said, 'What do you think?' And I said, 'It is good, and as long as I live, I shall know that he is utterly good.' "

Miss Sanderson tried to get an interview with Father Divine. He did not grant her one. On a bright May day, she sailed back to England. In early July, she was back in America. Father's spirit drew her back. She knew that she could not live unless she learned more about him.

In 1936, Rita Sanderson took up temporary residence in a Harlem heaven. She saw Father whenever she could at the public banquets, but she never spoke to him privately. She steeped herself in Father's messages and spent almost all of her waking hours in reading and rereading the *New Day*. After a few months in heaven, she returned to England where she stayed for close to three years. Then, in 1939, she officially resigned from the Christian Science movement to become a true follower of Father Divine. How rapidly she adjusted is illustrated by an incident that occurred soon after she entered heaven.

She was entering one of the cars of Father's caravan, to travel from a New York City heaven to the Kingston, New York one, when somebody accidentally closed the car door against the palm and fingers of her right hand. The pain was intense. The hand began to bleed.

A follower who sat beside Miss Sanderson was frightened by the sight of the blood. "Oh, how awful," she whispered tensely, "you'll have to do something."

Miss Sanderson only smiled at the other woman's concern. "It never happened," she said.

"But it's bleeding," the woman persisted.

Miss Sanderson stayed calm. "That is not a fact."

"It is a fact," the woman argued.

Miss Sanderson pursed her lips as she does up until today when she is displeased. "There is only one fact in the universe," she told the woman beside her, "and that fact is Father Divine."

It was Miss Sanderson's Christian Science which equipped her to such a quick realization of Father Divine. For Christian Science and Divinism have many points in common. As a matter of fact, many of the tenets of Father Divine are Christian Science tenets which he has adopted and exaggerated.

Divinism and Christian Science both believe that God, being all, is the only real substance, and that everything else is unreal. In the Divine and the Christian Science concepts, matter is nothing beyond an image in the mortal mind, and it cannot have a real existence. Father Divine is only a few steps ahead of Christian Science when he presents himself as a true and living God beside whom all matter is nothing.

Even the no-sex tenet of Divinism has its almost-twin in Christian Science. Mary Baker Eddy, the founder of Christian Science, regarded sex in procreation as something less than ideal. As man progresses, she intimated, sex needs will begin to disappear. In the resurrection there will be no marrying or giving in marriage. As a matter of fact, sex and marriage will continue only until mankind has truly learned its lesson that God is the father of all. It is only because that Christian Science lesson has been well learned in the kingdoms of Father Divine that the Divine theory of sex and marriage can be more radical than the Christian Science one is.

In death and in illness, too, the theories of Christian Science and Divinism are more apart quantitatively than they are qualitatively. Christian Science believes just as Father Divine does that anyone who is sick or believes he is has not attained salvation. Mary Baker Eddy, like Father Divine, has stated that "sin alone brings death, for sin is the only element of destruction." The idea only differs insofar as Mrs. Eddy believed that man has not yet attained the state in which he can demonstrate eternal life and overcome death, while Father Divine believes that man, as exemplified by the angels in his heaven, has already attained that state.

Because of the basic philosophical similarities of Divinism and Christian Science, Rita Sanderson cherishes the thought that all of her years of Christian Science have served only to equip her for Father.

"Christian Science is the half-truth and Father Divine is the whole truth," she says.

"I have found the whole truth," she wrote her family in 1939, the year she officially affiliated with Father. "Believing that these are the last days and that much will happen in the last year, I feel that it would be a tragedy to withhold from you whom I love the very best good news (Gospel) that could be imagined."

Miss Sanderson's conversion, shared in that year of 1939 with many other Christian Scientists, heralded a new type of useful devotee toward extending heaven's sphere of influence. Miss Sanderson and her former Christian Science friend Miss Johnson and her former Christian Science friends known today as Miss Universal Holiness and Miss Plain Holiness and Miss Loving Presence and Miss Soul Healer have brought a new kind of devotion to Father Divine. Their Christian Science discipline has given them an intellectual as well as an emotional realization of the meaning of Divine discipline. Since most of them speak well and make an excellent impression, they can interpret Father's discipline both to followers who are not nearly so capable of understanding it and to outsiders who view it condemningly.

This is another one of Father's most dedicated corps. They have given up comfortable lives as Christian Science practitioners with all that that entails in the way of status and recognition and have settled, because of their strong spiritual convictions about Father, for far less of all three.

Certainly, they are less comfortable from a purely physical standpoint. Certainly, they receive less recognition as mere followers of God who are on a par with all other followers than they did when they were individual interpreters of Christian Science practices. Their status in the movement is not much. Father Divine treats them with respect and assigns important jobs to them, but his true favors are granted only to the younger, more attractive white women to whom Miss Sanderson and the others like her must bow down and maintain a humbleness of manner. The fact that they do bow down, with seeming ease, is another proof of their sincerity of purpose.

Not so sincere but every bit as enthusiastic are a few older women followers who have not come to Divinism by way either of Christian Science or of other types of spiritual recognition. These are the women whom one can pick out at a glance as the ineffectual ones for whom Divine heavens provide the necessary protection of institutional living. These are the few on whom one-sided observers have based their characterizations of all white followers as psychotics. They are the eccentrics, the peculiar women who have been made aware of their peculiarities by the world outside the Peace Mission gates. They are the misfits and the weaklings. They are the frightened ones whose fear has always shone bright on their faces. They are the sensitives and the old women who want to be little girls again. They are the ones who might have ended up—and sometimes do—in mental hospitals instead of Divine heavens.

Mrs. Arthur Brockmorton, despite heaven's respect for soap and bathtubs, seldom washes. She has no concern with such amenities as hanging slips and brassière straps that peek out from under her low-necked dresses. She has a small face that might have passed for elfin in her younger days, and prickly white hairs sprout from her chin. She is in her early sixties, or maybe in her later ones, and she sports the modern, teenage hair style with bangs and a horse's tail.

"How old do you think I am?" she asks every new visitor to heaven.

Once an elderly minister with a morbid sense of humor answered her in a serious tone, "I think you must be in your early twenties."

Mrs. Brockmorton grew coy. "I'm older than that," she admitted.

Mrs. Brockmorton is one of heaven's sensitives. "When I talk about Father," she says, "I tremble with enthusiasm. My hand shakes. My whole body shakes." She trembles for illustration.

"I was born of an English father," Mrs. Brockmorton tells about herself, "not at all the spiritual type, and an

American mother who really was all spirit, spirit, spirit. General Ethan Allen was my great-great-grandfather, and I had a cousin who married into the Betsy Ross family."

Mrs. Brockmorton's husband, Arthur, was, she says, a great painter. He was an Irishman, and shortly after she married him he took her to England to live. He was a fine man "with a beautiful body," but "he had a love for grammar which was strictly of this world" and which kept him from developing the spiritual interest which his wife claims to have developed early in their married life.

Arthur and Mrs. Brockmorton maintained a studio in England primarily for the accommodation of struggling artists of talent. There were always laden tables set up in the studio with all the food and drink any young artist could desire.

Mrs. Brockmorton, herself, was an artist of no mean note, according to her present recollection. She was an actress and a writer. She still writes today—poetry mostly. Some of the followers who are "real appreciative of talent" enjoy her poems.

Mrs. Brockmorton can "unify beautifully with them. They vibrate when they read my poetry. My, how they vibrate! Their hands shake and their eyes fill with tears. It is sweet, sweet, sweet."

Mrs. Brockmorton was converted to Father Divine through reading a *New Day*. The spirituality and the sheer poetry of his speech delighted her. She recognized him first as a fellow artist. Then, from the authoritativeness with which he spoke, she recognized him as God.

"I love heaven," she says. "I love the angels. I love God. I love everybody and everybody loves me. Father has made me good, sweet, lovable, kind, sympathetic, and smart. I am happy, happy, happy."

It is possible that Mrs. Brockmorton is happier in heaven than she ever was before. Certainly, she is more secure there than she must ever have been any other place.

She says, "As soon as I knew Father was God, I knew I was lucky, lucky, and that was my lucky, lucky day."

Mrs. Brockmorton is right. She was never so fortunate as she was on the day she recognized Divine's divinity. For that was the day on which she attained her own security.

Not only did she receive a God at hand that day and a father who would protect her, but she also received a home and a family of sisters and brothers who, so long as she continued to profess faith in Father Divine, would never be perturbed by her small eccentricities. She functions in heaven, a respected person, not *too* atypical of the group at large, whose fantasies are never criticized. So long as she does not indulge in sex, cigarettes, liquor, or profanity, so long as she continues to profess her faith in Father, she is cherished as one of God's angels on a par with any other one ... except the young virgin ones.

[20]

"—ROSEBUDS OF MY HEART"

Father's young virgins, particularly his young white virgins, are truly his chosen people. He dispenses to them, and only to them, a whole font of doting love. He even sings sentimental songs to them.

"Blessed are ye, rosebuds of my heart," Father sings.

> *I have graced thee with purity.*
> *You have been blessed to behold the body of God,*
> *In all his deity.*
> *My love has bestowed on thee a pure heart.*
> *Thy purity causes nations to be healed of all illness.*
> *Thy hearts shall open to the world,*
> *The doors where glory is reigning.*
> *Blessed are ye, rosebuds of my heart,*
> *Your purity, my deity to the world is proclaiming.*

Father says that his young girl followers are "the wonders of this world," and he treats them like the wonders he considers them to be. They are the ones who occupy seats at the banquet tables that are closest to Father's own. They are the ones who are privileged to serve as members of his secretarial cabinet and to be in his presence as often as is Mother Divine in the Second Body. And they are the truest zealots of the movement.

If Father's older white women followers would be regarded as fanatics by the mortal world, his younger ones would be thought of as super-ones. Their rigidity and self-assurance, their firm belief in the right of Divine and the wrong of everyone else, their self-sufficiency, their righteous contempt for mortal things, and, above all, their colossal conceit, are hardly believable to people who have not experienced the closest contact with them.

Miss Sweet Time is a typical, young white follower. She is nineteen years old. She is tall and very slender. She has burned-wheat-colored hair which she wears in a long glamor bob. She has cat-green eyes and a wonderful velvet complexion which, naturally enough, has never known make-up. Her dresses, though, are tight and figure-hugging, as she can well afford to have them be, and she wears spike heels and the sheerest of nylon stockings to point up her inordinately good-looking legs.

Since she works outside heaven and is thrown into contact with young men, many more than she cares to enumerate have tried to date her.

"They would be considered handsome," she says coolly, "if one regarded them with mortal standards. I don't though. I look at them and I shudder at the whole idea of even carrying on a conversation. By my standards, they are terribly homely. I compare them to Father Divine, that's the reason why. I look at their faces and then I think of Father's beauty. And all the boys look the same to me then, not like boys at all but only like big blobs of butter."

It is easy for Miss Sweet Time to turn down dates with blobs of butter. "I just tell them, 'My religion forbids me to associate with those of the opposite sex.'"

Most of the young men accept Miss Sweet's ultimatum right off. There is something in the stiff stance of her body and in the cool, studied tone of her voice that belies her delicate appearance and makes them know she has a will of steel and will not ever be broken down by the likes of them.

"Long ago, when I was a small girl," Miss Sweet says, "I cast all human feeling out of myself."

It required a bit of restraint to do that then, but now Miss Sweet is past the stage where she needs to discipline herself for "resistance of any human advances." She wants nothing to do with anyone except Father Divine and the angels who surround him, and she makes that fact overwhelmingly clear.

"If ever I thought of a mortal man," she tells, "and I certainly cannot conceive of myself doing that, it would be the blackest sin any angel could commit. I am one of Father's sweethearts. I am one of Father's brides."

Miss Sweet Time is one of the brightest of Father Divine's young women—at least according to mortal standards. Three years ago, she graduated from high school as the most honored member of her class—the girl who, because she made the highest scholastic record, was chosen to make the valedictory speech. She got a job immediately after graduation as a private secretary. She earns seventy dollars a week today. She is a businesswoman, too. For the past three years she has been investing her savings, well over two thousand dollars annually, in Peace Mission properties.

"It's a grand feeling to be independent and to be able to invest money for aiding God's work," she says.

Miss Sweet was first brought to Divine banquets when she was little more than three years old. Today, she maintains that she still retains keen memories of her first sight of Father. How could she forget that first sight?

"A spiritual birth is more important than a mortal one, isn't it?" she asks in proof of her point. Her voice is not questioning. It is quietly positive.

Miss Sweet's mother was the one who introduced her to Father Divine.

"The so-called mother was an idealist." All the contempt in the world is in Sweet's voice as she talks. "And a seeker after truth. Before she found Father Divine she was a Christian Scientist. It took her too long to recognize Father's divinity. She was a sad soul, I remember, never knowing what was what."

Miss Sweet had always held her father somewhat responsible for her mother's sadness.

"He was uncouth and a money-grubber. All he thought about was making more money, even though he had enough. There was nothing spiritual about him. He was pretty mean to the so-called mother."

Miss Sweet's mother and father were always arguing about sex. Miss Sweet always heard them.

"I don't like cold women," the father used to say. "I never did. Yet, I had to go and marry one. An iceberg, in fact."

The mother used to say, "I try."

The father used to laugh, and the sound of his laughter used to fall harsh on Miss Sweet's ears.

Miss Sweet's mother used to talk to her when she was a small girl and long before she had any comprehension of what the problem was. It was hard indeed to be a woman, she said, and to be forced to fulfil the filthy physical duties with which women are called upon to pay for their board and room.

The physical life of Miss Sweet's mother and father was tragically typical of the physical lives of the mothers and fathers of many of the young white girls who make up Father Divine's present corps of dedicated virgins. These mothers, like Miss Sweet's mother, in their forties and fifties and sixties today, belong to the past generation's middle-class white culture which imposed strict standards for sexual behavior. Sex was dirty to Sweet's mother. It was ugly. And any lady, who was a lady, would rather die than enjoy sex or seem to be enjoying it. Miss Sweet's father did not have the sensitivity to cope with his wife's feelings. Neither did so many other husbands whose wives became mothers of virginal Divinites.

Sweet Time's mother recalls with shaking horror her physical relationship with "the so-called husband." So do most of the other mothers. They say that their husbands never treated them tenderly, even in the earliest days of their marriage.

"I was deflorated by my so-called husband," Miss Sweet's mother tells with bitter feeling, "devirginized. He never asked me did I want to, you know—just did whatever he wanted because he thought I was his property, which I was."

In different words, the mother of white Rosebud, Miss Glorious Illumination, tells the same story about her husband. So does Rita Sweet's mother. And Lovely Life's. And Longevity Joy's. And Joy M. Joy's.

Sweet Time's mother and the mothers of so many other Divinite virgins tell that, in a very real sense, they sold themselves to their husbands, not for money exactly, although money entered into it, but, more importantly, because if they hadn't married their husbands they might have been "old maids."

"Naturally," Sweet Time's mother says, "knowing as little as I did in those days, I couldn't be an old maid. It wasn't long after I married, though, that I realized I just never should have done it."

She kept telling Sweet Time she never should have done it.

"I hope and pray," she used to tell her, "that you'll never be in the kind of position with any man that I am in with your father."

Miss Sweet, knowing back when she was little that she never would be in that position, felt little sympathy for her mother.

Today she still feels little sympathy. What a weak woman the mother had been, Sweet tells. There she was, and in the palm of her hand, waiting for her, in effect, was Father Divine. The mother had known Father Divine to be God. He had condescended to reveal himself to her. And what had she done about the revelation? Absolutely nothing! Just gone on living at home with a husband whom she loathed and attending banquets. Why had she been so stupid? Why hadn't she just picked up and left the home and moved into heaven where she belonged? To this day, Miss Sweet cannot understand why not.

Oh, the mother tried to explain to her all right. She said she felt a responsibility to her, Miss Sweet Time, and for her two sisters. That was ridiculous, though, really. What was responsibility to children when it was compared to recognition of God in a human body? All these years for the sake of children, no more, Miss Sweet's mother had lived in a house instead of a heaven. "Deluded woman," Miss Sweet says about her mother today.

From the time Miss Sweet Time was nine years old and had been attending banquets for five years, she knew that, for her, compromise between Father and people in the world outside was an impossibility.

"I lay in my bed," she says, "in the house of my so-called father and thought about God. Every night, I thought the same thoughts."

It was when she was nine that she first completely rejected her mother as she had done her father years before and accepted Father Divine, as other children, those who already lived in heaven, did.

"Father Divine is my mother and my father," she told the mother then.

Miss Sweet Time was thirteen years old when her conviction about Father's divinity made her certain that the only life she could ever live would have to be lived in a heaven. She did not wish to remain a part-time follower. She wanted to go "all the way with Father Divine."

"I am going to give up the mortal life," she told her mother.

The mother was frightened. Her behavior was paradoxical. On the one hand, she was thrilled with Miss Sweet's strong recognition of Father's divinity. On the other hand, she was frightened to have her leave home.

"You are too young. Wait a few years," she pleaded.

Sweet Time said, "No."

"A baby like you——" the mother said.

"I'm not a baby."

Sweet Time's mother begged her. "Just a few years. That's all I'm asking you to do—wait a few years. Just until you're able to deal better with the girls in school. They'll make fun of our belief and make it hard on you. You're too young to be so set apart."

Sweet Time listened politely to her mother's arguments. She knew she would not adhere to them, though. The mother was foolish. What did she mean, talking about "too young"? Father Divine, himself, had told Miss Sweet that nobody was ever too young to know her own heart. He had assured her that she would be welcome in heaven. Her mother's talk about "set apart," that was foolish too. Of course, she was set apart and that was the way she wanted to remain—set apart from the other girls she knew who did not believe that Father Divine was God. Father had once explained that to her in a long interview.

So Sweet Time packed her clothes and completely cut herself away from what remained to her of the mother's apron strings. She moved into a Divine Peace Mission. From the day she left her home until now, six years afterward, she saw her mother only at banquets.

"Peace," she told the mother on these occasions.

Sweet Time and her mother have never, in the last six years, had a conversation that took longer than half an hour. They spoke the last time two years ago. The mother wished to tell Sweet Time that the "so-called father" had died.

"He passed," she said simply, never pretending a regret she did not feel.

Sweet Time was not regretful either. "The way he lived was death," she said.

From the day she arrived at the Divine Mission, Sweet Time knew fulfilment and happiness. It wasn't long until her good looks and her bright mind, which enabled her to make the most beautiful testimonies to Father Divine, earned her a place of honor in the movement. The other girls admired her, the older women catered to her, and Father granted her many special considerations. When he came to her mission, he sometimes sought Sweet Time out for long talks limited to just the two of them.

Once, during a talk with Father, Sweet Time asked him to fulfil a desire that had been growing stronger and stronger inside her.

"If I could have a spiritual name," she said, "I would be so happy, Father dear."

One night, shortly after Sweet Time had spoken to Father, the spirit unfolded a name. She lay in her bed just thinking about Father and how good he was to her, when a light flashed in front of her eyes. As soon as she became accustomed to the light, she noticed that there were letters written inside it. S-W-E-E-T T-I-M-E.

One of the first moves Sweet Time made after her revelation was to request that her school records take account of her spiritual name.

"At first," she tells coolly, "I had a bit of trouble over my name. Some of the students would say stupid things to me. It didn't matter, though. What they thought never was important to me. Nobody could ever make me believe now that anything in the outside world is greater than this life and they couldn't then. After all, I didn't need them to be my friends the way other girls needed each other. In this life I live, I need no friends except the ones who are my sisters right here. And, of course, the one who can never fail me. He is everything! My only ambition in life is not to fail him."

Sweet Time made a testimonial recently in which she described her complete dedication to Father.

"You took me in as a young child," she cried, "hovered over me, fed me, clothed me, asking for nothing save my heart which I am striving to give you daily in deeds and actions. Keep me ever humble and meek, for I love you and will always strive to be a real true daughter born of the loins of your holy heart!"

All the other young girls echo Miss Sweet's testimony in somewhat less effective words of their own. They tell Father over and over that he and heaven are far preferable to mortal parents and the mortal world.

"I would never live any place but here in God's own presence," says Miss Beautiful Bliss, seventeen years old, who was brought by a follower-mother when she was two. "I go to school and watch the others living in mortality. Tragic things are always happening in their families, like fighting, like babies being born—— Here, nothing tragic ever happens. Here, we live in happiness with you, Father. I will always do as you say and never, never disappoint you."

At least three hundred of these young women live in Philadelphia, Newark, and New York as close as they can get to Father Divine. Even at first sight, despite the variety of physical types, there is an expression that is disconcertingly similar about all of them. This is most apparent when they are anywhere in Father's vicinity. Then they tilt their heads, one head tilted like every other one, and look at Divine rapturously, expectantly, yet petulantly, too, in the same way that baby girls look petulant when they flirt with their fathers sometimes.

Almost all of Father's young women wear the same patina of sweetness. They look placid to the point where you want to do something to destroy their placidity. They look poised, and their poise is a morbid thing because it is induced by a hothouse maturity. Their faces are not sad or touching or tortured the way some of the older faces are. Looking at them one time only, you can tell how it is that, for them, there are no problems left to be conquered. They have no mental stirrings. They know nothing of the frustrations and confusions that other young people experience in the process of growing up—and it shows on their faces.

In heaven, even the teen-agers are not gauche. Strangely, though, their grace is not a pretty thing. You view it and you do not like it. You do not like the un-gauche teen-agers because, looking at them, you must discern the un-wholesome reasons behind what they are. You must know that the calm faces come because the minds are never rest-less, never wondering.

Father's young girls, far more than his other followers, are like stagnant pools whose prime function is to mirror their God.

Father had made it clear to his young followers that that *is* their only function—to mirror him. They are nothing. He is everything.

The proudest moment in the life of one of Father's young girls comes on the day when God formally recognizes her purity and permits her dedication to him. It is on this day that she becomes a Rosebud, which is Divine language for a dedicated virgin, and takes the "Rosebud Pledge to God":

We pledge our hearts to love you,
Our strength to serve you,
Our minds to be focused directly upon you,
Our lips to praise you,
Our lives to be sacrificed unto you,
Our sacred honor to acknowledge you in all our ways,
That we may be with you throughout all eternity,
One spirit, one mind and one body,
Lost and absorbed, once and forever, in your holy will!

It is the Rosebuds, Negro and especially white, whom Father uses for decorative purposes. They are seated around him at the dinner table, one white, one colored, to illus-trate racial integration. They ride together, seated the same way, in cars that follow the Divine one. They are the major-ettes of the movement.

In previous days, when Father conducted city parades, the young white girls marched in the most conspicuous posi-tions, twirling batons much as mortal-minded majorettes do. Today, Father has dispensed with the city parades, but young girls' military formations are still engaged in during the times when he and scores of followers visit the country estates in Pine Brook and Kingston. Then, the Rosebuds, in spruce majorette costumes, lead the formations.

Father is pleased to report, though, that attractive as his

young girls look, they could never be mistaken for mortal-minded ones. For the Buds' majorette skirts are modest enough to cover their calves.

Father Divine, although he permits figure-hugging dresses for his young girls, sets a different kind of fashion for non-street clothes. The majorette uniforms have been the least influenced by his style requirements. The Rosebuds' bathing suits have been the most influenced. They are a throwback to the days of the gay nineties, with high necklines and skirts down to three inches below the knees.

"Evangelical bathing beauty suits," Father has named his creations.

More important than their mere decorative functions are the Rosebuds' designation as God's official choral group. They make public appearances in other churches and before club groups and have, in years when Father was openly seeking public approval, made radio appearances. Not only are the Rosebuds the singers of the movement's songs, they also compose them. Some of the songs are beautiful. Whether songs of praise to Father Divine or whether songs inspired by anger against the injustices Negroes have suffered in America, the Buds' songs are no orthodox hymns. They are original, colorful, completely alive outpourings. Often they attain the very heights of folk art.

All Rosebud song composers prefer to remain anonymous. "No credit is due," they will tell you if you attempt to give them individual recognition for songs they compose. "It is all Father."

Father Divine does not need to be as modest as his Rosebuds. He discusses his own musical compositions in glowing terms. There is one story he likes particularly to tell the Rosebud composers, about a song he created himself at the movement's inception, back when he was in Sayville.

"It was a song composed by the spirit of my presence. I brought it forth. Representatives of the Victrola Company guaranteed $50,000. But I would not sell my gift, my word, for a million dollars."

Miss Sweet Time comments on Father's victrola company story.

"He would not sell his song for a million dollars, but he gave it to us, to me and the other Rosebuds, for nothing. Isn't it wonderful?"

You see Miss Sweet Time, you look down at the good figure in the tight dress and at the good-looking legs, and you listen to her speak, and it becomes difficult, even in view of everything you know about Father's followers, to connect the two, Miss Sweet Time and the words she is speaking.

Miss Sweet says, "Father gives so much for us. Oh, it isn't just that song he wrote and gave us. It's everything. Recently, he gave me a chance to sacrifice for him. Do you know the joy in that word—sacrifice? It is glorious."

One night, Miss Sweet tells, she and six other Rosebuds were going to a party. They left the heaven and started driving west. Miss Sweet was in the driver's seat.

"It was a hot summer evening. People were sitting outside. As I drove up the block, I saw a gang of young men and boys swarming in the street. They swarmed in front of the car. I had to slow down. They clambered all over the car, on the running boards, all over. Then they began to yell, 'You and that white bride.' Mad because Father had married someone of that complexion. It did not make me angry. I cried, 'Peace!' I told the boys to get off the car. I started to move it. A boy hanging on my window spat right into my face. While I was parked, a big man came over to the car. He was of the darker complexion. He struck me with his big fist. I didn't feel any resentment. I didn't feel the malice. It would have to return to him. It was wonderful. I am so happy to be able to sacrifice to make up a little bit for all the sacrifices Father is always making for us."

You look at Miss Sweet Time as she concludes her story and you ask her, aware that you are taking the good will she feels for you now and risking its loss, "What sacrifice is he making for you?"

"What sacrifice?" Miss Sweet's indignation as she repeats your question threatens to overcome her vaunted calm. "What sacrifice? Why, every moment that Father spends here in this wicked world so that he can save us is sacrifice. That song he could have sold for a million dollars but gave it to us instead, that's sacrifice. See the mystery?"

You look at this young girl, bright enough to have been chosen valedictorian of her high-school graduating class, and it comes to you all of a sudden that, strangely, shockingly, you do see the mystery.

21

"INTELLECT STANDS
AS A BAR!"

The mystery is this . . . that all of Father Divine's followers, whether they are stupid or whether they are bright, try
to follow to the letter a strict Divine enjoinment.

"Intellect stands as a bar," Father states, "unless you
bring it into subjection."

Sweet Time has no problem with her intellect. That is
why Father's interpretation of his sacrifices makes sense to
her.

There are many followers, like Sweet Time, who find
their intellects easy to subject. These are lucky. There are,
however, some few who are unfortunate enough to have
intellects that are not easily quelled. These suffer from
conscience and from Father's disapproval.

"Sometimes you think you've accomplished your heart's
desire," follower Chester Belstrom explains sadly. "You
think you have really succeeded in keeping your intellect
down where it belongs and it makes you very happy. Suddenly your happiness is shattered though, because your
intellect annoys you once again and you find yourself
thinking. One encouraging thing, though, you know that,
with Father's spirit helping you, you can put up a fight
against intellect and really win it. I am still fighting. So is
my brother LaVere."

Chester and LaVere Belstrom are schoolteachers. They
hold Ph.D. degrees in Education. Chester received his from
the University of Minnesota, LaVere his from the University of Colorado. After they'd been in Philadelphia for two
years, LaVere and Chester "got into severe trouble with
God. Our cursed intellects were responsible."

"One week," LaVere tells, "a stern statement that Father
had made to a group of Rosebuds appeared in the *New*

Day. Father had said that music was a creative outlet and that rehearsing interfered with creativity."

Chester says that he and LaVere were "absolutely chagrined" when they read Father's statement. "For," he tells, "we were and still are in charge of the men's choral group and orchestra and we had been used to holding rehearsals often. We knew that even though Father was seemingly disapproving the Rosebuds' rehearsals, he also had a right to disapprove of ours. If musical rehearsals were not in Father's mind and spirit and we had been holding them, we were not in his mind and spirit either."

"It frightened us to think of it," LaVere tells. "We requested an interview in order to talk the whole terrible thing over."

At exactly 4:50 A.M. on April 20, 1950, Anno Domini Father Divine, Chester and LaVere Belstrom, who had been waiting for six hours, were summoned into Father's office for the coveted interview. Its tone was typically Divine. Despite the elusiveness of Father's statements, however, and despite the confusion of the statements of Drs. LaVere and Chester, one important fact stood out. The Belstroms were ashamed of their college-trained intellects and Father was contemptuous of them for being college trained.

"Peace, Father," Chester opened the talk nervously. "We came to see you in regard to our rehearsals, to see whether or not they are in your mind and spirit."

Father answered, "Well, you should know whether they are or not. Each of you should know."

LaVere spoke up:

"Well, according to the message as given to the Rosebuds, we considered that we would sort of go out on the wings of your love, in a way of speaking, and trust in our singing by discontinuing our rehearsals, if they are not in your mind and spirit."

"Well, it is up to you," Father said, "whatsoever you want to do. Almost anything anyone is in and it becomes to be a part of them it would feel to them as if it is the ideal and the only thing—but it is up to the individual. Of course, I had not mentioned you—you all—when the subject came up, especially. But if you take it to be you and take or consider it is applicable, why, maybe it is."

"Well, that is the way a number of us felt, Father." Chester's voice was apologetic.

Father relaxed. He smiled. How many rehearsals had the teachers been holding, he wondered.

They had been holding two a week, one for the band and one for the chorus.

Father smiled again. "This rehearsal business," he said. He turned to Chester.

"Well, do you ever finish, both you and Mr. LaVere—of course, you are professors—do you ever finish so you don't have to do the same thing all the time by practice? I mean, can it ever be finished so you will be expert at it and that it can be demonstrated extemporaneously?—that it will be just automatically worked without any thought of anything? Like a person learns the alphabet all over and over all the time. Perfection should be attained some time. That is what I—the way I considered—if it is from that angle of expression one is supposed to demonstrate. And when that is attained, as with the alphabet so with any other course, or what I might say, unfoldment of culture. It should be sometime developed to perfection!"

Chester attempted to explain the point of view that had caused him and LaVere to hold rehearsals. It wasn't that they rehearsed to achieve perfection. They knew that only Father's spirit could grant impeccability. Sometimes, though, the Divine band and chorus, which had so many untrained voices and instruments, sounded "cacophonous." He explained, "In our rehearsals, about the only thing we have been working toward is the unification of vowel sounds that we might sound in unity."

"Blending of tone so that one person does not stick out of the choir; so that all the voices are blended and sound as one," LaVere added.

Father said the teachers were right. He said that in a chorus all the voices should sound as one, and in an orchestra all the instruments should. But, he asked, didn't Mr. LaVere and Mr. Chester think that these effects could better be achieved by trusting in his spirit than by holding mundane rehearsals?

"It is up to the individuals to be persistent and be governed by the Inner Urge," he said. "As I was saying, so many times about great—almost, you might say, super-

natural learned people—cultured educators and speakers—
and if they—yes, if they have to have a manuscript, to me
they are not cultured."

Dr. LaVere Belstrom agreed with utter sincerity. He
said, "That is something for all the world to hear."

Dr. Chester Belstrom said, "Amen!"

Like Chester and LaVere Belstrom, most of the Father's
white male followers who are today fighting to subject their
intellects come from middle-class or highly privileged
homes.

Schoolteacher Robert Baldwin is a recent recruit. He
says, "Why did I come to Father? I came because his love
drew me like a magnet and I could not stay away from
him. I heard about him through my so-called mother."

Robert Baldwin lived in Chicago with his father, three
brothers, and his mother, who had been a truth-seeker all
her life. "She was in Bahai and Unity," he tells, "and I
think there were several years when she was a member of
the I Am movement, too. But no religion satisfied her until
she found Father Divine. That was fourteen years ago. She
used to take the *New Day* at home, read it regularly. I
began to read it, too. So did my three brothers. It never
really impressed me in those days. I read it because the so-
called mother requested that I do so, and I loved her so
much I wanted to carry out her every request. My brothers
read it for the same reason. The so-called mother was the
most important person in all our lives. She was wonderful,
good, kind, always ready to listen to your troubles and
advise you. She had the broadest shoulders of anyone I've
ever known, any mortal being, that is, and you could always come and lay your troubles on her shoulders."

Robert used to have many troubles to bring to his
mother. His troubles began away back when he'd been a
little boy, smaller than most and far gentler. Somehow,
he'd never been willing to stand up for his rights or able to
fight with boys his own age but bigger who seemed always
to want to fight with him. He used to come crying home to
the so-called mother, ashamed and not knowing how to
handle the shame.

Robert's mother used to hold him close to her, stroking
his head, just stroking and stroking it.

"It's all right, darling," she'd say, "don't you worry about those bullies. Mama's got you now."

When Robert was fourteen, he was still puny, but he was very bright. Scholastically, he was far in advance of the other boys his age, already an upper sophomore in high school. There was a tremendous boy named Joel in his class.

One day, Joel picked Robert up in his arms, "just picked me up like I was some kind of an unfeeling thing, and held me high up until the other boys began to laugh at me. Then he dropped me."

At home, the so-called mother cradled Robert in her arms and said comforting words.

When Robert Baldwin was sixteen years old, he was in college, majoring in Education. That was the year three boys named Mark, Bill, and Charlie caught him in the locker room almost every day and made him listen to dirty jokes, telling one filthy joke after another.

"Goddam you, laugh!"

Robert wouldn't laugh.

"Laugh!" the boys insisted.

Robert wouldn't, and one humiliating day Charlie punched him in the nose, making it bleed.

The so-called mother treated the bloody nose and told Robert she was "proud of me for resisting the evil influences in college."

When Robert was only twenty-one, he got his first teaching assignment. It was at a "tough" school, and his mother was worried about him. Robert loved it, though, in spite of all the difficulties he encountered. It was hard adjusting to the other teachers and their slovenly work habits, "the way they watched the clocks, always so eager to leave at three."

Robert was a dedicated teacher, the first to arrive in the morning and the last to leave in the afternoon. The other teachers mocked at his devotion, laughing right in his face. Their laughter hurt him, he tells today, but not as much as the children's laughter did. "Because it was the children who were the important ones in those days B.F.D."

Robert went on teaching and living at home until 1941. That was a black and terrible year. That was the year his so-called mother died. Robert and his three brothers were sadder and lonelier than they'd ever been. Out of respect for their mother, they began to read the *New Day* seriously. Strangely, without the so-called mother there to interpret it, it became meaningful as it never had been before.

Today, Robert Baldwin says, "The so-called mother used to tell me, 'Someday, you'll find Father Divine, and when you find him, your life will be full.' She was always right."

In 1942, a year after his mother's death, Robert Baldwin was drafted into the army. He entered as a conscientious objector and spent most of his time in the medical corps and working as a chaplain's assistant. England was his first assignment. While he was there, he met four women Divinites who lived together in Croydon, a suburb of London. "They were wonderful to me," he says. He spent all of his off-time in their quiet home. One of the ladies, Miss Sweetness, reminded him of his mother.

Robert Baldwin knew, when he left the army three and a half years after he entered it, that the world, with its vulgar, striving opportunistic people, was not the place for him. He wanted to live a quiet, holy life such as his so-called mother had prepared him for. More important, he knew that Father Divine was indeed God. As soon as he left the army, he went straight home where he belonged— to Father's Philadelphia headquarters.

"I love Father with all my heart," he says. "He is my security."

Father Divine is the security of all his young men followers. It is the same for most of them as it is for Robert Baldwin. They love him with all their hearts. He is their protection from a ruthless world.

It is dangerous to ascribe a rationale for a whole group of human beings. The deepest reasons why Robert Baldwin and LaVere and Chester Belstrom and all of Father's other white men are affiliated with the Peace Mission movement are no more authoritatively known than are the reasons why Father's other members are tied to Divinism. There are certain extremely surface indications, though.

To begin with, there is the physical appearance of Divine young men. They may be stout or slim, tall or small, blonds, brunettes, or redheads—no matter what their physical variables are, they look somewhat alike. At first, you don't know why they should look alike. As many types here as anywhere, you tell yourself. And then, after you've been with them for a time, the reason why one of these young men appears to look like all of them hits you. It is the strange air of kindly spirituality they all have in common. In heaven, this spirituality is called gentleness. The world outside might call it effeminacy.

The point in addition to appearance that most of these men share is the attachment they had for their mothers who were Father's initial discoverers. Most of their lives were bound by the limits of the homes these mothers controlled and the unusual standards they set.

Robert Baldwin tells, "The so-called mother was not ever of this world."

Neither was Robert Baldwin ever of this world—quite. He never knew the companionship of women. He thought all women were "out to fleece" him. Many of Father's other young followers thought the same way too. Robert Baldwin and the other men never wanted ordinary male companionship either. Most men were too virile to suit their refined tastes, and too vulgar. Heaven's chasteness may be the prime attraction for most of Father's young men.

Rash observers have sometimes described Father's young white men followers as "homosexual." On first glance at these men in their heavenly milieu, this would be an easy conclusion to come to. Many of them appear unvirile and devoid of sex appeal as the outside world prescribes it. Few of them in their late twenties and early and late thirties and forties have ever known the love of women or even dreamed of knowing it. And the Peace Mission movement, with its enforced sexual segregation, offers an excellent opportunity for overt homosexual behavior.

These facts, however, are not enough to warrant judgment. They are really superficial. But a fair observer will look deeper than surface fact. He will talk to these men, and, if Father Divine has instructed them to, they will talk honestly to him and bare their instincts and emotions as few men in the mortal world would ever dare to bare themselves. They will tell him how it is and why it is that they have come to Father. And when they do that, honestly, as they are impelled to, the observer will be bound to admit that the majority of them are not overtly homosexual. True, they have never desired women physically. On the other hand, they have not ever desired men either so far as they know—at any rate from a physical standpoint. And the happy mental and spiritual companionship which many of them have found with other Divinite men could probably be found with Divinite women as readily, or even more readily—if Father once passed the word that would permit them to seek it.

Which is not to say that there is no overt homosexuality or desire for it in the Peace Mission movement. Of course there is some; there must be. And its practice is written all over the stances and faces of some followers. It is apparent in the hungry way in which women sometimes stare at other women, at their breasts and hips and legs. It is just as apparent in the way men stare at other men, at their bodies instead of at their faces.

On August 16, 1952, Father gave an address to his followers that some of them interpreted to be aimed at stamping out overt homosexuality and that elicited important comment within the movement. He said:

". . . I do not want anyone under the Peace Mission movement who claims or whomsoever you may be that claim to be believers or even sympathizers, going into others' private rooms that you are not assigned to; rooms that you do not sleep in. . . . Some of you so-called sisters and some of you so-called believers and followers, some may even have the audacity to call themselves Rosebuds, will not stay away from others' rooms—from the other Rosebuds' rooms, other sisters' rooms, when they are not occupying those rooms. From now, henceforth, I want any of you to report any brother or sister visiting another brother's rooms. I am talking about if it is a brother visiting in the other brother's rooms and they have no legitimate cause—or, if it is not necessary for them to go in there, just to socialize and visit, let it be known and they can get elsewhere to stay!"

The young men in Father's movement deny any homosexual practices. The more worldly ones point up that Father's tenet of denial of the flesh effectively outlaws homosexuality.

In a way it does, but only in a way. It is true that, since Father's word is law, and since Father says that any fleshly lust is sinful, overt homosexuality in the Peace Mission movement is not so often practiced to its ultimate as it is in other institutions that segregate the sexes. It is equally true, however, that, even if there is not rampant overt homosexuality, there is very definitely a homosexual pattern among the men which Father encourages as a practical aid toward maintenance of the idea of his divinity. He causes his male followers to worship him in exactly the same fashion and with exactly the same intensity as his female followers do.

LaVere and Chester Belstrom consider themselves as much "brides of Father Divine" as the most feminine Rosebuds do.

Father's men followers praise him as his women followers do, with warm words that lovers use to their sweethearts. An outsider listening to them might be inclined to laugh at first. But the laughter wouldn't last long. It would soon be replaced by disgust if the outsider were not a sensitive person, or by pity if he were. For the worship of Father's men, just as much as the worship of his women, has a naked sexual glare.

White John Robert rises from his seat at the banquet table. He has never seen Father before. Now he looks at him, and all the love in the world is apparent in that look. It is a sweet, pure love-look John Robert gives to Father, but there is another quality in it too, a quality of passion leashed under control.

"Father dear," he cries out, "now that I have at last looked upon you, I know that no picture can do justice to your beauty."

By rights, John Robert and his words should seem funny. And when Father Divine, as he always does on such occasions, glances into a small mirror beside him on the table and obviously agrees with John Robert's talk about his pulchritude, it should seem funnier still. It does not seem funny, though. It seems tragic.

Neither does it seem funny when an outsider reading the

New Day is drawn to a gossip column written by Kitty Blue, the movement's Winchell, and comes across this item, presented with the utmost naturalness and acceptance of "this is the way it ought to be":

"What particular soldier," Kitty asks, "serving in the Air Corps, on leave for Christmas, is getting back into the old routine, crooning a love song to Father?"

You read this, and it should seem funny, and it does in a way—but only in a way. For the naked emotions of the crooning soldier are too morbid to be laughed at.

And you would never laugh at the sight and sound of Brother Samuel, attractive young white man from Chicago. He was overwhelmed by his first sight of Father.

"Peace, Father," he stammered, "I—want—to thank you for—the—opportunity—to be here—and—look—upon—your—glorious—body." His voice broke. "I—want—to—thank you—Father," he began again. Then, in a shaking voice with tears streaming down his face, he said, "Oh God!" And sat down, burying his face in his hands.

Neither can you laugh at the song which Father's young men's group always sings to him. The words of the song are the words of a sweetheart who has at last found his only beloved.

> *What did I long for? I never really knew—*
> *Finding your love, I found my adventure,*
> *Seeing your smile, my heart beat the faster,*
> *All that I want in all of this world is you.*

You talk to Robert Baldwin about that song and attempt to imply the significance that it has for you. Robert Baldwin does not respond to your implication. On purpose or not, he claims not to understand you. He says, "Of course, that song represents the feeling all of us have about Father. It enables us to express our love. Through it, more than through ordinary words, Father can know that he is the only one who matters."

22

"FATHER CAN'T NEVER DIE!"

To Robert Baldwin and to Father's other white male followers, every bit as much as to his white women followers and his Negro men and women followers, Father Divine is what the young men's song calls him—all that they want in all of the world. Their dependence on him is a difficult thing to view.

It is not the homosexual dependence alone that seems morbid, for the women's dependence seems as morbid as the men's does. Almost instinctively, every time you are faced with the followers' dependence—and you are faced with it every moment of every day you spend in heaven—you think, "Father Divine is no young man. He is in his seventies at the very least. What will happen when he dies?"

You ask that question of Robert Baldwin. "When Father Divine dies, what will happen to the movement and to all the angels?"

"Father cannot die."

"But if he could?"

"He couldn't."

Robert Baldwin remains poised and unperturbed.

You leave him and you approach a white woman follower who has been with Father for sixteen of her fifty-four years. Her name is Lovely Life.

"Peace, Miss Life."

"Peace."

"I want to ask you a question."

"Of course."

You don't make any pretenses with her. You don't lead up to your questions. You merely ask, abruptly, "If Father Divine died, what would happen here? What would you do? What would all the other followers do?"

"Father Divine could never die."

"Suppose he did, though?"

"He wouldn't."

You don't like yourself for what you're doing to Lovely Life. Still, you persist with her. "Please, Miss Life, just *suppose* he did."

"It's a silly thing to suppose. It just could not happen, just could not happen, that's all."

"But, suppose——"

"It's too silly——"

"But——"

Lovely Life looks hard at you. "Leave . . . me . . . alone," she warns. She walks away from you. She walks through the foyer where you have been standing with her and into the small "Sisters' Sitting Room." She walks through the sitting room and into the women's toilet. You follow her there. There are no doors in Divine toilets, and you see Miss Life go into the second cubbyhole, stand in front of the toilet bowl, and throw up. . . .

You go to her, trying to make up in some little measure for this terrible thing you have done to her. You watch her for a moment with her pinched, pale face. Then you put your hand on her forehead, trying to ease somewhat her retching process. She tears herself away from the touch of your hand. She goes on throwing up. She finishes. She lifts her head to look straight into your eyes.

"Don't . . . touch . . . me," she whispers.

The whisper is more expressive than a scream could be. It is hissing hatred at you: "Don't touch me!"

You walk out of the toilet. You shut the door behind you. You go through the Sisters' Sitting Room again and through the foyer where you first approached Miss Lovely Life. You walk outside, and the people you see look wonderful to you. You walk for blocks and blocks, trying to escape the picture of what you have done to Lovely Life. You try to make excuses for yourself to yourself. I didn't know, you tell yourself, I really didn't know. All the time you know you should have known. You've seen enough of Father's followers. You've observed their overwhelming needs. Of course you knew. You think of Lovely Life again and of her answer to your question, and you know

that she is one of the less hopeless ones after all. Somewhere in the depths of her mind, she can at least conceive
of Father's death. Robert Baldwin is more hopeless than
she; he cannot conceive of it at all—not even in the depths
of him. If Father dies, what happens to him?

Outsiders to the movement, visitors to the banquets,
have often speculated about Father's death. Conceiving of
the movement as "phony," however, their speculations
have been along the line of "who would take over," rather
than the effect on the followers. That somebody would be
bound to "take over" is an unquestionable fact to most
outsiders. They are certain that Father has chosen and is
grooming his successor.

He is not.

Father Divine is too profound a believer in his own
philosophy to make plans for dying. Since he knows he will
live forever, he does not think about successors for his
movement. It is obvious, in considering the persons who
are today, and have from the movement's inception been
closest to the throne, that Father Divine has *never* thought
in terms of successors. His lieutenants have never been
publicized and are not being publicized today, except as
they can serve as Father's foils. Always, he insists that they
recognize and verbalize, as Mother in the Second Body
does, his "allness" and their "nothingness." They have always done that.

Since the movement's inception, Faithful Mary has been
the only one who challenged this position of "nothingness,"
and she received harsh punishment for her effrontery. Father's two wives have never objected to their positions.
Peninah was satisfied to be God's housekeeper, and Sweet
Angel is humble about being his attractive contrast.

A few people believe that if Father Divine were to die,
Sweet Angel could take his place. But Sweet Angel is not
bright. She would need to be manipulated, utilized as Father uses her, as a symbol. She is utterly naïve, as befits a
virgin bride. Her naïveté is charming in her present position. It would be stupid if she were to become a substitute
for Father. The followers could never conceive of her as
anything but what she is today. They could never accept
her as anything else. Sweet Angel, while she is very possi-

ble as Mrs. God, would be reduced to the very nothingness she claims for herself if Father Divine were not in the picture.

Next to Sweet Angel in proximity to Father are his secretaries. But none of them could hope to replace him. There are some who are sufficiently bright and able. Dorothy Darling, Saint Mary Bloom, Jane Shaneweiss, Anita Daire, Willingness Charity are all well trained, with good executive potentials. They know all the details of heaven's inner workings and are responsible for a great many. But they, like Mother in the Second Body, have lost themselves in Father. Ever since they first began to service Divine, they began to think of themselves as anonymous. It is hardly likely that they could divorce themselves from their long-imposed roles of anonymity or that they would want to. Father's secretaries, like Father's wife, trust entirely in his divinity. If that trust were shaken, so would they be. In the face of that, they would not try to save the movement. They would be too tragically busy trying to save themselves.

Next to the secretaries in proximity to Father stands John Germaine, executive secretary of all the branches of the Peace Mission movement both here and abroad. If Father Divine died, Mr. Germaine could possibly be able to utilize the confidence Father has placed in him for taking over the movement. But it is inconceivable that, even if he could, he ever would. For Mr. Germaine has such faith in Father's divinity that he meaningfully says, "Nineteen hundred years ago, when Father first came to the earth in his sonship degree as the Christ, why, I was right here by his side." This is Mr. Germaine's fondest illusion. If Father died, it would be lost to him. So would all of life. He would not want to continue with the movement then. Certainly, he would not want to lead it.

That is the case with all of those who are close to Father. They are idealists. They are honest and sincere in their convictions. They are certainly not using Father Divine for reasons the mortal world could define as opportunistic. If Father Divine died, and proved he was not God in reality, they would be unable to bear the thought and would want nothing to do with the movement. Then, no amount of money could hold them there.

Which means that if the Divine Peace Mission movement is to be continued after Father's death, only an outsider, one not presently emotionally involved with Divine but one who still has a thorough understanding of him, could attempt to take it over and administer it.

There are only two such people alive today: Father's past attorney and his present one.

Arthur Madison and Austin Norris are both brilliant enough to move any mass they desire to move. As Father's trusted attorneys, they both have a thorough understanding of the movement and the psychology of its recruits. They are both, today, highly respected by the followers. But neither of them would be interested in copying after Father. They are too mortal, and the restriction of a divinity such as Father symbolizes could hardly be worthwhile to them.

Presuming that, for some fantastic reason, either Mr. Norris or Mr. Madison, or Mother in the Second Body, or any one of Father's able secretaries, or John Germaine would wish to take over the Peace Mission movement— they never could. For the followers could not ever accept a new symbol in place of this most satisfying old one. How could a new person ever hope to replace Father unless Father had carefully laid the groundwork for his replacement? And Father has never given his followers even a theoretical rationale for his disappearance from their midst. He has never, for one thing, stressed reincarnation. As a matter of fact, in all the years of his leadership, his virgin bride is the only example he has ever presented of reincarnation. Nor has he prepared his followers with other theories. On the contrary. He has gone on telling them that death is visited only on the wicked. He has gone on telling them that their security, their only security, is the knowledge of his ever-presence.

The entire Peace Mission movement, past and present, has been built around the base of personal loyalty to Divine in his own body. That is the reason why it could not ever endure as a movement if he were not alive to guide it.

That is why, even if an effective enough leader were found, it would still have to disintegrate and fall apart.

If it were to fall apart, then, what about the men and women who make up the Peace Mission movement? If it were to fall apart, what about the angels, who consider themselves incapable of living or taking a breath without the intervention of their good God? *What will happen to them?*

You ask them, handling the others with more care than you handled Lovely Life. You question the white followers first, spending one day with the men and one with the women. No one else reacts to your question as Lovely Life did. No one is disturbed—outwardly, anyway.

"Father Divine can't die."

"Father won't ever die."

"You don't seem to understand, young lady. Father is God, and God can't die."

"Your question is too ridiculous to deal with."

Universal Vocabulary pities you intensely. She speaks in a tone to indicate her pity. "How I wish your eyes could be opened to the truth," she says kindly. "It would not be necessary for you to ask such a question."

"Father Divine won't die."

"Father can't ever die."

"He's God."

All day, for two days, you get the same answers from hundreds of white followers. "Can't die!" "Won't die!" "Never, never die!" Your head begins to swim with the sameness of their answers and the extent of their confidence. You begin to envision the event of Father's death and to visualize their disillusion. You see them, broken up, unconfident, miserably unable to give up the shell of their life with Father even while they recognize it to be only a shell. You see them that way, and you begin to think of the Negro followers, and you cease being so sorry for the white ones.

For, in comparing them with the Negro followers, you understand again what you understood before your conversation with Holy Life. Father's white followers, despite the overwhelmingness of their feelings for him, are basically intellectual rationalizers. Intensely as they need Father, if he were to die today, most of them could rationalize his death tomorrow. If the need is strong enough—and the need in this case would be survival itself—these people can rationalize anything. Father Divine is an authority-figure which most of them need desperately. But there are other authority-figures in other religions. And just as deeply as they have given of themselves to Father Divine, just so deeply can they give to others.

Miss Lovely was once a Christian Scientist. Before that, she'd been a Unity woman. Before she'd entered Unity, she'd steeped herself in Yoga. All her life she has intellectualized, not felt. You talk to her and you think her conviction in regard to Father is intense. And it is, of course. But then you realize that she was just as convinced about Yoga and Unity and Christian Science as she is about Divinism—before she became unconvinced. You realize that if Divinism should ever fail Miss Lovely, she would find another outlet.

It is the same with the vast majority of Father's other white followers. Although they are today even more fanatic than the Negro followers, the record shows they have always been fanatics in every cult they have joined.

Rita Sanderson was as devoted a Christian Scientist as she is a Father Divinite. If Father should die, it is not unlikely that she and her sisters in the faith could return to what they now characterize as "the half-truth" and be better, more convinced Christian Scientists for all their interlude with Divine.

When one talks about Father's white followers, the question of what will happen to the Rita Sandersons and the other adept intellectual rationalizers cannot be of great concern. Undoubtedly, the vast majority of them will find some way to heal the scars Father's death will leave them with. Among the white followers, the concern must be about the few, like Mrs. Arthur Brockmorton, who, if they were not living in Divine Peace Missions, might be living behind the walls of insane asylums. The question is: what will happen to these pitiful ones, these old ladies who conceive themselves as little girls again, and these ragged men who think they are the illegitimate sons of John D. Rockefeller? For them, will there ever be another heaven as tolerant as this one? That *is* questionable. It might be that the death of Father Divine will result in some new white patients for mental hospitals.

The tragedies of the Mrs. Brockmortons would not, however, be the worst in the movement if Father Divine should die. The worst tragedies would take place among the great bulk of depressed Negroes who have never been taught to rationalize and for whom Father Divine represents the salvation.

Sociologists Abram Kardiner and Lionel Oversey, who have spent four years investigating "the personality he [the American Negro] acquired while being obliged to adapt to extremely difficult social conditions," define what Father Divine's movement has meant to Negroes:

"It was the needs of the lower-class Negro which prompted the cult into existence and which the organization attempts to satisfy. In this sense it is the only Negro indigenous religion. We regard this movement less a religion than a folk-cult in which Father Divine is hardly more than the catalytic agent. If this is so, then this movement represents a considerable degree of self-assertion on the part of the lower-class Negro. It is a part of Negro protest with all its illusory and contradictory trends; but it is a protest in fantasy only and as such it dramatizes this protest and gives it articulate form . . . by denying reality and forcing new values in a make-believe world."

Where else than in the Peace Mission movement can Negroes achieve the values they've achieved in heaven? The good economies? The fine father? The husband-provider? The God, who is personally concerned with them? Where else can they achieve the thrilling self-dignity? If Father Divine leaves them, where will they ever find those values again?

Can any Negro do what Rita Sanderson can—return to another religion? Can he become a Baptist again if he has left the Baptist Church for Father, or a Methodist if he has left the Methodist Church? Not ever. For the Baptist and Methodist religions, which have attracted greater numbers of Negroes than any others, as well as the other religions with smaller Negro membership, have never belonged basically—or even partially—to the Negroes. The religion which Negroes brought from Africa with them was destroyed in slave days along with every other aspect of their culture. And the white man's church, although it has admitted them, has never influenced them. Thus, the white man's religion has never truly served the Negro's needs.

It is only the cults, the store-front churches, which have taken Negro needs into account. But once a Negro has known Father, he can never find his answer in a cult again. What can an ordinary store-front church offer a Divinite? Escape? Only very temporarily, only very momentarily. For while an adherent may spend half his night in a store-front church where there is life and color and sociableness, he knows—even while he is participating in a service—that, at its conclusion, he must return to the devastating routine of living as a Negro in a white man's world. What else can a cult offer, what besides escape? A sense of self-dignity? Not really. For even during the tensest moments, everyone from the preacher on down knows, deep in his heart, that, despite the singing and the shouting and the self-recognition, he has not changed by majority standards.

Actually, all that the cults and the store-front churches offer their congregations is a too temporary release for pent-up emotion. How can this satisfy Divinites? No cult except Father's has called reality false and given truth to a dream. Divinites who have known the dream want nothing to do with the bitter truth. The cults, while they are not truth, are not dream, either. So, in the event of Father's death, they could not ever be nearly enough to provide even a partially efficacious substitute.

If the doors of religion, legitimate and otherwise, would be closed to Divinites, what group affiliations would then be open to them? The National Association for the Advancement of Colored People? The National Urban League? Any one of the other agencies set up for the attainment of civil rights for Negroes? No. The programs of these organizations are carried out on a sophisticated level by paid and volunteer personnel who are themselves sophisticated and highly educated. Despite their most sincere efforts, their touch is now and always has been for the upper and middle classes. Their programs are hardly understandable to the vast majority of Divinites, who if they had not been naïve could never have joined Father's movements in the first place. How can Father's followers go along with the programs of the practical race relations agencies, programs which call for striving and for sacrifice to attain a mere part of the equality which they have already known *in toto* without any sacrifice or striving?

If affiliation with Father Divine makes any other affiliation impossible, what adjustment would be tenable for Divinites if Father should die? Certainly, they are not strong enough within themselves to live lone lives and like them. Neither can they ever again relate to other people, to husbands or wives, to sons or daughters, to mothers or fathers. They have never, even before they joined Father, been able to relate to other people adequately. If they had been, it is likely that they would be, today, outside instead of inside the Peace Mission gates. Their experiences before they joined Divine, coupled with experiences afterwards, have permanently incapacitated them for sex or marriage or family obligation. Even if they should be forced to give up Father, they could not ever dream of taking on sex or marriage or family obligation.

In the very face of a first question—"What would you do if Father died?"—Mr. Laughing Light, who left a wife and two children when he joined Divine, answers the subsequent question, "Would you return to your wife and children?" with a supercilious smile.

"Never! Never do that thing! Never get married up again with the so-called wife or any other wimins."

Maybe, long years ago, before he thought of joining Father Divine, if Mr. Light had had the opportunity of assuming the financial care of his wife and children, maybe if his own childhood had not been messed up by a working mother and a jobless father, maybe if he had had love and sympathy and understanding in childhood, maybe if he had had psychiatric therapy in adulthood—if most of the circumstances that had been in his life had not been, and if most of those that had not been, had—it is possible that if he lost Father Divine, he could have visualized relating to someone else. American racial patterns and Father Divine have, between them, once and for all, precluded such relationships for Mr. Light and all his "brothers and sisters in truth."

What, then, would be left to Divinites if Father should die? In losing him, they would lose, in one single, terrible swoop, their husband, their wife, their lover, their child, their mother, their father, and their God. Who in this world would be able to sustain such a loss?

It may be that the question of what would happen to Divine Negroes if Father should die starts out as an interesting theoretical question, but it must end as a terrifying prospect. Father's Negro followers make it that. You talk with them, as you have with the white followers, individually and in groups. Their answers, differently worded, naturally, are still startlingly alike.

Sixty-nine-year-old Love Dove, who, back in 1929, left a "so-called husbin'" and five "so-called chillun" on a tenant farm outside Augusta, Georgia, regards you unbelievingly at the beginning of your conversation with her.

"Ya'll mus' be crazy," she says, "real good 'n crazy. Father ain't never gonna go away from usn's. We got to have him too bad."

She keeps talking that way, calling you crazy, until, all of a sudden, something you say—you can't put your finger on exactly what it is—convinces her that, no, you aren't crazy. You watch her face the fact of your sanity and it is a devastating thing to see. If ever you have seen fear on any person's face, if ever you have known tragedy, you know you have never really seen it until your talk with Love Dove. You backtrack. How can you help it?

"It's all right, Miss Dove. Father won't die. You're right when you say he can't." You smile, and your smile seems artificial to you, but you go on smiling anyway. "You're also right when you say I'm crazy. It was certainly a crazy question I asked."

Love Dove is wound up, though. Something, some gnawing thing, tells her you're not as crazy as you say you are.

"If Father dies," she tells you in the calmest kind of a voice, "I sure 'nuff would never be callin' on myself to be goin' on livin' in this empty ol' world. I'd be findin' some way of gettin' rid of the life I never been wantin' before I found him."

If Father Divine were to die, mass suicides among the

Negroes in his movement could certainly result. They would be rooted deep, not alone in Father's relationship with his followers but also in America's relationship with its Negro citizens.

This would be the shame of America.

AFTERWORD

The newspapers reported Father Divine's death on September 7, 1965. In reading and hearing about it impersonally through the media, I had to recollect my predictions concerning what would happen to the movement and the followers, especially the black ones, when Father Divine died.

Five years later, when the book was about to be republished, I was asked to write about the state of the movement in 1970. I knew that I could not expect to be received in Philadelphia or at Woodmont, but my husband, Arnold, and a psychologist-sociologist friend, Dr. Paul A. Fine, agreed to seek to learn firsthand what were the current major elements of the movement. I asked them to give particular attention to these questions:

1. How had Father Divine's physical death been rationalized?

2. Had Mother Divine developed far enough beyond the puerile virgin bride I'd known to be able to replace Father as the fountain of leadership of the movement?

3. What had happened to the ordinary angels—the plebeians—especially the black ones? Had there been, as I predicted could have been the case, mass suicides among those whose entire lives had revolved around loyalty to Divine in his personal body?

4. Who are the movement's leaders, para-logicians, and philosophers today?

5. How vital, compared to when I knew it, is the movement today?

6. In the light of the black revolution in America, where does the contemporary movement stand?

Arnold, under the pseudonym of Dr. Alvin Karp, sociologist, and Paul spent many hours in two mission headquarters, the Divine Lorraine Hotel, where I'd visited and lived, and Woodmont, the movement's country estate in nearby Conshohocken, where Mother and the secretaries reside. The following are their reactions and answers to my questions, evolved during two visits they made to the Divine Lorraine Hotel on Sunday, March 22, 1970, and to Woodmont four weeks later.

ARNOLD HARRIS
CONCERNING THE DIVINE LORRAINE HOTEL,
MR. CHILD AND MOTHER DIVINE

We arrived at the Divine Lorraine at about seven o'clock. It's still a fine hotel; the lobby is spotless, freshly painted. The proper Divine signs, doubtless there in your time, were all around. A little old lady, an extremely light-skinned black woman, sat at the front desk and greeted us enthusiastically: "Oh, you're the two visitors we're expecting." I had the feeling from her attitude of friendliness that visitors weren't as usual as they had been, that our coming was really an important thing to them, and that they'd been looking forward to us since I had called to make our appointment.

She said, "Please wait a moment and let me call someone to get you." I thought at first sight that the person who came to us could have been John Germaine. His name, the Divine name, was Mr. Child. He was, of course, curious—but carefully curious—about why we were there. I told him I'd had some exposure to the movement in the fifties and had more or less a sense of its value in those days. He said, "Oh, yes, that's interesting."

Paul said, "If I could ask you a personal question, when did it come to you?" And Mr. Child answered, very simply, "I was a victim of Little Rock in 1954. I was a school administrator there." That was his answer, and I believe he was telling us that his attitude as an integrationist had made his position untenable, or else that some other, new force was needed to create change among human beings, and that force was Father Divine.

After we'd talked for a while, he took us up to the tenth-floor ballroom where about fifty people were gathered. The man–woman relationship obviously hasn't changed since your time there—the men were on the right side of the room and the women were on the left. Most of them were considerably older people. There was only one strong, vital individual present—a younger woman who could have been in her thirties or forties. She participated in the service by reading a sermon Father had delivered in 1931.

I say *service,* but this was not a service in the sense that you knew services to have been. It was a get-together with people singing and giving vent to their "burning spirit," as Mr. Child put it. You could call it a family party, albeit a large one, of the angels living in the Divine Lorraine Hotel. The four-piece band of piano, trumpet, and two electric guitars served as accompaniment. The guitars were played by two young white fellows in their early twenties. The piano player and trumpeter were black and older, and the younger fellows were very involved, without question. Remembering your description of the children of members of the movement, I noticed that one of the young men might well have been Miss Anita's son, Kenneth Daire. He would be about that age.

The songs were the dominant feature of the evening. In between, people would rise and give testimony to Father much as they'd done while he was alive. Mr. Child made a brief speech, really aimed at us, in which he said that the gates of heaven were always open and that they were pleased to have interested people come. He made a big point, however, about their not attempting to convert anyone. He said that there was no necessity, and no real use, for proselytization. The spirit, the burning spirit, has got to be within you. It can only come from inside. Paul and I were invited to say a few words, and we said—and we meant it—that, though we were from another world ourselves, we appreciated the warmth and beauty of this one, the singing, the joy, and the spirit Mr. Child had spoken about.

There was more singing after our talks, and then Mr. Child invited us downstairs to the banquet. It was held in what had once been the bar of the hotel, and it was not at all the kind of banquet you and I have attended, with several hundred people. Big platters of food were being passed along long lines of tables with the accompaniment of shouting and singing and testifying. I guess the only similarity would be in the seating arrangements for men and women angels. The Lorraine bar is a big oval with booths on both sides. The men sat to the right and the women to the left. The food was placed in platters on the bar, one side of which was for men and the other for women. No one needed to tend the food because everything was organized for self-service—you walked by as at a buffet and helped yourself. There was no ceremony of any kind. The door was open, and people walked in; got in line; picked up their napkins, silver, and dishes; and partook. The food wasn't as ample as it was twenty years ago, but there was still plenty, and it was unusually good —cauliflower in cheese sauce, luscious liver-and-bacon done to a crisp, chicken, beef, vegetables, cake, and several kinds of ice cream. Payment for one's meal is the same as it always was—whatever you wish or can afford.

I might say, though, I didn't see any down-and-outers, not only at the banquet but in the hotel generally. In fact, the very genteel lady at the desk seemed to have a sharp eye for drunks and other derelicts. We saw her order one drunken man out very nicely and politely but also quite firmly. We saw no evidence of the helping hand, and the feeling Paul and I got from both the people generally and from Mr. Child himself was (and these are my words, not Mr. Child's): "We are no longer seeking out the poor and the derelict and the criminal element, as was the case in the early days. On the contrary, we ourselves have succeeded spiritually and in every other way, and we aren't looking for new people unless they are as special as we are and fit to be part of our little aristocracy." It's all very ingrown and, quite obviously, a dying movement. The people are generally old, the same black followers we knew twenty years ago. There certainly aren't nearly as many as there were then. The general mood is that of a respectable, middle-class movement, and there is little or none of the black, lower-class vitality of twenty years ago. I saw few people I would have characterized as having a life force so intense that they might have been driven to suicide when their center, Divine in his body, left them.

Obviously, it was not possible to discover whether or not there was any validity in your concluding that there might be mass suicides among the black, lower-class followers after Father's death. There may well have been. If so, the burials would have been undertaken with the same secrecy we knew in earlier days, and the world would never have learned about them. Of course, there may not have been any, but the black followers we met gave the impression they were light-years away from the problems of thievery, sloth, and degradation that characterized so many of the followers you knew. They were a part of the movement of their time, and today's black followers—and white ones— are a part of the new theology. I won't talk about the new theology, because Paul explains it in detail. The only point I want to make here is that today's angels see themselves as a spiritual elect—and an earthly one as well—much more conclusively than did the old-time angels.

I asked Mr. Child (Paul and he were talking about the new theology), "Tell me, in the context of what you were just saying about spirituality and the spiritual purpose of the Peace Mission movement, how do you compare what it is doing and where it is today with the situation when you came in 1954?"

He answered that in 1954 there were still many people in the movement who did not take it seriously from a spiritual viewpoint. They came for the singing and dancing, and primarily because they wanted to be taken care of. Now it's shaken down to the few; the chaff are gone. All but the most spiritually complete people have fallen away. "We now have infinitely more meaning for creation and the world."

When I continued to press him away from the spiritual and on to the earthlier aspects, finally naming the words "social purpose," he said simply that there had been a need for bread in the early days and Father, therefore, provided the bread; he met the need. Under the circumstances of today's world, however, bread is no longer a need. The need of today's world is for a spiritual elect, and it is this the Peace Mission movement has become. He said, "Look at some of the people who are approaching God, Himself, in their qualities and capacities. You'll see their holiness in their faces. Look at Mother Divine when you meet her. Look at the people around her, the Rosebuds, for instance, if you want to experience true spirituality."

To talk about Mother Divine, I must first describe Woodmont, where we met her. It, like the Hotel Lorraine, is largely unchanged. The mood is of the traditional estate, with its hundreds of acres of rolling hills planted and manicured beyond belief. Not a flower or a shrub is out of place. It is literally heavenly, and even more appropriately possessed today than it was as the home of Mr. Wood, steel magnate of Conshohocken, whose mills it still overlooks in the valley below. We were shown into the solarium, which was luxuriant with all kinds of potted plants, carpets, statuary, and paintings. And there were fresh flowers, beautiful fresh flowers, expensive flowers—long-stemmed roses and rare chrysanthemums. It was meant to duplicate heaven, to be heaven, and it was.

We were taken to Mother's office, a large, quiet, and quite traditional room. Dorothy Darling was there, still taking notes, and there was a black secretary. Mother was greatly changed. She no longer had that doll-like quality she had had as a younger person. Since Paul had never seen her before, his first impression of her might be significant. He said, "I expected a doll-like person from the photographs, and she has a stronger face than that. I wouldn't call her a woman of great character but she's a woman of character."

I think she's acquired regality since we knew her. Those years of being hailed as a queen have obviously had their effect. She's gained some weight and is an imposing figure now. She held her chin high while we talked and was a very gracious lady with us. She obviously took pleasure in describing Woodmont and its antecedents. She emphasized the beautiful vista and said the place was predestined as a heavenly headquarters.

She is better-spoken than she'd been when we knew her, though she still doesn't give the impression of a cultured woman. She is not cultured and not contemplative in the sense that Mr. Child, say, gave the impression of being. I

must say, though, that there is nothing phony about her—
no air of pretense. She's still the symbol of the wedding of
God and the church. She describes herself as the spotless
bride with even less emotion and spontaneity than used to
be the case. I didn't get a sense of grief or of personal
involvement, as I guess befits a living symbol.

I asked her, as I had Mr. Child, about the social significance of the movement—its presence as a living force and
its activity in these times of incredible turmoil. She didn't
give an adequate answer. She was simply at a loss for
words. She stumbled and made some vacuous and unre-
sponsive answer. Mr. Child, who sat behind us during the
interview, protectively took over for her and answered the
question. His analogy was that what we are experiencing
now is the time between the birth of Christ and the
Epiphany. On the surface, everything is quiescent, so you
think nothing is happening. But there will be a burst of
glory when you least expect it. Mother nodded to Mr.
Child's answer and didn't react very emotionally to it, or to
anything else. In fact, the only time we saw her react with
any passion was when I asked her feelings about your
book. She literally excoriated you, saying you'd written so
many untrue things. When Paul asked her to name specific
untruths, she didn't answer except to say, with great indignation, that you had treated Father Divine as a man and
tried to assign human origins to him. That was your unfor-
givable sin.

DR. PAUL A. FINE
    CONCERNING MOTHER DIVINE, WOODMONT,
    AND THE BANQUET AT THE DIVINE LORRAINE HOTEL

When Mother talked about your assigning Father human
origins, I answered her in what I thought would be an
acceptable way—I said that in previous visitations of God's
spirit and his taking on a reality form among men, much
attention is paid to the stories of origins. Moses in the
bullrushes is a story of great importance; the Virgin
Mary's giving birth to Christ is a story of great importance.
All believers in God have long accepted these stories of

divine origin. I asked, "What are your stories about Father's origin?"

She was tongue-tied. She couldn't answer my question because she couldn't feel what I was saying. Dorothy Darling made an attempt to get her off the hook, but it wasn't too successful. She appeared infinitely more intelligent than Mother, but her ability to feel really wasn't much more adequate. Neither of them *felt* the question the way Father must have when he answered your question about his origins: "I was combusted one day in 1900...."

While this vigorous man was ready to give you an answer out of his own spirit, out of his own emotionality, the women were not even ready to feel the question. Certainly, they weren't ready to feel this all-important event. And neither could they feel the less important ones. Arnold and I asked our questions, not only about Father's origins, but also about other theological aspects that I'll examine later within their own framework. We constructed our questions in terms of Father Divine's own theological structures and views. And Mother simply was not prepared to field anything like that. So the sense of discomfort grew in all of us. I fell into silence. Arnold handled the situation with some gentlemanly remark about the beauty of the estate, which led to our being shown through it again.

Soon a bell rang, and we went into the dining room to our side of the table, where our seats were fairly close to Mother. After we were seated, Mother picked up a big, old-fashioned silver bell and rang the living hell out of it. There was a fierce note in her ringing and her whole stance changed to being almost masculine. Her chin became more determined as she rang.

She sat at the head of the table beside Father's empty seat. I say Father's seat is empty, but he's there to Mother and the other followers. He's there. Every dish is tendered to him before Mother blesses it to pass on. It is quite an experience to watch her sitting at the head of the table and passing the food with her benign smile. The speech of Father's they chose to play at dinner was the one in which he presented Mother, soon after the marriage, as the spotless virgin bride. And she talked about herself this way with no emotion or sense of grief over Father's loss.

But, then, Father is as much with her and with the other angels today as when he was alive. His body lies in the Woodmont shrine, which people come to view. But it is only his fleshly body that is buried, his spirit lives on.

It was not Mother who gave us this concept but Mr. Child. He explained the whole present meaning of the movement in our first half-hour with him; and every other experience we had, both in Woodmont and at the Divine Lorraine Hotel, brought his words to life. Speaking as the movement's philosopher, he said that we, of the world, are incarnated in fleshly bodies. He quoted Father as saying that our world of perceived reality is a world of problems which we invent for ourselves. Racism, age, poverty, political problems—all this has been invented by the human mind. Our salvation from such problems is to simply recognize that they don't exist. We must transcend to the higher reality, the higher plane of consciousness. We must enter heaven, and it is not in the sky. He was very specific about this. Father Divine's heavens are still not earthly showplaces. Heaven is here on earth for those of us who are able to realize that it is here. And to come to that perception one must begin by intuiting the spirit of God. Everyone can intuit the spirit because it is more or less within us all. The spirit may not be crystallized or purified in us all, but it is there waiting to come to fruition if we will permit it. But our human wills prevent us from meeting the spirit. Only the elect, and they are few, have relaxed their wills sufficiently.

These elect must permit the spirit to bring them into heaven. They no longer live on the earth. Divinites no longer live among men and women. The followers obviously are as persuaded as they ever were of this and also of the need to cast off husbands, wives, and children—precisely, actually, not symbolically. "That thou shalt love the Lord thy God with all thy heart," Mr. Child told us, "is with all thy soul and thy might. Single-mindedly!" One gives himself over to God. And in this transubstantiation, this transfiguration, one literally leaves the world, and is in heaven here and now.

The attitude toward procreation has not changed either. It is the same as it was at the beginning . . . when the

Kingdom of Heaven arrives on earth there will be no death, and, therefore, no need for creating new people. Mr. Child voiced this eloquently, and all the angels expressed it in their testimonials. They illustrated his philosophy. He pointed this up to us, pointed up the followers acting out their intuition. I asked him how he distinguished between intuition and emotion. He answered that intuition is simply that which brings us into, or raises us to, the new consciousness. But if the new consciousness, once intuited, remains on the level of intellect, it becomes pale and hypocritical. The emotion is the deeper resonance, the deeper expression within the spirit, within the soul of the voice you find.

I couldn't help thinking as I listened to him that kids today are talking in more or less the same vein. You can do your thing in your way and nobody has a right to stop you if it doesn't coincide with his way. Bring out your own spirit, the voice within yourself.

The testimonials themselves were not the wild pandemonium you describe in your book, but there were some remainders of it. It wasn't just singing and shouting but a person feeling free, as he certainly must have when Father was there, to stand and speak to the brothers and sisters as the spirit moved him. Allowing the voice of God to speak through him, because then, to some degree, he is God. And there were the beaming, smiling, delighted faces of people who were practiced in letting themselves go.

One of the witnesses was an old woman in her seventies, a big woman, with a harsh, growly voice. She testified, as she must have done for the thousandth time, as though what she was saying was fresh and new. I would like to hear it again and again and again to see how fresh and new it does sound to an insider. But, at least to the ears of a stranger, it sounds fresh and new. And she testified, as though she were a newcomer, that she had been deeply involved in theology since she was a child. She said that her father was a preacher but that she'd found formal religion very unsatisfying until she experienced this new spirit through Father Divine and grasped the new way and felt herself freed. She used words to that effect, and then she did a jig. An old lady, her legs are quite busted up, and

I thought she would collapse. It was frightening primarily because it was rather different from the joyous outlet of the majority. It was not done in the spirit of joy. It was foot-stamping in a sort of seizure, something like a temper tantrum. She was like a child going into a fury and kicking her feet and being unable to stop. But that was her way. It was her thing, and it was perfectly acceptable.

Another woman, also white, was interesting to me because she said that she came from my hometown, Seattle. I know where she comes from very well—Queen Ann Hill. It is a settlement of old people whose children have grown up and gone away. They live in very modest, little houses. All of Queen Ann Hill is a hotbed of the John Birch Society. To leave must have taken a good deal of dissatisfaction and some courage on this lady's part. She had, for a long time, been part of the movement in Seattle, though peripherally. You could say she was torn between heaven and Queen Ann Hill. She knew she couldn't go on that way, so she came to Philadelphia to enter heaven. And she testified to what Mr. Child told us; she no longer dwells in her mortal body, or lives in the mortal world.

There were many elderly, white-haired women of her type, not so much the Christian Science and Unity seekers-after-truth one knew from the old days, as they were typical WASP personalities out of rigid, cold backgrounds like hers. As I watched those ladies smiling, beaming, saying "Peace," I couldn't help comparing them to others I knew of similar backgrounds—prim, proper, straight, upstanding members of the silent majority. It is impossible for such people to talk to you for five minutes without revealing their fear of the foreign, the black, the young—of change itself.

Of course, in a very real sense they and all the Divine people are also obsessed. But their obsession, in which they have left all of the past behind, makes them warm rather than cold, kind rather than cruel, friendly rather than hostile. Mr. Child put it well, I thought, when he said, "Why do we here dwell in harmony? Because there is friendship between the races in America? No. The reason we are in harmony here is because we know there is no racism. There is no racism as there is no age or sex."

And then he commenced talking about the celibacy in heaven, to detail its deeper meaning to himself. And somehow, it was a very chilling moment. He said, "I had a wife. Many of us had wives and children. I loved my wife. But I reached a point in my recognition where I knew I had to go beyond the mortal way. I knew the whole relationship, the only relationship, the entire relationship is with God. And therefore, there is no time for relationship with people."

Then he said several things, the most telling of which seemed to have come directly out of *Doctor Strangelove*. The Colonel in *Doctor Strangelove* explained that, yes, he liked being with women, but not at the expense of his vital essence. The one thing he had to preserve, above all, was his vital essence. Exactly that language was used. When men and women are together sexually, there is a giving up of the vital essence. The vital fluid, the vital energy, is necessary for man's relationship to God. That is why, he said, "when you are through with what you call making love, you still feel unsatisfied. You feel tacky." He expressed a clear sense of revulsion. He said he had felt himself to be "dirty, to be dirtified," by sex, that he could feel the sweat of love-making on his body and feel his gorge beginning to rise.

He explained that the sexual love we, of the world, are talking about really has nothing to do with divine love. He said of the motto "make love, not war" that that love is a kind of war. There will be no peace on earth, no harmony, until we give up all earthly relationships and transcend to the higher form of consciousness. That is how the theme kept coming up over and over. You'll see from the following testimonies how every talk, every action, so clearly illustrates what he expressed to us in three minutes.

An old Jewish lady, the exact antithesis of the WASP types, was there. She was the very typical kind of Jewish mother—a sweet-faced, pleasant-looking, articulate, bright, interesting woman in her sixties. She could have come from any orthodox Jewish home in Brooklyn or the Bronx. She informed us that she'd been raised in the orthodox theology of Judaism and explained the idea of the Divine elect in her terms. She listed, by name, which none of the others of us could have done, the twelve tribes of Israel and then multiplied the number twelve by twelve thousand. It came to the magic number of 144,000, and that is the number of the Divine elect.

Mr. Child hastened to explain that we were not to take the number 144,000 seriously but reiterated that, certainly, there was an elect, that would prove Divinism to be repeating Christ's way. Father Divine first drew the people with works of the world, as was the case during the years you were exposed to the movement. But those works, as exemplified by Father's feeding of the hungry, had no other purpose than to draw the people. But what must be understood and is not, sufficiently, is that such attempts to draw people are not, and never were, for the good of their human bodies. They have one purpose and only one, and it is to draw people who otherwise might not achieve exposure closer to the burning spirit. It is simply to bring people nearer to God's transcendent spirit. That, and only that, was the aim of the works of the world that Father engaged in when you knew him.

The first stage has now been accomplished, Mr. Child went on. The movement is in its second stage—preparing the elect (who have absorbed the burning spirit) to permit the spirit to emerge, and making the Divinites' intuition ready to reveal God's spirit as Christ did. This second stage is the one of purification. Christ illustrated his meaning by using the image of Gideon's army, who were to be the Christian soldiers. Gideon had gathered a mighty host around him, and God had said there were too many. Then they took their long and arduous trip, and many fell by the wayside. Even afterward, however, there were too many. They came to a river bank (and here Mr. Child got mixed up and he realized the story was bombing and finished it up without much further detail). He said that God told Gideon at the river bank that those who came to the river bank and threw themselves on the water and lapped the water like dogs, also would have to be eliminated. But those who would hold their swords in their hands and drink with their eyes, those are the ones whom you want.

Of course, this definition of an elect also served to explain the disintegration of the movement as exemplified by the comparatively small number of followers. Mr. Child reminded me of the philosophers and spokesmen of the Communist party during the days of its crushing obliteration. They also spoke with great hope and optimism, saying their sacrifice as individuals was part of the inevitable historical movement which was bound eventually to lead to the great days of the dictatorship of the proletariat. I see the same kind of thinking among Divine philosophers.

It is a refusal to recognize defeat as a possibility even while you are in the very midst of experiencing it. When you have a purification, a stripping down to Gideon's army, you can't lose under any circumstances. The smaller your membership, the more convinced you can be of your validity.

Which brings us, of course, to your initial question of who and where is Father now. Mr. Child's answers were long and drawn out. He explained that there had been several times during the thousands of years of man's history when God's spirit had realized itself in the human body. He had generally chosen an improbable figure, in the worldly sense, for this realization. Moses was one—and where could you have found a more improbable figure, from the Egyptians' viewpoint? Moses was the deliverer, the giver of the law. God took that form in him. Sometimes he comes as the Christ in a man's body, the Son to symbolize our mutual childness. And sometimes He comes as the Father, as He did with Divine.

From the viewpoint of improbability, Father, like Moses and like Christ, was wrong for our Establishment. He was the wrong color and the wrong size and so far ahead of his time that he was castigated as Christ was. It was the same with Father as with every figure in whom God was manifest, throughout history. Father's in the pattern. So is his relationship with his, our, time and society. The embodied essence of the Great Spirit initially attacks the Great Pharaoh, the powerful Pharaoh, the Establishment. And it is defeated. And then the Spirit turns its forces; it no longer strikes against the Establishment, but rather finds its reincarnation among ordinary people, in the lives they lead. And that is what has occurred here among the ordinary people who are incandescences of Father Divine.

And Mr. Child's reaction to your question, "Where is Father now?" is merely part of the reaction to the question, "Who is Father?" It is so obvious to them. Father is the spirit of God. And he is at present in heaven as he ever was, because he is within Mother and Dorothy Darling and the WASP women and the orthodox Jewish lady. And he is within all the black followers here in this transcendent place on earth. He is everywhere. He is everywhere. He is all. Will he be back? Of course, though not in the body he resided in before.

Mr. Child said, "He is also in you." If I do an unselfish act, if I sacrifice myself on any level, then Father Divine is me. He is a supremely transcendent, incandescent incarnation of the spirit. That is all.

I became a little teasing, a little rough, after he had said that God was also in me; I responded, "Well, such an expression of your theology is very gentle and humanitarian." He approved this interpretation of the gentle side, and then I hit him with my basic observation: "Your portal of entry into the movement, though, is very rigid and harsh." He hesitated at that, then replied,

Yes, it is harsh until you begin to know God as children know Him. We are all children in heaven. There are no adults. We don't have children—we *are* children. And this is what we must realize. When we give in to our childlikeness and recognize our childishness in relation to the Heavenly Father, we will find our way through the portals you describe as rigid and harsh into the new transcendent place of life—heaven here on earth. As soon as we relax our own wills, black or white, according to your earthly terminology, we will find our way very simply, through God's will for us.

Index

Note: Spiritual names of individuals are alphabetized under the first element of the name.

Abdul Hamid, Sufi (Eugene Brown), 49, 54–55, 80–81
American Civil Liberties Union, 189
American Jewish Congress, 189
Anna Dearone, Mr. 173–75
Answer Man, The (Bruce Chapman), 5
Arata, Mr. (district attorney), 28, 31
Associated Negro Press, 183
Associated Press, 183
Atlanta, Georgia, 188
Austin, J. C., 203

Baker, George. *See* Father Divine
Baldwin, Robert, 334–37, 340, 341, 343
banquets, xxi–xxiii, 66–67, 74, 227, 274, 355–56
Barefoot Prophet (cult leader), xi
Barnes, Nellie. *See* Miss Jonathan Matthew
Beautiful, Miss (Mary Mason), 100–102, 158–59, 304
Beautiful Bliss, 326
Beautiful Heart, 164–71
Beautiful Love, 176–82
Beautiful Peace (Jean Johnson), xxvi, 153–55, 193, 209
Becton, George Wilson, x, xi, xii
Bell, Marguerite, 235
Belstrom, Chester and LaVere, 222, 331–34, 336, 339
Bible Institute, 245–46
Birdsall, Jessie, 57
Black Star Line, xviii
"Blessed are ye, rosebuds of my heart," 319
Blue, Alex G., 34, 39–40
Bowan, Tessie, 120–21
Boyer, Reverend Charles, 241–42
Braden, Dr. Charles, 120
Brigantine Hotel, 240
Bright Light, Miss, 169
Brockmorton, Mrs. Arthur, 315–17, 347
Brown, Eugene. *See* Abdul Hamid, Sufi
Brown, Thomas, 85–93
Brown, Verinda, 85–95, 97, 180, 300
Buddhist Universal Holy Temple of Tranquility, 49
    See also Temple of Tranquility
Buncha Love, xxvi, 89
Buncha Sweetness (Leila Slaughter), 155–58
Burrows, Rose, 29–30

Caldwell, Ethel, 144
Carole Sweet, 285–87, 300
Chapman, Bruce. *See* Answer Man, The
Charity, Miss, 255–56, 271, 272
Charity Love, Miss, 169, 170
Charles Cheerfulness, 142–43
Charmed Life, Miss, 102
Cheerfulness Good, Mr., 104
Child, Mr., 354–58, 359, 361–62, 365–66
Church of the Living God, 12–13
  See also Temple(s) of God
Christian Science, and Divinism, 313–14
Circle Mission Church, 234, 235, 237
communism, 202, 207–208
Connely, Mrs., 35
consecrated dime ceremony, xii
Copeland, J. P., 10
Cox, Lillian, 36–37
Craster, Dr. Charles V., 125–26
Crown Publishers, xxvii
cult leaders, x–xii, 48–50, 54
cults, xi, 349

Daddy Grace, xi, 50, 54, 55–56
Daily Worker, xiv, 207
Daire, Anita Nadler, 162, 258–65, 344
Daire, Kenneth, 162, 183, 258, 260–62
Daire, Kenneth, Jr., 162–63, 258, 260, 355
Daire, Robert, 162, 258
Dancing Soul, 149–51
Daniel in the Lion's Den, Mr., 103–104
Denny, Robert, 239
Determination Charm, 142
Devine, Major J. *See* Father Divine
Diamond, David, 307

Dineen, Judge Benedict J., 94
Divine Lorraine Hotel, xxi, 227, 234, 354, 355, 358
Divine Riviera Hotel, 227, 232, 234, 240
Divine Tracy Hotel, 227, 240
Divinism
  compared to Christian Science, 313–14
  vibrating, 117–18
Divinism, tenets of, 26, 88, 120, 122–25, 143–47, 355–57, 361–62
  on bank accounts, 88–89
  on human reproduction, 119
  on insurance policies, 88–89
  on race relations, 22, 24, 36–38, 97–98, 130, 363
  on rejection of relationships of mortality, 13, 125, 149–170
  on sex, xix, 14, 23, 99–118, 313, 364–65
  visualization of the positive, xxiii, xxiv, 128–32, 141
  on vocabulary, 130–32, 182
  See also Righteous Government platform
Dorothy Darling, xxi, xxv, xxvi, 252–53, 262, 271, 272, 273, 284, 285, 344, 358, 360
Duryea, Justice Charles, 31–32

Ebenezer Baptist Church, 203
Ecker, Frederick H., 189
Eddy, Mary Baker, 313
education: of Negro in South, 219, 224
Eisenhower, Dwight D., 193–95
Emancipation Proclamation, 213
"Endeavor Pledge" of Sweets, 249–50
Equality Smart, 188, 190

Everjoy, Sister, 24
Ezekial Light, Brother, 88

Faithful Heart, 235–37
Faithful Mary (Viola Wilson),
  xv, 71–83, 85, 256, 284,
  297, 343
  death of, 83
  repudiates expose, 81
  testifies for Verinda Brown,
    93, 94
  ultimate break with Father
    Divine, 75
  writes expose, 77–79
Faithful Mary Extension
  Heaven, 52–53
  also known as Faithful Mary
    Kingdom, 74
Father Divine
  accused of assault and bat-
    tery, xv, 77
  and communism, xiv–xv,
    202–208
  death of, xxxiii, 353
  disciples of, 11, 15, 18
  early background of, 4–5
    assistant to Samuel Morris,
      7
    reborn as the Messenger, 8
    arrested, 9
    arrives in New York City,
      11
    moves to Brooklyn, 13
    marries Sister Penny
      (Peninah), 14
    moves to Sayville, 15
    in Sayville, 17–44
  as healer, 23, 28, 36, 43, 62–
    63, 73, 78, 108, 122, 124,
    129, 139, 252, 255, 362,
    363
  and income taxes, 4, 55, 243
  judgment against for
    Verinda Brown, 94
  marriage of to Sweet Angel,
    xix, 266–68, 271–82

and money, 93, 243–46, 305
moves headquarters to
  Philadelphia, 95
and music, 328, 332
as Negro mass leader, xix,
  xxxi, 190, 202
personal magnetism of, 54,
  305
and photographs, 182–83
physical description of,
  xiv, 2, 131, 305
and politics, xiii, 193–209
possible effect of his death
  on followers, 341–52
possible successors to, 343–
  46
as presidential candidate,
  211–12
and press, 181–84
as protector-provider, 113
and the psychiatrists, 86
and race relations, xiii, xiv,
  xx, 15, 189–91, 208, 281
relations of with public
  health and social agen-
  cies, 126
and retribution, xxvii–
  xxviii, xix, 41, 43, 55,
  80–81, 83, 85, 160, 168–
  70, 171–91, 263
secretaries to, xxii, xxv,
  xxix, 227–65, 344
and work load, 131
See also Divinism; followers;
  Peace Mission move-
  ment
"Father Divine is my Father,"
  23
"Father Divine: Man or God?"
  (Prodigal Son's article),
  300
"Father drew me safe back
  home," 81
"Father is on the mountain,
  Father is in the sea,"
  164

"Father is the doctor," 24, 122

"Father, oh, Father, give me the victory," 108, 109, 110

Father's Sweets, xxix
    See also Father Divine: secretaries to; inner cabinet

Faust, Helen, 38

Fern, Miss, 211, 219–20, 222, 224

Fine, Dr. Paul A., xxxiv, 353–67

followers (angels), xiii, xvii–xviii, xxx, 1–4, 69, 355–57
    attitude of toward retribution, 169–70, 171–91
    children, 158–70, 171
    confessing among, 67–68, 362–63
    converts from Christian Science, 24, 314–15
    happily married, 88
    lower-class Negroes, xxxi, 19–20, 112–13, 158, 348–52
    Negro men, 104–105
    possible effect on of Father Divine's death, 341–52
    white, 19, 303–17, 346
    women, 341, 365
    young virgins (rosebuds), 319–30
    young white men, 336–41

Ford, James W., 203

Fu-Fu-Tan, Madame, 49

Gans, Rita, 199

Garner, John Nance, 201

Garvey, Marcus, x, xvii, xviii, 15

Germaine, John, xxvii, 145, 195, 232, 344, 345

Gladys, Miss, 222

Glorious Illumination, 322

"God, Incorporated," 52

Goldberg, Elaine, 51

Good John, 145

"Goodness and love and justice and truth" (Mother's song), xxiv

Good Truth, 142

Gottlieb, William, 75–76

Great Love, 158–59, 254–55, 257

Green, Martha, 164–71

Guthrie, Thomas, 26–27

Gutley, Fred, 26, 35

Gutley, Peter, 35

Haislip family, 214–15

Halleck, Annie, 35

Handsome Is As Handsome Does, Miss, 266–71

Happy Heart, 46

Happy Love, 73

Harlem: conditions in, x–xii, xvii, 42, 45–48
    cult leaders in, x–xii, 48–50
    depression in, 42, 64
    Father Divine moves heaven to, 44

Harlem, Negro Metropolis, x–xi

Harris, Arnold, xxxiv, 353–67

Hartshorne, Judge Richard, 153, 158

heavens, x, 52

Henderson, Reverend, 6, 7

Hepburn, David A., 302

Hickerson, Saint John the Vine, 8–9, 12–13
    on Father Divine, 5, 7, 12

Hill, L. Baron, 34

Holy Grace, 211–18, 221, 223–24

Holy Life, 346

Holy Light, 113–18

Honest Disciple, 107, 108

Honey Bee Love, 242

Hopeful, Miss, 145
Hoshor, John, 5
Houses of Prayer, 55
Humility, Mr., xxvi
Hunt, Agnes, 37
Hunt, John West, xv, 258
    See also Prodigal Son
Hunt, Mrs. John (mother). See
    Mary Bird Tree
Hunt, Warner, 129, 288, 292–
    94, 300, 301, 302, 303,
    308

impersonality, concept of, 70–
    71
inner cabinet, 248
    See also Father Divine: secre-
    taries to; Father's Sweets
intermarriage, 278, 282–84
Internal Revenue Bureau, 55

Jackson, Andrew, 283
Jackson, Robert, 45
Jacob Jeremiah, Miss, 169
Jaynes, Clara, 278
Jefferson, Thomas, 283
Jehovia, Father. See Morris,
    Samuel
Jenkins, Charles, 121
"Jesus'll lead us," xvi, 45
Jewett, Delight, xv, 297–99,
    300
Jewett, Lee (father), 298–99
Joe Patience, 142, 183
John Devout. See Hunt,
    Warner.
John Lamb, Brother (Maynard
    J. Matthews), 19, 37,
    299
Johnson, Miss, 314
Johnson, Mrs. Amelia, 153–
    55
Johnson, Henry Lincoln, xix
Jonathan Good Heart, 238
Jonathan Matthew, Miss

(Nellie Barnes), 59–63,
    69
Jones, Dorrie, 105–13
Jones, Joe, 5
Jones, Robert, 152
Jones, Vernon, 105–13
Joseph, Mr., 129, 131
Joy M. Joy, 322
Justice, Miss, 162
"Just to hear you tap your
    beautiful feet," 139
"Just to look at you," 2

Kardiner, Abram, xvi, 283,
    348
Karp, Dr. Alvin. See Harris,
    Arnold.
Kaufman, Mrs. Angela, 179–80
Kingston Hospital (Kingston,
    N.Y.), 78, 266
Kitty Blue, 340
Konner, Kevah, 173–74
Krum Elbow estate, xv

La Guardia, Fiorello, xiii,
    196–97
Latham family. See Lyon,
    Mary Sheldon
Laughing Light, 350
Lawson, Bishop, H. C., 54, 56–
    58
Lee, Henry, 64–69
Lee, Jim, 64
Life Longevity, 285–86
Light-o'-love, 80
Lincoln, Abraham, 195, 213
Lincoln, Leroy, 190
"Listen, world, we want you
    to know," 140
Little Child Again, Miss, xxvi
Long, Huey, 172
Longevity Joy, 322
Love Dove, xxii, 351
Lovely, Miss, 347
Lovely Best, Miss, 123–25, 274,
    275, 309–10

Lovely Heart, 42
Lovely Life, 220–21, 228, 322, 341–43, 346
Lovely Rose of Sharon, Miss, 145
Lovely Thought, 142
Loving Jeremiah, 163–64
Loving Presence, 314
Lowell, William W., 93, 95–96
Lyon, Mary Sheldon, 304–308

Madison, Arthur, 39, 198–99, 239, 243, 345
Mahood, Joseph, 35–36
Margaret, Miss, 246, 247
Margaret Faith, 237
Mark of Oppression, The, 283
Marvelous Heart, 280
Mary Bird Tree (Mrs. John Hunt), 129, 288, 294–95, 301, 303
Mary Lena, 152
Mary Loveheart, 133–42
Matthews, J. Maynard. *See* John Lamb, Brother
Mays, Reverned E. A., 208–209
Mays, Jack, 142
McCook, Judge, 93, 94
McKay, Claude, x, xi, xiii
McLaughlin, Judge Charles B., 94
Metropolitan Life Insurance Company, 188–91
Metropolitan Museum of Art, 307
Miami Beach, Florida, 187–88
Mikado of Japan, 181
Miller, Brother, 173
"The Mills of God Are Grinding On," 186–87
"Monster Glory to Our Lord" celebration, 42
Moonbeam, Miss, xxvi
Morris, Samuel, 6–9

Mother in the Second Body. *See* Sweet Angel.
Mother's twin. *See* Miss Peaceful.
Munimum, Amiru Al. *See* Abdul Hamid, Sufi.
Mussolini, Benito, 181

National Association for the Advancement of Colored People, 189, 282, 349
National Urban League, 349
Nazareth Mission Church, 234
Negroes, migrations of from the South, 45, 64
Negro press, 32, 45, 196, 276–77, 282, 299
New Day, xxxii, 64, 98, 116, 161, 170, 204, 217–18, 221, 256, 272, 293, 295, 300, 310, 316, 331, 334, 336, 340
Newport, R. I., 179–80
New Star Casino, 198
See also Righteous Government Convention.
New York *Age*, 56, 57, 276–77
Nicey Love, 142
Norris, Austin, 96, 228–29, 234, 239, 241, 243, 253, 308, 345
"Not Only Equal But the Same," 198
numbers racket, xii, 48, 49, 64

O'Brien, Mayor, 196–97
Ochs, Adolph, 172
Oklahoma, 188
Onward Universe. *See* Brown, Thomas
Our World, 300, 302
Oversey, Lionel, xvi, 283, 348

Palace Mission Church, 234, 307

Panken, Judge Jacob, 153, 158
Patience Budd, 131–32, 306–308
Paul, Priscella, 57–59, 87
Paul Selfless, Reverend, 237–38
Peace, Miss, 154, 246, 247
Peace Dove. See Lyon, Mary Sheldon
Peaceful, Miss, 258–59, 281
Peaceful Love, 242, 244
Peaceful Rachel, 235
Peace Mission co-operatives, 4, 51, 228, 232–33
    boards of trustees, 235–39
    hotels and rooming houses, 53, 230, 232, 240
    real estate holdings of, 233–34
    restaurants, 53, 229–30
    other businesses, 53, 231–32
Peace Mission movement, xi, 199, 228, 303, 345–46
    celebrates Father Divine's second marriage, 274–76
    changes in after Father's death, 353, 356-58, 361, 366–67
    employment agency, xiii, 17
    finances of, 53, 69–70, 227
    free banquets, 14
    homosexuality in, 337–39
    neighborhood problems, 17–44
    real estate holdings of, 4, 53
    rehabilitation of criminals, 142
    and schools, 211–25
    sexual segregation in, 338
    See also Divinism; Father Divine; followers; Peace Mission co-operatives
Peace Mission school (New York), 219–25
    gradings, 223
    teachers, 222
    teaching methods used by, 221, 223
Peninah (Sister Penny), 4, 11, 70, 71, 265, 343
    and banquets, 14, 15, 75, 78, 91
    death of, 266, 275
    marriage to Father Divine, 14
    reincarnation of, 266–68, 274
Philip Life, 246, 247, 274
Philip Light, 125
Pine Brook Hotel, 227–28
Pius XI, Pope, 197, 201
Plain Holiness, 314
Poise, W. M., 83
Prodigal Son (John West Hunt), 286–302
    See also Hunt, John West

Quiet Devotion (Rita Delap), 79–80, 284–85
Quiet Dove, 172

Rapid Integration, Miss, 150–51
Raskins, Mrs., 110–12
Ready Love, 287
Rebecca Grace. See Brown, Verinda
"Red Tide, The," 188
Refuge of the Christ Church, 57
Reid, Maybelle, 5
"Retribution," 175–76
Rita Sweet, 322
Righteous Government, Mr., 104
Righteous Government Convention (1936), 197–201
Righteous Government platform, 199–201

Ritchings, Edna Rose. *See* Sweet Angel

Robert, John, 339

Robert Right, Mr., 132

Rockaway Beach, N.Y., 180

Rockland Palace, xiii, 42, 44, 81, 197

Rogers, Mr. (Sayville resident), 26, 31

Rogers, Will, 172

Roosevelt, Eleanor, 282

Roosevelt, Franklin Delano, 197, 201

"Rosebud pledge to God," 327

Ruth, E., 247–48

Saint John Sincere, Miss, 129–30, 131

Saint Mary Bloom, 235, 251–52, 271, 272, 273, 307, 344

Saint Nicholas Palace, 198
See also Righteous Government Convention

Samuel, Brother, 340

Sanderson, Rita, 310–14, 347, 348

Sayville, Long Island, 15–44

Sayville vs. Father Divine, 32–40, 42

Schwaner, August, 26

Shadd, Reverend Albert E., 272–73

Shaneweiss, Jane, 251, 344

Sharkey, C. J., 173–74

Sheldon, William Hill, 304, 307

"Shorty George." *See* La Guardia, Fiorello

Sincere Satisfying, Mr., 89

Slaughter, Jim, 155–58

Slaughter, Leila (mother). *See* Buncha Sweetness

Smile All the While, Miss, 102

Smile-a-While, 288

Smith, Justice Lewis J., 33–42

Smith, Roger, 152–53

"Snoofy." *See* Abdul Hamid, Sufi

Snow White, 242

Snowdon, Mrs., 7

Sober Living, Mr., 228

Soul Healer, Miss, 314

Stark Happiness, Miss, 169

Sterrit, Anne, 145, 222, 255

Stevenson, Adlai, 194–95

store-front churches, 65, 349

Strength Determination, Mr., 295

Stuyvesant Town (New York City), 188–91

Suffolk County News, 17

Sunbeam Willing, 142

Sunny Side Up, 284

Sunshine Love, 253–54, 257

Sweet Angel (Edna Rose Ritchings), 3, 80, 248, 265, 343
  after Father's death, 358–60
  background, 269–71
  described, 268–69
  as reincarnation of Peninah, 268

Sweet Devotion, 220

Sweet Dove, 224, 284

Sweet Heart, 256, 270–71

Sweet Music, 126–28

Sweetness Love, 102, 230

Sweet Notion, 18

Sweet Peace, 220–21

Sweet Soul, 102

Sweet Time, 320–26, 328–30, 331

Swettman, Claire, 34

Temple of Tranquility, 49

Temple(s) of God, 13

"Ten Commandments of the Sweets," 249, 250–51

Texas, 188

"There Goes God! The Story of Father Divine and

His Angels" (McKay article), xiii–xiv
Thomas, James C., 32, 34, 39
Thunder Territo, 147
True Love, 235
True Sincerity, 235
Truman, Harry S, 195
Tucker, Officer, 31

Uni-Presence, Miss, 129, 131
Uni-Presence, Mr., 172–73
United States Treasury Department, 243–44
Unity Mission Church, 234
Universal Cheerfulness, 199
Universal Holiness, 314
Universal Light movement, 80
Universal Mind Substance, 37
Universal Vocabulary, xxvi, 2, 287, 346

Valdosta, Georgia, 9, 11
Victory Dove, Miss. 89

Wagner, Robert F., 201
Washington, George, 195, 283
West, Mrs. Lorraine, 126–28
"What did I long for? I never really knew—," 340
White, Poppy Cannon, 282–83
White, Walter, 282–83
white press, 32
White Rosebud, 322
Whittley, Rita, 299
Willingness Charity, 344
Wilson, Lillian, 20–25
Wilson, Viola. See Faithful Mary
Winecoff Hotel, 188
Wisdom Smiling, Mr., 89
"Woe, Children of Sinful and Perverse Parents," 159–60
Woodmont, 353, 354, 358
World's Gospel Feast, xi–xii

"You've got to make 100," 249

15-303